HELIGOLAND

Jan Rüger is Professor of History at Birkbeck, University of London. He is the author of *The Great Naval Game: Britain and Germany in the Age of Empire* and joint editor of *History after Hobsbawm: Writing the Past for the Twenty-First Century*.

Praise for *Heligoland*

'An engrossing and accomplished history that uses the island of Heligoland to trace the complex course of Anglo-German relations across two centuries. Rüger offers a daring account that brilliantly uses micro-history to find the bigger picture.'

Wolfson History Prize Judges

'Fascinating.'

Neal Ascherson, *London Review of Books*

'Resonant... a prism through which to view the entire span of Anglo-German rivalry, conflict and, eventually, reconciliation.'

Martin Kettle, *The Guardian*

'Rüger's book brilliantly spins a far bigger history out of one small, half-forgotten place. For so long the fault line between two powers, Heligoland deserves to be rescued from oblivion; it has found an admirable historian.'

Ben Wilson, *The Sunday Telegraph*

'Utterly fascinating... impeccable, original, scholarly and superbly written'

Simon Heffer, *Literary Review*

'The whole book is studded with unexpected gems about extraordinary people... a fine tale.'

Max Hastings, *The Sunday Times*

'Riveting'

Ian Hernon, *Tribune*

'Engaging... More people should know Heligoland's story for the echoes it has today.'

The Economist

'Monumental'

Die Zeit

'Visitors today may be quite unaware of Heligoland's curious history or of the weight of symbolism it once bore. Day trippers come now to enjoy the bird watching, the 1950s architecture, the duty-free cigarettes. Before setting out, they should read Mr. Rüger's fascinating book.'

The Wall Street Journal

'Pacey and erudite... succeeds admirably.'

European History Quarterly

'Masterful... fascinating... this is microhistory at its best.'

Mariner's Mirror

'Jan Rüger's new book takes the North Sea island of Heligoland as a lens through which to examine Anglo-German relations over the past two centuries. The result is an entertaining and illuminating study full of colourful detail, that traces the phases of co-operation and hostility between the two powers over the decades from the Kaiser to Hitler and beyond.'

Richard J. Evans, author of *The Pursuit of Power: Europe 1815–1914*

'A brilliant and subtle history of Anglo-German relations, told through the evocative study of a contested island. This fascinating book is a triumphant demonstration of the power of microhistory.'

Christopher Clark, author of *The Sleepwalkers: How Europe Went to War in 1914*

HELIGOLAND

BRITAIN, GERMANY, AND THE
STRUGGLE FOR THE NORTH SEA

JAN RÜGER

OXFORD
UNIVERSITY PRESS

Great Clarendon Street, Oxford, OX2 6DP,
United Kingdom

Oxford University Press is a department of the University of Oxford.
It furthers the University's objective of excellence in research, scholarship,
and education by publishing worldwide. Oxford is a registered trade mark of
Oxford University Press in the UK and in certain other countries

First published 2017
First published in paperback 2019

Impression: 1

Published in the United States of America by Oxford University Press
198 Madison Avenue, New York, NY 10016, United States of America

British Library Cataloguing in Publication Data
Data available

Library of Congress Cataloging in Publication Data
Data available,

ISBN 978-0-19-967246-2 (Hbk.)
ISBN 978-0-19-967247-9 (Pbk.)

Printed and bound in Great Britain by
Clays Ltd, Elcograf S.p.A.

For Paul and Anna

Contents

List of Illustrations

Die Insel ist wie ein zu kleiner Stern.
Rainer Maria Rilke, 'Die Insel (Nordsee)'

Figure 0.1 The North Sea with Heligoland in the south east. Detail from *A Map of the Island of Heligoland* by G. Testoline, 1810.

Prologue

Between Worlds

Out in the North Sea, five hours north-west of Hamburg and 300 miles off the east coast of England, sits Heligoland. In good weather its imposing cliffs can be seen from more than a dozen miles, rising abruptly to eighty feet above the crashing waves. It is a steep, triangular bastion of an island. Half a mile to the east lies a flat sand dune, Sandy Island, which looks like a geological accident that could be washed away by the North Sea at any moment. In between these twin islets ebbs and flows a relatively calm stretch of water, sheltered from the north-westerly wind by the cliffs. Sailors have relied on this natural harbour ever since humans began to cross the sea between Continental Europe and the British Isles.

For generations Britain and Germany have collided in this archipelago half the size of Gibraltar. The two nations' pasts are etched into the rust-coloured, blotched sandstone cliffs. Wherever you turn, Heligoland's scarred landscape reveals the imprint of war: the craters and broken rock formations, the iron and concrete remnants of Germany's naval stronghold, built and demolished with equal determination, the overgrown ruins of the dream of sea power, bombed again and again. In 1947 British forces set off here the largest non-nuclear explosion on record, blowing up what was left of Hitler's island fortress. In its ruins a long history of Anglo-German conflict was meant to come to a conclusive end. Pressed in Parliament on why it was not prepared to give Heligoland 'back', the Attlee government declared that the island represented everything that was wrong with the Germans: 'If any tradition was worth breaking, and if any sentiment was worth changing, then the German sentiment about Heligoland was such a one'.[1] Above all, the outpost stood for a long tradition of militarism which London was determined to see buried forever.

But long before it became Germany's North Sea bulwark and was fought over in two world wars, Heligoland had been Britain's smallest colony, an inconvenient and notoriously discontented border island. Its location at the fringes of Europe, where the British empire ended and the German-speaking world began, intrigued geographers and colonial officials. In 1888, Sir Charles Prestwood Lucas, the head of the Dominion department at the Colonial Office, described Heligoland as

> the point at which Great Britain and Germany come most nearly into contact with each other, and...the only part of the world in which the British govern-ment rules an exclusively Teuton though not English-speaking population.[2]

'Contact' was an understatement. A web of laws and customs made it impossible to draw a clear boundary on the island between the British empire and the different Germanies that existed in the long nineteenth century. For the Germans flocking to the colony ever since it opened its spa resort in 1826, Heligoland was just outside the Fatherland, but very much part of it.

From early on this was an island of the mind as much as an island of rock and stone.[3] Poets and painters, from Heinrich Heine in the 1830s to Anselm Kiefer in the 1980s, styled the outpost as a monument of German identity. However different these constructs of nationhood were, they focused on two aspects in common: Germany's boundaries and its relationship with the sea, the latter almost inevitably involving the British. German sentiment about Heligoland was thus always in part a sentiment about Britain, its naval power, its attitude towards Europe, and its role in the world. For generations the island symbolized a German desire to be equal with and to be recognized as equal by the British. Having acquired it from Britain in 1890, the German government turned Heligoland into a fortress that expressed this ambition, a showpiece of the grand strategy that was meant to force Britain into acknowledging Germany as a world power. But the Kaiser's battle fleet, built up over two dec-ades, did little to compel the British to give way.

Heligoland, demilitarized after the First World War, became a symbol of this failure. For the Nazis it was a metaphor of the Fatherland's shameful humiliation by the Allies, 'a silent warning', as Joseph Goebbels had it, demand-ing revenge.[4] After he took power, Hitler had the fortress rebuilt and vastly expanded as an icon of Germany's will to be bold with Britain. Comprehensively destroyed by the RAF, the island's ruins turned into an emblem of German victimhood and nationalism after the Second World War. When the UK released it into German hands in 1952, Chancellor Adenauer proclaimed that his country had 'finally been given back a piece of soil to which we Germans are attached with so much love'. The island would now show to the world that the Germans had overcome the past: 'Peaceful Heligoland, set in the seas between Germany and Britain, will be in future a symbol of the will to peace and friendship of both nations.'[5]

For the British Heligoland provided a lens through which to interpret Germany. The island was a 'parable' for the Anglo-German relationship, wrote Austin Harrison, the editor of *The Observer*, in 1907.[6] The meanings of this metaphor changed dramatically in the course of the two centuries, as the relationship of the two countries was transformed. When the Salisbury government ceded the colony to the Kaiser, it was proclaimed as a token of friendship, heralding a new era of Anglo-German collaboration. Only from the turn of the century did Heligoland change in the British imagination. The forlorn colonial enclave, that 'gem of the North Sea', became a dark rock symbolizing the German menace.[7] H. G. Wells, Erskine Childers, and a host of lesser writers used the outpost as a symbol of the German threat—and Britain's failure to stand up to it.[8] Giving the island to the Kaiser had been a momentous mistake, argued Winston Churchill and Admiral John Fisher. Their mantra, 'no more Heligolands', meant: no more concessions, no more appeasement.[9]

Situated at the fault line between imperial and national histories, this rock in the North Sea provides an apt location from where to rethink the Anglo-German past. Most histories of this relationship focus on the two world wars. There is no scholarly account that spans both the nineteenth and the twentieth centuries.[10] This absence of a long-term perspective has created a misleading picture: the nineteenth century appears as a mere prehistory of the catastrophes of the twentieth century. We have grown accustomed to a narrative that uses the period between the Congress of Vienna (1814–15) and the First World War as the foil against which to narrate the 'rise of antagonism'—a dramatic shift from unity to enmity, from 'friend to foe'. Yet for most of the nineteenth century Britain and Germany were neither joined in comprehensive alliance, nor locked in conflict. This was a decidedly ambivalent relationship long before Bismarck founded Imperial Germany and Wilhelm II decided to build a battle fleet against Britain. What took place in the decades before the First World War was not an inevitable shift towards enmity, but an increase in both cooperation and conflict. Under radically altered circumstances, this state of interdependence re-emerged after the Second World War. In order to appreciate this, the traumatic periods of violent conflict need to be inserted into the longer history of Anglo-German coexistence—in this book from the Napoleonic Wars to the Cold War.

Such a longer time-frame prompts us to see the past as more than a national construct. The first chapter of this book opens a window onto a time when 'Germans' and 'Britons' were still uncertain denominations. Those who cooperated across the North Sea to defeat Napoleon rarely identified themselves according to the national categories that were cemented only towards the end of the nineteenth century. For many of them local and regional sentiment was far more decisive. The inhabitants of Britain's North Sea colony were a case in point. Wedged in between the British empire and the German nation state, the Heligolanders were keen to cultivate a separate, independent identity. In August 1890 they were told that they had turned from subjects of the British empire into citizens of Imperial Germany. Yet they still had to be 'made German', as the German Foreign Office agent sent to the island put it.[11] Their story is as relevant to this book as the view from Berlin and London. It mirrors the many episodes in the Anglo-German past in which refugees and migrants have played key roles for both countries. If anything has characterized this relationship consistently through the past two centuries, it is that people never stopped moving between the German- and English-speaking parts of Europe. They more than complicate the national framework within which so many British and German histories operate.

Following the arc of the Anglo-German relationship as it spans the past two centuries allows us to appreciate the many ways in which Europe and the British empire were bound up with one another. We are used to thinking of the two as opposite poles: historians and politicians alike have fostered a narrative in which the empire allowed Britain to disengage from Europe, as if the two were clear-cut opposites, with Britain in a position to choose one over the other. This is very much a twentieth-century idea, reflecting, more than anything, Britain's changed global position after the Second World War. The imperial project was never isolated from Europe, nor did it allow Britons to isolate themselves from Europe. The UK's trade was never exclusively with either Europe or the rest of the world, it was with both. The same was true in strategic terms: colonial expansion hinged on calm in Europe, while overseas conflict typically went hand in hand with European instability.

Just as empire and Europe were not two separate spheres between which Britain could choose, national and imperial impulses were not neatly separated in modern Germany, either. The unification and dynamic expansion of the Bismarckian nation state in the second half of the nineteenth century took place in a global context in which the British empire played a key role.[12] At the very time when borders became invested with new national symbolism, the wealth of nations depended more and more on the movement of goods and people across boundaries.[13] The case of Heligoland is typical of this paradox. It offers a history of both the transnational relationships that bound nineteenth-century Germany and the British empire together and the reverse process in which the world of Anglo-German collaboration was challenged by the 'nationalizing process' that accelerated towards the end of the nineteenth century. After 1890, when Imperial Germany acquired Heligoland in return for colonial concessions in Africa, nation and empire were to be symbolically disentangled—in the very period when Britain and Germany were becoming more interdependent than ever before.

In making an islet in the North Sea the main character of a history of Britain and Germany, this book builds on a tradition of scholars who have studied small settings in order to reflect about large historical issues.[14] There is no doubting the miniature scale of the locale at the heart of this book, Britain's smallest colony, rarely inhabited by more than 3,000 people.[15] Heligoland was 'the quaintest little spot imaginable', wrote a British diplomat in the 1870s.[16] It had 'the ingredients of one of those miraculous-looking islets pictured in fairy-tale books', commented a British traveller in the 1930s.[17] German visitors agreed: the cliffs, the beach, the small town, complete with church spire and lighthouse, made for the perfect image of a *Heimat* by the sea.

Exploring this local world and the attraction it held for contemporaries allows us to get away from the Olympian vision that characterizes so many historical narratives.[18] All too often the main actors in histories of international relations are exclusively statesmen and politicians. But the 'rise and fall of great powers' took place not only in the ministries of Whitehall and Wilhelmstraße, it was also manifest in the everyday lives of people and their places. Heligoland allows us to uncover this local history of Anglo-German conflict. 'Local', though, should not be taken to mean in isolation from the bigger picture.[19] For microhistories to work, they have to engage simultaneously with small settings and large contexts. This book does so by crisscrossing between local, regional, national, and imperial archives, reaching from small record offices in the north of Germany and the south of England to the large national archives (mostly in Britain and Germany, but also in Denmark, Australia, Canada, and the USA). The book does not neglect the perspective from the political cockpits in London and Berlin, but it refracts this view through the everyday life of the Heligolanders and those involved with them, amongst them spies, smugglers, soldiers, and traders. Their voices interrupt the flow of dispatches and memoranda swelling the files of the Colonial and Foreign Office archives. We gain a richer sense of the past if we listen to them, directly caught up as they were in the Anglo-German struggle for the North Sea.

History, as the great French historian Fernand Braudel once wrote, likes to 'make use of islands'.[20] He meant this in a geographical sense: islands had, he thought, functioned throughout history as stepping stones for trade and migration. But the same is true in metaphorical terms. From the moment Heligoland entered the European stage during the Napoleonic Wars, to the time when it slowly exited that stage towards the end of the twentieth century, it was never only a geographical reality in which people lived and died, but also a product of the imagination. The book engages continuously with both these worlds. It explains the role this outpost played at the edge of the Continent, where empire and Europe met. And it explores the myriad ways in which people in the past have thought about the island, in order to make sense of Britain, Germany, and the sea in between them. A vast archive of artefacts allows us to do so: paintings, poetry, literature, music, maps, charts, travelogues, photographs, films. *Heligoland* binds these diverse sources together 'under the name of a place'.[21] It reveals in roughly chronological order the personal stories and official dealings, the decisions and events, the culture and the politics that made this cliff-bound island a microcosm of the Anglo-German relationship.

I

Edge of Europe

George III, Britain's long-reigning and now ailing monarch, had never heard of Heligoland. On 9 December 1806 his government, the 'Ministry of all the Talents' led by William Grenville, came together to discuss the war against Napoleon. Since Nelson's victory at Trafalgar the French navy, or what was left of it, posed little threat to Britain.[1] There remained the Danish fleet, so far kept out of the war by the government in Copenhagen. But with the French army advancing through northern Germany Denmark's position of neutrality looked increasingly precarious. In October 1806 Napoleon had decisively defeated the Prussian army at Jena and Auerstedt. Soon enough, he would be in a position to threaten the Danish with occupation. If they gave in and became French allies, their fleet could be turned against Britain. In this situation, Grenville's cabinet concluded, 'it may eventually become necessary to take possession of Heligoland in order to secure a safe position for your Majesty's ships'.[2] The navy should blockade the North Sea outpost now: it was paramount that the Danish should not turn it into a fortress. George III agreed. On 10 December he ordered his fleet 'to prevent any reinforcements from being thrown into that Island'.[3]

Edward Thornton, Britain's man in northern Germany, had recommended this course of action for some time. Thornton was the minister-plenipotentiary to the Circle of Lower Saxony—a patchwork of territories that had belonged to the Holy Roman Empire, but were now being violently reorganized by Napoleon. With the French advance into northern Germany, Thornton's daily duties had become almost entirely taken up with intelligence gathering. Relying on a sprawling network of informants, he was busy supplying London with reports about Napoleon's moves. In November 1806, with the French about to occupy Hamburg, Thornton had to leave his headquarters for the neighbouring Duchy of Holstein, which, governed by the Danish, was still neutral. From here he continued to send intelligence reports to London. Heligoland played a key role in this activity. His couriers and spies used it as a convenient stepping stone: within the reach of the Royal Navy but just outside of Napoleon's sphere of influence. One of them, John Sontag, a military intelligence officer, reconnoitred the island in July 1807. He urged London to take the outpost 'should a rupture with Denmark appear inevitable'.[4]

On 11 August 1807, expecting the French to occupy Holstein any day, Thornton thought 'it my duty to hasten to England'.[5] All British vessels had left the duchy's ports a week earlier, but he had arranged for a boat to take him into the Bight where the commander of the British warships on blockading duties was expecting him. On 14 August he went aboard HMS *Quebec*, together with three of his staff. From there Thornton eventually transferred to another warship for the passage to London. As he sailed out towards Britain he passed Heligoland, that 'elevated, barren, rocky spot'.[6] When he arrived in London Thornton was summoned by George Canning, since March 1807 foreign secretary.[7] Canning was one of the key figures in the

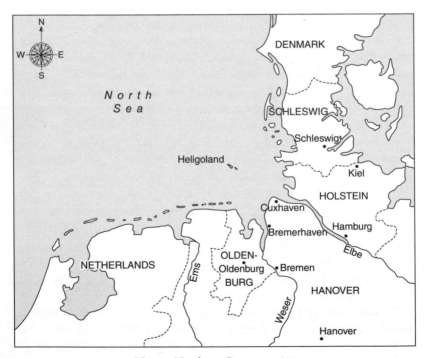

Map 1 Northern Germany, 1807.

new government headed by the Duke of Portland, which had taken over from Grenville's 'Ministry of all the Talents'. Advocating a hard line against Denmark, Canning had been instrumental in the government's decision to send the Royal Navy to the Baltic to secure control of the Danish fleet. But the show of force had not persuaded Denmark to enter an alliance with Britain. The Danish, under immense pressure from Napoleon, had rejected the British ultimatum. Since mid-August the two countries were at war, with British naval and military forces advancing against Copenhagen.[8]

Taking Heligoland in this situation seemed 'of special importance', Thornton agreed with Canning. It was paramount that Britain should deny the Danish and French the strategic stronghold:

> By its position and great elevation, compared with the low, shoaly and danger-ous coast of the North Sea, it is absolutely necessary for every vessel bound to or from the Hever, Eider, Elbe, Weser and Jahde rivers to make the Island of Helgoland.

If it was owned by the British, a 'squadron of the King's ships could regulate from hence the blockade of the principal rivers of the North Sea'. At the same time the island could function as an outpost from where to under-mine the Continental system through which Napoleon had cut off all trade between Britain and the rest of Europe. As Thornton explained, Heligoland was close enough to the mainland for 'merchandise to be conveyed in small vessels to the Continent'. Yet it was sufficiently removed from the coast for the Royal Navy to be able to control its access. For intelligence gathering too the island was 'a point of essential importance to his Majesty's Government'.

Capturing the island would not, Thornton believed, be difficult. The rock was garrisoned by a small number of Danish soldiers. There was a larger militia made up of Heligolanders, but they were unreliable. Thornton pre-dicted that they would 'yield to the first summon of any maritime force', as that force 'would put an immediate stop to the preoccupations of the inhab-itants, and cut off all the means of their subsistence'.[9] Canning was per-suaded and the Admiralty prepared orders on the same day: in parallel to the British assault on Copenhagen (which was to begin on 4 September), Heligoland was to be taken by 'the earliest and best means'.[10]

The officer charged with the task was Vice-Admiral Thomas McNamara Russell, commander-in-chief of the North Sea squadron. A detachment of his ships was already blockading Heligoland when the Admiralty's orders reached him by dispatch boat near the Dutch coast. Russell set sail immediately

and arrived at Heligoland on 4 September, anchoring his flagship HMS
Majestic with its seventy-four guns in full view of the town. So far the
Danish commandant had refused to capitulate, despite being cut off from all
support. As Russell wrote later,

> I was making my arrangement to storm him with the marines and seamen of
> the squadron if he did not instantly surrender, for at this time the value of the
> island to us is immense. At six pm, however, he sent out a flag of truce, desiring
> that an officer might be sent in the morning to treat on articles of
> capitulation.[11]

Russell agreed and sent a deputation on shore with a letter for the governor,
imploring him not to 'sacrifice the blood and property of your inhabitants
by a vain and impotent resistance; but that you will by an immediate surrender avert the horrors of being stormed'. As it turned out, Major Karl
Johann von Zeska, the island's commandant, was not in a position to mount
much of a defence. He could rely on his company of Danish soldiers, but he
was unable to motivate sufficient numbers of the Heligolanders to fight. As
Thornton had predicted, the latter were keener to save their families and
livelihoods than to die for the Danish crown. Von Zeska gave in and negotiated the handover. This was less heroic than the government in Copenhagen
had expected, but it meant that he was able to gain a number of important
concessions.[12] Russell granted his request for safe passage to the Continent
on his word that he and his troops would not take up arms against the British
again. Von Zeska tried in vain to gain a written assurance that the island would
return to Denmark after the war. This was out of the question for Russell, but
he agreed to far-reaching concessions with regard to the islanders' position.
The Heligolanders would not have to do service in the British navy or army
against their will. They would enjoy freedom of religion and their property
rights would be safeguarded. Importantly, Russell agreed to guarantee the privileges which they had enjoyed under the Danish crown.[13] Conveniently for the
Heligolanders, the articles of capitulation left these privileges undefined—
the document was to become the islanders' most treasured constitutional
record, invoked whenever they tried to gain concessions from their rulers.

At 4.30 p.m. on 5 September the Danish flag was lowered and the Union
Jack hoisted. The British had taken the island without a shot being fired.
Russell sent the Danish prisoners with a flag of truce to Holstein. The
Heligolanders, he declared, 'shall become subjects of Great Britain with all
the universally known advantages peculiar to that character'. Russell installed
one of his officers, Corbet d'Auvergne, as acting governor and told him to

'see that the inhabitants are treated with the greatest kindness; to conciliate their affections; and secure their attachment to our government; as I hope it [the island] will never be given up'.[14] Before he set sail again, Russell sent a report to the Admiralty:

Heligoland continues to be governed like our colonies by a governour [sic], a council, and an assembly. It contains three thousand three hundred souls, with a majority of females by three hundred. It is possessed of a secure haven, formed between it and Sandy Island, for vessels of twelve feet draught of water, and a safe roadstead for twenty sail of the line the year round.

In order to demonstrate how useful the natural shelter would be for the navy he added: 'It blows tremendously hard at this moment at W.S.W., which is nearly the least sheltered, yet we ride easy with a scope of two cables'.[15]

What begins here, in September 1807, is the story of an outpost at the edge of Europe in which Britain and its empire were bound up with the Continent. Heligoland belonged to a string of islands which Britain occupied during the wars with France: Corsica, Elba, Malta, Sicily, and the Ionian Islands (though Corfu remained French until 1814). Together with Gibraltar, acquired in the early eighteenth century and vigorously defended during the Napoleonic Wars, they were catalogued as Britain's 'European possessions'.[16] For some observers these acquisitions signalled a new departure in Britain's relationship with the Continent. Gould Francis Leckie, an enterprising writer who spent much time in Sicily, was one of the most influential amongst them.[17] In his *Historical Survey of the Foreign Affairs of Great Britain*, published in 1808, he portrayed these outposts as part of an 'insular empire' that would allow Britain to refrain from too much engagement with the Continent, while ensuring its maritime supremacy. This mirrored a broader conception of the empire as a realm that stood in opposition to Continental Europe, an idea which proved attractive for many commentators in the nineteenth and twentieth centuries. The Continent, unstable and plagued with revolution and tyranny, was something Britain would do well to stay away from. The empire would allow it to do just that. As long as the Royal Navy dominated the world's maritime thoroughfares Britain would not need to meddle in Continental politics. It could concentrate on expanding its empire and worldwide trade.[18]

But Leckie's idea of an 'insular empire', and the broader 'blue water' strategy which it reflected, were based on a false dichotomy. Empire and Europe were not clear-cut opposites, nor was Britain in a position to choose one

over the other. Its shifting and ill-defined imperial project was bound up
with Continental Europe economically and strategically. Britain's trade was
rarely exclusively with either Europe on the one hand or the colonies and
the rest of the world on the other. Rather, the movement of goods, finances,
and people was typically triangular, involving Continental as much as overseas locations. Nor did the empire allow Britain to disengage from Europe
strategically in any sustained fashion. On the contrary, overseas expansion
hinged on European stability, just as European instability typically resulted
in overseas conflict. Most London governments in the late eighteenth and
early nineteenth century were all too aware of this: playing a strong role in
Europe and expanding the empire were intrinsically linked rather than
opposed interests. This interdependence was encapsulated by Britain's
European colonies, scattered as they were around the shores of the Continent.
Their occupation was aimed at supporting the fight against Napoleon—
they were testament to the expressed British will to tilt back the balance of
power in Europe. Rather than symbols of withdrawal, George III's 'European
possessions' became hinges between empire and Continent, much like their
royal family seat of Hanover itself.[19]

In the case of Heligoland this became obvious soon after the takeover of
September 1807. While most of the press applauded the occupation, some
critics argued that it did not go far enough. Charles Pasley, who visited the
island in November 1807, wrote a particularly acerbic critique in his influential *Essay on the Military Policy and Institutions of the British Empire*.[20] Pasley,
an engineer officer and later a well-regarded general, could not understand
why the 'conquest of that worthless lump of red clay, called Heligoland, is
received with the greatest applause and joy in England'.[21] Britain, he thundered, was far too hesitant—it had not nearly enough military ambition.
Heligoland was a symbol of 'this unmanly timidity': rather than occupy all
of Denmark, the government had gone for a small rock in the North Sea.[22]
But Pasley's argument, clad in much rhetorical flourish, overestimated
Britain's capability to counter Napoleon on land. While its navy was able to
see off the French threat, its army did not have the strength to challenge
Napoleon on its own. In 1807 an all-out invasion of the Continent was
likely to lead to disaster. Britain had to wait until enough governments had
turned against Napoleon and a coalition had emerged that was prepared to
act. To this end it was crucial that Britain supported those ready to rise
against Napoleon through 'guineas and gunpowder': arms supplies, subsidies,
covert operations, and targeted expeditions.[23]

Heligoland was key for this policy. It was to be the gateway for Britain's engagements in northern Europe and the linchpin for its efforts to break Napoleon's blockade.[24] As soon as the island was secured, London sent military and diplomatic staff out to set up the infrastructure for infiltrating the Continent. The first of these agents arrived on 2 October 1807 and reported back that the communication with the mainland was 'entirely cut off'.[25] It took almost a month before the British had worked out how to go around the French and Danish gunboats patrolling the entrances to the Rivers Elbe and Weser and the harbours in Holstein. By 29 October the acting governor was confident 'that with the greatest secrecy being observed we may obtain any intelligence that Mr Canning wishes to have from the Continent'. The Heligoland boatmen seemed particularly good at evading enemy craft and landing mail or cargo covertly. What was more, they seemed to be loyal:

> I am happy to say that the inhabitants of this island are sober, good people, and seem well disposed to their present government, and may be made by proper means very useful in obtaining any intelligence.[26]

In January 1808 Canning appointed Edward Nicholas, a career diplomat, to 'take charge of all correspondence with the Continent'.[27] This was an innocuous description, considering the range of tasks Nicholas was charged with: running a network of informants and agents on the Continent, directing covert operations, conducting counter-intelligence measures, orchestrating pro-British propaganda amongst the French and their allied troops, organizing the transport of troops to and from the Continent, smuggling armaments and channelling secret payments to allies and insurgents.

Nicholas had worked in a similar if less wide-ranging capacity under Edward Thornton until the French had occupied Hamburg in November 1806.[28] He was now to be solely responsible for supervising Britain's intelligence gathering and covert missions in the German-speaking lands. As long as Heligoland provided the closest and most reliable outpost through which to communicate with the Continent, he was also in charge of the government's European correspondence. As Canning explained, 'all letters of every description whatever which pass between this country and the Continent are to be delivered in the first instance to the care of Mr Nicholas'.[29] It was through Nicholas that the cabinet and the king were informed about the course of the Napoleonic Wars in these years; and it was through him that most covert initiatives against the French were to be taken. Canning sent 'despatches from Mr Nicholas' to George III at least once a week, often more frequently and, if they were urgent, late at night. 'I lost no time in reading to his Majesty the intelligence from Heligoland', was a typical response from Windsor.[30]

From February 1808 until June 1812 'der Konsul', as the locals called Nicholas, resided in Heligoland. Officially he was employed by the Foreign Office on a 'special mission' during this time, with the rank of a minister-plenipotentiary, equivalent to an ambassador.[31] Reporting directly to Canning, he was given far-reaching powers. All arriving and departing ships had to have a passport signed by him. No one who was not from Heligoland could reside in the island without his permission. All mail to and from the island had to go through him.[32] This last aspect was pivotal, since the government's communication with the Continent depended on it. As Nicholas told the governor, 'I am the only person authorized to judge of the propriety or impropriety of what letters are to be delivered'.[33] Few of his contacts on the Continent knew him by his real name. Those who did were under strict instructions not to use it in any correspondence that could be intercepted. Nicholas warned Charles Hamilton, who took over as governor in February 1808, 'that it must be at your peril if you open, cause to open or detain any letter addressed to His Majesty's Ministers or myself under their or my seal or false names'.[34]

For four and a half years Nicholas was the *éminence grise* of the island, making the governor look like a subordinate officer. Hamilton complained bitterly to the Colonial Office that his authority was being undermined, but the Foreign Office routinely overrode the Colonial Office's objections in this regard. Nicholas, in turn, left Canning and his successors in no doubt about the lowly qualities of the governor, whom he described as naive and slow. The governor, he scoffed, did not even speak German.[35] In many ways Hamilton and Nicholas could not have been more different. Hamilton was averse to too much work and took up to two months' leave every year. Nicholas relished his mission and seemed continuously at work. Only once in the fifty-three months during which he resided in Heligoland did he ask for leave, on health grounds. The Foreign Office flatly denied the request— he was irreplaceable given the 'present critical situation of affairs in the North of Germany'.[36] Hamilton and Nicholas differed markedly also in the attitude they took to the islanders. Hamilton, with more than a hint of colonial paternalism, thought of them as 'poor people entrusted to my care' and repeatedly defended them as loyal subjects.[37] Nicholas, in contrast, disliked the Heligolanders with a passion. They were notorious, he wrote to Canning, for the 'little confidence they merit'.[38] Officials on both sides of the North Sea were to judge them in similar terms throughout the nineteenth century and beyond: as a selfish and narrow-minded island people who failed entirely to appreciate the need to align themselves with their masters.

Nicholas had not only been given far-reaching powers, but also considerable financial clout. He needed a continuous flow of funds to pay couriers and informants, bribe the enemy's officials, and reward the Royal Navy's officers. 'The nature of the service I was charged with', he explained in August 1813, 'required constant naval protection to the boats I employed, certain civilities were due and expected by the officers in return for a disagreeable and at times dangerous service'.[39] On a quite different scale were the funds required by the allies and insurgents whom Britain supported against Napoleon. Occasionally bullion and guineas could be shipped from England for these purposes, but that was risky and took a long time. Nicholas needed to be able to pay highly fluctuating sums at short notice to a range of beneficiaries on the Continent. For this he enlisted the help of the Hamburg merchant bankers Parish & Co. The house had been set up by John Parish, the son of a ship's captain from Leith in Scotland, who had emigrated with his family in the mid-eighteenth century. Parish had made vast profits in international trade and finance, making him one of Hamburg's richest men. His luxurious lifestyle was proverbial—'pärrisch leben' became a Hamburg idiom for sparing no expense.[40] From 1795 Parish was involved in masterminding the transport and financing of British troops fighting the French on the Continent and in the colonies. When he retired and moved to England in 1806, his sons took over the business. Nicholas knew them from his time in Hamburg and had established a particularly good relationship with John Parish junior and his brother Charles, who was prominent amongst the merchants circumventing the French blockade. Early in 1808 the Parish brothers arranged an account under a false name on which Nicholas and anyone he authorized could draw.

Agents coming from Heligoland were thus able to get funds in Hamburg, similarly the couriers and informants whom Nicholas used on the Continent. John Parish junior also facilitated larger payments on credit for troops and insurgents fighting Napoleon. He was arrested twice on suspicion of aiding the British, but swiftly released and never charged. It helped that his brothers Richard and David were busy organizing international transactions for the French in Paris and the Americas—just like the Rothschilds, with whom they competed, the Parish brothers were careful not to alienate any of the great European powers.[41] The well-oiled system, for which Parish & Co charged a handsome commission, continued throughout Nicholas's time in Heligoland. When he returned to London in 1812, Nicholas still had debts of 49,444 Mark Banco with Parish 'on account of secret service'.[42] (Mark Banco was the Hamburg unit of account. The sum, roughly £4,800 at the time, amounted to about five times Nicholas's annual salary.[43]) The Foreign Office footed the bill without hesitation, just as it rarely queried the 'extraordinary expenses' which Nicholas incurred.[44]

The collaboration between Parish and Nicholas illustrates the distinct Anglo-German character of much of the covert action that was conducted through Heligoland. 'Anglo-German', that is, in a loose, cultural rather than strictly bi-national sense: the agents, informants, couriers, bankers, merchants, and officers with whom Nicholas worked came from a range of backgrounds, many of which did not fit into the national categories that became entrenched later in the century. Most of them spoke both English and German. Many of them had strong links to England, Scotland, Ireland, or Wales on the one hand and to Hanover, Holstein, the Hanse cities, Prussia, or other German states on the other. The 'extraordinary Anglo-German symbiosis', created by the French threat and epitomized by Heligoland, should not be mistaken for a pact between two nations.[45] It was both more and less than that: a dense network of (almost exclusively) men for whom local and regional identities mattered as much as supra-national constructs such as the House of Hanover. Some had strong, others only vague feelings for whatever they identified as 'Germany' or 'Britain'. What held them together was opposition to Napoleon, for political, personal, or commercial reasons. In many cases, that of John Parish included, all three applied.

The King's German Legion, which used Heligoland as a recruitment base and arms depot, was a case in point.[46] The Legion, an integrated part of the British army, had been set up to recruit volunteers from the German-speaking lands who had fled the French. Friedrich von der Decken, one of the many officers in the Legion who served both on the Continent and in Britain, was responsible for the covert operation.[47] The largest proportion of his recruits came from Hanover, but it would be wrong to see the Legion as a mere Anglo-Hanoverian vehicle. Those who joined it via Heligoland came from a wide range of backgrounds, mostly northern German, but also Prussian, Bavarian, and Austrian.[48] Major Kentzinger, the commander of the Legion's base on the island, had agents who brought volunteers from as far as

Figure 1.1 *A View of Heligoland from Sandy Island.* Hand-coloured aquatint by Robert and Daniel Havell, 1811.

the Tyrol.[49] As long as they spoke German he also took on deserters, draft-dodgers, and prisoners of war who had escaped the French.[50]

So successful was the King's German Legion at attracting men from German states that Continental governments, keen not to offend the French, warned their citizens not to be lured to Heligoland by the British.[51] Practically all recruits for the Legion, once interviewed and checked by an army surgeon, were sent to the Legion's headquarters in England. From there they were dispatched to support British campaigns all over Europe. Units of the Legion fought in Spain, Sicily, and at Waterloo, where they famously defended the stronghold of La Haye Sainte until they ran out of ammunition.[52] Epitomizing the peculiar Anglo-German collaboration prompted by the Napoleonic threat, they were loyal both to the English king and to the various Germanies that they identified with.

The recruits of the King's German Legion who made their way from the Continent to Heligoland crossed paths with the agents and couriers who took the opposite route. By spring 1808 Nicholas and his confidants had established a network that was reliable enough for large-scale covert missions. The first of these was masterminded by Canning and Arthur Wellesley (the later Duke of Wellington) in May 1808 when the Madrid uprising caused serious difficulties for Napoleon in Spain. As news of the insurrection spread through Europe, Canning tried to fan the flames. Could Spanish troops stationed in northern Europe be encouraged to defect from Napoleon and join the resistance in the Peninsula? The Marquis of La Romana, commanding a division in Denmark, was known to harbour anti-French sentiments. If he could be persuaded, might the Royal Navy be able to evacuate him and his division, reported to be 37,000 men strong, and transport them to Spain? It was worth a try. Wellesley selected a Scottish priest whom he had used as an agent before for the mission. Father James Robertson (a 'short, stout, merry little monk') was an almost perfect choice: he was fluent in German, having spent many years in a Bavarian monastery; as a Catholic he would have more authority with La Romana; he would have a natural alibi as a travelling clergyman; and since he had no direct links to the government he could be disowned if things went wrong.[53] Wellesley told Robertson 'that, if the service on which you will be employed should succeed, you will be amply rewarded; and that, if in the execution of it, any accident should happen to you, your mother and your two sisters ... will be taken care of and provided for by Government'.[54] Robertson would report to a case officer, Colin Alexander Mackenzie, who had run similar missions before.[55] Mackenzie was to accompany him to Heligoland and stay there during the mission, liaising with Nicholas and Canning.[56]

Before leaving London Robertson assumed the identity of a Bavarian whom he had known and who had died in Britain without leaving any family behind. Mackenzie entered Robertson under this false name at the Alien Office, stating that he was instructed to convey him out of the country. On 4 July the couple went on board a packet boat at Harwich. 'A favourable breeze brought us in forty-eight hours to Heligoland', recounted the priest later.[57] Nicholas briefed them about the situation on the Continent and gave Robertson a letter for Parish, written with invisible ink, instructing the Hamburg banker to furnish the priest with the necessary funds. On 8 June Robertson embarked for the Continent. After some mishaps he made it to Bremen on board a contraband trader, avoiding French troops and customs officers. Using false papers, he travelled on to Hamburg, where John Parish provided him with money and intelligence. Via Altona and Lübeck Robertson eventually made it to La Romana's headquarters in Nyborg on the Danish island of Fyn (Fünen), keeping his superiors in Heligoland informed through coded letters. Mackenzie and Nicholas were thus able to send dispatch boats at the right time to London and the Baltic, where a fleet under the command of Vice-Admiral Sir Richard Goodwin Keats was waiting. It took Robertson some time to convince La Romana, but after several meetings the general agreed to the plan hatched by Canning and Wellesley. A final dispatch via Cuxhaven to Heligoland set in motion the evacuation. On 9 August La Romana escaped the French using all the ships available at Nyborg. His cavalry units had to leave behind their horses, shooting hundreds of them before embarking. Keats's ships brought La Romana's division to England, from where they went on to Spain.[58] In early October 1808 they landed in Santander and joined Wellington's campaign against Napoleon. It was a stunning success for British intelligence and military planning, much exploited in anti-French propaganda, orchestrated by Nicholas from his island outpost.[59]

Emboldened by the La Romana mission, London used Heligoland for a string of covert operations in which Britain and its Continental partners cooperated. In March 1809 the Portland government agreed to support a clandestine network of Prussian officers who seemed ready to rise against Napoleon—while their king, Friedrich Wilhelm III, was hesitating to commit himself against the French (Prussia had suffered a crushing defeat at Jena and Auerstedt three years earlier).[60] The insurgents' hopes rested on Major Ferdinand von Schill, who had fought an audacious guerrilla campaign against the French in 1806 and 1807.[61] Schill was now to lead an insurrection planned for Westphalia, which he hoped would spark a general revolution against Napoleon. Prussian and British agents made repeat journeys to and from Heligoland to negotiate the details. London agreed to supply arms and money via the island. Canning promised to send a British expedition to the Continent, should the insurrection be supported by the Prussian king.[62] In April 1809 Nicholas organized for Parish & Co in Hamburg to pay £20,000 up front to the insurgents via Augustus Maimburg, a captain in the King's German Legion who acted as an Anglo-Prussian go-between.[63]

Anticipating, as Canning told George III, 'a general rising throughout Westphalia and Lower Saxony', Heligoland was turned into a major weapons depot.[64] But much of this came too late. Schill began the revolt before having secured sufficient support, either in the Prussian or other armies. After some initial success, he had to retreat before Napoleon's troops. On 14 May 1809 Schill sent a courier to Nicholas requesting 20,000 muskets with ammunition as well as swords, pistols, and saddles for 3,000 men.[65] But none of these could be delivered in time and Schill withdrew to the Baltic coast. The British Admiralty was busy drawing up a plan to evacuate him and his troops when Nicholas was informed that Schill had been killed on 31 May 1809.[66] Those of his troops who survived were taken prisoner; only a few hundred escaped. Worse still, the Prussian king disowned Schill, quashing all hopes of a wider Prussian uprising.

Heligoland continued to be the Anglo-German headquarters for covert operations in northern Europe. To Canning's great regret, most of these followed a similar pattern: Britain would get weapons to the island and from there onto the Continent, but the uprisings they were meant to be used in fizzled out before British support could become effective. The abortive rebellion in Hanover in July 1809 was a case in point.[67] Two deliveries of arms and ammunition were shipped by convoy from Britain in mid-July.[68] The plan was to smuggle them to Hanover for an uprising which Canning hoped would distract the French from the expeditionary force London was about to send to Walcheren, the Dutch island in the Scheldt estuary. Nicholas organized for the weapons to be landed on the east Frisian coast, but the insurrection was aborted and the guns had to be abandoned. As Nicholas's agent wrote, French officers 'discovered our long train of waggons' and were soon 'in eager pursuit'.[69] In parallel with this, the British landing at Walcheren failed abysmally.[70]

A few more covert operations run from Heligoland followed, but, with bigger powers such as Prussia not ready to act, insurrections against Napoleon remained sporadic and weak in the German lands. It was a sign of the overall strategic situation that Heligoland was now used more and more for withdrawals. In August 1809 Nicholas managed to orchestrate the evacuation of Friedrich Wilhelm, the Duke of Brunswick Oels. The duke, George III's nephew, had raised a corps of partisans to fight the French and had briefly managed to re-occupy Brunswick. Vastly outnumbered, he fled with his 'Black Brunswickers' (so called because of the black uniforms they wore in mourning for their occupied country) to the North Sea. On 9 August 1809 they were evacuated to Heligoland from the River Weser amongst considerable chaos 'owing to the confusion of the moment, the Westphalians being on his rear [sic], and the Danes having occupied the other bank of the river'.[71] Within days a convoy brought the duke and his corps to England, from where they eventually joined Wellington's forces in the Peninsular War. George III was delighted about his nephew's rescue, which was duly celebrated in the press, but there was an unwelcome sense of déjà vu at Whitehall: the British were getting rather too much experience in evacuating troops from northern Europe.[72]

It was inevitable, given the prominence of such operations, that the French would try to put a stop to Britain's use of Heligoland. As early as

May 1808 Nicholas had reported that 'the enemy's secret agents' were trying to infiltrate the island under false German or English names.[73] In order to protect his network he set up special counter-intelligence measures. Travellers and merchants alike complained about the strict controls. Louis Ompteda, wrongly suspected of working for the French in May 1809, was one of them. Having been arrested together with two other travellers he found himself closely watched by an officer 'who seemed to perform the functions of a police agent':

> We were not permitted to speak with one another, or to approach the window, lest, perhaps, we might make secret signs to someone outside; we were scarcely allowed to move so great were at that time the precautions taken about Heligoland.[74]

The precautions taken by Nicholas paid off. In late August 1809 he arrested a French spy who had arrived on the island under the name of Herling. The Foreign Office had no doubt that this was 'a very active spy of the French government' known as 'Colville' or 'Lauda'. It asked Nicholas to 'send him to this country or detain him at Heligoland until you can receive instructions as to his future disposal'.[75] On 23 September Nicholas put Colville on a warship bound for England. The French agent 'still persisted in his story'. Nicholas had refrained from interrogating him further, trusting 'that he would come under much better hands' in London.[76]

In the wake of the Colville case the French made a sustained effort at cutting the routes connecting Heligoland with the Continent. While they were in no position to challenge the Royal Navy's squadron stationed off the island, they became increasingly effective at controlling the entrances to the Rivers Elbe and Weser. Again and again British detachments had to embark on missions to keep a check on Danish and French gunboats. To Nicholas's great regret, he did not manage to hold on to Neuwerk, a small tidal island close to the Cuxhaven coast which served as a stepping stone for his couriers. About thirty nautical miles from Heligoland, Neuwerk is exposed at low tide, so that visitors can walk to it from the mainland. Nicholas paid a generous fee to the lighthouse keeper who orchestrated the secret exchange of post on the islet. He would make a 'private signal' to the Heligoland boatmen, indicating that they could land and hide their secret mail.[77] Once they had left he would make a signal to agents on the mainland, who would then walk over the mudflats to Neuwerk and pick up the correspondence. This maritime dead drop worked smoothly until Neuwerk was used for the evacuation of deserters, which brought it to the attention of the French.

Initially Royal Marines were able to drive the French off the island again, but the navy's ships could not operate in the shallow waters and the French had the advantage of land access. Lord George Stuart, in command of the frigate HMS *Horatio*, was 'sorry to say' that his squadron could do rather little.[78] By November 1810 Neuwerk had to be given up.

Yet none of this put an end to the secret communication between Britain and the Continent. Nicholas was able to establish alternative routes to the Holstein coast and on to the Hanseatic cities, aided by staff at the Hamburg Post Office who were in his pay.[79] When his own agents or informants were arrested he managed surprisingly often to get them released, mostly through 'the timely application of a bribe'.[80] When this failed, the incriminating material could normally be 'purchased out of the hands of the French seizing officers'.[81] This was particularly important in cases where it concerned John Parish, Nicholas's banker on the Continent. When the cover of a Hamburg agent who knew Parish was blown he moved him 'out of reach of the French authorities'.[82] Nicholas was similarly obsessive about protecting any communication that could implicate the British government.[83] Only once during his mission did official dispatches from London come into the hands of the French.[84]

Nicholas's success in protecting Britain's secret communication with the Continent reflected the advantage he enjoyed over the French in running his Anglo-German network. His headquarters at Heligoland was out of Napoleon's reach—there was a brief scare late in 1810 that the French would try to take Heligoland, but the Royal Navy's command of the North Sea was never tested. At the same time, Nicholas's station was close enough to the Continent for his couriers to sail to the mainland and back within a day. Most of all, he could rely on a dense clandestine network in the coastal areas occupied by the French. This included not only outright agents, but also friends, associates, and informants, most of whom he knew from his days in Hamburg. His contacts ranged from officials and high-ranking officers to pub owners and fishermen. Nicholas rarely struggled to recruit locals willing to assist him, despite the dangers involved. This is partly explained by the generous payments he offered. Yet the goodwill he encountered reflected not only opportunism, but also a combination of patriotism and Anglophilia: many in the Hanseatic, Hanoverian, and Frisian territories were convinced that the British effort against Napoleon was aligned with their own interests. 'The whole of the coast from the Ems to the Elbe', Friedrich von der Decken wrote in December 1811, 'is inhabited by people who are not only anxious to have intercourse with England, but are sincerely attached to the English cause'.[85]

Nowhere did this symbiosis between British and Continental interests show more than in the vast smuggling activity that centred on Heligoland. Circumventing the Continental System, Napoleon's blockade of British commerce was pivotal for Britain's finances as well as its strategic prospects in Europe.[86] Smuggling had been accordingly high on Canning's agenda when he first suggested that the island should be taken, but many British merchants were initially hesitant. Nathan Mayer Rothschild, the Frankfurt-born founder of the famous London house, first contemplated smuggling via the island in October 1807. His father-in-law, Levy Barent Cohen, warned him:

> Regarding shipping to Heligoland, it is attained with too much difficulty to attempt anything. Some clever person is necessary to have on the other side, say the Continent, to give you information in what manner to manage this kind of business.[87]

What was needed was 'a friend there to arrange matters' so that 'you can introduce the goods to the Continent'.[88] While government initiative was essential in securing Heligoland, the problem described by Cohen was solved by the Hanseatic merchants who pioneered routes through which to land goods on the Continent. The Parish brothers were amongst them, acting as agents for British houses while also trading on their own account.

By the spring of 1808 an extraordinary network of Anglo-German merchants had begun to use Heligoland for large-scale smuggling. In May 1808 Canning asked Nicholas to set up a system allowing merchants from Britain and the Continent to reside on the island. This was because the 'applications which are daily made for passports to Heligoland . . . have become so numerous'.[89] By the summer of 1808 around 200 merchants, mostly from London, Hamburg, Edinburgh, Bremen, Liverpool, Frankfurt, and Manchester, had settled on Heligoland. Two years later Hamilton estimated that, together with their clerks and servants, the merchants made up about 1,000 foreign residents.[90] It was they who advised the government how to break Napoleon's blockade and they were the ones who shouldered the enormous risk involved.

At the core of their activity lay the island's Chamber of Commerce.[91] Nationality played no role in the Chamber—any merchant residing on the island qualified for membership. This included representatives of companies that had their headquarters in Britain or on the Continent.[92] Larger houses such as Rothschild, Oppenheim, and Parish were thus able to establish branches on the island, using agents and cover names.[93] The vast majority of merchants had British or Hanseatic-German backgrounds.[94] They voted for a president (a Hamburg trader) to lead the Chamber and a secretary (a London merchant) to assist him. What they had in common was commercial interest and a cosmopolitan outlook—many amongst them had family in and business ties to both Britain and the Continent. Consequently, the Chamber had decidedly little of a national agenda. As one critic wrote to Canning, 'the merchants that compose the same want patriotism'.[95]

Precisely this, not representing national interests, made the Chamber successful: it could speak for merchants from all backgrounds, including the handful of Scandinavian and exiled French ones that existed amongst the Anglo-German houses dominating the trade. From the beginning the Chamber succeeded in negotiating favourable conditions both on the island and in London. This included a passport system by which ships were cleared, allowing Nicholas's men to inspect cargoes and crews, while ensuring a swift landing of goods.[96] When the government changed this mechanism to a licence system, which was less flexible, the Chamber intervened to have it amended.[97] Importantly, it succeeded early on in lobbying London to provide naval protection. The Admiralty duly dispatched warships to guard the transports sailing in convoy across the North Sea.[98] And it reinforced the squadron at Heligoland tasked with patrolling the coasts of Holstein and eastern Frisia as well as the Elbe and Weser estuaries. Without this protection few of the boatmen making the hazardous journey to and from the mainland would have succeeded for long. Here is how a passenger described a typical trip:

> At midnight I was on the shore where the ship which was to take me was at anchor. I found my unknown [sic] on board immediately. He was no less a person than a Bremen smuggler, and owner of the cargo. There were also two young merchants from Hamburg who wished to proceed to Spain from England. The total ship's company consisted of the skipper, quite a common man, and a lad of sixteen or seventeen... After a time, when we were approaching the estuary of the Elbe, we heard the reports of cannon-fire, which on the sea has a peculiarly clear sound. I learned later on that it was an English frigate which had engaged some French gunboats at the mouth of the Elbe. At last, towards 3pm, we anchored off Heligoland.[99]

From early 1808 the covert trade rose dramatically. The Colonial Office was inundated with requests from merchants for land on the island. In April

Governor Hamilton warned his superiors that the 'mercantile establishments are already too numerous, considering the contracted space to be occupied, the number of foreigners necessarily employed as labourers from the continent, and that the supply of water is far from being abundant'.[100] 'The spirit of adventure is so great', he wrote in October, that the harbour was full of ships despite 'this critical and hazardous season'.[101] In November the Chamber of Commerce told the underwriters at Lloyd's that the Heligoland trade had reached 'an extent which the most sanguine mind could hardly have imagined it capable of reaching under the present extraordinary situation of the Continent'. Within twelve days 'upwards of one hundred and twenty vessels fully laden' had arrived from Britain, the 'aggregate value of whose cargoes cannot be less than eight hundred thousand pounds'.[102] In March 1810 Hamilton told the Earl of Liverpool that 'every spot unoccupied [on the island] has been appropriated to mercantile purposes'.[103] He calculated that goods in the value of four to five million pounds were on the island at any given time.[104]

Heligoland was now the most important covert trading outpost the British had apart from Malta, the smuggling centre of the Mediterranean.[105] The volume of trade can be reconstructed with some precision, as the Chamber of Commerce raised a levy on all goods landed on the island. The levy was used to fund the facilities run by the Chamber as well as pay for the harbour master and his men who orchestrated the stream of ships coming and going—up to 300 vessels a day in good weather. There were a few merchants who refused to pay or fell into arrears, but the vast majority complied with the system, so that the levies paid reflect the overall value of goods fairly reliably. Accounts exist for 1809 to 1811. They show that for these years a total of £215,837 was raised in levies. Given that the rate remained unchanged at 0.25 per cent, the value of goods registered in this way would have amounted to roughly £86.3 million, a little more than Britain's annual public budget for 1811.[106] These were extraordinary sums, exceeding even the value of goods being smuggled through Malta.[107] As the Chamber of Commerce explained to the Committee at Lloyd's, Heligoland was 'the only medium through which the North of Germany and the countries upon the Rhine can receive their supplies'.[108]

Heligoland's role became so notorious that Heinrich von Kleist, the Prussian playwright, devoted a long article to it in December 1810, defying the Prussian censors. According to his account, goods worth £20 million had been piled up on the island. The activity there exceeded 'all trading

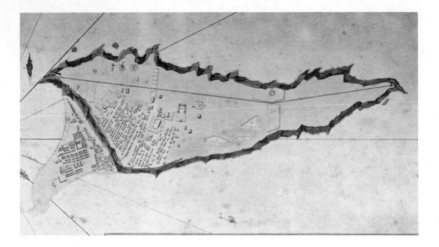

Figure 1.2 Bird's-eye view of Heligoland during the Napoleonic Wars. Detail from *A Map of the Island of Heligoland* by G. Testoline, 1810.

places of the Continent' and belonged to 'the most extraordinary and remarkable appearances of our time'.[109] The French were accordingly keen to stop the smuggling. Napoleon's police commissars warned in public announcements that 'any interaction with the English via Heligoland will be treated as treason'.[110] They even forbade the use of English in conversation or writing in the ports and cities along the coast. But despite their concerted efforts, the French failed to put an end to the clandestine trade. Their gunboats could never control the entire coast. As long as the Royal Navy did its bit, Governor Hamilton told Lord Castlereagh, the foreign secretary, then the smugglers would 'find no difficulty in landing their cargoes on the adjacent coasts'.[111] Practically all the smuggling was conducted in small ships, sailed at dusk or dawn by local fishermen who knew the waters better than anyone else. As John Rennie, the civil engineer, explained in a letter to the First Lord of the Admiralty, Robert Dundas:

> The vessels which generally carry on the trade between the island of Heligoland and the continent carry from 5 to 50 tons, are very flatt [*sic*] and drawn from 4 to 5 feet of water. They come in great numbers, so much so, that Mr Brown [the harbour master] says he has seen 800 sail (including open boats) at one time.[112]

The goods which the Heligoland smugglers ferried to the Continent showed how closely intertwined empire and Europe were in British trade.

The vast majority was colonial produce, shipped from India, east Asia, the Caribbean, and the Americas. A list from July 1812 provides a snapshot (in descending order of importance): coffee, sugar, tobacco, cotton wool, pimiento, pepper, cocoa, ginger, indigo, nutmeg, cinnamon, cardamom, treacle, gum, shellac, currants, raisins, rum, tea, rice.[113] Coffee was consistently on top of the lists of traded goods. In 1813 more than 11 million pounds of coffee were shipped via Heligoland, about a third of what Britain's colonies produced.[114] There was, as Patrick Colquhoun (a merchant who knew northern Germany well) wrote, 'a universal taste for coffee on the Continent, which pervaded all ranks of the people'.[115] It was colonial products such as coffee, followed by sugar and tobacco in traded volumes, which broke the Continental System—leading Marx and Engels to declare later that Napoleon had lost the war because of the Germans' love of sugar and coffee.[116] The covert trade in British manufactures was secondary in comparison to colonial products, rarely making up more than a fifth of the goods traded. As Charles Graumann, a prominent member of the Heligoland Chamber of Commerce, explained, the 'most flourishing' trade lay in exporting to the Continent 'the produce of her [i.e. Britain's] colonys [sic]'.[117]

As the clandestine trade revealed, it was not only commerce that linked Europe and the British empire in this North Sea outpost, but also the law. Most of the merchants were used to the rules that governed trade in commercial centres such as London, Edinburgh, or Liverpool. But the island's magistrates felt bound by a set of laws that had been in place before the British occupation. Only some of these were documented. As Hamilton observed in March 1808, 'certain regulations peculiar to the situation and circumstances of the inhabitants' had been established by custom and were never written down.[118] For most of the traders operating on the island this seemed arbitrary and unacceptable. There were 'numerous and complicated cases' which arose from this collision of legal traditions.[119] Most small conflicts could be settled informally within the Chamber, but a number of more serious cases raised issues that could not be ignored. All of these involved British subjects who argued that their rights had been abused and that Britain's laws should apply in the island.

This was not a particularly new problem for the Colonial Office. In other parts of the empire British rule depended also on laws and jurisprudence that were foreign to the English legal tradition. The lawyers at Whitehall repeatedly compared Heligoland to Malta and the Cape, where Continental European and British laws collided similarly.[120] What complicated the matter in Heligoland were two factors. First, Britain was at war with the state that had administered the rule of law in the island previously—Whitehall could hardly write to Denmark for legal advice. Second, the island's sudden commercial importance meant that a number of British subjects were affected who had the means and incentive—as well as the ego and education—to engage in lengthy legal battles. A sense of disbelief is palpable in their correspondence with the government: could a bunch of fishermen on a rock in the North Sea be allowed to use their own laws to pass judgement on established London merchants who were backed by City bankers and lawyers?[121]

The attorney general thought they could, as long as the decisions of the Heligoland court were based on pre-existing Danish or Holstein laws. This confirmed the position taken by the island's magistrates: all Heligoland laws continued to be valid unless explicitly abolished by new British laws. As the government's lawyers put it, 'until the King gives laws to a conquered country, they are governed by their own laws'.[122] The Foreign Office had recommended in 1807 that the island's 'internal government should be continued as exists at present without any alteration' and the articles of capitulation had been signed in this spirit.[123] Governor Hamilton accordingly sided with the magistrates against British residents in a number of cases.[124] Mindful that this alienated the British on the island, he repeatedly asked the Colonial Office for help.[125] In May 1811, the Earl of Liverpool assured him that the government would try to introduce in the island 'some form of judicature more consonant to the feelings of the British part of the inhabitants'.[126] Nicholas, who wisely stayed out of all legal conflicts, thought that this was urgent. 'The island is in a sad state', he wrote, 'and something should be done by Government'. Whitehall should either introduce English laws or send an official 'acquainted with the [relevant] foreign jurisprudence'.[127] But there was no such person at the Colonial Office and the solicitor general advised against abolishing the pre-existing law: 'The usual course, I believe, has been to leave the old laws in force until a treaty of peace takes place'.[128] The legal muddle continued, as did the governor's dependence on Continental laws.

As long as lucrative deals were to be made most of the merchants put up with these legal oddities. And lucrative deals there were, promising extraordinary profits. On average the smugglers could expect to make a 50 per cent gain on the value of goods, often more.[129] At the height of the smuggling trade, coffee could be sold in Hamburg at twice the London price. Some merchants operating from the island became very rich very quickly. Abraham Ellerman was ahead of everyone else in this respect. One of the first merchants to establish themselves on the island, he was elected as president of the Chamber of Commerce in 1808 and remained one of the most influential personalities throughout the war years. Ellerman exemplified the Anglo-Hanseatic symbiosis fostered by the Napoleonic Wars.[130] Born in Altona in 1775, he grew up in Hamburg, but was sent to boarding school in England. Like so many of the Hanseatic merchants, he had close contacts to the anglophone world. In October 1808 he married Eliza Georgiana Lang Hughes, the 18-year-old daughter of a British officer stationed on the island. Ellerman had learned the merchant trade working for the Parish brothers, but worked on his own account in Heligoland. Between 1808 and 1813 he had by far the highest turnover of all the merchants there, amounting to roughly £400,000 for the period 1809 to 1811. Assuming that he operated with a similar margin as most, he could have made a profit of as much as £200,000 in those three years alone.[131] He lived 'in great style and kept open house, priding himself upon not allowing any person of distinction or note to visit the island without having tasted of his hospitality…which was granted in a princely style', wrote his son later.[132]

But extraordinary losses could be made too. While Ellerman left the island as a rich man, many other merchants lost their fortunes in the Heligoland trade. There was no regular insurance against the risks involved. If underwriters could be found, their commitment was not in the form of legal contracts that could be enforced. As Nathan Rothschild was told, insuring cargo that was to go through Napoleon's blockade was done 'always upon separate slip of paper [sic] which is an honorable matter which cannot be brought to a court of law'.[133] Many cargoes were sent without insurance against capture, despite the risk posed by privateers and the gunboats of the French and Danish. The merchant ships sailing from Britain were soon armed, which deterred some privateers. A clerk working for Rothschild on Heligoland wrote in January 1812 that a British vessel had 'reported of being attacked by a French privatier [sic], though ready to counterattack with 24 armed men, the French privatier steered off without a fight'.[134] Smaller boats caught by French forces close to the shore could often be bought free, but there remained the underlying risk of having to write off an entire cargo. As Ellerman explained to the Committee at Lloyd's:

If the goods were seized by the Douaniers, gunboats or Gendarmes of the enemy, it has always been possible, except in four or five instances, to obtain their release for the payment of a moderate sum of money, which seldom exceeded the profit which could be had on the sale of the property. When captured by the Danes however the case became widely different since the loss was then absolute and irretrievable.[135]

It was not only the dangers arising from the smuggling itself, but also the unpredictable fluctuations in prices, which posed high risks. This was especially precarious for smaller houses entering the game late. Bodan and Skirving was one of them. Heligoland was 'very ruinous' for the Edinburgh merchants, who went bankrupt in 1811.[136] A larger number of insolvencies followed from late 1813 when prices fell sharply. James Forrest and William Miller, both from Leith in Scotland, were part of this wave. The drop in the price of coffee and sugar hit them hard, reducing their cash flow so much that they could not pay their debtors and had to file for bankruptcy in 1814.[137]

The fall in the smugglers' fortunes mirrored the decline in Napoleon's position in Europe. In February 1813 the Prussian king joined the coalition against the French. His troops now fought together with Austrian, Russian, British, Swedish, Spanish, and Portuguese forces. In June 1813 the largest transport yet went from Heligoland to support the allied troops with arms and ammunition.[138] On 13 October Russian forces captured Bremen. Three days later the Battle of Leipzig began, which marked the end of Napoleon's rule in German-speaking Europe. Decisively defeated, his troops retreated towards France. Only Hamburg, turned into a fortress under Marshal Davout, was held. In December 1813 more weapons were shipped from Heligoland for the troops involved in the siege of the city (which was to last until Napoleon's abdication).[139] At the same time London revoked the licence system which had given the Heligoland merchants a de facto monopoly. There was little left of Napoleon's Continental System, so Britain's blockade could be lifted too.[140] The days of covert trade were numbered. Within a few months the 'pleasing and fascinating melange' of Anglo-German merchants, officers, spies, and exiles had begun to leave the island.[141]

Late in 1813, more than six years after he had first fled northern Germany, Edward Thornton, Britain's envoy extraordinary, returned to the Continent. Lord Castlereagh had charged him with negotiating a peace treaty with Denmark. Thornton had clear instructions: London would be prepared to give back all occupied Danish possessions, except Heligoland. This had been

Canning's position throughout the war. As early as October 1807 he had told Count von Bernstorff, the Danish foreign secretary, that Britain would not return the island. Then Bernstorff had rejected all such 'insulting offers'.[142] Now Denmark was prepared to cede Heligoland 'in order to restore peace', as Frederick VI, the Danish king, put it.[143] In the Treaty of Kiel, signed on 14 January 1814, he granted the British crown 'full and unlimited sovereignty' over the rock in the North Sea.[144] While this only confirmed the fait accompli presented by the occupation of September 1807, it was more than a formality: Britain now had a legal claim to the outpost. Later in the year the cession was made public in Heligoland when announcements in Danish and German were posted in the town. They contained a declaration by Frederick VI, relinquishing his claim on the island and releasing his subjects from their oath of loyalty to the Danish crown.[145]

London's determination to keep the island expressed an underlying belief in the importance of Continental Europe for Britain's geopolitical position. If the wars against the French had shown anything it was that Britain could not win against European threats by retreating onto an 'insular empire'. In 1814 this was the fundamental lesson drawn from the Napoleonic experience and it was what gave Heligoland its strategic value. Ever since Vice-Admiral Russell had taken it in September 1807, the island had been a key component of Britain's Continental commitment. London had used it in every way possible to fight Napoleon and support the European resistance against him. Maintaining a presence here, at the edge of the Continent, signalled that Britain would do so again, if necessary. It also demonstrated a rather large amount of confidence in the Royal Navy. In keeping the outpost, which was so much closer to northern Germany and Denmark than to England, London showed little doubt in its ability to see off any future naval challengers from across the North Sea. With hindsight it seems astonishing that this was to prove an accurate assumption for the entire nineteenth century.

2

Nation and Empire

When John Hindmarsh arrived in Heligoland in October 1840 he was instantly disappointed. The contrast to South Australia, the colony he had previously governed, could not have been starker. This North Sea island seemed permanently enveloped by bad weather.[1] And it was small, very small—'scarcely more than a rock'.[2] Yet what seemed fascinating was the way in which the British empire and 'the people of Europe' were bound up with one another here.[3] The weights and measures used in the colony were not the imperial ones, as standardized by Parliament in 1824, but those common in most German states. The most widely used currency was the Hamburg Mark Courant. Practically all accounts on the island, including that of the public debt, were held in that currency. Important public notices were displayed in German and English. German was spoken in church, in court, and at school.

Intrigued by the European character of his colony, Hindmarsh spent much time researching its history. It seemed obvious to him that the interweaving of colonial and Continental structures had begun during the Napoleonic Wars. But much of the Anglo-German symbiosis prompted by the French threat had since disappeared. Practically all of the merchants, officers, and spies had left Heligoland after France's defeat. A new generation of residents and visitors had since begun to give the island a novel character. His colony, Hindmarsh thought, was becoming more German.

This had started in the 1830s when the island had been frequented by radicals and revolutionaries who appreciated the colony as a safe haven from where to propagate a new Germany. Ludolf Wienbarg, who coined the title *Junges Deutschland* ('Young Germany') for the literary and political movement, thought of the British colony as his 'Switzerland'.[4] 'Only where England's proud flag is hoisted' could those persecuted on the Continent for their political views live 'in peace'.[5] The colony was close enough to the mainland for him and other politically minded poets to stay in touch with developments in Europe. Yet it was at a safe distance from the hands of the Continent's police forces. The island consequently turned into a hotbed of radicals who, under the watchful eyes of the British governor, dreamt of German nationhood and revolution.

Heinrich Heine was the first of a line of prominent writers who decamped to the island in order to escape censorship and police surveillance. Heine stayed twice, in the summers of 1829 and 1830. He was 'tired and desperate for peace and quiet', he wrote.[6] In the German lands it was impossible to relax, for fear of the police. But in the British colony he found a safe haven from the 'guerrilla war' he had been involved in. What he appreciated about the island was not only its political freedom, but also its qualities as a holiday destination. 'You have no idea how much I am enjoying the *dolce far niente* here', he enthused.[7] Heine filled this sweet idleness with reading, writing, and long conversations with other visitors.

It is this combination of literary exile and seaside holiday that forms the backdrop to Heine's *Helgoländer Briefe* (*Heligoland Letters*), a series of fictional letters written from the island which he published later as part of his political manifesto *Ludwig Börne: Eine Denkschrift* (*Ludwig Börne: A Memorial*).[8] The letters linked anecdotal travel observations with political and philosophical reflections, much in the style of the *Reisebilder* (*Travel Pictures*), which had established Heine's reputation as a travel writer. The *Reisebilder*, published between 1826 and 1831, were based on Heine's journeys through Europe, but they went beyond mere travelogues. Written in a sarcastic-ironic tone, they contained an acerbic critique of the reactionary politics dominating in the German-speaking states. At the same time Heine's *Reisebilder* and his Heligoland letters had, like much of the literature of the *Junges Deutschland*, a deeply romantic dimension: the longing for nature and the call for political freedom went hand in hand. Heine's depiction of Heligoland and the sea offers key examples of this romanticism, which was to be much imitated by writers following in his footsteps:

> I strolled along the beach on my own at dusk. All around me prevailed festive silence [*feierliche Stille*]. The high-arched sky resembled a gothic cathedral. The stars hung like countless lamps, but they burnt dimly and tremulously. The waves roared like a water organ: stormy chorales, painful, desperate, though now and then triumphant. Up above me an airy procession of white cloud formations that looked like monks, all of them moving along with bowed heads and a sorrowful look, a sad parade.[9]

Throughout his travel prose Heine links such emotional images with political and religious discussions. The main, dominant themes that run through
his letters from Heligoland are freedom and revolution. He learned of the
July revolution in 1830 while residing in the island. 'It is still all like a dream',
he wrote. 'Lafayette, the *tricolore*, the Marseillaise . . . it is as if I am drunk'. The
events in Paris had hit the guests like sunstroke (*Sonnenstich*). 'I know again
what I want now', he exclaimed, 'I am the son of the revolution'.[10] Even the
islanders seemed to be jubilant about the French king's abdication, hailing
it as a victory for the poor.

Heine clearly enjoyed his time in Heligoland, but the colony also
reminded him about everything that he felt was wrong with Britain. The
governor, '*dieser Stockengländer*' (literally, 'this stock Englishman'), was a case
study in the uninspiring character of the English. Heine felt he 'could smell
the boredom which Albion's sons emit everywhere'. He had experienced
this in Britain itself, but also with the British abroad. Indeed, every Englishman
he had met had given off 'a certain gas, the deadly, thick air of boredom'.
The English believed that this unfortunate feature was a product of their
country rather than themselves. In order to escape it, they went on long
European journeys, but in vain: it was impossible to shake off the boredom
of Britain. So 'they travel through all countries, get bored everywhere and
return home with the *diary of an ennuyée* [*sic*]'.[11]

It was not only boredom Heine accused the British of in his letters from
Heligoland, but also a raft of stereotypes designed to set them apart from
Continental nations and in particular the French, to whom Heine felt closest.
Just like the Americans, to whom they had passed on all their bad habits, the
English were hypocritical and materialistic. While professing to be pious
believers, their true religion was material gain. Money was 'their sole, almighty
god'. What this showed, Heine thought, was the lamentable effect freedom
had had in Britain and the United States. For all the political liberties that the
English and Americans had gained, they had failed to use them for any higher
purpose. Instead, they were obsessed with material gain and ridden with
egotism. Freedom, in its anglophone variety, seemed like 'a bad dream'.[12]

Heine was followed by a succession of radicals and revolutionaries who fled
the Continent to the island in the wake of the 1830 revolutions. Easily the
most notorious amongst them, certainly in the eyes of the British authorities, was Harro Harring. In contrast to most of the authors associated with
the *Junges Deutschland*, Harring had not only written about freedom, but he

had also fought for it in a number of revolutionary uprisings. He had been a prominent participant at the Hambach festival in 1832, at which more than 20,000 students had demonstrated for the unification and democratization of Germany. *Persona non grata* in most German states, he fled to Switzerland. Expelled from there, he travelled through numerous other countries before taking refuge in Heligoland in November 1837.

Harring clearly presented a step too far for Henry King, the then Heligoland governor. For years King had tolerated the politicized poets who came to his island to propagate a democratic and united Germany. After all, these political tourists spent handsome sums during their exile, which helped to reduce the colony's public debt. But Harring was in a different league: not content with enjoying Britain's freedom, he seemed bent on preaching revolution in this colonial outpost too. Acquaintances described him as a 'demagogue by profession'.[13] King decided that he should be moved on, lest he create problems with neighbouring countries or, worse, politicize the islanders themselves. Constitutional government and democratic elections were dangerous ideas for a colony in which the inhabitants had no vote and no say in who governed them. On 6 April the Court of Magistrates ordered Harring to leave the island within seventy-two hours. The governor confirmed the decree on the next day, but Harring refused to go. Instead he entered into a lengthy debate in which he accused the governor of acting arbitrarily and violating basic human rights. King would have none of it and asked London to send a warship to remove the revolutionary.

Harring, awaiting deportation, promptly penned (in verse) a critique of British liberties, which was published the same year in London.[14] He felt insulted and betrayed by the English, he exclaimed. Like so many liberals on the Continent he had thought of Britain as a beacon of law and justice. While all over Europe revolutionaries had fought hard (and often in vain) to establish human rights and equal laws for all, the British had enjoyed their long-existing liberties. But clearly the rule of law did not extend to the empire, not even to a colony that consisted exclusively of Europeans. He was bitterly disappointed with the 'freedom' granted to him in this outpost. Heligoland, where he had hoped to find peace, seemed now like any Continental 'state in miniature'. Without legal representation and without a trial he had been banned from the island. 'The King' (i.e. the governor) had even 'threatened me with Botany Bay'.[15]

All this made 'Rule Britannia' sound cruelly ironic: 'Britons never shall be slaves' seemed to imply for Harring that it was perfectly acceptable if others *were* slaves. The rule of law was a privilege not of all humans, but of those lucky enough to have been born British. So he sat 'betrayed and mocked on England's "free" rock':

> Ich sitz verraten und verhöhnt
> Auf Englands 'freiem' Felsen hier... [16]

On 6 June 1838 HMS *Partridge* arrived at Heligoland. A detachment of marines bound Harring (who was apparently armed) in ropes and took him on board. He was deported to Britain, where he continued to accuse the government of acting tyrannically in its colonies. 'Give me back my precious weeks', read one of his accusatory poems, 'which you have taken from me by breaking England's law'.[17] The Colonial Office was keen to establish the legality of his deportation. In August 1838 it obtained legal advice that 'there can be no doubt that Harro Harring was lawfully removed from Heligoland'.[18] This was based not on British law (which would never have approved the governor's proceedings), but on pre-existing Continental laws which still applied in the island—for once the colony's position at the fault line between different legal traditions worked in favour of the governor. Harring, who felt 'robbed' of his rights and freedoms, moved on. He travelled through a number of countries, none of which granted him asylum. In May 1839 he returned to Heligoland, only to be expelled again. After spells in France, Holland, and Brazil he spent time in the United States, from where he contacted the governor in Heligoland to ask whether he might be allowed to return. But Governor Hindmarsh, King's successor, made it clear that the 'mischievous monomaniac' would be 'immediately expelled'.[19]

Harring's story, which soon featured in tourist guides and travel diaries, did nothing to stop the influx of political radicals to the colony. There was a real danger, the magistrates wrote to London, that 'our island may become a hiding place of revolutionary ringleaders, of discontented, baseminded and inflammatory subjects'.[20] The police on the Continent, too, were keenly aware of the island's function as an exile for those censored in northern Germany. In 1837 the 'Göttingen Seven' had been suspended, all of them prominent professors who had protested against the revocation of the Hanover constitution. In the wake of their dismissal, an increasing number of politically active academics and intellectuals were forced to publish from outside their home states. Heligoland became an ideal location for them, so much so that the Hanover police employed informants on the island to keep an eye on their activities.[21]

On 21 August 1840 a Hanoverian officer reported that more than 100 delegates had been welcomed on the island by groups of like-minded radicals from other German states. Most prominent amongst them had been one 'Professor Hoffmann from Breslau, a born Hanoverian and known liberal poet'. Led by him, the gathering had 'wined, dined and sung songs':

> Hoffmann gave numerous liberal and revolutionary speeches and made offensive references to the measures taken by our government. Many toasts are reported to have been raised with veiled attacks on His Majesty [the king of Hanover] and his government... Hoffmann got the most rousing applause and used every opportunity to show much enthusiasm for the cause of the opposition as well as display his intelligence, wit and eloquence.[22]

Few other figures did more to anchor Heligoland in the national imagination than the eloquent Professor August Heinrich Hoffmann. Publishing under the pen name 'Hoffmann von Fallersleben', he had become famous for his *Unpolitische Lieder*, a collection of poems that were anything but 'a-political'.[23] Widely read and recited, the songs turned into one of the most successful critiques of contemporary Germany. They were promptly censored in most German-speaking countries. Like Heine and Harring before him, Fallersleben was forced to publish from outside the Prussian- and Austrian-dominated sphere. Heligoland was an outpost from where he could do so. It allowed him not only to converse, as he put it, with 'oppositional men' from all over German-speaking Europe, but it also meant that he could have unrestrained meetings with his Hamburg publisher Julius Campe.[24]

It was here, in a British colony, that Fallersleben wrote the *Lied der Deutschen*, which was to become Germany's national anthem. Fallersleben later styled the origins of the song as a deeply emotional occasion on which the experience of nature had forced him to think about German nationhood:

> As I wandered in solitude along the cliffs, with nothing but the sky and the sea around me, I felt so uncanny and I had to write, even if I did not want to.[25]

This retrospective romanticization suggested an image (the creative soul feeling the nation in unison with nature) that could have come straight from Caspar David Friedrich, by then already the most influential German landscape painter. It worked all the better here since Fallersleben was imagining Germany from the edge of the Continent. The sea separated him from the patchwork of *Kleinstaaten* and illiberal regimes that he hoped would one day be superseded by a unified Fatherland. There is no reason to suggest that Fallersleben did not genuinely feel this romantic combination when he

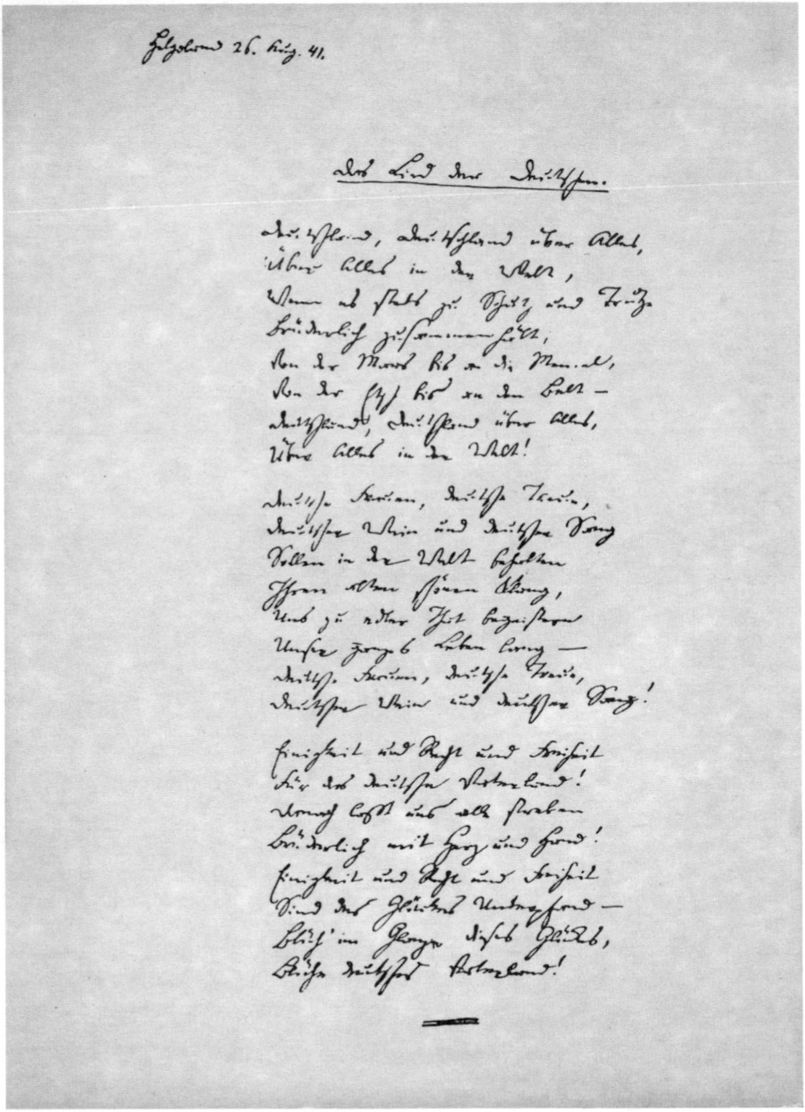

Figure 2.1 'Das Lied der Deutschen'. Manuscript by August Heinrich Hoffmann von Fallersleben, Heligoland, 26 August 1841.

wrote 'Deutschland, Deutschland über Alles' on 26 August 1841. But the self-styled image of the solitary poet staring at the sea and feeling the urge to write 'the nation' needs to be augmented by the picture of Fallersleben on holiday, having a good time with the rich and privileged. Amongst the acquaintances whom he cultivated on the island were aristocrats, bankers, and factory owners, whose interests lay not so much in discussions about politics or poetry, but in drink and entertainment. Fallersleben joined them happily. 'I developed an admirable ability to open bottles of champagne', he recalled.[26] This was no contradiction—wining and dining went hand in hand with dreaming the nation. Indeed, the *Deutschlandlied* was a drinking song long before it became a solemn anthem. The second verse offered a toast to German women and wine; and the original Heligoland manuscript included a variant ending which called for the audience to raise a glass to the Fatherland.[27]

As with so many of his political poems, Fallersleben set the words of the *Deutschlandlied* to an existing song which he could expect most educated Germans to be familiar with. His choice, a catchy tune composed by Joseph Haydn, showed how politically aware (and ambitious) Fallersleben was. Haydn had composed the song in honour of the Austrian emperor, Francis II, to the words of Lorenz Leopold Haschka's poem 'Gott erhalte Franz den Kaiser' ('God save Kaiser Franz'). Later used by Haydn in the second movement of his 'Emperor' string quartet (Opus 76, no. 3), the tune had turned into the unofficial anthem of the Habsburg empire, a popular parallel to the English 'God Save the King'. Fallersleben thus took a monarchical anthem and turned it into a song that challenged monarchy explicitly. *Einigkeit und Recht und Freiheit* ('Unity and Justice and Freedom'), the chorus at the heart of the 'Song of the Germans', clearly referred to the French revolution and its rhetoric of *égalité, fraternité, liberté*. Germany, united and free, was to be above princes and kings, hereditary rule and absolutism; and it was to be united in defence of itself (as well as in drinking wine and adoring its women):

Deutschland, Deutschland über alles,	Germany, Germany above all else,
Über alles in der Welt,	Above everything in the world,
Wenn es stets zu Schutz und Trutze	When, always, for protection and defence
Brüderlich zusammenhält,	It stands brotherly together,
Von der Maas bis an die Memel,	From the Maas to the Memel,
Von der Etsch bis an den Belt—	From the Etsch to the Belt—
Deutschland, Deutschland über alles,	Germany, Germany above all,
Über alles in der Welt!	Above all else in the world!

Deutsche Frauen, deutsche Treue,	German women, German loyalty,
Deutscher Wein und deutscher Sang	German wine and German song
Sollen in der Welt behalten	Shall retain, throughout the world
Ihren alten schönen Klang,	Their old beautiful sound,
Uns zu edler Tat begeistern	And inspire us to noble deeds
Unser ganzes Leben lang—	For the length of our lives—
Deutsche Frauen, deutsche Treue,	German women, German loyalty,
Deutscher Wein und deutscher Sang!	German wine and German song!
Einigkeit und Recht und Freiheit	Unity and justice and freedom
Für das deutsche Vaterland!	For the German fatherland!
Danach lasst uns alle streben	For this let us all strive
Brüderlich mit Herz und Hand!	Brotherly, with heart and hand!
Einigkeit und Recht und Freiheit	Unity and justice and freedom
Sind des Glückes Unterpfand—	Are the pledge of fortune—
Blüh, im Glanze dieses Glückes,	Bloom in the splendour of this happiness,
Blühe, deutsches Vaterland!	Bloom, German fatherland![28]

Fallersleben read the completed text to Campe on 29 August 1841. Campe bought it on the spot and returned to Heligoland five days later with the first proof. On 5 October it was sung publicly for the first time—by a crowd of students and patriotic gymnasts (*Turner*) marching through Hamburg in honour of Carl Theodor Welcker, a prominent liberal professor. The Prussian government censored the publication of the *Lied der Deutschen*, but it could do little to prevent its growing popularity. The song became a rallying cry for the opposition in the German lands, demanding national unity, freedom, and the rule of law. Hand in hand with this liberal vision went a claim for 'German' territory. This tension mirrored the irredentism that was inherent in most national liberal writing of the time. It was significant in this context that Fallersleben told the British governor that he had no doubt Heligoland would be German one day.[29]

By 1844 the colony had become so notorious as a safe haven for national liberals and political radicals that the Austrian Chancellor Metternich appealed to the British not to allow the enclave to become a place from where 'trouble' would be 'exported to the states of the German Federation'.[30] The government of Sir Robert Peel was hesitant about restricting the movement of Continentals to Heligoland, not least since they brought much-needed income to the colony. But London was also keen to avoid an overspill of the revolutionary spirit to Britain and its empire. So it agreed

with Metternich that it would be a bad idea if a free press were to be established in the colony. The locals hardly needed a German newspaper preaching revolution and nationalism, nor should the island be allowed to turn
into a source of 'political libels in Germany'.[31]

Governor Hindmarsh confirmed that applications had been made for the
establishment of a free press on the island. But he had dismissed all such
suggestion: 'I considered that in a small community of fishermen a newspaper would be useless'. What was more, it would only make the island 'the
focus of attraction for all the discontented spirits in Germany'.[32] But surely,
he was asked, was a free press not 'consistent with the principles of the
British constitution'?[33] Hindmarsh's response was telling, since it made direct
use of the island's position between empire and Europe. Although Heligoland
was a British possession, he replied, it was governed by Continental laws, a
circumstance he deemed 'fortunate' since it meant that no press could be
established without his consent.[34] The Colonial Office and the Foreign
Office approved.[35] Just as with the deportation of the demagogue Harring
before, they were happy to exploit the legal peculiarities of the island for the
suppression of free speech. The exiles on the island could be under no illusion: the political freedoms they associated with Britain did not apply in its
North Sea colony. Yet they continued to use Heligoland as a safe haven.

What attracted them was not only the absence of the Continental police,
but also the island's qualities as a seaside resort. As a British magazine observed
in May 1848, the colony had

> gradually become one of the principal and most fashionable of German
> watering-places, being visited during the season by Hamburghers, Prussians,
> Hanoverians, and people from the several German States, who flee for two
> months of the year from the prevailing despotism of their countries to a for-
> eign island, where they can think, speak, and act with freedom.[36]

Seaside tourism and revolutionary exile had gone hand in hand ever since
Jacob Andresen Siemens had persuaded the governor to allow him to set up
a bathing establishment in 1826.[37] From modest beginnings the *Seebad* rose
quickly to prominence. German travel guides noted it first in the 1830s,
British colonial handbooks in the 1840s:

> The climate is mild, and resembles that of the midland counties of England, the
> heat and cold being tempered by the sea breezes; the air is pure and very salu-
> brious, whence Heligoland has been much frequented by visitors from all parts
> of Germany, Prussia, Poland and Russia, since the erection of the baths in 1826;
> they are considered by physicians as the most efficacious in the North Sea.[38]

By then the baths had turned into the colony's main source of income. In 1846 Hindmarsh told the Colonial Office that there was 'a visible improvement in the pecuniary circumstances of the inhabitants within the last few years, owing to the growing reputation of the island as a watering place and the consequent influx of visitors from all parts of Germany'.[39]

Theodor von Kobbe, a prominent author and liberal lawyer who holidayed in Heligoland regularly in the 1830s, epitomized the educated, affluent traveller whom the island attracted. Friends had recommended the resort to him. The air, unpolluted and free of pollen, was reinvigorating—spending the summer on the island could heal most respiratory diseases, he believed. The sea water, which had a higher salt content than on the coast, was good for weak nerves and helped against most skin conditions.[40] Heligoland's isolation also made it, Kobbe was convinced, a creative place. He was not the only one who thought so. Visitors noted that the island attracted especially 'poets and singers'.[41] Tourist guides described the bohemian spirit amongst the holiday-makers:

> But the most frequent and numerous visitors are the artists, authors, musicians, prima donnas and heroes of the stage. They all escape from their newspaper articles, books, notes, concerts, operas and great engagements in order to refresh and strengthen their frail nerves, weakened voices and damaged lungs on this isolated, solitary island.[42]

The guide went on to give a long list of prominent literati, actors, and authors who descended on the island regularly. What they enjoyed most (if authorities such as Fallersleben and Heine are to be trusted) was 'dolce far niente'. This was a well-established trope in the travel literature of the romantic age—Stendhal had famously described the Italians as particularly successful at 'sweet idleness' in *Vie de Rossini* (1824).[43]

'Dolce far niente' was also what the German-speaking aristocracy was after in the summer months. In the late 1840s Heligoland began to feature in the travel plans of the upper classes. The spa authorities started to publish a daily list of newly arrived guests, reflecting an increased interest amongst visitors to know who was holidaying alongside them on the island.[44] These *Kurverzeichnisse* gave not only the name of each visitor and where they were from, but also their occupation. From the 1850s they increasingly listed landowners and aristocrats. Their visits provoked problems for the governor, who asked the Colonial Office for advice with regard to etiquette and precedent. In June 1858 Governor Pattinson urged London to send the flags needed to honour the elevated guests of the current season. 'At present', he wrote, 'we have here Their Highnesses the Prince Leopold of Saxe Coburg and Gotha and the Prince Hermann of Saxe Weimar: both, I believe, related to the Queen'. The Grand Duke of Saxe Weimar was expected to join them any day. The Crown Prince of Saxony had arrived earlier and 'was received with the salute due to his exalted rank'. Amongst the list of other dignitaries soon to arrive were the Princes of Thurn and Taxis, Esterhazy, and Reuss.[45]

These illustrious guests had somewhat different expectations from the academics and literati who had first discovered Heligoland as a destination. By the 1850s the island had its own spa physician, Dr Heinrich von Aschen, who was popular with rich patients in northern Germany. As the governor explained to the Colonial Office, it was important that Aschen be given 'a certain rank and standing as a British official' to impress the noble guests.[46] In August 1858 he was sworn in as physician in ordinary to Her Majesty in Heligoland.[47] The Colonial Office noted it as another Anglo-German oddity that the colony now had a German doctor who was appointed by the queen to look after German guests.[48]

Successive governors hailed the rise of the *Seebad* as the source of financial salvation, but it also brought unexpected problems. For some time in the 1850s the island attracted guests who were intent on ending their lives. In some cases, Dr von Aschen concluded, this could be explained as the result of mental health problems. The rock's isolation and the high cliffs may have accentuated such suicidal tendencies. Other guests suffered from serious conditions which they hoped to overcome—or else kill themselves. As Aschen wrote in 1859, one Dr Paulsen of Holstein 'came here determined either to be cured or to destroy himself: not succeeding in regaining his health he shot himself in the presence of his wife'.[49] Criminals and conmen too were attracted to the increasingly popular *Seebad*. A steady influx of wealthy guests and the absence of a regular police force seemed an irresistible combination.[50] But in the eyes of the London government none of this mattered nearly as much as the worst of vices that the guests were cultivating in the colony, gambling. A Hamburg newspaper wrote in 1856 that the island's *Spielbank* made huge daily profits.[51] *Roulette* and *rouge et noir* were particularly popular. A reader of *The Times* reported from a visit to the island that to his 'disgust' he had found 'a roulette table kept open to the public without any attempt at secrecy'. He found it hard to believe that a British colony should belong to the few places where 'these satanic institutions' were still being tolerated. Worse still, this seemed to be for 'mere pecuniary

Figure 2.2 *Ansicht der Insel Helgoland.* Oil painting by Georg Christian Perlberg, 1839. Neue Pinakothek, Munich.

motives'.[52] In July 1859 Governor Pattinson had to admit that gaming tables existed in the *Conversationshaus* and some of the hotels. He was quick to assure London that it was only guests who did 'the thing'. He himself had never profited 'directly or indirectly by the play which goes on here'. But this did not cut it with the Colonial Office. Gambling was frowned upon all over the empire. The colonial secretary, the Duke of Newcastle, left the governor in no doubt that it would need to be stopped in his colony too. In July 1859 he instructed him to 'take immediate steps for the suppression of gambling'.[53]

Pattinson's reply showed how much the island had become part of the Continent's travel culture. 'There can be no doubt', he wrote back, that 'games of chance' existed on the island. In fact, 'it would be idle and foreign to the truth were I to conceal the fact from Your Grace's knowledge'. Gambling had gone on ever since Heligoland had become popular with European visitors and 'successive governors here, I believe, had been compelled to shut their eyes to a state of things they were impotent to put down'. He knew that it was wrong, but he was convinced that public gambling should be allowed. Practically all German spa towns, from Baden Baden to Norderney, had a *Spielbank* or casino. Without gambling Heligoland would lose guests and much-needed income. What was more, closing down the gaming tables would

> divert the gambling into other channels where the play, instead of being openly and fairly carried on, would go on in an underhand manner to the demoralization of half the island, for I beg to apprise Your Grace that for the three or four summer months during which strangers resort to Heligoland for health or recreation, every house becomes more or less a place of entertainment, a lodging house or a hotel: and although the present state of things may be considered illegal, I feel convinced that secret play would be carried on unfairly and perhaps to a ruinous extent.[54]

So the gambling continued. The governor made sure that the island's magistrates knew that London considered it illegal. At the same time he did nothing to encourage them to actively stop it. Like all his predecessors since the late 1820s he turned a blind eye to an activity which seemed so offensive to the Victorian age, but was indispensable to the highly lucrative bathing establishment. Outraged visitors reported repeatedly in the next few years that gambling went on publicly in the island, but not until the 1870s were the island's gaming tables to close—Heligoland was to be the last of Britain's colonies to rule out gambling, a testament to its peculiar position at the edge of Europe.[55]

The prominence of Britain's smallest colony as a holiday destination reflected the rise of spa towns and seaside resorts all over Europe.[56] 'Taking the waters' had become a routine summer occupation amongst the affluent and leisured classes—Heligoland was only one amongst dozens of destinations on the Continent's spa circuit. But the island differed from other watering places: it was more isolated and more naturally striking. 'The location, removed from the Continent in the middle of the sea', was what made Heligoland special, wrote Theodor von Kobbe.[57] He enthused about the sunset and the 'appearance of this rocky island, its richness in form and colour, which presents continuously new pictures to the enchanted eye'.[58] But the experience of nature that he and other visitors had in mind went beyond enjoying the postcard views. The isolation and all-round exposure to the elements prompted them to reflect about nature and life in more existential ways. Numerous tourist guides promised this *Naturerfahrung* ('experience of nature') to the educated traveller: 'Here we find nothing but the long stretch of the sea'. At dusk, when the last glimmers of the sun sank behind the waves, 'we are overawed by a notion of endlessness, an idea of the boundless universe in which we live like atoms on a corn of dust'. The individual facing this display of nature's greatness seemed terribly and infinitely small.[59]

It was depictions such as this that helped to turn Heligoland into a 'natural monument', a site where travellers could expect to have a more direct and intensive experience of nature than elsewhere. From the 1830s the island was increasingly canonized as such a *Naturdenkmal* by writers, poets, and novelists. At the same time Heligoland became a popular *sujet* for romantic painters. Christian Morgenstern and Eduard Schmidt repeatedly depicted the dramatic red cliffs, rising abruptly above the crashing waves. In the style of Caspar David Friedrich they rarely failed to include a figure in the foreground, dwarfed by the imposing power of nature.[60] J. M. W. Turner portrayed the island in a similar fashion in a watercolour which was used as an illustration to Thomas Campbell's poem 'The Death Boat of Heligoland'.[61] Clarkson Stanfield, one of Turner's rivals, depicted the island later in *A Skirmish off Heligoland*.[62] Yet these prominent British examples remained exceptions: turning the North Sea rock into a cultural icon was a

Figure 2.3 *Düne bei Helgoland*. Oil painting by Christian Morgenstern, 1854. Hamburger Kunsthalle.

predominantly German activity. A stream of paintings, drawings, poems, letters, essays, and books established the island as a 'natural monument' in the German-speaking lands.

Cultivating Heligoland as a *Naturdenkmal* did not necessarily imply claiming it as a German monument.[63] This is particularly well illustrated by the example of Johann Wolfgang Goethe. Goethe, not only a famous poet and playwright, but also a prominent naturalist, showed 'great interest' in Heligoland and its 'peculiar location'.[64] He was particularly fascinated with the island's geological characteristics and corresponded with a number of scholars on the subject. He was too elderly to travel to Heligoland himself, so he asked for rock specimens to be sent to him.[65] Descriptions of the island 'with beautiful samples of un-organic and organic nature' delighted him.[66] He collected specimens of the Heligoland cliffs and fossils from its shores and he discussed essays on the island written by naturalists such as Kaspar von Sternberg and Johann Martin Lappenberg.[67] Heligoland was a 'remarkable point on earth', Goethe wrote in May 1827.[68] It exemplified 'the endless charm of eternal nature'.[69] He displayed no inclination to read this status in political or national terms. What could be experienced in the island, he suggested to his correspondents, was the *Weltgeist*, the 'world spirit', not the German spirit.[70]

While Goethe, who died in March 1832, showed little interest in ascribing national meanings to 'that remarkable island',[71] the generation of authors who came after him displayed a more ambiguous attitude. The poets and professors who dominated the culture of the *Vormärz* (the period before the German revolutions of 1848) were grappling with different cultural, territorial, and ethnic ideas of 'Germany'. Culturally, for most of them, Heligoland seemed to belong to the German Fatherland. In some descriptions the islanders themselves appear as German or proto-German. The journalist and literary critic Ludolf Wienbarg explained what he saw as the Heligolanders' remarkable honesty as a trait that was 'rooted in the German tribal character [*im deutschen Stammcharakter*]'. Exposed to the sea, they were 'free and honest amongst themselves'. This was part of their 'good German nature'.[72] In Wienbarg's depiction Heligoland offered a motif that brought together nature and nation in a pre-modern idyll. This was mirrored in the romantic paintings of the period which typically showed the island with a number of fishermen engaged in their 'natural' occupation. Here was a miniature Germanic Ur-*Volk*, freedom-loving and deeply rooted in its *Heimat*.[73] By no means all of the authors writing about the island made this link between nature and nation. But for many of them the island seemed to belong at least culturally to 'Germany', however they defined that construct. Heine and Fallersleben certainly left no doubt that they thought it unnatural that Britain should own the outpost.[74]

There was nothing peculiarly German about the link between nature and nation which these authors claimed. 'Natural' monuments and 'natural' boundaries featured prominently in most nationalist discourses of the nineteenth century. Nor was it a particularly Germanic utopia that the nation's roots were to be found in small, 'untouched', quasi-tribal societies, which lived in harmony with nature.[75] Both German and British authors depicted the Heligolanders as 'pure' and 'unspoilt'. Travel guides spoke of them as innocent, almost childlike creatures.[76] This interpretation featured strongly in a report submitted to the Colonial Office in 1854 by George Milner Stephen, Hindmarsh's son-in-law and secretary. The islanders, he wrote, were timid and 'unaccustomed' to the contemporary world. They were not even used to defending themselves.[77] This view of the Heligolanders persisted for decades to come. In the 1870s British visitors still wrote about them as an isolated and naive community of fishermen—when most of them had long turned into shop owners, innkeepers, and hoteliers.[78]

Governor Hindmarsh had little time for such idealizations, which he thought were based on romantic novels and outdated guidebooks. The Heligolanders, he wrote, had perhaps once been a 'pure' people, but that had changed dramatically in the recent past. The islanders had become 'mixed' and 'spoilt', first by the merchants and smugglers of the Napoleonic Wars, then by the tourists and travellers frequenting the island. The worst influence had been that of the political refugees. The 'more extensive intercourse of the Heligolanders with educated strangers' and 'the influx of doubtful political characters who annually resort hither have induced a growing dissatisfaction' amongst the islanders, he wrote in February 1846. The Heligolanders were, in other words, being politicized by the Continentals.[79] This reading made it possible to blame the Heligolanders' demeanours on the neighbouring nations—exposed to the vices of the Continent, the islanders had developed a dishonest and profit-minded side. Such interpretations naturally presupposed that the islanders had been 'unspoilt' or 'innocent' at some point in the past. German nationalist authors such as Wienbarg made a similar assumption when they wrote of them as a miniature *Volk* supposedly kept pure through geographical isolation. Yet it is difficult to see when exactly that could have been the case. While the mobility of the islanders was undoubtedly less pronounced than that of people living on the Continent, nevertheless they too had married, moved, and migrated. As one guide put it, 'the current Heligolanders appear, like the current Germans, no longer to have a pure origin [*reine Abstammung*]'.[80]

The revolutions which broke out all over the German lands in the spring of 1848 lent new urgency to the question of where Heligoland belonged. One of the key questions facing the revolutionary, pan-German parliament in Frankfurt was how Germany was to be defined. Where were the nation's boundaries to be drawn? This was a conflict–ridden issue, given the ethnically diverse borderlands that sat around the fringes of the German Confederation. In the north this involved Denmark and the duchies of Schleswig (or Slesvig) and Holstein, which had historical links with Heligoland (Danish ownership of the island had been based on Denmark's king ruling over the two duchies in personal union). In March 1848 Frederick VII, under pressure from revolutionary crowds in Copenhagen, announced a new, liberal constitution which foresaw Schleswig as an integral part of Denmark, cut off from Holstein. The Germans in both duchies rose up, demanding independence. They were supported by Prussia and, after abortive talks in London, by the Frankfurt parliament. While Danish and German armies fought a series of battles on land, Denmark set up a blockade of all German ports.

Heligoland was to be at the centre of the ensuing naval conflict, involving Britain as a passive participant. The Danish North Sea squadron, Hindmarsh wrote, 'can be seen from the island most of the time'.[81] The Frankfurt parliament hurriedly put together a new 'imperial' fleet, the first national German navy, commanded by Karl Rudolf Brommy. Its colours, the pan-German black-red-gold tricolour, were not recognized by the British and Brommy's ships initially strayed into the colony's three-mile territorial jurisdiction, but there was never a question of Britain becoming involved.[82] On 4 June the German *Reichsflotte* engaged the Royal Danish Navy off Heligoland, with Hindmarsh and the islanders watching from ringside seats. The outcome was a draw which left the Danish blockade intact. The Imperial German fleet remained undefeated, but did not attack again.[83]

The episode, which became known as the First Battle of Heligoland, was emblematic for British attitudes towards German–Danish conflict. Keen not to take sides, London was acutely aware of the potentially destabilizing effects that a new, unified Germany would have.[84] Disraeli had warned in April 1848 against 'that dreamy and dangerous nonsense called "German nationality" '.[85] Not all of his contemporaries were as disdainful, but few doubted that 'the German question' would eventually affect Britain. Liberal, parliamentary reform in Germany was to be encouraged, but revolution and radicalism ought to be avoided, especially if it led to a re-drawing of Europe's borders.[86]

There was thus relief in Britain when the German revolution proved short-lived. By 1850 the post-revolutionary reaction was well under way in most German states, temporarily defusing German–Danish confrontation. But the link between German unification and conflict with Denmark was not to go away—nor the significance of Britain's North Sea island for this conflict, as the Second Battle of Heligoland was to show in 1864. Britain's smallest colony marked the zone in which German and Danish naval interests collided. It represented the northern, maritime boundary of a future, unified Germany; and it signified the nation's violent conflict with Denmark, seen as one of the main opponents of German unification.[87]

Parallel to the rise of the German national movement, Heligoland thus turned into a site where British visions of empire and German visions of nationhood intersected. Both aspects were clearly on display in the lengthy essay that appeared in Charles Dickens's *Household Words* in 1855.[88] 'Look at the map of Europe', it urged its readers,

> there is a spice of humour in the choice of the spot. The advantages which it offers for the purpose are quite out of the common way. In time of peace, Heligoland is an advanced sentinel, who can constantly keep her eye open on what is passing in the north of Germany. In war, she is a little Gibraltar, from which, as a centre, Britannia can send her cruisers...[89]

But although this 'little jewel' was a 'sentinel of empire' it had a distinctly German quality to it. Even the waves seemed to 'express themselves in German on our tight little island, although the Union Jack does spread its colours above it'.[90]

The boundaries of the empire were remarkably porous here, allowing for the languages and laws of the Continent to influence life on the island directly. Again and again British visitors commented on the character of the island as a contact zone in between empire and Continent. As early as 1807, Charles Pasley, an officer in the Engineers, had observed that: 'They speak a language on this island peculiar to themselves, but are educated in German and English is very commonly spoken'.[91] Children were taught English at school (by German teachers), but few of the adults were so fluent as to allow it to be an official language. Even the magistrates insisted on communicating in German.[92]

The English of some of the islanders writing to the Colonial Office was so bad that the clerks at Whitehall asked them to write again in German.[93] When the Colonial Office asked the Metropolitan Police to second an officer to the island, it asked specifically for someone who spoke German.[94] In November 1852 Governor Hindmarsh submitted to the Colonial Office 'that there should be created an Office of Translator and Interpreter' in the colony.[95] 'There is constant need of someone to write German letters and to translate from German to English and the reverse and not one of the Magistrates are able to perform this duty'. This was made worse by 'the resort of strangers to the island' who only spoke German.[96] A translator would also help with the island's archive, which held the key to many disputes about past legislation. Practically all of these were documented in German. The clergymen, he explained in another dispatch, 'belong to the German Lutheran Church. The entire population belongs to this Church. The service of the Church is performed in German'.[97] All this, Hindmarsh argued, illustrated the Heligolanders' peculiar linguistic position—the Colonial Office eventually agreed and approved his request for a translator.

But the most powerful way in which Continental structures reached into the colony was to be found in the law. The occupation of 1807 had left the island's legal setup untouched. All pre-existing laws continued to be valid unless explicitly abolished by new British laws. Numerous cases arose in the 1830s and 1840s in which British legal interpretations collided with Continental ones. The most notorious was the salvage of the *Good Hope*, a commercial vessel which struck the island's rocks in December 1847. 'The ship was in a very dangerous position', recalled Governor Hindmarsh, 'without topmast, full of water, and without the means of getting off'.[98] Its captain was glad to have the crew rescued and thanked the Heligolanders who went out to him in their small boats, defying the storm. But he was shocked when the magistrates asked him to sign away a third of the cargo in return for being salvaged. He signed under protest:

> I, the undersigned J. J. Kelly, master of the ship *Good Hope*, from Cardiff bound to Bremen with railroad iron, do hereby declare and most freewillingly promise in consequence of my present distressed and dangerous situation, sitting on the rocks, I surrender my cargo to be saved by the authorities of this island for the third part of all that shall can or may be saved, and submit my said cargo to the rules and customs of the Island.[99]

Joseph Magrath, the owner of the *Good Hope*, was incredulous when he read this. So were the underwriters at Lloyd's, who had insured his ship, and the merchants at Rothschild's, who owned the cargo. Surely this was an act of piracy, 'illegal and contrary to all British law'?[100] The Colonial Office had to disappoint them. Yes, the islanders had a reputation for being ruthless wreckers, but their behaviour remained within the law.[101] The law, that was, which applied in the colony and which consisted of the decrees of Schleswig and Holstein as well as the customs of the island which had been in place before the British occupation.

Magrath and his City backers found this hard to believe. In January 1848 he went to Heligoland to get the islanders to agree to a substantially reduced claim. He returned after four months without success. The islanders' representatives insisted on 'a third of the cargo consisting in circa of 230 English tons of railway iron'.[102] Only upon payment would they release the full cargo and the salvaged *Good Hope*. Magrath and the underwriters at Lloyd's found it impossible to believe that the government could not 'protect British subjects and British property' on a North Sea island ruled by a British governor.[103] But they had to accept that it was the island's and not England's laws that applied in the colony. In significant aspects Heligoland continued to be ruled according to Continental laws, despite having been a British possession for more than forty years.

Empire and Europe were closely intertwined in Britain's smallest colony not only through laws and languages, but also through the people who came and went. The governors and their administrators linked the island with other parts of the empire through their careers, families, and personal networks.[104] Governor Hamilton, who served in Heligoland during the Napoleonic Wars, went on to govern Newfoundland. David Allan, who had been in charge of the army stores under Hamilton, became deputy commissary general in Sydney. William Lithgow, one of his clerks, went on to Mauritius as deputy-assistant of the accounts branch of the commissariat there. Later he took a similar position in New South Wales. When Hindmarsh was appointed to the governorship in Heligoland, he asked a number of officials who had worked with him in South Australia to join him. George Milner Stephen, who had been advocate-general and crown solicitor in Adelaide, became Hindmarsh's secretary (and eventually married his daughter).[105] Both Hindmarsh and Stephen were to go back to Britain for their retirement. Many colonial careers revealed such patterns, linking the North Sea colony with other parts of the empire as well as the British Isles. Edward Charles Frome had been surveyor-general of South Australia under Hindmarsh's successor in Adelaide before serving in Heligoland with the

Royal Engineers. He went on to become lieutenant-governor of Guernsey.[106] Some of the Heligolanders, in turn, emigrated to other colonies. An official initiative, supported by the governor, to send a hundred islanders who were 'anxious to emigrate' to New Zealand failed.[107] As New Zealand House told the Colonial Office, it had the 'express object of discouraging the occupation of land by paupers'. Only 'capitalists and persons of superior station' would be allowed to settle in New Zealand.[108] But smaller groups of islanders succeeded with their plans to emigrate, especially to the Australian colonies. Others went to work in Britain or served on British ships.

These links with Britain and its empire were more tenuous than those with the Continent, but they continued to develop. The Crimean War, which broke out in October 1853, provoked a renewed interest in using the island as a recruitment base. The Enlistment of Foreigners Act, passed by Parliament in December 1854, paved the way for foreign legions to fight under British command. In January 1855 the army began to set up barracks in Heligoland 'for the reception of men volunteering for military service in the Crimea'.[109] By April 1855 Hindmarsh was expecting several thousand recruits.[110] In reference to the King's German Legion of the Napoleonic Wars the new unit was called the British German Legion.[111]

The recruits arriving on the island came voluntarily, but this was the result of a well-organized campaign. Led by Major General Richard von Stutterheim, a network of agents was busy advertising the Legion to young northern Germans. The War Office paid Stutterheim, who was in charge of the base at Heligoland, a commission for each recruit accepted into the Legion. At the height of his activities he had close to 200 agents swarming the pubs and inns of the costal regions. This did not go down well in the northern German states and cities. The Grand Duke of Oldenburg was particularly annoyed when British warships were spotted picking up recruits.[112] He made public declarations warning his subjects not to be lured by the British, nor to travel to Heligoland.[113] Undercover officers followed Stutterheim's agents and their recruits. A number of young men under military age were arrested before they could reach the island. The government in Brunswick was furious when it discovered that soldiers serving in its forces were leaving their units to volunteer for the Legion in Heligoland. Several of them were given hefty prison sentences.[114]

Volunteers continued to flock to Heligoland, attracted by the prospect of good pay and a sense of adventure. Yet few of them got to see the Crimea, let alone fight: the war was over before the Legion could be deployed. As a result Heligoland turned into an Anglo–German waiting room in between Europe and empire. Needing to find a place for its German legionnaires, the London government settled large numbers of them in the Eastern Cape Colony in South Africa (where they promptly founded the town of Stutterheim). By July 1857 German newspapers reported that the Legion's Heligoland base was being dismantled.[115] The infamous *Werbezeit*, as the Germans had called the recruitment campaign, was over. Its unintended consequence was that Heligoland became anchored in the memory of German South Africans as a kind of Ellis Island of the empire, linked both to their Continental origins and the far-flung colony where they came to settle.[116]

The British German Legion was emblematic of the Anglo–German symbiosis that characterized Heligoland from the 1830s to the late 1850s. Rarely in this period did the London government show any concerns about the German influence in its North Sea colony. Officials regularly referred to the island as an odd or peculiar case that seemed to stretch the pluralistic character of colonial rule to new extremes.[117] But they did not see any political problems in these peculiarities. For most British observers the island's intriguing character was a function of its position in between Europe and empire. If anything it symbolized Anglo–German friendship. Governor Pattinson, who took over from Hindmarsh in April 1857, certainly thought so. In February 1859 he received news that the queen's daughter, married to Friedrich Wilhelm of Prussia, had given birth to a son. Pattinson promptly drew up an address, which a large number of Heligolanders signed. It exclaimed that 'the heart of England will beat and vibrate in unison, and with one accord, to that of the loyal Prussian Nation: and the joint prayers of the people of England and Prussia will be offered up to the Throne of Grace'. The birth of the queen's grandson Wilhelm (the future Kaiser Wilhelm II) reminded the governor of Heligoland's symbolic position in between 'the two great nationalities'. Both, the North Sea island and the newly born Hohenzollern-Saxe-Coburg offspring, epitomized the two nations' friendship. Pattinson was sure that the future would

> cement and bind together more strongly than ever, in the bonds of sympathy, and alliance, two great nations, already long united by the sentiment of religion, mutual respect, and enduring regard.[118]

3

A Matter of Sentiment

Amongst the artists and aristocrats who descended on Heligoland in the summer of 1855 was a tourist from Berlin who seemed curiously uninterested in the holiday season. Not for him the sunbathing and swimming, the 'dolce far niente' in the sand dunes. While others engaged in polite conversation, he marched up and down the island, measuring distances and taking notes. This was Colonel Gaertner of the Prussian Engineer Corps, sent by the government in Berlin to reconnoitre the island. What were Britain's ambitions in the North Sea? How valuable would Heligoland be in case of war? On 22 September Gaertner submitted a lengthy report on these questions to the Prussian minister of war, together with a thirty-one-page memorandum on 'English intentions'. Both were read by Otto Theodor von Manteuffel, the minister president and foreign secretary, as well as by Friedrich Wilhelm IV, the Prussian king.[1]

Gaertner's report signalled Berlin's growing interest in the British outpost. The island now lay at the fringes of Hohenzollern power, marking the point where Prussia's expanding influence met with Britain's strategic interests. London had kept strict neutrality during the war between Denmark and revolutionary Germany in 1849. Would it do so again? Or would it use Heligoland as a base from where to intervene in Continental conflicts? Apart from the British German Legion Gaertner noted few soldiers on the island. The fortifications seemed woefully inadequate to this engineer's eye. But, he conceded, as long as the Royal Navy commanded the North Sea there was no need for more artillery or troops in Heligoland. The island's main value was as a base from where to blockade the German North Sea harbours. To do so, the British would need no more than 'a few heavily armed warships, which can be supplied with everything necessary from Heligoland'. One day, though, he concluded, Prussia might be in a position to stand up to Britain with its own fleet.[2] This last point suggested a new departure: for the first time officials in Berlin were thinking of Heligoland and the North Sea as a potential theatre of Anglo-German conflict. Gaertner did not suggest that such conflict was to be expected any time soon, but he pointed to a future in which it was thinkable that Britain's command of the 'German Ocean' would be challenged by a Prussian-led fleet. In those circumstances Heligoland would become invaluable.

Colonel Gaertner's undercover mission marked the beginning of a period in which the Anglo-German relationship was to change fundamentally. Bismarck's appointment in 1862 as Prussian minister president led to a series of diplomatic and military moves aimed at supplanting Austria as the dominant force in the German lands. That Bismarck was able to shift the centre of power from Vienna to Berlin had much to do with the victories Prussia won over the next decade, first against Denmark (1864), then Austria and the southern German states (1866), and finally against France (1870). Yet Bismarck's success in exploiting the weakness of his opponents and unifying Germany under Prussian hegemony was dependent on British neutrality.[3] During none of the three so-called wars of unification did London intervene. Its tacit agreement to Prussian expansion was based on the hope that this would lead to a rebalancing of power in Europe which suited Britain's interests, especially overseas, where France and Russia were its main rivals. But would the British continue to act in such a benevolently detached manner as a unified Germany began to play a new role on the Continent?

Historians have traditionally been sceptical about the chances of Britain and Germany developing a long-term partnership in the second half of the nineteenth century. Paul Kennedy famously interpreted this period as the beginning of the 'rise of the Anglo-German antagonism': German unification provoked a seismic shift in the European balance of power; this, in turn, brought Britain and Germany, for generations united in friendship, into conflict.[4] While the idealists in both countries continued to cultivate the many ties that existed between Britons and Germans, the realists involved in foreign policy were increasingly aware of the underlying strategic conflict that set the two nations apart—a conflict which was to come to a head when Germany began to build a fleet that directly challenged the Royal Navy.[5] Yet this reading, which sees the First World War as predetermined by German unification, does not account for the complexity and open-ended character of the Anglo-German relationship in the Bismarckian period. No doubt, the foundation of the Kaiserreich in 1871 established a new continental power which had the potential to turn into a rival of Britain. But while clearly altered, this relationship did not have to deteriorate, let alone descend into antagonism and war. What took place in the second half of the nineteenth century was not an inevitable shift towards enmity, but an increase in both cooperation and conflict.

Whatever path the Anglo-German relationship would take, Heligoland was likely to be a bellwether for it. Berlin's new interest in the island expressed a sense of unease about Britain holding a strategic position so close to the mainland, at a time when Prussian-led Germany was expanding. At the same time the outpost was itself becoming more enmeshed with German affairs, prompting Berlin to establish new forms of cooperation with the British. Long before the island changed hands between London and Berlin in August 1890 it thus developed into a microcosm of the Anglo-German relationship. At its heart was to be a strongly felt ambiguity: interdependence and cooperation between the two nations grew at the same time as a sense of rivalry began to be associated with the cliff-bound colony.

Few characters illustrate this tension better than Henry Fitzhardinge Berkeley Maxse, governor of Heligoland from 1863 to 1881. Maxse replaced Richard Pattinson, whom the Colonial Office had regarded as an all-round embarrassment. The clerks reading Pattinson's dispatches had found them 'incoherent and illiterate' or 'very stupid'. T. F. Elliot, under-secretary of state at the Colonial Office, described Pattinson as 'a gentleman who indulged in such habits of constant intoxication that his despatches were often scarcely intelligible, and that he was a standing reproach to England in the eyes of the North of Europe'.[6] This was only slightly exaggerated—the Prussian envoy at Hamburg had told Bismarck that the incompetent Pattinson was an 'old naval officer fond of drinking'.[7] 'I could not possibly give him another appointment', had been the comment by the Duke of Newcastle, the colonial secretary, when he had recalled Pattinson: 'I fear the sooner he comes away the better'.[8]

Governor Maxse was cut from a different cloth. An efficient administrator, he had 'a laudable capacity' for understanding the intricacies of colonial rule.[9] The Foreign Office in Berlin saw him as energetic and ambitious.[10] While his predecessors had shown no interest in acquiring even the most rudimentary German (Pattinson confessed not to 'understand a word'), Maxse was fluent.[11] 'Fortuitous circumstances', he explained, 'have caused the German language to be almost as intimate to me as English'.[12] From a well-established upper-class family, Maxse had initially embarked on a military career. But, having been wounded in the Crimean War as one of the officers leading the Charge of the Light Brigade, he spent much time on the Continent studying German. In 1859 he married the renowned Austrian actress Augusta von Rudloff ('a very handsome, nice ladylike person', Queen Victoria thought when she met her decades later).[13] Their children grew up bilingually and were educated in Britain and Germany. The post in Heligoland allowed the Maxses to lead a life literally in between the two cultures.

The governor and his wife embraced the artistic tradition of their colony with Anglo-German gusto. During the bathing season they invited authors and actors to the island and organized a busy schedule of performances and readings. A succession of grateful poets and composers dedicated their works to the Maxses in return.[14] The governor moonlighted as a dramatist himself, switching between German and English. This was 'the only person' who wrote plays in two languages, concluded Lord Frederick Spencer Hamilton, Conservative MP and later the editor of the *Pall Mall Magazine*, who visited the island twice during Maxse's time:

> His German plays had been very successful, and two one-act plays he wrote in English had been produced on the London stage. He always managed to engage a good German company to play in the little Heligoland theatre during the summer months, and having married the leading tragic actress of the Austrian stage, both he and Lady Maxse occasionally appeared on the boards themselves, playing, of course, in German. It looked curious seeing a bill of the 'Theatre Royal on Heligoland', announcing Shakespeare's tragedy of *Macbeth*, with 'His Excellency the Governor as Macbeth, and Lady Maxse as Lady Macbeth'.[15]

In his spare time Maxse translated Bismarck's letters, dedicating their publication in English to Princess Bismarck 'with the sincerest respect and admiration'.[16] Like Lord Odo Russell, Britain's ambassador in Berlin, Maxse was well liked by the chancellor. Bismarck told his staff that he 'personally thought highly of the governor'.[17]

If all this made Maxse a picture-book Germanophile, he was very much a realist when it came to Anglo-German politics. His love was clearly for German culture, not the German state. He admired Bismarck, but this did little to blunt his critique of Prussian foreign policy. His intimate knowledge of Germany made him more rather than less critical of the chancellor: Maxse's dispatches regularly warned Whitehall about what he saw as

Bismarck's aim of Prussian hegemony in Central Europe. He was also a hard-headed colonial administrator, intent on consolidating British rule at a time when the colony was becoming more and more enmeshed with German affairs. Having taken up his governorship in June 1863 he embarked on a series of reforms aimed at improving public life and making the island less dependent on the mainland. 'Sir Fitzhardinge' was doing 'his utmost to anglicize the island', wrote an attaché at the Berlin Embassy after a visit to the island.[18]

By far the most ambitious of Maxse's many projects was the introduction of a constitution. There were several reasons why he was keen on a set of laws that would codify the island's system of government. London had recently begun to 'constitutionalize' colonial rule in various parts of the empire.[19] A string of colonies dominated by white settlers had been granted more rights, with the government encouraging a development towards 'self-government' or 'responsible government'.[20] This form of imperial liberalism provided the background against which the Colonial Office prepared the Heligoland constitution.[21] There was much lofty rhetoric about freedom and progress, combined with a dose of patronizing condescension which indicated that Whitehall was unsure whether its colonial subjects were ready for representative government. But at the heart of the gifting of colonial constitutions, here as elsewhere in the empire, was a straightforward bargain: political liberty in exchange for financial self-reliance.

All this was clearly on display during the discussions between the Colonial Office and Governor Maxse, which led to the draft of the constitution approved by the queen on 7 January 1864.[22] The islanders were 'primitive', 'illiterate', and 'trivial';[23] but they were also white and European, so they qualified for the same treatment as Britain's settler colonies. The clerks at the Colonial Office compared Heligoland especially to the Cape Colony.[24] This made some sense: South Africa provided one of the few examples where European and colonial British law intermeshed in a similar fashion, but the main motivation there was radically different.[25] The more fitting parallel was with those white settler colonies in Australia and Canada where self-government and financial independence went hand in hand.[26]

The new governmental structure for Heligoland had similar aims. Its main innovation was a 'Combined Court', which was to consist of a nominated Executive Council and an elected Legislative Council.[27] The franchise was to be restricted to property-owning men: 'Every male British subject above the age of 21 years and of sound mind shall be capable of voting for the election of representatives in case he shall be the owner of any house or land of the value of one pound per annum'. In a concession to the island's seafaring economy the owners of ships also qualified for the vote.[28] The colonial mini-parliament which they were to elect would have to shoulder responsibility for the difficult financial decisions which Maxse foresaw for his colony. This was the main reason why he was prepared to share power with the islanders. Maxse's many pet projects (compulsory education, an insurance scheme, a savings bank, a new hospital) all cost money. At the same time he was keen to repay the colony's mounting debts. Yet one of the key sources of income, gambling, was under threat of abolition. London was adamant that, as elsewhere in the empire, the gambling in Heligoland had to stop. Maxse agreed that the gaming tables were immoral and 'un-English', but revoking the licences would take away a large chunk of the colony's income. He wrote to the secretary of state:

> Whilst, Sir, it is impossible to condemn too deeply the establishment of anything approaching to gambling in a public manner in a British colony, the proceeds arising from such an establishment in Heligoland form at the present moment the almost sole source of revenue to the colony.[29]

The solution, as Maxse saw it, lay in taxation. So far, the Heligolanders had not paid any significant taxes. This anomaly was based on privileges granted to them under Danish rule, though their precise legal status was contested. Since the British had agreed in 1807 to respect the islanders' 'ancient rights', it seemed difficult to introduce taxation by decree. Much better to involve the population (or rather its male, propertied representatives) and offer them something in return: London would give them self-representation; they, in return, would pay taxes. It was a trade-off that had worked before in other parts of the empire. Maxse was confident that it would do so here too.

At the same time he intended the constitution to be an antidote to the rising German influence in his colony. Successive governors had lamented Heligoland's messy, conflict-ridden position in between different legal traditions.[30] The hotchpotch of Continental and colonial laws not only created problems for the island's jurisdiction; rather inconveniently, it also gave the Heligolanders a source of power in their dealings with the governor. Again and again they had insisted on privileges which they saw as their 'ancient rights' and which Maxse found impossible to verify. It was tempting to sweep aside this mess and curtail their access to jurisdictions outside Britain's reach. This was the political subtext to the self-congratulatory rhetoric by which he told the colonial secretary that the colony's old law, 'a remnant of the dark ages', was about to be abolished. The new constitution would finally 'meet the spirit of civilization'.[31]

Introducing a modern, London-crafted constitution would assert British rule at the edge of the Continent at a time when the map of Europe was being rapidly re-drawn. Tensions between Denmark and the German Confederation were running high over the Schleswig-Holstein question, which was to make the seas around Heligoland the focus of naval conflict again. On the face of it, this struggle was a traditional dynastic conflict, triggered by the death of Frederick VII, the Danish king, without legitimate issue. His successor, Christian IX, intended to continue the personal union between Denmark and the two duchies. But he faced a rival, Frederick of Augustenburg, whose claim to Schleswig and Holstein, while dubious, was supported by the German national movement. In November 1863 Christian IX, under pressure from his own, parliamentary government, took a step towards integrating Schleswig into the Danish state by creating a joint parliament for the two. This violated the London Protocol of 1852, which had enshrined the independence of both Schleswig and Holstein. National feeling in Denmark and the German lands ran high, fuelled by memories of the the war triggered in 1848 over much the same issue.[32] In January 1864, after some diplomatic manoeuvring, Austria and Prussia sent troops into Schleswig to uphold the duchy's independence. In parallel the Austrian and Prussian navies were sent to the North Sea to engage the Danish fleet.

Britain's North Sea enclave was to be located at the centre of the ensuing naval conflict. 'Heligoland is of such vital importance to either of the contending parties', Maxse wrote to London, that the island might come under attack.[33] The Colonial Office sanctioned his urgent request to reinforce the colony's defences, though the colonial secretary thought it was 'an ugly moment to make such an expenditure so near Germany!'[34] London was understandably keen not to be pulled into the conflict between Danes, Prussians, and Austrians. But such worries were unfounded. As in the previous Danish–German war both sides pledged to observe British neutrality. The Admiralty dispatched the frigate HMS *Aurora* to show the flag and keep an eye on what it regarded as a cat-and-mouse game between minor navies. The one symbolic British vessel was enough—neither the Danish nor the Austrian-Prussian fleets had the slightest interest in challenging the Royal Navy and its command of the North Sea. When they eventually squared up to each other off Heligoland, both sides made sure not to get too close to British territorial waters.[35] The result was a tactical victory for the Danish fleet, with the Austrian flagship under Admiral Wilhelm von Tegethoff withdrawing in flames on 9 May.

But the war was ultimately decided on land, and here Denmark was resolutely defeated. In October 1864 Christian IX signed the Treaty of Vienna in which he renounced all rights to the duchies. Schleswig and Holstein, historically closely associated with Heligoland, were now under joint Austrian and Prussian administration. It was against this backdrop that Governor Maxse inaugurated the new constitution in his colony. 'The gift which has been granted to you this day', he told the islanders, 'is inestimable, it is political freedom, and if properly used it is wealth and prosperity for the colony'. The subject of the island's debt followed closely behind: 'Your finances have not always been conducted in a manner tending to enrich this colony' (this was an understatement: without the parliamentary grant that London had paid for decades the colony would have long been bankrupt). 'The fault', Maxse told the islanders, lay in 'the system which from beginning to end was faulty in the extreme. It is in order to revise this system to arrange your law code and to place the happiness of the people on a substantial basis, that it has pleased Her Majesty to order the inauguration of the constitutional changes which I have announced to you'.[36] The new constitution was a gift that was to be honoured by voting for and paying taxes.

But to Maxse's great dismay the Heligolanders were less interested in political freedom than in avoiding taxation. The newly constituted 'Combined Court' did vote for the introduction of income tax. But a large number of the islanders refused to pay. This included some of their elected representatives, who declared that taxation was against their 'ancient rights'. For years a stalemate ensued, during which the governor was frustrated by the islanders' 'passive resistance'.[37] While Maxse threatened them with increasingly draconian consequences, they published a catalogue of complaints against him in German and turned to the Continent for help.[38] A deputation went on a tour of northern German capitals, ostensibly to ask for legal advice, but clearly intending to exert pressure on the governor.[39] This came in the wake of Prussia's momentous victory over Austria and its southern German allies at Sadowa (Bohemia) in July 1866. The Peace of Prague, signed a month later, gave Holstein and Schleswig to Prussia. The Hohenzollern monarchy now owned the strategically important stretch of land between the North Sea and the Baltic, which had maintained close links with Heligoland before the advent of British rule.

The Heligolanders were keenly aware of the altered power constellation. What their representatives pioneered here, in the 1860s, was to be at the heart of their political *raison d'être* for generations to come. In linking their own interests temporarily to the rise of Prussia as the pre-eminent German power, they gained much needed political momentum against their colonial rulers. The Colonial Office had to concede that this strategy was working:

> Heligoland is a little place inhabited by little people who are doubtless very illiterate and narrow-minded. It is however a community half Danish, half German, in the neighbourhood of a great and ambitious country which has sufficiently shown of late its affection for other such communities of more renown. This makes one view their petty disputes and difficulties with more anxiety than otherwise they might seem to deserve.[40]

If these islanders, whom German nationalists claimed to be part of the Fatherland, were in continuous conflict with their British rulers, would Prussia not come to their assistance? Bismarck left little doubt that he regarded Heligoland as German. The chancellor was, Maxse wrote, 'flattering the feelings of the people not only in Prussia but in all of Northern Germany' with his pan-German rhetoric.[41] Aware of these broader political implications, Maxse pleaded with the islanders, but the majority of them refused to give in.[42]

In October 1866 it looked to him as if there would 'soon be a complete state of anarchy' in the colony.[43] London was none too pleased. 'The state of affairs in the island', wrote Lord Stanley, the foreign secretary, 'has been for some years such as to cause considerable embarrassment to HM Government'.[44] It was not only 'the indisposition of the inhabitants to submit to any measures of taxation', which was deeply irritating, but also the governor's impotence in the face of the Prussian authorities. Even more annoying was the islanders' 'prowess', as Stanley had it, in publishing exaggerated grievances 'under which they allege themselves to be suffering'—and which were duly reported in the German press, portraying Britain as incapable of instilling order in the smallest of its colonies. There was no doubt that the government had to assert itself in 'this inconvenient island'.[45] In June 1867, the colonial secretary, the Duke of Buckingham, went to Heligoland with a naval detachment, incredulous at the complete lack of gratitude displayed by the islanders. He returned without having achieved much. Shortly afterwards another show of force was needed to prevent a riot.[46] By February 1868, the government had had enough. It revoked the constitution and took away 'from these islanders the political privileges for which they have shown themselves so little fitted'.[47] A colonial police force, the 'Coast Guard', was permanently stationed on the island to discipline them. All political concessions were annulled. There were to be no elections and no quasi-parliamentary institutions. Heligoland was a crown colony again, ruled directly by London through the governor.[48]

The irony of a colony consisting of a European miniature nation being issued a written constitution by a country that had none and then successfully resisting that imposition was not lost on the Continental press, nor on critics in Britain. Theodor Fontane, the novelist, lived in London as a correspondent for the Prussian government's press office at the time. In October 1866 he wrote an article on what he called 'the Heligoland question' for the Berlin *Kreuzzeitung*. The colony's affairs, Fontane thought, showed up bigger Anglo-German differences. He saw it primarily as another example of British double standards: Heligoland proved that the *Engländer* did not care for others to have the rights which they protected so anxiously for themselves.[49]

Much of the ensuing debate focused on the way in which the constitution had been abolished. Years later critics still cited the episode as a showcase for the abandonment of 'imperial liberalism'.[50] In 1876, Lord Roseberry castigated the government in the House of Lords for having acted 'in the most Cromwellian manner'. The Heligolanders were 'as much entitled to respect for their rights and liberties as were the inhabitants of Cromarty or Rutlandshire'. It was regrettable that the episode had demonstrated that there was a 'difference between our professions and our practice'. The German press in particular had highlighted 'that while we had preached the granting of constitutions all over the face of the earth, here was the case of our abolishing in the most summary manner the constitution of one of our own dependencies'.[51] British and German commentators angrily exchanged views about 'tyranny', 'autocracy', and a range of other attributes usually reserved for countries against which the British liked to accentuate the civilizing virtues of their empire. As Sedley Taylor, a fellow of Trinity College, Cambridge, pointed out, it was a curious role reversal that the Germans should be entitled to lecture the British about liberalism.[52]

Taylor became one of the fiercest critics of British rule in Heligoland. The Colonial Office disliked him with a passion, aware of the attention the 'noisy' and 'irresponsible' don received in Germany.[53] Taylor, a hopeful liberal candidate for Parliament, went to Heligoland in the summer of 1876 to study the effects of direct rule. 'He arrived', Maxse observed, 'primed by a

German friend from Hamburg and fortified by the contents of a German guide book full of eagerness to enquire into English personal government and despotism as established in the North Sea'. Taylor found the islanders to be poor and dissatisfied—the abolition of the liberal constitution of 1864 had clearly been a mistake. This opinion fitted perfectly with the view taken by much of the German press, which gave ample space to Taylor's criticism. As Maxse commented, 'the Germans are too delighted to get hold of an Englishman and a fellow of Trinity College Cambridge to back their views of Heligoland'.[54] Nor was Taylor alone. Adolphus William Ward, professor of history at Manchester and later president of the Royal Historical Society, argued the same case, alarmed that 'England, the guestland of the free, is giving so bad and despotic an example at the very door of Germany'.[55] His father, the diplomat John Ward, was even more caustic in his criticism. Maxse and the Colonial Office had 'proved themselves unable to manage a little German community of two-thousand five hundred souls'. It was no credit to the government 'that the discontent of these poor people should have required to be kept down by systematic coercion, whilst it was possible, by pursuing the opposite path of conciliation, to give them solid grounds for loyalty and attachment to the British crown'.[56]

Maxse wrote long letters to Taylor and Ward to justify himself: the Heligolanders were not made for self-government; the idea of them as freedom-loving subjects who had been wronged by their despotic governor was a travesty. These were tax-dodging opportunists who needed firm rule. 'All colonies must repress unrest and punish crime', he told Ward, doubtless only increasing the latter's suspicions about despotism in Britain's smallest colony.[57] Maxse urged the prolific Taylor to desist from creating more publicity. There were 'international reasons why a discussion of Heligoland in the papers is not very advisable', he told him.[58] But Taylor went on writing his articles, drawing on the material that discontented Heligolanders were busy sending him.[59] What was more, he continued to be quoted in the German press. There were plenty of authors on the Continent, Maxse noted, who had a 'desire to keep up a blister against England'. By criticizing London's rule in the colony, they were trying to impose a 'favourable view of Germany and its institutions' on the Heligolanders. They were 'flogging a dead horse', he thought.[60]

The debate over the abolished constitution and 'British despotism' marked a new departure in the role that Heligoland played between the two nations. For the first time the island had come to serve as a metaphor for broader Anglo–German contrasts: commentators in both countries now used it as a prism through which to view the differences between their nations. Yet while a sense of rivalry was beginning to be associated with the colony, Britain and Germany were more closely bound up with one another here than ever before. Nothing illustrated this better than the character of the law that operated in the island. Neither the liberal constitution of 1864 nor its abolition in 1868 had done much to counter the increasing influence of German jurisdiction in the colony. A diverse set of laws continued to exist from before British rule. The result was, as the lawyer Friedrich Oetker wrote, 'a mish-mash, such as is to be found in very few other places in the world. Apart from local regulations we have to deal with Roman, Canonical, German, Danish, Schleswig-Holsteinish and English laws and ordinances'.[61] The relation between these was complicated by linguistic difficulties. The legal process in the island involved three languages: the version of Frisian in which the locals conversed; German, in which all legal proceedings were recorded; and English, in which the governor issued ordinances and other legal documents to the islanders.[62] All this added to the complex inter-dependence between British and continental laws, prompting T. F. Elliot at the Colonial Office to conclude that no other colony could offer 'such curiosities of legislation'.[63]

These legal oddities continued after 1868 under direct rule. In fact, they intensified with rising numbers of cases being debated between London and the governor. Given all this, Maxse saw no other way than to involve the Prussian and Hanseatic governments. He regularly wrote to the ministries in Schleswig, Hamburg, and Berlin for legal advice. By December 1866 this practice had reached such an point that the British consul general in Hamburg suggested a German solicitor be appointed to decide legal disputes arising on the island. The Foreign Office was alarmed that key decisions affecting the running of a British colony should be 'at the mercy of a German lawyer', but could not deny that the expertise of lawyers on the Continent was needed.[64]

The law was clearly not an instrument here through which Britain simply exercised sovereignty over its colonial territory. Rather, it represented a cumbersome form of compromise, which signalled the frailty of London's rule. In order to govern the island, the British had to collaborate with the neighbouring German states. Instead of reasserting imperial rule and spreading British institutions, they had to accept a messy *modus operandi* in which the colonial government was dependent on Continental laws and jurisdiction.

More than anything else, this legal 'mish-mash' demonstrated the limits of Britain's imperial sovereignty in this island outpost at the edge of Europe.[65]

The Heligolanders themselves were actively engaged in this interdependency. From the 1860s they developed their own diplomacy 'from below' aimed at ensuring the continued involvement of both colonial and Continental authorities in their government.[66] A compromise between the two was best suited to preserve what the islanders' representatives thought of as their 'ancient privileges'. The fact that this strategy proved remarkably successful until well into the twentieth century should not be misread as evidence for the existence of an active form of colonial resistance. Nor were the Heligolanders natural-born anarchists, engaging in the 'art of not being governed'.[67] In fact, they were quite happy to be governed—even by a 'despotic' colonial regime—so long as that regime safeguarded the privileges that had propped up their local economy and hierarchy in the past.[68]

While the law thus continued to function as a hinge between colony and Continent, the British did what they could to connect the island more strongly with Britain and its empire. From the 1860s onwards they made an increased effort to bring Heligoland in line with policies that applied in other colonies. The abolition of gambling was a case in point. The islanders were lobbying London to let them continue with the lucrative gaming tables, which were so popular with German holiday-makers. But the Colonial Office insisted on the reform as an empire-wide project. Maxse, now supported by the Coast Guard and unencumbered by a colonial mini-parliament, drove through the abolition. When the last gambling house was closed, this was portrayed as a victory of the empire over a vice that continued on the Continent. As the government declared in the House of Commons: 'Gambling is no longer permitted in any of Her Majesty's Dominions. Heligoland and Hong Kong were the last two colonies where it existed'.[69]

It was not only such reforms that linked Britain's smallest colony with the rest of the empire. Just as had been the case earlier in the century, the officers and bureaucrats who served on the island continued to connect it with other colonies through their careers and lives: Maxse went on to govern Newfoundland; his successor, Sir Terence O'Brien, had been governor of British Ceylon in the 1860s and was to follow Maxse to Newfoundland after his stint in Heligoland. The way in which they ruled these far-flung places drew directly on their colonial experiences elsewhere: personal contacts and family allegiances continued to be at the heart of the vast patchwork that was the empire. While Maxse would write to Schleswig and Berlin for legal advice he was also in contact with governors in Jamaica, Gibraltar, the Cape, Sierra Leone, and Sri Lanka. In a range of matters including colonial prisons, public health, and education he collaborated actively with other colonies.[70]

While all this linked Heligoland with other colonies on the ground, the royal family provided the symbolic umbrella under which the islanders could imagine themselves in union with the rest empire. 'Dear Mama, … It is very gratifying to find your German subjects *so* loyal', Prince Arthur wrote to Queen Victoria during a visit in 1872 (thanking her 'so much for allowing me to use the Yacht').[71] Whether the islanders' loyalty was genuine or not, successive governors invoked it as something the Heligolanders had in common with the vast imperial family. When Prince Leopold, Victoria's youngest son, died in March 1884, the islanders were told (in German) that in grieving for the queen's loss they should feel part of 'the three hundred million subjects of the British empire, of which race, belief or colour they may be'.[72]

But by far the most tangible link between colony and empire lay in the Royal Navy. Heligoland's *raison d'être* as a British possession was the navy: so long as the Admiralty thought it needed the outpost in case of war with Europe, Britain would hang on to it. Keeping Heligoland, in turn, relied on the navy's uncontested command of the North Sea. Neither London nor the governor ever seriously doubted the fleet's ability to deter an attack on the colony. Nor did the Heligolanders themselves, for that matter. They showed their confidence in the Royal Navy by staking their sons' futures on it. Following persistent lobbying, they were allowed to put their boys forward for a career in the navy. A doctor mustered them and the governor signed off on their qualifications before a cruiser picked them up. Aged between 12 and 14 years they were unlikely to see their parents for years to come.[73] Maxse kept the islanders informed of the progress their sons made in the service and publicized their successes in examinations.[74] This was part of a wider strategy to publicly link the island with Britain and its empire through the fleet. From the 1870s onwards Maxse and his successors repeatedly asked the navy to 'show the flag' in the colony. Like other such rituals, these spectacles were designed to impress audiences at home and abroad with the unity and prowess of the empire.[75]

But no amount of naval demonstrations and official visits could disguise the fact that German influence was on the rise in Britain's outpost. After the foundation of Imperial Germany in 1871 cooperation between colony and Kaiserreich was increasingly formalized on a range of matters including education, religion, transport, communication, banking, finance, policing, health, and law. German bureaucracy and its quest for 'harmonization' now reached deeply into the colony's messy affairs. In June 1873 the island was de facto incorporated into the Reich's postal system. German regulations, weights, and tariffs were introduced. In postal terms Heligoland was *Inland*, Britain was *Ausland*.[76] All of this, posters announced in both languages, was done 'for the convenience of the German visitor'.[77] The colony's stamps were issued both in German and British currencies and were printed by the government press in Berlin. Maxse got the German post master general to concede that the queen's head would still be shown on the curiously Anglo-German stamps, soon to feature prominently in philatelists' collections.[78]

When a new common currency was announced in Germany in 1873, Maxse told London that he did not want it in the colony—for symbolic reasons.[79] The colonial secretary, the Earl of Carnarvon, agreed: British currency should be used consistently in all parts of the empire. Where there had to be foreign currency, 'it should exist side by side with English'. Yet Heligoland was 'an exceptional case': it depended 'entirely on its German

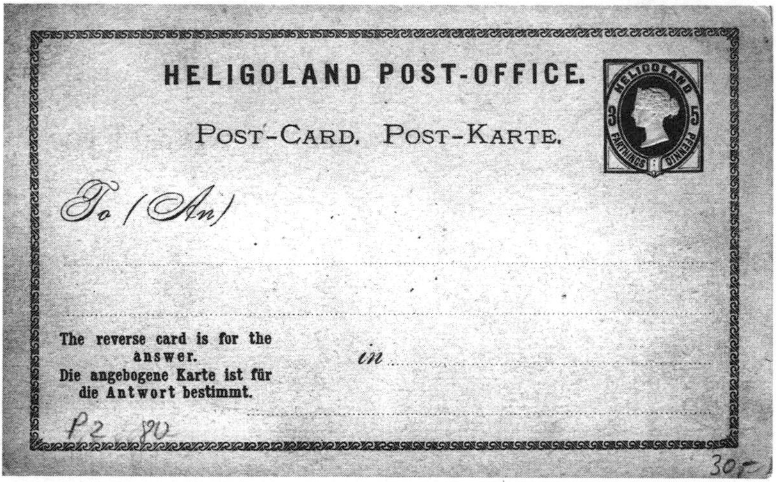

Figure 3.1 Heligoland postcard issued in British and German currencies, 1876.

connection'.[80] So the new German Mark became the colony's official currency. Whitehall officials noted for the first time that there was 'a tendency towards the Germanization of Heligoland'.[81]

As if encouraged by such progress, the Berlin government suggested more measures by which the colony's affairs could be aligned with German public life. The Kaiser's Embassy in London regularly notified Whitehall of changes in German law and asked that the colony's laws be changed accordingly. The officials at Whitehall were irritated: 'The fact that there is a "deviation" in the Heligoland laws from subsequent legislation in the German Empire does not appear to be conclusive proof that the Heligoland laws require amendment'.[82] But in most cases they complied with the German request. Governor Maxse agreed that for practical reasons it was 'expedient to assimilate the Heligoland laws', though he was fully aware that this led increasingly to a 'community of arrangement between this colony and Germany'.[83]

Remarkably, the 'community of arrangement' extended to combating Socialism. In May 1878 Bismarck introduced the first draft of his Anti-Socialist Law in the Reichstag which instituted a ban on all public meetings of the Social Democrats. In response, Wilhelm Liebknecht and August Bebel, the party's founders, hatched a plan to use Heligoland as a place of exile. The inner circle of the Social Democrats as well as deputies and functionaries were to decamp to the island, following in the footsteps of Heinrich Heine and Hoffmann von Fallersleben in the 1830s. However, London made it clear that it would not tolerate 'a large body of foreigners coming over to hold meetings which [are] forbidden in their own country'.[84] In a move which showed how closely enmeshed Britain's colony had become with Germany's internal affairs, Disraeli's government dispatched a warship to intercept any vessel that the Social Democrats might use to get to the island.[85]

In financial matters, too, the colony became almost intractably bound up with the Kaiserreich. For public projects that required private funding, such as a new telegraph line, the colony became the co-owner of an Anglo-German company which had its seat in Berlin.[86] German shareholders dominated in the company, which was backed by Hamburg banks. Eventually, the colonial government was bought out and in 1888 the German government suggested it take over the entire company. The Colonial Office had long warned against the colony's communications being 'in the hands of Germany', but commercial considerations overrode political ones.[87] A number of similar ventures saw German investment in transport, mining, and shipping.[88] The London government had no objections to German banks opening branches on the island—so long as they did not call themselves 'colonial'.[89] Heligoland's cash reserves, in the meantime, were held by a Hamburg bank.[90] Hoteliers and restaurateurs were queuing up to invest in the island's booming tourism. 'German capital', Whitehall officials concluded in 1884, was 'tending to flow into the island'.[91]

Given all this, was it not predictable that the Germans would want to acquire the colony? Maxse had noted as early as 1865 that Bismarck seemed to be coveting the North Sea outpost. By 1869 the Foreign Office assumed that Berlin was stirring pro-Prussian sympathies on the island in order to create a case for its 'German character' and eventually lay claim to it.[92] Such speculation increased with Prussia's war against France, which broke out in July 1870. The French fleet sailed into the North Sea to blockade the German ports. Again Heligoland lay at the centre of naval conflict. Britain kept strict neutrality, but Maxse could not prevent German spies from using the island as a lookout from where to monitor the French fleet, which sought in vain to engage what there was of a Prussian navy.[93] It was against this background that politicians and journalists speculated for the first time about the usefulness of the island in German hands. In September 1870, when Moltke's armies had just defeated the French at Sedan, Maxse wrote to London:

> There is not the slightest doubt that Prussia and Germany envy England the possession of Heligoland to which they naturally attach much importance. Articles in the German newspapers have often appeared calling upon Germany not to forget her 'youngest child' meaning the British possession of Heligoland.[94]

This tendency increased after the Prussian-led foundation of the Kaiserreich in 1871. Wilhelm I, the German emperor, put Albrecht von Stosch in charge of the new Imperial Navy. In November 1872 Stosch drew up an ambitious naval programme in which he highlighted Heligoland's strategic value. When Bismarck presented the naval bill to the Reichstag five months later, Odo Russell, Britain's ambassador to Berlin, alerted London. 'It is the first time Prince Bismarck has officially declared the possession of Heligoland by a foreign power to be disadvantageous to Germany'.[95] To be sure, the bill had not announced any plans for Germany to acquire the island—but it did highlight that Berlin was thinking of the British outpost as lying squarely in its own sphere of strategic interest.[96]

It was around this time that Maxse began to see a threat in the Germans living in his colony.[97] There was a danger that the islanders were being pushed aside by the new German residents. Many of them were gaining the island's *Bürgerrecht* (citizen's rights) through marriage:

> Whilst in former times the marriage of a Heligoland girl with a foreigner was invariably out of affection and where the advantages were generally on the part of the former, the matter has now become totally different.[98]

Germans, he warned, 'now come in needy circumstances to Heligoland, marry a Heligoland girl, claim to be Heligoland *Bürgers* and bring up large families in a German sense'.[99] It was not only the new immigrants whom Maxse saw as a threat. He also suspected Heinrich Gätke, his long-standing senior clerk, of undermining his rule. Gätke was 'a most excellent official', Maxse told the colonial secretary, but 'being a born Prussian [he] has naturally strong sympathies with that country'. And he harboured a 'contempt for the Heligolanders' which made him favour German rule.[100]

There was no doubt that Gätke held considerable power as government secretary and official translator. As his cousin, the novelist Theodor Fontane, put it, Gätke was Heligoland's secret king and *Inselpatriarch*.[101] But nothing in the records suggests that Gätke actively worked against British rule. Maxse's suspicions are more convincingly explained as a reflection of his own growing sense of besiegement. His position as an Anglo-German 'in-betweener' seemed increasingly anachronistic, given the national rhetoric which dominated in the German press, eager to see the island united with the Fatherland. In September 1881 Maxse agreed reluctantly to the governorship of Newfoundland.[102] After almost twenty years in Heligoland he left the island with much regret.[103] En route to taking up his new post he stopped in London to brief his designated successor, Sir Terence O'Brien. Bismarck, Maxse told O'Brien, had 'made up his mind to have Heligoland'. The Germans had 'long been scheming to get the place and have their plans quite ready for turning it into a northern Gibraltar. They have for years been undermining our influence in the island'.[104]

Bismarck had set his sights on Britain's North Sea colony as early as 1870, but he had no interest in alerting London to his desire. Repeatedly he instructed his diplomats to discourage any impression that Berlin coveted the island.[105] In March 1876 he told Count Georg Herbert zu Münster, the German ambassador in London, 'not to touch upon the topic of Heligoland'. He was to 'avoid the impression that one is thinking about the acquisition of the island'.[106] At the same time he encouraged Münster to see how far his

British contacts might be led to mention the topic themselves. Three months later, in June 1876, Bismarck's son Herbert, his right-hand man at the German Foreign Office, sent instructions that officials should publicly deny that 'we had initiated or conducted any negotiations about Heligoland'. The aim was to avoid the impression 'that we had set our minds on it [*als ob wir uns darauf gespitzt hätten*]'.[107]

Yet despite Bismarck's caution it became the worst-kept secret in Anglo-German relations that Berlin was keen to get the island. In December 1881 a private meeting took place between George Strachey, the British chargé d'affaires at Dresden, and Richard Fleischer, the owner-editor of the *Deutsche Revue*, a conservative-liberal monthly. It was one of those Anglo-German encounters destined to be misread on both sides. Fleischer claimed that he was authorized to enquire whether London would 'treat for the sale of Heligoland'.[108] There was no way for Strachey to ascertain whether this was Berlin putting out feelers (Bismarck was known to use trusted journalists for this purpose) or whether this was just another Heligoland-obsessed member of the Prussian establishment speaking for himself. If it was the former, Strachey lanced the Bismarckian *ballon d'essai* with some force. He told Fleischer that 'it was inconceivable that the Queen's Government would surrender British territory'.[109] The island would be British for generations to come. Fleischer back-pedalled promptly, but not without letting Strachey know that he considered 'the acquisition of Heligoland by Germany to be a mere question of time'.[110] His sentiment was echoed by much of the Berlin press, which, encouraged by leaks from officials, was confidently discussing the German future of the British colony.[111] Alarmed by all this, Whitehall officials were for the first time talking of 'the Heligoland question'.[112]

Bismarck moved quickly to quell all speculation. He told his cabinet to stop encouraging articles on the topic: there ought to be as little public impression that the government was involved as possible.[113] At the same time he asked his mouthpiece, the *Nord-Deutsche Allgemeine Zeitung*, to publish an article to rein in the press: 'No political writer of any other country, who desired to advocate the acquisition of foreign territory, would endeavour to accomplish his ends by publishing the desire for this acquisition and painting it in the brightest colours'.[114] The verbal slap on the wrist of Germany's expansion-eager journalists was a typical Bismarckian tactic. Behind the scenes he agreed with them that Heligoland should be German. But officially he was, as the British ambassador observed, 'throwing cold water on their wishes'.[115]

Whether Fleischer had acted on his own accord or whether he had been instructed by Bismarck, the outcome of his initiative showed how careful the German Foreign Office would have to be. The island provoked huge emotions in the German press. But public attention, Bismarck told Admiral Stosch, could 'only have the effect of reducing the chances of an acquisition of Heligoland'. Nor was the British reaction to Fleischer's gambit encouraging. As Strachey put it unambiguously, 'no English Government would venture to entertain any such project as this of the cession of Heligoland'.[116] Strachey was only a second-rank diplomat, but neither the Foreign Office nor Lord Russell, the ambassador in Berlin, had contradicted his reply. The episode underlined Berlin's weak position: despite official denials, its desire for the island was all too obvious; yet it had little to offer in return or, conversely, with which to exert pressure on London.

Two years later, in 1884, Bismarck was confident that Germany's position had improved. Berlin had supported London in a number of colonial disputes against Britain's main rivals France and Russia. This had been without any immediate payoff for Berlin. London, Bismarck told Münster, would continue to need Berlin's support. 'Because of its geographical position, England has to fear significant danger in Europe only from France, in Asia only from Russia'. Germany was in a position to act as a counterweight against both. The chancellor felt that this was a good moment for an overture. 'We believe that our attitude . . . towards England's opponents or rivals is more important for England's policy than the possession of Heligoland'. Emperor Wilhelm I signed off on the initiative, which, Bismarck was sure, would be well received by German public opinion if it succeeded. He instructed Münster to sound out Lord Granville, the foreign secretary: by ceding the island, Britain would secure Germany's continued good will and friendship. The Reich would in particular support London in Egypt, a hotspot of colonial competition where Britain was eager to protect its vital trade route through the Suez Canal.[117]

Münster was delighted. Acquiring Heligoland, he replied, had been his *Lieblingsidee*, his 'favourite idea', for some time.[118] But his enthusiasm dimmed when it became clear that the Gladstone government was in no mood to cede the island. Granville told him that the question would have to wait— there was a growing concern in Parliament about signs that Germany wanted to pursue a colonial policy.[119] 'So are we not allowed to do that?' was Bismarck's annoyed response, scribbled into the margins of Münster's dispatch. As if to underline its displeasure with the budding of German colonialism, the Gladstone government dragged its feet over an unrelated issue: Berlin had asked London to accept its claim over Angra Pequena (Lüderitz Bay) in South West Africa; London was not forthcoming with an answer and did little to stop the colonialists at the Cape from extending their influence into the area. Bismarck ordered Münster abruptly to take Heligoland off the agenda.[120] He had thought of its acquisition as 'a favour of the kind which we can only ask for from a truly friendly and well-meaning government'. But the attitude taken by Gladstone in South West Africa indicated that Britain did not (yet) see any need to court German friendship.[121]

London and Berlin had read their relationship strikingly differently: German good will was not nearly as important for the British as Bismarck had assumed. The open-ended promise of Germany's support in colonial questions would not buy Britain's North Sea rock. Clearly, Germany would need more diplomatic capital. Bismarck told his staff not to mention the island any more. At the same time he made sure that Granville and Gladstone got the message that German support could not be taken for granted. To Bismarck the episode had highlighted that Germany's overseas influence had to be taken more seriously. He had been famously averse to 'colonial adventures', but his reaction to the abortive Heligoland talks in 1884 shows that this was not a dogmatic position. Colonial and European theatres were closely interlinked: concessions in the one could be offset by gains in the other. Germany would not 'artificially' build colonies, but 'if they emerge, we will seek to protect them'.[122] In February 1885 Berlin put the territories in East Africa acquired by Carl Peters, the German colonial pioneer, under German protection. Possessions in New Guinea and the neighbouring 'Bismarck Archipelago' followed in May that year. This endorsement of colonial engagements was not an end in itself, but a means of improving Germany's position vis-à-vis the other powers. Europe and a closer engage-ment with Britain remained at the heart of Bismarck's policy. London and Berlin, he believed, had a shared interest in checking France and Russia—an interest which might well lead to a formal alliance one day. Heligoland was to be a function of this anticipated Anglo-German future: it came into the spotlight whenever there was movement in the two nations' relationship.

So far officials in London had routinely denied that they would consider ceding Britain's North Sea colony. In March 1885 Earl of Derby, the colonial secretary, told his staff that Count Münster, the German ambassador, had 'more than once mentioned the subject privately to me, but got no encouragement'.[123] Yet there was no unanimity within the political establishment on this point. Later that month Sir John Eldon Gorst, Conservative MP for Chatham and solicitor general under Salisbury, moved in the Commons that Heligoland be offered to Berlin. Gorst argued that the island was creating more problems than it offered opportunities. The Germans seemed particularly 'sentimental' about the outpost. Should it not be given to them? Sir Henry Holland, who was to be colonial secretary from 1887 to 1892, disagreed. Gorst's motion was 'most unwise and uncalled for'. Heligoland was of strategic importance. Getting rid of it would save only 'a very small subsidy'. 'Are we to throw over the Heligolanders for such a gain?' he asked rhetorically.[124]

It is worth quoting from the ensuing debate since it highlighted the key issues which, for almost a century to come, were to dominate British thinking about the island and the German quest to own it.[125] Holland was vitriolic in his critique of the motion. It was 'a strange proposal to hand over this island to the Germans without ascertaining the views and wishes of the islanders'. There was

> no desire on the part of the people of Heligoland for the proposed annexation. They had prospered and thrived under English rule, and he was certain that they did not desire to come under German rule and German law, including conscription for military service. He was not prepared to sacrifice these people for the purpose of pleasing and conciliating the German people, however desirable it might be to do so.[126]

In later debates Heligoland was to serve as the first example of 'appeasement': as a misguided concession which had only encouraged Germany's appetite for expansionism. But here, in 1885, 'pleasing and conciliating' the Germans had positive connotations. Holland had nothing against the idea. He simply objected to the islanders not being asked. Five years later, with Holland (now Viscount Knutsford) as colonial secretary, the Salisbury government was to do exactly that: 'sacrifice' the Heligolanders without consulting them.

While Holland and other MPs rejected Gorst's motion vigorously, they agreed with him on one point: there was a peculiar 'German sentiment' about this small island. When Heligoland was ceded five years later, Salisbury explained its value as mainly 'sentimental'.[127] The Germans looked at the island 'from a sentimental point of view', argued Sir James

Fergusson, the under-secretary of state for foreign affairs.[128] And no doubt, the Germans—or rather 'a certain class' amongst them, as Maxse pointed out—*were* sentimental about Heligoland.[129] Generations of poets and painters had cultivated the island as a national icon. There was wide agreement in the German press in 1890 that the Germans had always had a distinct fondness for the 'sentimental island'.[130]

But the idea that Berlin coveted Heligoland as a matter of sentiment distracted from underlying hard-headed strategic considerations. For Bismarck and most in his government the island's value was defined by the projected Kiel Canal and its function for the Imperial Navy. Ever since 1864 Prussia had planned a waterway through Holstein in order to be able to move the fleet between the Baltic and the North Sea without having to go around Denmark. After unification the project, which had the support of Wilhelm I, moved up the political agenda. By 1878 a detailed scheme was ready, which foresaw Kiel and Brunsbüttel (at the mouth of the Elbe) as the eastern and western end points of the canal. From 1883 its construction was being actively planned; works began in June 1887. From the beginning Heligoland played a pivotal role in official thinking about the canal.[131] 'The value of this island as a strategic position', Governor O'Brien explained, lay in 'the great advantage it offers as the site for a naval fort to cover the entrance to their [the Germans'] four main rivers including the Baltic Canal'.[132] This was why 'the possession of Heligoland by Great Britain' was 'such a thorn in the side of Germany'.[133] German diplomats were careful not to mention any of this publicly, but in their internal dispatches they used practically the same words. Germany had to be 'Herr vor der eigenen Tür': in command of its own front lawn, Münster wrote. 'To this end', he explained, 'two things are mostly necessary: the possession of Heligoland, the natural outpost of Germany's coast and rivers; and the construction of a large canal between the Baltic and the North Sea'.[134] It was this underlying strategic consideration, not any sentimental feelings, which motivated Bismarck to seek the acquisition of the island.

At the same time, the colony's value for Britain was becoming questionable. Until well into the 1860s the assumption at Whitehall had been that Heligoland would play a strategic role—most likely against France— as a stronghold for blockading, smuggling, and arms-running. With the dramatic change in technology in the second half of the century this scenario began to look increasingly outdated. A modern navy would be able to maintain a blockade of northern Europe without having to rely on the island as a shelter. At the same time it seemed doubtful that the outpost could be held without heavily fortifying it. And even if it was transformed into a second Gibraltar, Britain would have to commit a large fleet to the North Sea to defend the colony in times of war. Discussions between the Admiralty, the Foreign Office, and the Colonial Office in September 1869 brought this out for the first time: Britain's smallest colony had begun to pose more strategic risks than it offered benefits.[135] In October 1886 the Colonial Defence Committee concluded that 'the naval and military importance of Heligoland has ceased to exist under modern conditions'.[136]

If strategically the island was no longer much of an asset, culturally it was a lost cause—or so Governor O'Brien, Maxse's successor, thought. In November 1887 he wrote a long dispatch to London, in which he vented his frustration:

> Heligoland is not like one of our larger and more prosperous English-speaking colonies where a foreigner soon gets merged into the population of a people which from community of interests and, other causes is drawn towards and attached to the mother country. Here a German remains a German imbued with his national feelings and, probably with the covetousness exhibited by his countrymen for the possession of the island, he and his surroundings therefore become the hotbed for the nourishment of anti-English feeling and would be but too ready tools should the occasion arise to get up a demonstration against our rule.

A new generation of Heligolanders was growing up for whom Germany was no longer a foreign country, but part of their everyday experience. As O'Brien explained, 'German, if not the language of the people, is that of our Church and of our laws while it is that of our visitors and of those with whom the Heligolanders mostly come in contact'. This was made worse by the fact that 'the principal officials, the government secretary, the clergyman, doctor, school teachers, in fact most of those who can influence the minds of the young are German'.[137] In depicting all this as a threat, O'Brien betrayed the same siege mentality that Maxse had shown. There was a strong sense that the symbiosis of British colonialism and German nationalism, which had defined the island from the 1830s onwards, was coming to an end.

All this made it more likely that London would eventually cede the island—if the price was right and the context of the Anglo-German

Figure 3.2 *Dolce far niente auf der Düne*. Drawing by Emil Limmer, published in *Illustrirte Zeitung*, 1887.

relationship conducive.[138] In the late 1880s there was a sense of openness to this relationship which is easily misread in hindsight. Bismarck and Salisbury were not engaged in an early form of antagonism, the one trying to push Germany towards hegemony, the other trying to contain it. Theirs was a strong and reliable partnership which expressed both dependence and distance: dependence, because London and Berlin shared underlying interests and cooperated effectively; distance, because they were seemingly unable to come to a formal agreement which would have given their well-functioning relationship a more long-term basis. Heligoland expressed this tension. While Bismarck hoped that its eventual acquisition would be part of a larger Anglo-German treaty, Salisbury thought of it mostly as capital that could be used for colonial bargaining. This contrast came to the fore in early 1889 when Bismarck made an alliance offer designed to bind the two nations together in opposition to France. Paul von Hatzfeldt, who had taken over as the German ambassador to London in 1885 and was seen as 'the best horse in the diplomatic stable' by Bismarck, put the idea to Salisbury on 15 January: a treaty could take different forms, but at its core would be the commitment to help the other nation in case of war with France.[139] The reply was hesitant—the prime minister asked for time, but not for details. As if to underline that he was serious about the offer Bismarck declared in the Reichstag that Britain was Germany's 'old and traditional alliance partner, with whom we have no contentious issues'. No treaties existed between the two nations, 'but I wish to continue with the close contact which we have now had with England for at least 150 years'.[140]

Two months later Salisbury told Bismarck junior, sent to London for talks, that he was unlikely to find a majority in Parliament for an alliance, as much as he agreed with the overall idea. 'Meanwhile we leave it on the table, without saying yes or no: that is unfortunately all I can do at present'.[141] But while shelving Bismarck's idea of an alliance in Europe, Salisbury encouraged colonial talks, especially on South West Africa. British and German interests overlapped considerably here. In April 1884 Berlin had put the territories acquired by Adolf Lüderitz, a Bremen merchant, under its protection. London however owned the most important harbour in the region, Walvis Bay (in modern Namibia), which had been annexed by the neighbouring Cape Colony to forestall German influence. Perhaps the Germans could be persuaded to give up on their protectorate? As Joseph Chamberlain told Bismarck junior only days after the prime minister had politely rebuffed the alliance offer, 'we have an interest in stepping in your shoes there which I am sure will prove too tight for you'. As compensation he suggested Heligoland. Herbert Bismarck was delighted, though he made sure not to 'show how much satisfaction I felt'.[142] Chamberlain, later colonial secretary under Salisbury, suggested talks with the prime minister. In April Hatzfeldt followed this up with Salisbury who mentioned the island again as an object for a potential swap. Hatzfeldt was optimistic, but suggested that 'we should not make the impression that we put much value on the possession of the island'.[143] Bismarck agreed.[144] His son instructed the staff at the Berlin Foreign Office not to push the issue: 'If we show too much desire, we are driving up the price and might disrupt the entire endeavour'.[145]

It took Bismarck some effort to get Wilhelm II, the new emperor, to toe the line. Wilhelm II had ascended to the throne in June 1888, after the death, in quick succession, of his grandfather, Wilhelm I, and father, Friedrich III. Hearing that the British had suggested swapping parts of South West Africa for Heligoland, Wilhelm II urged action. This was an opportune moment and the island was strategically 'of the highest importance'.[146] Could the negotiations not be sped up? Bismarck junior reiterated in a secret dispatch that this would be a mistake.[147] His father agreed. Taking the initiative would show Germany as *begehrlich* (covetous). This would drive the price up and make an agreement less likely. 'One has to wait for the moment when England needs *us*. So far *we* need England'.[148] He warned emphatically that 'any German initiative in the matter' would be disadvantageous. 'I urgently advise against it, in the interests of succeeding at a later date'.[149] Eventually the Kaiser agreed and followed Bismarck's line, begrudgingly.[150]

The episode was telling for several reasons. It highlighted the tensions between Bismarck and Wilhelm II—the Kaiser had vaguely defined ambitions to govern more directly, while Bismarck was keen to keep the young emperor at arm's length.[151] This conflict translated into the conduct of foreign policy where the Kaiser favoured a less open-ended approach than Bismarck: if Germany wanted Heligoland, it should say so and secure its acquisition rather than wait endlessly for a more favourable agreement. But the talks of spring 1889 revealed also just how little the chancellor and his aides thought of the Reich's possessions in Africa. The protectorates carried 'very little weight', Herbert Bismarck wrote in a memorandum that was endorsed by his father. 'If we keep South West Africa, we will be forced to invest more than hitherto in policing, defence and administration; and for now there is no expectation that trade and capital will follow our flag'. He was confident that 'the acquisition of Heligoland would be so popular at home' that a swap would be 'acceptable'.[152] There is no indication here that Bismarck senior and junior would have hesitated to sell a significant part of the Reich's colonial possessions in Africa in exchange for a rock in the North Sea.

Nine months later, in March 1890, Bismarck resigned, after almost three decades at the helm of Prussian and German politics. Wilhelm II appointed Leo von Caprivi as his new chancellor—'a typical Teuton of the hugest, most impressive type', the Berlin correspondent of *The Times* commented.[153] Caprivi was determined to depart from Bismarck's policies. One of his key early decisions was not to renew the Reinsurance Treaty with Russia. This created a sense of pressure in Germany's foreign policy which had not existed under Bismarck: stronger ties with Britain were much more of a necessity now. For the Kaiser's new government Heligoland was the symbol of this rapprochement. Its acquisition would demonstrate Anglo-German friendship and herald a broader alliance. Behind the scenes the Kaiser pushed hard for the acquisition. As he recalled later, he had dreamt of the happy day when Heligoland 'would become German again' ever since he had first visited the island in 1873.[154] He was determined not to let the opportunity pass, now that Bismarck had gone—'without Heligoland the Baltic Canal has no meaning for our fleet', he told his ministers.[155]

All this put Salisbury in a strong positon during the talks which began in May 1890. Discussions about colonial spheres of influence had continued on ministerial level after Bismarck's departure. Now the prime minister connected them with the Heligoland question again.[156] The thinking in his cabinet was summed up in a memorandum used by Viscount Knutsford during the negotiations: 'Heligoland may be looked upon as a great make-weight in any future bargain with Germany, but it may fairly be reserved for a very big consideration'.[157] Salisbury put a range of demands on the table, amongst them that Germany would allow Britain to establish a protectorate over Zanzibar off the coast of East Africa. This was, as Hatzfeldt reported, a new and 'very important' request.[158] Germany did not have a legal claim to Zanzibar, but had a strong presence there, linked to its protectorate on the adjacent mainland (modern Tanzania). The German East Africa Company, led by Carl Peters, was pushing to extend this presence. To allow the British to claim Zanzibar in this situation was a big ask, all the more so since Salisbury had demanded additional German concessions, including the pro-tectorate over Witu (or Swahililand, in present-day Kenya) and a free hand in Uganda. But he had offered Heligoland in return. As far as Berlin was concerned, that was all that mattered. Adolf Marschall von Bieberstein, the state secretary at the German Foreign Office, told Hatzfeldt that the North Sea outpost had 'the greatest importance'.[159] The far-reaching colonial concessions demanded by Salisbury could be accepted. 'We will still regard the acquisition of Heligoland as a profit', Marschall wrote.[160] Hatzfeldt sug-gested holding back in order to negotiate a more favourable deal. But Caprivi and Marschall, pushed by the impatient Kaiser, would have none of it: they were 'ready for an immediate agreement'.[161]

There were some questions in the Salisbury cabinet about the wisdom of giving up Britain's North Sea colony, but these were overcome by the Admiralty's clear stance. The navy did not want to hang on to Heligoland. Defending the rock would be a huge challenge and Britain did not need an outpost close to Germany in case of war. If the navy had to blockade north-ern Europe, it would do so at distance. Salisbury found it more difficult to convince the queen, who was clearly outraged by the idea of ceding any territory. On 9 June she wrote to the prime minister:

Have received your account of the Cabinet. Understood from Lord Cross that nothing was to be done in a hurry about Heligoland, and now hear it is to be decided tomorrow. It is a *very serious* question which I do not like.

1st. The people have always been very loyal, having received my heir with enthusiasm; and it is a shame to hand them over to an unscrupulous despotic Government like the German without first consulting them.

2nd. It is a very bad precedent. The next thing will be to propose to give up Gibraltar; and soon nothing will be secure, and all our colonies will wish to be free.

I very much deprecate it and am anxious not to give my consent unless I hear that the people's feelings are consulted and their rights are respected. I think it is a very dangerous proceeding.[162]

Salisbury was quick to address the queen's demands, but he never committed to consulting the islanders. Their rights would be 'carefully reserved', the treaty would stipulate that none of them 'will be subject to naval or military conscription' and that 'every person wishing to retain his [*sic*] British nationality will have the right to do so'. By 11 June London and Berlin had agreed on a draft treaty, but the queen still hesitated. Closer cooperation with Germany was 'valuable', but 'that any of my possessions should be thus bartered away causes me great uneasiness, and I can only consent on receiving a positive assurance from you that the present arrangement constitutes no precedent'.[163] Salisbury assured her that no precedent was intended.[164] On 12 June Victoria finally gave in, though not without having a last word: 'I sanction the proposed cession or almost exchange. But I must repeat that I think you may find great difficulties in the future. Giving up what one has is always a bad thing'.[165]

Salisbury dispatched Percy Anderson, the head of the African department at the Foreign Office, to Berlin to discuss the remaining details. For days Anderson and his counterpart Friedrich Richard Krauel pored over the map of Africa. Using red and blue ink they re-drew the continent's boundaries, demarcating Britain's and Germany's spheres of influence.[166] The British got Witu, the Somaliland coast, and a free hand in Uganda. Importantly, they would be allowed to claim Zanzibar. Berlin received rather less—the 'Caprivi Strip', connecting German Southwest Africa with the Zambezi River, was one of the few real gains. But in German eyes this was outweighed by the cession of Heligoland. On 1 July Malet, Anderson, Caprivi, and Krauel signed the agreement.[167]

The negotiations had gone smoothly ('They don't seem to have the sledge hammer method of the Bismarcks', commented Philip Currie, permanent under-secretary of state at the Foreign Office),[168] but they led to an embarrassing public relations mishap. Caprivi was obliged to hold back with official declarations until the British Parliament had ratified the treaty. Yet the draft agreement had already been published.[169] For six long weeks—it must have seemed like an eternity to the chancellor—the German press debated the agreement without Berlin being able to issue an explanation. The mainstream conservative and liberal press welcomed the treaty more or less cautiously.[170] But Caprivi faced strong criticism from two directions: the colonial lobby and Bismarck. 'We have swapped the bathtub Heligoland for the three kingdoms of Witu, Uganda, Zanzibar', thundered Carl Peters, the colonial pioneer who saw his hard-won acquisitions in East Africa being bartered away.[171] His 'bathtub Heligoland' became a much-quoted Anglo-German quip, echoing the comment by the explorer Henry Stanley that Britain had got a new suit in exchange for an old trouser button. It was out of opposition to the treaty that Peters co-founded the Pan-German League (*Alldeutscher Verein*), pledging to oppose any future government that did not follow the path of colonial expansion. The league was to play a key role on the Wilhelmine radical right, pioneering a new form of political agitation and challenging the government for years to come.[172]

But Bismarck's sniping was more immediately worrying for Caprivi. The former chancellor was much admired amongst the national-conservatives who supported the government. The newspapers were keen to hear Bismarck's opinion—he was all too pleased to oblige, feeding them his vitriol. The Kaiser's foreign policy dilettantes had made a classic mistake by being too eager and obvious, he railed. Salisbury had dangled Heligoland in front of Caprivi and the Kaiser. The two had promptly capitulated, neglecting Germany's interests. Never would he, Bismarck, have given the British a free hand in Zanzibar. And besides everything else, the value of the rock in the North Sea was questionable.[173] Yet the truth was that the talks leading to the treaty had begun under Bismarck himself. He too had been prepared to swap colonial possessions for Heligoland, convinced of the value of the island, which he had described as *ur-deutsch*. There was a direct continuity between the talks started and aborted repeatedly under Bismarck and those seen through by Caprivi. The main difference was that Caprivi had been prepared to pay a higher price.[174]

Bismarck's criticism proved useful for the Salisbury government as it took the Heligoland bill through Parliament. The former chancellor's objections, widely reported in the London press, underlined just how lucrative a deal Salisbury had got. There was little danger that Parliament would not approve it, though the opposition launched a debate ('of the guerrilla order', Salisbury thought) in both Houses.[175] Most of this re-hashed the arguments exchanged on the last occasion when 'the Heligoland question' had reared its head. Why had the islanders not been consulted? Were they being betrayed in order to conciliate the Germans? Salisbury and his ministers defended the treaty resolutely: it 'removed far away any chance of jealousy' with Germany, that 'great and friendly nation', while allowing Britain to expand further in Africa.[176] Everything possible had been done to protect the Heligolanders. They would be able to opt for British nationality; and Berlin had pledged to safeguard the colony's existing laws and customs. Salisbury was confident that the islanders would welcome the cession. There was no 'trustworthy evidence' to suggest otherwise, he told the Lords.[177]

This was disingenuous—all dispatches from the colony indicated that the islanders were opposed to German rule.[178] Salisbury was challenged on this point repeatedly, especially by Roseberry and Granville, but he would not disclose his 'necessarily confidential' sources.[179] Eventually he conceded that 'there is no way of being absolutely sure of the assent of the Heligolanders, expect by mode of taking a plebiscite'. That however was out of the question. Consulting colonial subjects was 'not only singularly alien from all our practice, but also, what is more important, a precedent full of risk and difficulty with regard to other portions of the Empire'.[180] Plebiscites were un-British and a threat to the empire—this was to remain the official position until well into the twentieth century. On 28 July the Heligoland bill passed the Commons by a majority of 148.

When Caprivi explained the agreement to the German public the next day, the future of the Anglo-German relationship was high on his agenda. What mattered most was that conflict with Britain had been resolved, heralding a new era of friendship and cooperation. 'Above all', the agreement would 'strengthen the good relations' between the two countries.[181] Most German newspapers followed this line, while lamenting the loss of overseas territories. Commentators in both countries predicted that a political alliance would be the next, natural step. The *Standard* (not yet called *London Evening Standard*) was confident

> that the crowning ceremony of the Anglo-German Convention will give a fresh and lasting ratification to the sentiment of kinship with which it is only natural that the English and the German people should regard each other.[182]

Yet this narrative, which portrayed the cession of Heligoland as a stepping stone towards a brighter Anglo-German future, gave too much significance to the treaty. This was, first and foremost, a colonial agreement—a function of the Scramble for Africa rather than the Concert of Europe. The talks leading up to it had shown the Anglo-German relationship to be business-like and normal, but a formal alliance had never been in the offing. The agreement underlined that Britain, while happy to strike deals in colonial matters, remained deeply hesitant about European alliances. Whether the Anglo-German link would become closer as a result, as Caprivi and the Kaiser confidently predicted, remained to be seen. The real prize, the Anglo-German alliance envisaged by Bismarck, remained as elusive as before.

4

Making Germans

On 19 June 1890 Rudolf Lindau, a senior diplomat and successful novelist, travelled from Berlin to Heligoland. Adolf Marschall von Bierberstein, the state secretary for foreign affairs, had selected him for what was to be a delicate mission: Lindau was to prepare the Heligolanders for their takeover by Imperial Germany. Sending an agent to soften up the islanders had been London's idea. Percy Anderson, Salisbury's chief negotiator, had warned Marschall about anti-German sentiment. Berlin, he told him, ought to 'anticipate agitation in Heligoland by taking steps to conciliate certain of the influential islanders'.[1] Lindau was the ideal choice for this task. He had been involved in the manipulation of public opinion for decades, first as the director of Bismarck's press office and now as the head of the press department at the German Foreign Office. And he knew Heligoland well, having spent many a summer there.[2]

Lindau realized soon after his arrival that he faced an uphill struggle with this small offshore population. 'I think', he wrote to Berlin, 'that if a vote were to take place as to whether Heligoland should stay with Britain or be given to Germany, the vast majority of Heligolanders would decide for the status quo'.[3] There was, of course, to be no vote—the cession of the island had been decided without consulting the inhabitants. British journalists, however, were busy conducting an unofficial plebiscite. Lindau could do little to prevent the result—a clear vote for remaining British—from being published.[4] Colonial rule had suited the islanders' identity politics: London had accommodated rather than challenged their *raison d'être* as a miniature island people in between two large powers. Their main political aim in August 1890 was not to be united with the Kaiserreich, but to preserve against this state the privileges and special regulations that they had enjoyed under British rule. Despite being economically almost entirely dependent on Imperial Germany they were keen to stress their separate identity and independence from German ideas of nationhood. The Heligolanders, Lindau concluded, still had to be 'made German'.[5]

Making the islanders German was crucial, from Berlin's perspective, for political and cultural reasons. Much of the publicized rationale for the acquisition of Heligoland depended on the purported ethnic link between them and the Reich. The official memorandum stressed that

> Germans of all tribes have felt for many generations the pain of a foreign power ruling over German soil so close to the mainland. They felt the pain of a truly German tribe which, ripped apart from its homeland, was left to languish.[6]

Yet this rhetoric could not hide the fact that it was far from clear where the Heligolanders belonged ethnically or nationally. The case for their Germanness rested on their Frisian origins. In nineteenth-century racial thinking the Frisians represented a supposedly 'pure' or 'untouched' ethnic group, constituting a link back to the early Germanic 'tribes'. Yet even the anthropologist and biologist Rudolf Virchow, who argued this case with some force, had to admit that the Frisians were 'mixed'.[7] Already in 1856 Karl Reinhardt had observed in his book about the island that 'the current Heligolanders, like the current Germans, appear to have no pure origins'.[8] Writing fifty years later, the linguist Theodor Siebs went a step further: the Heligolanders were in language and customs closer to the British than to the Germans.[9]

If it was therefore unconvincing to claim the Heligolanders ethnically as Germans, it was all the more important to make them German in sentiment. On 1 August 1890 Adolf Wermuth, a high-ranking Prussian civil servant, joined Lindau to prepare the takeover. Wermuth was to be the new German governor, ruling Heligoland on behalf of the Kaiser until it could be fully incorporated into Prussia. He introduced himself to Arthur Barkly in English—the British governor spoke no German and very little French—and found that it would be easy to deal with him. Things were 'rather more complicated with the islanders'.[10] Wermuth had a hard time explaining the treaty to them. Most of the Heligolanders remained sceptical, he noted, though they seemed to like the idea of being exempted from military service and most forms of taxation. Many of them complained that they had not been consulted—Barkly had told them about the cession only after the treaty had been signed.[11] This had made an impression on them which 'can hardly be styled favourable', the governor thought.[12]

The handover would have to be accordingly well orchestrated, impressing the islanders as much as the Kaiser and the wider public. There was no established protocol for a takeover of this kind. London and Berlin cobbled together a programme which combined elements of military and civic ritual—and which was to be revived in the second half of the twentieth century when Britain developed more of a routine in handing over colonies.[13] On 9 August Karl Heinrich von Boetticher, the secretary of the interior, arrived to formally receive the island from Barkly. Wermuth thought it was a moving, almost religious occasion:

> The ladies of the British governor in their light robes are looking down upon us from the balcony on the first floor, full of interest. Down beneath them stand the two representatives, facing one another... To their side the guard of honour made up of English marines has taken position, guarding the Union Jack... The ceremonial words of transfer are being spoken. As soon as they have been uttered, at half past three, the German flag rises next to the British on the flag pole. It is greeted by the English with a 21-gun salute. At the same time Herr von Boetticher proposes a toast to Queen Victoria, Mr Barkly one to Kaiser Wilhelm. All participants join in. It was one of the rare moments when one feels a shiver running down the spine. We departed from the ceremonial site hesitantly. But until nightfall the British and German flags flew merrily next to each other in the breeze. At night both were lowered together.[14]

The inevitable banquet followed, before Barkly embarked on HMS *Enchantress*, with his family and household on board. 'Island taken over' was the lapidary message Boetticher sent to Berlin by telegram.[15] At 11.40 p.m. the last British ship, HMS *Calypso*, left Heligoland. Its commander had been told to make sure to bring away the last Union flag that had flown over the island.[16]

On the next morning Wilhelm II arrived to take possession of his 'imperial island'.[17] After the obligatory fleet review the Kaiser came on land, entourage and ministers in tow, and went up to the *Oberland*. From here, the plateau amongst the cliff tops, he took in the majestic, all-round view of the sea, that 'German ocean'.[18] The navy's chief minister held a religious service, which was followed by a parade of 3,000 soldiers. Then the Kaiser spoke. 'I, Wilhelm II, German Emperor, King of Prussia, reincorporate this island with the German Fatherland'. Twenty years had passed since the war against France, which had unified Germany. Now 'the last piece of German soil' that had remained outside the Reich was being added. He then addressed the islanders present, who were easily outnumbered by the assembled troops. 'Heligolanders!', he exclaimed:

By the community of race, language, customs and interests you have always had much in common with your German brothers...With all the more joy does every German welcome with me your re-union with the German people and Fatherland...May the return to Germany, the participation in her glory, her independence and her freedom prove a constant blessing to you and your descendants.[19]

According to the programme for the imperial transfer, the Heligolanders would now symbolically offer the island to the Kaiser. Wermuth had bribed a number of local women into presenting a Heligoland-shaped bouquet of flowers to the Kaiser and paying homage to their new ruler.[20] The islanders promptly thanked 'our sublime and generous' Queen Victoria for her many years of beneficial rule before expressing their joy at being incorporated into Germany. On Wermuth's insistence the delegation proclaimed that 'we feel already through descent, language and customs as one' with the Reich.[21]

All this skirted carefully around the main issue: the Heligolanders' nationality. For decades German observers had commented on the islanders' lack

Figure 4.1 Wilhelm II takes possession of Heligoland, 10 August 1890.

of national sentiment. This miniature people had the tendency 'not to be loyal to their rulers', the Hanoverian officer Friedrich von der Decken had written in 1826.[22] Numerous reports by Prussian officials had come to the same conclusion: whether governed by the Danes or the British, the islanders had never developed a sense of national belonging. Now, in August 1890, they had literally overnight changed from subjects of the British empire into German citizens. As Arthur Stadthagen, lawyer and Social Democratic member of the Reichstag, pointed out, they had woken up on 10 August as 'compulsory Germans'.[23] But, thanks to the treaty clause which Salisbury had insisted on, they had the right to choose to become British subjects again.[24] This option—which stood in contrast to the more draconian regulations that had applied in Alsace-Lorraine, annexed by the Reich in 1871—would be available for two years and could be exercised through notification of the local authorities.[25]

This meant, theoretically at least, that the Kaiser's future bulwark against Britain could be inhabited by British subjects. Consequently, the Berlin government went out of its way to dissuade the islanders from making use of the option. Boetticher, the secretary of the interior, quipped in the Reichstag that the Heligolanders had not yet 'acquired a taste' for German military service and taxation.[26] The government promptly exempted all those born before 1890 from conscription and ensured that the islanders would continue to enjoy extensive tax privileges. Combined with the Kaiser's considerable generosity, this would surely result in a heightened loyalty to the German nation state.[27] But lest too many of the islanders still felt inclined to opt for British citizenship, Berlin created a number of bureaucratic hurdles. Some of the Heligolanders protested against what they saw as intimidation: the local authorities made them feel 'very nervous about expressing their wish to remain British subjects'.[28]

What was more, there were strong financial incentives not to opt for British citizenship. British Heligolanders had to pay the regular poll tax levied on foreigners in the Reich—120 Marks for tradesmen, shopkeepers, and hoteliers. This was perhaps not 'a monstrous sum', as one of the enraged British observers wrote to the Colonial Office, but it was a significant deterrent (a single trip from Heligoland to Hamburg cost 7 Marks in this period).[29] Nor were British Heligolanders eligible for the lucrative local privileges. As the consul general in Hamburg wrote, many islanders 'who had the intention to opt for British nationality were deterred therefrom' out of fear that they would lose out financially and be 'regarded and treated as aliens'.[30] If this was not enough, the imperial secretary of the interior declared that in regarding British Heligolanders as foreigners the government retained the right to deport them if they 'became inconvenient'.[31]

To the government officials in London all this indicated that the islanders had become victims of the Germanization strategy that was on display in other border regions of the Kaiserreich, too. As one of the clerks in the Colonial Office wrote,

> I fear that Germany is carrying out in Heligoland the same kind of policy that has been so successful in the *Reichsland* where not a quarter of the people now speak French and that I believe Prussia adopts in the Polish provinces.[32]

The comparison with the German–Polish and German–French border-lands was apt, despite the different scales involved. Imperial Germany, founded only in 1871, resembled a patchwork of identities and loyalties. The unitary idea, embodied by the Kaiser and the imperial state, was in con-tinuous conflict with older traditions. Nowhere was this clearer than in the border regions, where the Kaiserreich's ambition to create a homogeneous nation state met with the reality of ethnically diverse populations who did not fit neatly into national categories. This was the case not only in Silesia and Alsace, but also in Schleswig, where a Danish minority existed.[33] Berlin made a concerted effort to Germanize these regions through language, edu-cation, law, and religion. Heligoland mirrored this strategy. Whatever the islanders themselves felt, they had to be seen to be Germans, guardians of the nation's northern boundary.

The government in London decided that it could do little more than look on as its former subjects were bullied into becoming Germans. The Colonial Office felt strongly that Berlin should be reprimanded. It seemed 'that the German government has violated the agreement in spirit if not in the letter', argued Edward Wingfield, assistant under-secretary, in November 1892. The treatment of the Heligolanders was 'thoroughly German and not indicative of nobility', agreed C. A. Harris, one of his clerks.[34] He recom-mended that 'we might expostulate' with Berlin 'even if we receive a diplo-matic snub'.[35] But while many at the Colonial Office felt that London should stand up to Berlin, they also acknowledged that Whitehall had a share in the blame for the fate of the islanders. 'I think we have hardly done our duty by the Heligolanders', Harris wrote.[36] 'I quite agree that we have neglected [them]', Wingfield replied, adding hastily that 'of course it was the duty of the Foreign Office to see that they were protected'.[37] He had a point: none of the staff at the Foreign Office involved in drawing up the treaty of 1890 had thought through how the 'nationality question' would work out in practice. Giving the islanders the right to 'opt for Britain' was one thing, establishing the mechanism by which this option would be exercised was another. The Foreign Office had left the implementation to the German authorities and had failed to ask about the consequences awaiting British Heligolanders. There was, as Rosebery admitted, 'no clause in this agreement binding the German Government not to tax as aliens those natives who opt for British nationality'.[38] Belatedly, the government got assurances from Berlin that it would consider the children of fathers who opted for British citizenship also as British citizens, but it established no rules that would prevent the Germans from discriminating against them.[39] In a rather lame gesture, the Foreign Office asked Berlin to put up posters on the island reminding the inhabitants of their option to become British.

Berlin fobbed off all queries nonchalantly. On the day of the handover, Marschall wrote to Malet that 'no decision has as yet been arrived at with regard to the execution of the provisions of the Anglo-German agreement ensuring the right of option to natives of Heligoland'.[40] This was extraordinary for an administration that had planned all other steps of the island's takeover minutely in advance. When London complained a year later about the grievances of its former subjects, Berlin answered that these must have been invented by British newspapers.[41] Islanders who intended to remain British 'have not in the least been influenced or in any other form been prevented from opting for England'.[42] The allegations, for which London had several witness reports, were 'entirely without foundation', Malet was told in Berlin.[43] Complaints from islanders and the consul general in Hamburg continued to reach London, but Whitehall decided it could do little more. 'I think we must let it drop', wrote Wingfield at the Colonial Office, concurring with his clerks.[44] Malet, the ambassador in Berlin, thought so too.[45] In February 1893, the Marquess of Ripon, the colonial secretary, agreed with Rosebery, the foreign secretary: as long as Berlin kept carefully within the agreement, there were 'no grounds on which a remonstrance to the German Government could be based'.[46]

It was unsurprising, then, that only a minority of the Heligolanders opted for British nationality. Most of them left the island, migrating to Britain, but also to Australia and the USA, where some of them had relatives. Those British citizens who stayed on the island were being made to feel like strangers in their own home. As one of them, John Franz, wrote, he felt 'in

all matters pushed down as a British citizen'.[47] He had been born and
brought up in the island, was married with three children, and owned a
small family business. Yet, like all other British subjects, he had been declared
a *Schutzbürger* by the island's authorities. As an alien he could be deported if
necessary and had to pay a special poll tax.[48] In common with other
Heligolanders, Franz had never needed any documents when going to the
mainland before 1890. Now he depended on a formal letter from the consul
general at Hamburg, a 'passport' requesting the German authorities to allow
this 'British subject, native of Heligoland, travelling on the Continent to
pass freely without let or hindrance'.[49]

Other Heligolanders, too, continued to live a curious existence in
between the nations, causing much bureaucratic confusion. Otto Müller
was one of them. Born in Heligoland in 1852, he had left the island before
its cession, had lived in London, and then served on board British ships. It
seems he was somewhere on an ocean when, unwittingly, he became
German. No one told him about the cession or the option of asking for
British nationality within two years. It took the Home Office and the
Foreign Office in London several rounds of legal discussions before they
came to a conclusion about Müller's nationality. Having gone through all
cases which they could find on the question of the national status accorded
to inhabitants of conquered or ceded territory, the lawyers decided that
Müller was German. As the Foreign Office explained to the Home Office
in January 1901, Müller 'owes allegiance to the German Emperor'. He had
to 'be regarded as a natural born British subject who has become an alien'.[50]

The bureaucracies in London and Berlin went on struggling with cases such
as Müller's.[51] The question of nationality complicated a range of otherwise
straightforward administrative acts. But most of all, it intruded into the personal
lives of the Heligolanders. They were made not to think of themselves as one
group, defined by where they had been born and brought up, but as individuals
who were defined by nationality, a status which was decided upon by the governments in London and Berlin. This nationalizing effect reached deep into
the islanders' everyday lives and charged key moments, including marriage,
divorce, and death, with a new meaning, as we shall see. Yet the ideologically
motivated and bureaucratically expressed ambition to create a homogeneous
nation state never succeeded fully in this Anglo-German borderland. In the
personal histories of the Heligolanders Britain and Germany continued to be
bound up with one another. Only in the 1950s—after two world wars and
the demise of Imperial, Weimar, and Nazi Germany—was there to be a sense

that the Heligolanders had been 'made German', with a majority of them expressing a clear preference for German rule.

While the Heligolanders continued to lead an existence in between empire and nation state, the government started a series of initiatives aimed at incorporating the island into Germany. As far as the bureaucrats in Berlin were concerned this was first and foremost a legal process. In December 1890 the Reichstag passed a bill of laws entitled 'Unification of the Island of Heligoland with the Prussian State'.[52] A raft of German and Prussian laws now applied in the outpost. German legal historians took this to be the moment when colonial law had been superseded by the German legal code. Britain's regime had only been an 'interim', wrote Ernst von Moeller, convinced of the island's 'German character'.[53] But the idea that colonial law had simply ceased to exist was a fallacy. The Germans found—just as the British had when taking over the island at the beginning of the century—that it was impossible to sweep aside existing laws, no matter which tradition or language they belonged to. The island's capitulation in 1807 had stipulated that London would respect pre-existing laws. The same applied now. Berlin had explicitly acknowledged this in the treaty with London: 'Native laws and customs now existing will, as far as possible, remain undisturbed'.[54]

This stipulation was the source of all sorts of headaches, Wermuth wrote.[55] As much as the German state liked to pretend otherwise, the law was not a straightforward instrument through which it could exercise sovereignty over its newly acquired territory. Rather, the laws that applied in the island resembled a compromise in which the British colonial past and the German present coexisted. Nothing demonstrated this better than the tax privileges of the Heligolanders: the island's duty-free status was based on an exemption that had first been codified in the colonial period. The island's marriage laws, too, expressed a colonial legacy. Throughout the British period, getting married had been significantly easier in Heligoland than on the Continent. Bride and groom did not have to give public notice of their intention and the governor routinely dispensed with asking parents for permission. Until the turn of the century the island remained a 'paradise for lovers', a destination for elopers from all over northern Europe.[56]

August Strindberg, the Swedish playwright, was one of them. In late April 1893 he travelled to Heligoland with Frida Uhl, an Austrian writer who acted as a muse to a number of European literati around the turn of the century. Strindberg, who was 44, had been married previously. Uhl, who had turned 21 only weeks earlier, was uncertain whether her father, the editor of the well-respected *Wiener Zeitung*, would approve. So she and Strindberg opted for a discreet wedding in Heligoland. The local priest was still the same as in the colonial period: Heinrich Schröder, who had a reputation for asking few questions. The Strindbergs were not the only ones who appreciated this—Schröder officiated at up to six weddings per day in the summer season (the writer Ernst Jünger's parents travelled to the island all the way from Heidelberg to get married). With a minimum of fuss, Schröder declared Strindberg and Uhl husband and wife on 2 May 1893.[57] To Uhl it seemed as if Heligoland was still English.[58]

The colonial past thus remained alive in the island's laws and customs—at the very time when the German government moved to symbolically disentangle the British empire and the Kaiserreich. British magazines ridiculed the 'smoke and enthusiasm' and seemingly endless visits by which the Kaiser celebrated his new island, but Germanizing Heligoland went beyond rhetoric and ritual.[59] A concerted effort to write the German Reich into the story of Heligoland became obvious soon after August 1890. Street names were changed, bilingual teaching and record keeping stopped, new public buildings and monuments erected. Not all of this was government-sponsored. The new Hoffmann von Fallersleben monument, which turned into a site for national pilgrimage, was funded by public subscription.[60] Much of the town's transformation was driven by private and commercial as much as official initiative. Heligoland now experienced its own, belated *Gründerzeit*: a new style of architecture took hold, mostly neoclassical in character, displaying confidence and aspiration. Next to the modest older houses, which had low roofs and bare brick walls, rose taller buildings with white stucco façades, suggesting a grandeur that had been lacking so far. British visitors were impressed:

> Shops abound, and many pretty buildings, pensions, and hotels, and the first-named are well-stocked with a variety of products suitable for presents and as mementoes of the pretty little island... Returning to the foot of the rock, after an all too brief sojourn, we found a pleasant beach and elegant casino, with all the necessaries for spending a delightful evening by the sea, at the foot of the cliffs, and to the strains of a band; or, in the day-time, leisurely to bathe, or fish, or read, or bask in the sunshine on the fine clean sand, with the ever-present North Sea stretching away beyond the limit of vision.[61]

The new *Kurhaus* (assembly rooms) took pride of place, opposite the now extended pier. As tourist guides noted with approval, new facilities were being built everywhere, amongst them a theatre, yachting harbour, indoor swimming pool, and monumental aquarium, run by the new Royal Biological Institute. The 'imperial island' was visibly shaking off its colonial past.[62]

A similar desire to distance Heligoland from its association with the British empire characterized the myriad ways in which popular culture embraced the 'German island'. A wave of guidebooks, histories, and picture books appeared after 1890, celebrating the new 'crown jewel of the German Sea', the 'Imperial Island', or the 'Kaiser's Island'.[63] There were special coins, stamps, and a range of other souvenirs, depicting the island as a sea-girt piece of Germany that had been reunited with the Fatherland.[64] Part of the motivation for this Heligomania was profit-driven. Tourism to the island was booming. Visitor numbers rose rapidly and exceeded 100,000 per year after the turn of the century. As a British visitor observed, there was a new-found prosperity in Heligoland: 'All classes of island shopkeepers are having highly prosperous times'.[65] But there was plenty of voluntary initiative too, indicating that the fascination with the newly German island was more than a commercial one. In the wake of the takeover new associations and clubs were founded which evoked the island in their title. This ranged from the Hamburg *Club Helgoland* (main objective: 'to have a good time amongst friends') to the *Berliner Thor- und Fußball-Club 1897 Helgoland*, which enjoyed some success in the German first division after the turn of the twentieth century and celebrates Heligoland in its name to this day.[66] Patriotic singing societies, gymnasts' associations, bowling clubs, and veterans' societies discovered the island as a destination for their excursions, as did schools, lobby groups, and political parties. Many of them had special postcards and albums printed to commemorate their trip.[67] So popular did these excursions become that they turned into a subject of mockery—a *Helgolandfahrt* was only complete if its members had been sea-sick once on the way to the 'German island'.[68]

The popularization of Heligoland went hand in hand with its decline as a spa for the grand and noble. As Robert von Benda, a national liberal politician, explained in the Reichstag in December 1890, 'a very distinguished and rich society' (in which he clearly counted himself) had once patronized the island.[69] To his great regret this had changed recently, with only the occasional prince and princess visiting Heligoland. Those aristocrats who still came did what they could to set themselves apart from the bulging numbers of day trippers and middle-class nobodies. Princess Sophie, the

Grand Duchess of Saxe-Weimar, whose fondness for the island almost matched the Kaiser's obsession with it, had a special sedan chair shipped to Heligoland, courtesy of the Hamburg Senate.[70] In this palanquin, made out of wicker so as to float, she would be carried to the beach and into the water, thus avoiding the crowds.

The grand duchess and her wicker chair were remnants of an older age of genteel spa tourism. Few of the noble guests returned, especially not after 1892 when cholera, rampaging in Hamburg, briefly reached the island. (The grand duchess was swiftly evacuated by the navy.[71]) Instead of aristocratic spa circles a new form of mass tourism began to dominate, with day trips and short stays in high demand.[72] The travel diaries of visitors were now more likely to note the prices paid and bargains made than the sights of aristocrats on holiday.[73] As a British visitor observed,

> although princes and the higher nobility of Germany no longer come to Heligoland for a summer stay as they did when it was English, the number of trippers and excursionists who stay three days or so has vastly increased. Every industry connected directly or indirectly with the eating and drinking which German tourists demand is flourishing.[74]

While the island was rapidly losing its status as a destination for upper-class tourists, it continued to attract poets, painters, and professors. A new generation of writers discovered Heligoland in the decades before the First

Figure 4.2 View of Heligoland from Sandy Island, 1890.

World War, keen to connect with the island's literary tradition. Theodor Fontane, Franz Kafka, and August Strindberg were amongst them.[75] What attracted them was not the refuge from censorship and police surveillance which had brought Heine and Wienbarg to the colony in the 1830s, but the island's reputation as a creative enclave and site of natural beauty. Reaching Heligoland had become much easier, with daily steamers running services from a number of ports. What had not changed was the sensation of leaving the Continent behind and arriving a few hours later at the red cliffs out in the North Sea. For decades writers had rhapsodized about the sea-girt isle as a 'natural monument', a site where one could expect to have a more direct and intensive experience of nature than elsewhere. This promise of 'being closer to nature', away from modern life, was still at the heart of what literary-minded travellers sought when they embarked on a holiday on Heligoland.

None of them craved this solitary experience more than Rudolf Lindau, the German Foreign Office official who had prepared the island's takeover in 1890. Lindau had begun to frequent Heligoland in the 1870s, using it for extensive writing holidays. Mark Twain, Ivan Turgenev, and a host of other international authors corresponded with him in his island retreat. In 1902, having retired from the diplomatic service, he settled on Heligoland for good and devoted himself entirely to his literary career. It was, he wrote, as if he had left Germany and lived 'in almost complete isolation from the outer world'.[76] It suited him perfectly:

> Never for a moment have I regretted that I chose Heligoland as a place of rest. Once I have been on the Continent for four weeks I long to be back in Heligoland. I have no use for so-called entertainment any longer; but I need peace and quiet. Nowhere do I think the quiet to be more beautiful than here.[77]

From this self-imposed literary exile Lindau continued to write and correspond with an illustrious circle of writers. When he died in 1910 he was buried, according to his wishes, in the Heligoland cemetery on the *Oberland*.[78]

Nature and distance mattered in another, more mundane, sense for a growing number of the academics and artists who descended on the island every summer. In the summer of 1894 Otto Schultz, a genial entrepreneur from Hanover, had discovered that a few days in the pollen-free island had cured his hay fever. In 1897 he founded the *Heufieberbund von Helgoland*, which was to make the outpost a Mecca for hay fever sufferers. Aby Warburg, art historian and scion of a family of Hamburg bankers, was one of the prominent members of this association.[79] Between the early 1890s and the First World War Warburg went to Heligoland practically every year. As soon as he reached the island he felt Heligoland's 'wonderfully restorative air'.[80] By 1906 his annual ritual of going to the island had become somewhat unreal, like a play—he called it the 'Heligoland Sneeze Theatre': 'every 12 months the curtain lifts and draws again'. But his visits enabled him to get better— or so he told his wife, who would stay at home with their three children.[81] Yet Heligoland offered not only a refuge from the dreaded hay fever, it was also an inspiration for Warburg's work. Repeatedly he used the island as an analogy, in both his correspondence and his academic work.[82] For Warburg as for so many others, Heligoland continued to be an island of the mind, a symbol which served as a vehicle for their own ideas and world views.

It was not only writers, but also painters who cultivated Heligoland as a 'natural monument' in the decades before the First World War. Johann Joachim Faber, Eduard Schmidt, and Christian Morgenstern had established the North Sea outpost as a *sujet* in the first half of the nineteenth century. Artists such as Walter Leistikow, Gustav Schönleber, and Georg Brandes continued that tradition now. While they developed new styles, they focused on the same striking features of Heligoland as their predecessors had. Leistikow, a founding member of the Berlin *Sezession*, was a good example. He painted the island in darker colours and more schematically than the generation of Romantic artists had. Both his oil painting of 1889 and the gouache of 1890 depicted the island as emptied of individuals. There is very little left of the picturesque and parochial here—the main role of nature, devoid of human activity, seems to be that of a melancholic mirror, a func- tion which was to be at the heart of many of Leistikow's arresting landscape paintings.[83]

While Leistikow seemed to give the island a new meaning as a *Naturdenkmal*, the mainstream of artists continued to depict it in the estab- lished Romantic genre. Perhaps the best known was Friedrich Preller (the Younger), whose *Sonnenaufgang bei Helgoland* celebrated Heligoland as both imposing and idyllic. Preller's painting was popularized by Ferdinand Avenarius, the editor of *Der Kunstwart* (a leading arts journal), who pub- lished it in a long print run. Preller and many others who painted Heligoland after 1890 consciously referred to the earlier generation of art- ists and writers who had discovered the island as a symbol of a future Germany in the 1830s and 1840s. For them, clearly eager to continue the

Figure 4.3 *Helgoland*. Oil painting by Walter Leistikow, 1889.

Figure 4.4 *Sonnenaufgang bei Helgoland*. Drawing by Friedrich Preller (the Younger), 1904.

tradition associated with Caspar David Friedrich, the particular appeal of Heligoland was that it offered a motif that brought together nature and nation in a pre-modern idyll.

A similar desire to incorporate the island into an older tradition of German Romanticism was evident in Anton Bruckner's composition *Helgoland*, perhaps the most striking example of the Heligomania that flourished in the 1890s.[84] This was Bruckner's last completed work, a 'symphonic chorus with large orchestra' in which he styled Heligoland as a proud Germanic island threatened by invasion. The islanders implore the intervention of God, who unleashes a powerful storm over the North Sea, destroying the enemy and restoring peace. The story is told through surging and cascading strings, brass, and chorus, evoking wind and weather as much as violent conflict. After an imposing orchestral interlude the chorus repeats over seventy bars the final words 'Oh Lord, free Heligoland praises you'—a prime example of nineteenth-century musical monumentality.[85]

What is intriguing about Bruckner's grandiose ballad is not only its monumental character, but also its national context. *Helgoland* was written for the fiftieth anniversary of the Vienna Male Choir, to whom Bruckner dedicated it. It was first performed at the *Hofburg* in the presence of the Austrian emperor Franz Joseph. In short, *Helgoland*, the composition, was really rather Austrian. What was German about it was the national association. Bruckner clearly saw himself as part of a German nation which went beyond the boundaries of Bismarck's *kleindeutsches* Reich and included parts of Austria-Hungary. In fact, when August Silberstein, on whose poem Bruckner based his composition, had written his 'Helgoland' in the 1860s, 'Germany' had had no clear territorial boundaries. Instead, an ethnic and cultural definition applied for Bruckner as for Silberstein, a 'tribal' idea of Germanic nationhood, which comes through in other examples of Bruckner's work, too, and which he shared with composer Richard Wagner and much of the Wilhelmine cultural elite.[86] Both the monumental character of the work and its evocation of an ethnically defined Germanness was to ensure its popularity with leading Nazis a generation later.

The example of Bruckner's *Helgoland* and much of the cultural embrace of the island after 1890 show the immense appeal that the wind-swept rock in the North Sea had as a national monument. As British commentators observed, there was a 'very deep and real' sentiment amongst Germans for the island.[87] A number of important sources of identification came together

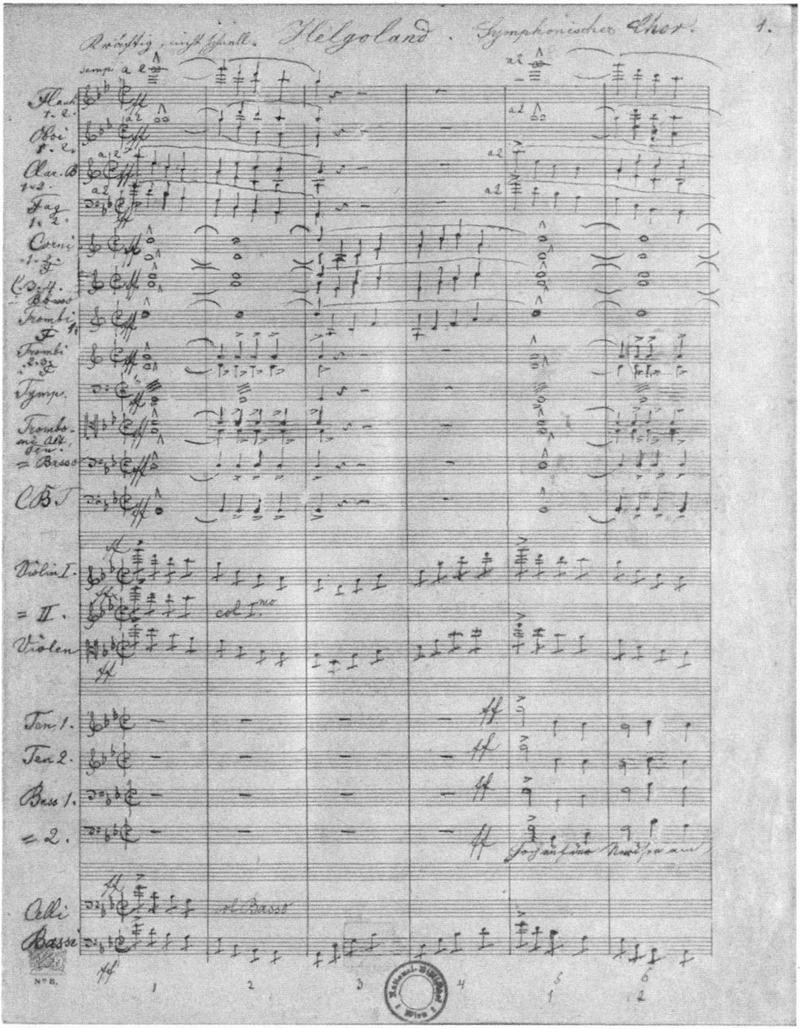

Figure 4.5 Original score of *Helgoland* by Anton Bruckner, 1893.

in this sentiment: the older, national liberal tradition, represented by Hoffmann von Fallersleben, for whom the island had been an exile from a despotic and fragmented Germany; the triumph of unification, achieved against the Danish (to whom Heligoland had once belonged) as much as the French and Austrians; the romanticized depiction of a pre-modern unity between nation and nature, which imagined in the Heligolanders a Germanic *Volk* that lived in harmony with the sea, untouched by the forces of modernity. The island's appeal as a commercial site mattered similarly, signalling profit as much as national prestige. All this was heightened by geography and geology: this was Germany's only deep-sea island, an outpost in the North Sea marking the maritime borders of the Reich. Its imposing cliffs, rising 40 metres vertically out of the sea, were the nearest thing the Germans had to the White Cliffs of Dover. In literature, music, popular culture, and official rhetoric Heligoland symbolized the point where Germany ended: a sentimental reminder of the nation's boundaries; a symbol of welcome and farewell for crews and passengers leaving the Fatherland or coming home from abroad.

Yet while the island turned into a monument to German nationalism, its colonial past continued to be bound up with it. This was the case on Heligoland itself, with its peculiar laws and customs. And this was the case in those territories that had been swapped for the island. The East African sultanate of Witu posed a particularly stark reminder. While Heligoland turned German in August 1890, the protectorate over Witu passed to the British. There was no ceremony or public occasion marking the handover. In fact, there was no handover. Berlin and London were agreed that 'Germany withdraws in favour of Great Britain her protectorate'.[88] But they failed to communicate this to Ahmad ibn Fumo Bakari, the sultan whose sovereignty both governments had pledged to respect. On 9 September 1890 Salisbury reminded Berlin that the sultan ought to be informed.[89] Marschall, the foreign secretary, confirmed that he would 'lose no time' in doing so. But whatever the Germans told Fumo Bakari, it came late and in a condescending manner.[90] Nor did it help that the British were painfully slow to take on their new role: the official notification placing the sultanate under British protectorate was only published twelve weeks later.[91]

All this played a crucial role in the circumstances that led to the death of nine German colonialists in September 1890—deaths which, in turn, led to more violence and destruction a month later.[92] In early September Andreas Küntzel, a colonialist from Bavaria, arrived on the coast of Witu with a group of German labourers and craftsmen. It is unclear whether he knew of the change in the protectorate. If he did, he showed no sign of understanding the implications. His main aim was to set up a saw mill and export timber. The sultan had no objections, but asked Küntzel for a letter from the British consul general. Küntzel ignored the request; for the sultan, however, a letter from the British was crucial: it would have confirmed under whose authority the project was being undertaken, so that he could seek redress in case conflicts arose. The letter would also have recognized the sultan's role as the regional ruler to whom European colonialists had to present their credentials if they wanted to settle in the sultanate. This must have seemed all the more important to Fumo Bakari as his position was weakened through the slow transition from one colonial protector to another. He had traditionally been a reliable client of the Germans. Bismarck's Memorandum on the German Protectorates of 1885, a key document of German colonial policy, spoke of the sultan's strong interest in a 'good relationship with the German Empire'.[93] This interest was based on his long-standing conflict with Zanzibar, a centre for the slave trade. Witu, in contrast, had offered a home to former slaves who had fled from Zanzibar and elsewhere. Being under a German protectorate had given the smaller Witu much clout in its struggle with the otherwise more powerful Zanzibar. The removal of this patronage came at a time when the sultan was struggling to enforce his rule in some parts of Wituland, with growing dissatisfaction being stoked by regional strongmen.

Küntzel thus challenged the sultan at a time when Fumo Bakari was facing considerable instability caused in part by the recent Anglo-German colonial swap. Küntzel had no time for these intricacies and instructed his men to start building a camp. He ignored requests by the sultan to stop, repeatedly it seems. The simmering conflict was acerbated by language issues—no one amongst the Germans spoke or read Swahili. There was one local translator, but he was frequently sent to different locations and was, crucially, absent when soldiers arrived with a letter from the sultan. The Germans sent the letter on to the nearest colonial station to have it translated. This took too long for the soldiers, who escorted the colonialists to Witu. Here things got out of hand. While Fumo Bakari sent for a German agent to mediate, he had Küntzel's group disarmed and effectively detained in the town. He then seems to have lost control of the locals guarding the Germans. According to a number of witnesses the conflict reached boiling point when Küntzel swore publicly against the sultan and his representatives in the afternoon of 14 September. He did so in the main town square in front of the sultan's flag, using 'vicious swear words'. Amongst other things, he called the sultan 'son of a whore'.[94] The next morning Küntzel led a breakout, but he was held back at the town gate. Witnesses disagreed whether the first shots were fired by the Germans or the locals who had been charged with guarding them. There was a short fight, with casualties on both sides. All but one German (who survived injured in a hideout) were killed.

The news of what the German and British papers were to call 'the Witu massacre' reached Berlin on 23 September. The press was outraged, but applauded Salisbury's immediate decision to send an expedition under the command of Sir Edmund Fremantle to Witu. The investigation of and response to the death of the nine Germans was to be an Anglo-German enterprise. 'Joint action' was what Marschall called it.[95] There were limits to this—the British were de facto in charge once the military expedition had been ordered—but both Caprivi and Salisbury were keen to be seen to be cooperating throughout. From the very beginning the diplomats on the spot were consulting directly with one another, as did the governments in London and Berlin. Within days the British had sent a gunboat with German officials on board to the small island of Lamu, just off the coast of modern-day Kenya. Its mission was to collect evidence and evacuate European nationals in the area. The only surviving German witness was brought to Zanzibar and interviewed. The official line taken by both governments was that the sultan was responsible, if not directly then indirectly. Even if he had not condoned the murders, he had 'allowed them to take place', as Marschall told Metternich, the German ambassador in London.[96]

The full report, received in Berlin three weeks later, revealed a more complex picture. Gustav Michahelles, the German consul general in Zanzibar, concluded that much initial responsibility for the conflict lay with Küntzel. At least indirectly his report also highlighted the power vacuum left by the mismanaged transition from one protectorate to another. Berlin, in contrast, was keen to blame the sultan for the murders. The British consul general in Zanzibar, Sir Charles Euan Smith, also saw him as 'the author of the violence'. Michahelles was not convinced. This was, he wrote to Chancellor Caprivi, 'an interpretation which I cannot agree to'.[97] In his opinion the Germans who had been killed were at least partly responsible themselves. The sultan had not intended any animosities, but had been unable to control the local population, which had been outraged by Küntzel's behaviour. The whole episode was a 'regrettable event'.[98]

The Caprivi government displayed little intention to wait for the outcome of the investigation. On 3 October Berlin told London that it had to

insist on 'immediate punishment'.[99] Salisbury suggested a military expedition. Berlin agreed and instructed Michahelles to liaise with the British
commanding officer. The aim was to ensure 'revenge as fast as possible'.[100]
By the time Michahelles's report was received in Berlin (24 October) the
expedition was well under way. The officer in charge, Admiral Edmund
Robert Fremantle, the commander-in-chief of the East Indies Station, was,
the British ambassador wrote, 'anxious to act without delay'.[101] He arrived
with his squadron at Zanzibar on 13 October and requisitioned troops who
would support the British marines and Indian police forces under his command. On 21 October this combined force arrived at Lamu, where Fremantle
declared martial law for the entire sultanate. Fumo Bakari was given an ultimatum to come to Lamu and deliver those responsible for the murders. He
refused to do so. On 24 October Fremantle 'began hostilities', as Michahelles
put it, by sending detachments out to burn down a number of villages. He then
advanced against Witu. There was repeated fighting on the way, with a few
British injured and between 50 and 100 of Fumo Bakari's men killed. By the
time the British-led force arrived at Witu the sultan had fled. On 28 October
Fremantle occupied Witu, 'burning and destroying the town, and blowing up
buildings with guncotton till 3pm', as he noted in his journal.[102] Afterwards he
had 'quite a nice dinner, with a bottle of champagne to celebrate our victory,
which I should have enjoyed more but for a splitting headache, due to sun,
anxiety, and smoke of the burning town'.[103] When back at sea he had some
doubts, but remained convinced of the expedition's necessity:

> I am not so satisfied with such wanton destruction as we had to effect but it
> was in the bond, it is in accordance with African custom, and the lesson it will
> read to the Arabs on this coast is patent.[104]

Fremantle could console himself that he had done what the Germans would
have done: 'set an example', as the mouthpiece of the Berlin government
put it.[105]

It is impossible to think of Heligoland without this colonial dimension. In
German and British discourse the island remained linked to those territories in Africa that had been 'lost' or 'gained' in exchange for the North Sea
island. While over the next two decades Heligoland turned into a symbol of
Anglo-German conflict, there remained a dense set of common imperial,
racial, and cultural assumptions which united Britain and Germany. That
Britons would avenge the death of Germans in Africa may seem remarkable

in hindsight, but it went without comment at the time—so strong was the shared imperial mindset. It was the honour of Europeans, defined in terms of race and gender, rather than of Britons or Germans, that had to be restored. As Sir James Fergusson, the under-secretary of state for foreign affairs, put it in the Commons, it had 'unquestionably' been Britain's duty 'to inflict punishment for murders of white men'.[106]

5

Island Fortress

The early 1890s were the closest the Anglo-German relationship ever got to a honeymoon. Both governments propagated the cession of Heligoland as evidence of the two nations' affinity.[1] Most of the press followed their lead. The handover symbolized 'like nothing else the tight bond of friendship between Britain and Germany'.[2] The treaty was 'the basis for increased unity between England and Germany in all great questions of politics'.[3] It had given 'a fresh and lasting ratification to the sentiment of kinship' between the two nations.[4] Given all the talk about Anglo-German friendship, officials in Paris and St Petersburg began to worry that a broader alliance between Britain and Germany was on the cards.[5]

Yet within little more than a decade Heligoland had turned into the opposite: a metaphor of Anglo-German rivalry and enmity. In the British imagination it changed from a forlorn yet charming outpost, that 'pearl of the North Sea', into a dark rock symbolizing Germany's threat to Britain.[6] Numerous authors used the island as a metaphor of what had gone wrong with the Germans. H. G. Wells did so in *The War in the Air*,[7] but by far the most prominent example was *The Riddle of the Sands* by Erskine Childers, published in 1903. At the heart of this genre-defining best seller was a journey of discovery: Charles Carruthers, a Foreign Office clerk, accepts an invitation for a yachting trip from Arthur Davies, an old chum from his Oxford days. The cruise takes them across the North Sea to the German coast where they realize, little by little, that the Germans are preparing to invade England. Heligoland is part of this preparation. In Childers's depiction, it represents a monumental mistake made by a complacent political establishment in London. 'And, to crown all, we were asses enough to give her Heligoland, which commands her North Sea coast', says Davies, pointing to the island as a symbol of the need for Britain to 'buck up' and face the German threat.[8] The sea itself was renamed in relatively short order as a result of that perceived threat: until well into the 1880s Heligoland had routinely been described as lying in the 'German Ocean'; now, at the turn of the century, most British officials and cartographers preferred the neutral term 'North Sea'.[9]

Heligoland thus came to symbolize the seismic shift that took place in the Anglo–German relationship in the two decades before the First World War. This shift was neither inevitable nor accidental. It took deliberate decisions made in specific circumstances for the Anglo–German relationship to take a turn for the worse. Nothing illustrates this better than the German naval programme inaugurated in 1898. Building up a powerful navy was likely to raise eyebrows in Britain, but it did not have to lead to an arms race that was to threaten European peace. Russia, France, and Italy were also building up their fleets. Japan and the USA, too, were busy projecting prestige and power through naval expansion. The German fleet was, in this respect, no exception. Its architect, Alfred von Tirpitz, appointed by Wilhelm II as secretary of state for the Imperial Navy in June 1897, was at pains to stress this. In order to protect its trade and colonies Germany had to be able 'to make its power felt beyond territorial waters', he wrote in one of the foundational texts of the new fleet.[10] 'Since Germany has remained particularly backward in regard to sea power, it is a vital question for Germany as a world power and a great and cultivated nation [*Kulturstaat*] to catch up with what has been missed', he told the Kaiser in September 1899. Greater naval power was 'essential if Germany does not want to go under'.[11]

None of this was terribly contentious. Most international observers agreed that it made sense for the Kaiserreich to acquire a bigger navy, given its expanding trade and colonial commitments. What made the crucial difference was the kind of fleet Tirpitz wanted. He thought of the navy not primarily as a weapon for colonial conflict, but for war in the North Sea. Britain was 'the most dangerous enemy at the present time', Tirpitz told the Kaiser when he presented his plans for the new navy on 15 June 1897. Britain was also 'the enemy against which we most urgently require a certain measure of naval force as a political power factor'. The German fleet was to be this 'political factor'. Once it had reached its full capacity, it would act as a lever, coercing Britain into accommodating Germany as an equal power on the world stage. This pressure would only work if it was directed against the British Isles themselves. Hence it was necessary to concentrate on battleships, designed for service in the North Sea.[12]

On 26 March 1898 the Reichstag passed the last section of Tirpitz's bill. The foundations of the Kaiser's new navy were laid. Germany was to build a battle fleet of such strength that attacking it would pose too high a risk for the Royal Navy. This 'risk theory' was a key component in the Tirpitz Plan. Rather than having to fight the Royal Navy in battle, the Kaiser's fleet would be an instrument of deterrence, creating the leverage over Britain that had escaped the Kaiserreich so far. Tirpitz's gamble was twofold: first, that Britain would for a crucial initial period not realize what the German battle fleet was really being built for (this was the 'danger zone', the *Gefahrenzone*, during which Germany had to 'keep quiet and build ships');[13] and, second, that when the British finally woke up to the threat, they would not find the means necessary to rise to the challenge. This was a hugely ambitious and risky strategy. But for Tirpitz and the Wilhelmine leadership it was also a rational response to the dilemma that defined Germany's international position. Once Berlin had decided not to renew the Reinsurance Treaty with Russia (1890) and once Russia had entered into a new alliance with France (1892), two fundamentals of Bismarck's foreign policy had gone: the isolation of France and the containment of Russia. Bismarck had always hoped for an Anglo-German alliance, but he had been able to be patient. His successors felt that they could not afford this luxury—Germany's security was in flux now, with Austria-Hungary as its only reliable partner.

The Tirpitz Plan was part of a political strategy that was meant to overcome this dilemma through a 'policy of strength' (*Politik der Stärke*). It was no coincidence that the appointment of Tirpitz came at the same time as Bernhard von Bülow took over as state secretary at the Foreign Office. The two men were to be engaged in the same project: establishing Germany as a world power on an equal footing with the other imperial nations, most of all Britain. It was in support of Tirpitz's naval bill that Bülow gave his famous Reichstag speech about Germany's 'place in the sun':

> We certainly do not feel the need to have a finger in every pie. But we believe it is inadvisable to exclude Germany from the outset from competition with other nations in lands with a rich and promising future. (Bravo!) The days when Germans granted one neighbour the land, the other the sea, and reserved for themselves the sky, where pure doctrine reigns (Laughter—Bravo!): those days are over... In a word, we do not want to put anyone into our shadow, but we too demand our place in the sun.[14]

The speech signalled a new departure in Germany's foreign policy. How much this was the case became clear when Joseph Chamberlain, the colonial secretary, put out feelers for new alliance talks in March 1898. On the surface this was the same project that Salisbury and Bismarck had mooted a decade earlier: both nations needed stability in Europe and had few colonial conflicts with one another. Theirs was a 'natural alliance', Chamberlain suggested in 1899:'I cannot conceive that any point can arise in the immediate future which can bring ourselves and Germany into antagonism of interests'.[15] His initiative betrayed doubts, heightened by the South African War, about Britain's capacity to maintain its empire without any reliable partners in Europe. But Bülow, promoted by the Kaiser to imperial chancellor in 1900, was not seriously interested. For him the cession of Heligoland was not a basis on which to build, but a point of departure.

Rather than strengthen Germany's ties with Britain, Bülow intended to remain aloof. His policy reflected the expectation that Tirpitz's fleet would act as a coercive tool in the near future, prompting the British to make more concessions than they were offering now. Throughout the negotiations Bülow remained non-committal, upping German demands repeatedly. In the end, he demanded a British promise to defend not only Germany, but also Austria-Hungary, in case of war. But that was more than Salisbury was willing to give.[16] When the gap between German demands and British concessions proved too big the talks were abandoned. 'R.I.P.', Bülow wrote under the final entry in the files documenting the negotiations.[17]

The notion that Britain would be ready for more wide-ranging concessions once the threat of the Imperial Navy had reached its full capacity became an *idée fixe*, repeated by Tirpitz and his staff like a mantra whenever Anglo-German relations reached a critical point. As late as October 1911, Eduard von Capelle, one of Tirpitz's most loyal assistants, was to argue that Britain needed Germany as an alliance partner and could not afford to keep building ships at Germany's pace. 'Our approach', he wrote, should be:'give England the cold shoulder and don't chase after her! England must and will come to us'.[18]

Heligoland played a key role in this strategy. The island's position at the entrance to the Elbe and Weser, as well as to the Jade Bight (on which lay the Wilhelmshaven naval base), predestined it as a defensive stronghold. It was to protect not only the approach to Germany's most important ports (above all, Hamburg and Bremerhaven), but also the entrance to the Kiel Canal. For Germany, Heligoland was 'the key to the North Sea and the key to the Baltic', explained Admiral Sir John Fisher, Tirpitz's ardent opponent at the Admiralty in London.[19] Fortifying it with heavy artillery and establishing a base for torpedo boats and submarines on the island would give the Germans the capability to unite their naval forces without hindrance through the canal, which connected its Baltic and North Sea stations. Turned into a fortress, Heligoland would make a British blockade of the German North Sea coast exceedingly difficult. And it would function as a safe haven for the Kaiser's navy, which could withdraw under Heligoland's long-range guns if threatened by the British fleet.

But the Tirpitz Plan prescribed more than a merely defensive role for the island. As the Kaiser explained in November 1897, his battle fleet would be 'leaning on Heligoland', from where it could break out at 'any moment' to sail against 'the English coastal cities': 'Only if the mailed fist is thus held before his face will the British Lion hide his tail'.[20] A series of naval war games and battle plans employed this idea, using the island as the rendezvous point from where to commence operations against Britain.[21] The Tirpitz Plan itself foresaw the island as a stepping stone towards Britain, suggesting the anticipated theatre of war. It was, in Tirpitz's words, 'between Heligoland and the Thames' that the new fleet would have to 'unfold its greatest military potential'.[22]

All this presupposed that Heligoland would be turned into a heavily armed fortress. Berlin had begun to plan the island's fortification even before Britain had ceded it. As soon as the Anglo-German treaty was signed, these plans were put into practice. In October 1890, Chancellor Leo von Caprivi instructed the Prussian authorities that Heligoland was 'of particular importance' as 'an advance position' and would have to be heavily fortified.[23] The Kaiser signed off on a comprehensive scheme in June 1891. Work began almost immediately, concentrating on two areas: the cliff tops of the *Oberland*, where a line of heavy, long-range artillery was to be embedded into the red rocks, and the south point of the *Unterland*, where the main naval harbour was to be built.[24] The two were to be connected by a massive tunnel, through which supplies and ammunition could be brought up to the island's plateau, towering 40 metres above the sea. Here, where Heligoland offers commanding 360-degree views of the North Sea, the main garrison was established, complete with barracks, parade ground, depots, and a field hospital. All this was vastly expanded after the turn of the century when the Tirpitz Plan came into effect.

By the time the naval race with Britain reached its climax, the island's fortification had resulted in physical change on an unprecedented scale. Easily half of Heligoland was taken up by military installations. A sixth of the island had been tunnelled under or dug into, with bunkers and depots carved deep into the red rock. While the cliffs of the *Oberland* were now part of a fortress of reinforced concrete and steel, the southern point of the island, the *Unterland*, was dominated by the new naval base which, having been extended by 20 hectares into the sea, accommodated separate harbours for torpedo boats and submarines as well as a naval flying squadron. A range of lower defensive positions was established to supplement the artillery on the cliff tops. All around the island massive searchlights were set up, designed to detect the enemy at night. It would have required a fair amount of creative imagination for tourists to recognize in all this the 'natural beauty' that had been the subject of so many romanticist paintings. For British visitors the change was ominous. This 'is not the Heligoland which I knew', wrote William George Black, Glaswegian lawyer and politician, after a trip in June 1911.[25] When he had first visited in 1886, Heligoland had been 'an ideal little community' of Frisian cottages, surrounded by the North Sea. Now it was the site of 'enormous military industry', that had transformed the island through 'the most able and clever engineering'.[26]

While an army of workers was busy turning Heligoland into a German Gibraltar, Tirpitz was keen to promote the opposite image. The island, he told his staff, should be used as a symbol of the British threat. This was an endangered German outpost in a sea dominated by the Royal Navy. Without a strong fleet, 'the German island' would be defenceless, just as it had been in the late summer of 1807, when the British had taken it as part of their operations against Denmark, culminating in the naval expedition to Copenhagen. For the Kaiser and his admirals, Heligoland was inseparably linked to the historic fate of the Danish fleet: the island was a constituent part of the Wilhelmine 'Copenhagen complex', the fear that the Royal Navy would suddenly appear in Heligoland Bight and do to the Germans what it had done to the Danish a century ago.[27] The historical parallel was misleading, but conveniently so: it suggested German victimhood rather than aggression. Tirpitz played on this fear with some virtuosity. In 1902 he penned a detailed script for an adventure novel, imitating the invasion stories that were so popular in Britain. In direct reference to *The Battle of Dorking* by George Tomkyns Chesney, he suggested *Battle of Helgoland* as a title. The book's aim, Tirpitz wrote, was to 'make clear to the German public that it is underestimating the danger of war with Britain'. The plot followed the development of increasing Anglo–German tensions (caused by the British press, not the German navy), which leads to all-out war at sea and ends with 'our fleet annihilated' and 'German influence on the seas dead'.[28]

The spy fever which gripped Heligoland at the height of the naval race was used by Tirpitz and his press office for the same purpose: to talk up the British threat. After the turn of the century a number of British officers went, privately, to the island.[29] The most notorious case was that of Bernard Frederick Trench and Vivian Brandon, who reconnoitred the island in August 1910. When they were arrested the German police found 'numerous notes about Heligoland' in their hotel room. 'It appears that they had been able to work very much without being disturbed', Alfred Tapken, the head of naval intelligence at the Admiralty in Berlin noted critically.[30] In December 1910 the Imperial Supreme Court sentenced them to four years in prison. A similar case, involving Bertrand Stewart, an army officer 'on holiday' in Germany, followed a year later.[31] The main aim of these well-publicized 'spy trials' was to mobilize support for the navy in Germany. This was well understood in London.[32] Nothing illustrated the need for Germany to be strong at sea better than the image of Heligoland as an endangered outpost where British agents were at work. Obligingly, German magazines portrayed the island as a stepping stone from where the British were spying out their 'German cousin.[33]

As a consequence of the Tirpitz Plan Britain had become the crucial factor in Germany's foreign policy. But it would be a mistake to assume that the reverse was also true, that Germany was the main consideration of London's diplomacy. From the British point of view, Berlin's *Weltpolitik* was only one of a number of challenges arising at the beginning of the twentieth century. Bülow's talk about securing a 'place in the sun' was irritating, but not nearly as worrying as the reality of Russia and France encroaching on key British spheres of influence in east Asia and northern Africa. It was about these flash points, where the empire seemed acutely under threat, that British foreign policy was concerned during the initial years of the Tirpitz Plan.[34] However, this did not mean that a general priority of imperial over Continental considerations existed. The two arenas continued to be closely interdependent: a shift in the European concert of powers almost always necessitated a reconsideration of the global, imperial picture and vice versa.[35] It was the coming together of changes in both theatres that led British foreign policy to focus more strongly on Germany. Russia's defeat in its war with Japan in 1905, forcing it into a period of retrenchment and reform, was the watershed.[36] It diminished the Russian navy and reduced the threat to British interests in

Figure 5.1 'John Bull: I must just ask my officers to see if my German cousin is well'. Caricature in *Ulk*, 1911.

east Asia. It also meant that the rising position of Germany on the Continent was less likely to be checked by St Petersburg. Consequently, key figures at the Foreign Office, who had hitherto played down the German challenge, began to change their mind. When the Marquess of Lansdowne, foreign secretary from 1900 to 1905, who had long found Berlin to be merely 'an irritant', left office, he was convinced that Germany was now following an aggressive policy that directly threatened Britain.[37] Edward Grey, his successor, had come to this conclusion earlier, but it was not until after the Russo-Japanese War that his concerns were more widely shared amongst politicians.[38]

Even when the German threat had become more of a priority at the Foreign Office, its attitude towards Berlin remained related to its assessment of other powers and the relation between Britain's imperial and Continental concerns. This can be seen particularly well in the character of the Anglo-French *Entente*. The agreements signed by France and Britain in April 1904 were aimed at settling overseas conflict between the two powers, not unlike the Anglo-German treaty of 1890. While Delcassé, the French foreign minister, hoped from the beginning that the agreements would lead to a political alliance, most British politicians were adamant that they would not. From their point of view the *Entente* was a temporary alignment to meet specific problems, not a defensive alliance.[39]

What made the colonial rapprochement the basis for Anglo-French cooperation in Europe were Berlin's efforts during a number of crises to force Britain to take a stance against France. The first of these was triggered when the Bülow government decided to intervene against French attempts to establish a stronger presence in Morocco. Britain, Spain, and Italy had secretly agreed to France's move, which ran against the Madrid agreement of 1880. Germany had publicly stated that it followed an 'open door' policy in Morocco, so the French initiative could be seen as an affront. Bülow and Friedrich von Holstein, the head of the political department at the Auswärtiges Amt (the German Foreign Office), persuaded the Kaiser to sail to Tangier to show the flag in March 1905. Yet the grand gesture, aimed at driving a wedge between the *Entente* partners, backfired. Lansdowne told Metternich, the German ambassador, that he could not predict if Britain would remain neutral if Germany attacked France.[40] Holstein, convinced that to back down would 'have the same consequences as to dodge a duel',[41] insisted on a conference, which convened in Algeciras from January to April 1906. At Algeciras it became clear that it was Germany that was isolated, not France. Only Austria-Hungary supported the German claims. Berlin had to accept a compromise, while France was formally given the right to extend its influence in Morocco. In the course of the crisis the British and French military held their first informal talks about wartime cooperation. While these remained, in Grey's words, 'provisional and non-committal',[42] they showed that the *Entente* was beginning to develop a defensive dimension.

It was now that Heligoland took on a broader political meaning. Eyre Crowe, senior clerk at the Foreign Office, was the first official to use the island as a symbol of 'the German problem'. In his influential Memorandum on the Present State of British Relations with France and Germany, written in January 1907, he argued that—whatever the intentions of German foreign policy—it was wrong to think that concessions would 'conciliate' the Kaiserreich.[43] The example of Heligoland showed this forcefully. It marked, in Crowe's narrative, one of the earliest moments when Britain had shown a misguided 'spirit of accommodation' vis-à-vis Germany. Instead of cementing the 'reassertion of Anglo-German brotherhood', as intended in 1890, the island had become a symbol of the Reich's menace against Britain.[44] In hindsight, the cession of the colony could thus be seen as the first of a series of occasions on which, in Crowe's words, 'England's spirit of accommodation' had been deeply misguided.[45] Heligoland had become an example of appeasement *avant la lettre*.[46]

Crowe's interpretation was echoed by Austin Harrison, the editor of the *Observer*. Heligoland offered a 'parable' of what had gone wrong with the Germans, he wrote in *England and Germany*, a book published later in 1907. Recalling a heated discussion he had had with a particularly rotund German while on holiday in Heligoland, he concluded the book by warning his readers about the dangers of 'the New Germany'. This was a materialist, expanding, vulgar nation now, rapidly leaving behind the cultured and self-restrained 'Old Germany':

> Let us all do justice to the splendid qualities of the German nation, let us sympathise with them in their national mission; but let us know that a great Power and Empire are rising in Europe, with a great Navy to create and complete it. It came into the world through the throes of battle. All that it is, all that it has achieved, it owes to force, and on force it relies for all that it hopes to achieve. In the centre of Europe the great German sociocracy stands for Kaiser, might, and dominion, for what is known as *Machtpolitik*. The Germanic problem still awaits solution. Its issue is largely our own.[47]

Harrison was not the only prominent commentator for whom Heligoland encapsulated 'the German problem'. When the journalist and author Robert

Blatchford wrote a series of articles on modern Germany for the *Daily Mail* in 1909 (later reissued as a best-selling booklet), he seized on the same imagery. For him, Heligoland was emblematic of the Kaiserreich more generally. Machine-like and methodical, this 'nation of soldiers' was 'working night and day' to turn the erstwhile peaceful British colony into a menacing fortress. The ceaseless building activity and the secrecy that enshrouded the island expressed 'the German motive for hostility to Britain'.[48]

But not only did the island undergo a transformation in the British imagination. The Heligolanders themselves were also rediscovered: as a freedom-loving miniature nation, overpowered by militarist Germans, who disregarded their rights, formerly protected by the British empire. Giving the island to the Kaiser had, in this reading, been a twofold mistake: strategically, because Heligoland now stood in the centre of Anglo-German conflict; and morally, because the islanders had been betrayed. Combining the benefit of hindsight with self-righteous indignation, this interpretation identified with the islanders as victims of German aggression—they were a reminder of what happened when you failed to confront the Reich's expansionism.[49] Herbert Beerbohm Tree, the actor and theatre manager, echoed this sentiment when he told German critics (who had asserted that Shakespeare was best performed in Germany) not to treat the Bard as a 'literary Heligoland'.[50]

By the time the Second Moroccan Crisis broke out the idea of Heligoland as a metaphor for German *Machtpolitik* was well established in British political discourse. In May 1911 Paris sent a military expedition to Fez, ostensibly to relieve the besieged sultan. Britain was in no hurry to support the French, who were arguably contravening international agreements. Again Berlin tried to capitalize on potential disagreement between the *Entente* powers, dispatching a gunboat, the *Panther*, to the port of Agadir. But when Bülow ignored London's initiative for mediation the Asquith government decided to send a strong signal of support for France. Arthur Nicolson, permanent under-secretary of state at the Foreign Office, promptly invoked Heligoland as a reminder of why London ought to take a more offensive stance. What had the Germans done when Britain had given them the North Sea island? As soon as they had 'got Heligoland into their hands', they had converted 'the innocent harbour of refuge...into a very formidable fortress'. There was 'no reason to doubt' that they would follow 'a similar procedure' with any territory conceded on the Moroccan coast.[51]

On 21 July 1911 Lloyd George, hitherto seen as one of the 'pacifists' in Asquith's cabinet, gave a belligerent speech at the Mansion House. A situation 'in which peace could only be preserved by the surrender of the great and beneficent position Britain has won by centuries of heroism and achievement' would be unacceptable, he exclaimed. The sabre-rattling continued on both sides until a compromise was found, giving Berlin some territorial compensation, though much less than German public opinion had expected. France, in contrast, was allowed practically full control over Morocco, precisely what it had aspired to. The result of the crisis was a German climb-down and a strengthened Anglo-French *Entente*. Moreover, during the crisis the British and French general staffs secretly agreed on a number of operational details, which foresaw British forces on the Continent in the event of war. Grey, in parallel, assured the French 'that in the event of Germany attacking France or wilfully breaking off negotiations British public opinion would side with France and would enable the British Gov[ernment] to support France'.[52] The crisis, willingly escalated by Berlin, had resulted in the increased isolation of Imperial Germany. 'No more Heligolands', Admiral Fisher wrote to Churchill in the aftermath of the crisis. What he meant was: no more concessions to the Germans, who seemed bound to use any advantage they could against Britain.[53]

None of this implied that Britain and Germany were locked in antagonism. True, in the wake of the Agadir crisis Britain and France reached new levels of strategic cooperation. But Grey emphasized that the *Entente*, celebrated in public as something more substantial than it was in diplomacy, did not amount to an alliance: the military and naval talks between London and Paris remained decidedly non-binding.[54] It was never his idea to permanently isolate Berlin.[55] True, Germany's posturing combined with the naval competition made a rapprochement difficult. But a resurgence of the Russian threat might well make it necessary to cooperate more with Germany again and less with France. In such a scenario, and given enough time, Heligoland might well be re-invented, its legacy as a menacing fortress no more than 'unpleasant memories' in the popular press.[56]

While British diplomacy thus continued to retain a degree of flexibility towards Germany, the stance taken at the Admiralty was bold and unambiguous. What mattered most for the leadership of the navy was that the century-old British domination of the sea continued, despite limited budgets and rising international challenges. When John Fisher was appointed as First Sea Lord on 21 October 1904 (Trafalgar Day, naturally), he was convinced that in order to achieve this balancing act, the navy needed sweeping reforms. The 'revolution' on which he embarked with much bravado was not aimed directly and certainly not solely at Germany.[57] Even HMS *Dreadnought*, which was to turn into a floating embodiment of Anglo-German conflict, was not exclusively thought of as an answer to the Kaiserreich. By building an entirely new type of battleship, bigger, faster, and more heavily armed than all its predecessors, Fisher threw down the gauntlet not just to Tirpitz, but to all potential rivals. The aim behind *Dreadnought* was to create a bold instrument of power that would deter any nation in the world from challenging British maritime superiority. As he put it in February 1905,

> if you 'rub it in' both at home and abroad that you are ready for instant war with every unit of your strength in the first line... then people will keep clear of you.[58]

HMS *Dreadnought* was the key instrument in this deterrence strategy aimed at sustaining the status quo against competitors in Europe and the world.

It was the German decision to take up the *Dreadnought* challenge that provoked a quantum leap in Anglo-German naval competition. This was, after the inception of the naval programme in 1897/8, the second decisive moment for Tirpitz and the Kaiser's navy. It was clear now that Germany would not be able to 'quietly' build up its navy until it had reached a size that would be too risky for the Royal Navy to attack. The launch of HMS *Dreadnought*, staged with maximum publicity on 10 February 1906, showed that London would not let it come to this: it was prepared to mobilize unprecedented resources to maintain its maritime superiority. Different options were open to the German government by which to react. It was possible to redirect the naval programme, to change its anti-British focus. But Tirpitz never contemplated this course of action. Supported by the Kaiser, he instead decided to accept Fisher's challenge: Germany followed suit and built a Dreadnought fleet against Britain. This momentous decision was taken by Tirpitz without any meaningful involvement of the German Foreign Office or the Treasury. The Kaiser's prerogative, which exempted naval and military matters from civilian control, made this possible. Just as with the decision to build a fleet against Britain taken in 1897, the structure of government in the Kaiserreich had a crucial impact on the Anglo-German relationship here.

In his memoirs Tirpitz portrayed the launch of HMS *Dreadnought* as a great opportunity for Germany, allowing for a new naval race on equal terms.[59] In reality it was the Imperial Navy's fatal moment. While stiffening opposition in Britain, Tirpitz's decision to build a Dreadnought fleet resulted in a financial crisis at home. Huge additional investments in naval infrastructure were necessary: the Kiel Canal had to be widened, dockyards and construction plants had to be altered, the fortifications at Heligoland upgraded. All this demanded new funds. The battleships themselves, whose tonnage and gun calibre increased with every round of the arms race, absorbed unprecedented economic resources. It mattered not so much what these floating behemoths would do in war, but what they cost in peace: the outcome of the Anglo-German arms race would be decided by the fiscal prowess of the states building them. It was highly significant that the Asquith government managed at this time to see through difficult tax reforms, allowing it to put its well-established income tax on a new basis, while Germany struggled to introduce such a system.[60]

The key to the British success in the naval race lay here, in the government's ability to raise the necessary revenue without losing its domestic political support. This came much to the surprise of Tirpitz, who had always argued that the British state would be unable to finance a naval race at the rate the Germans would.[61] While his staff still advised ministers that Britain would be forced to 'give in', Tirpitz admitted privately in early 1909 that his grand strategy was unlikely to succeed, should the British further increase the number of Dreadnoughts they were to build.[62] This moment came only months later, when the Parliament in London, under pressure from an intense public campaign, agreed to a budget that allowed for eight new battleships. The climax of the Anglo-German arms race was reached. While Tirpitz continued with his programme, he began to voice doubts even to the Kaiser, on whose support he depended so much. In a remarkably frank conversation, he told Wilhelm II in October 1910 that it was feasible that the fleet for which he was responsible would represent 'from the historical point of view a mistake' and that 'Your Majesty's naval policy [may be] a fiasco'.[63]

Tirpitz was able to hold sway for two more years. In February 1912 Richard Haldane, secretary of state for war in Asquith's cabinet, came to Berlin to sound out the possibilities for a naval agreement.[64] Would London and Berlin be able to agree on a formula limiting their navies? Theobald von Bethmann Hollweg, who had succeeded Bülow as chancellor in 1909, was unable to rein Tirpitz in over the German position. Supported by the Kaiser, the admiral insisted on a 2:3 ratio in naval power and nothing less than British neutrality in case of a European war as the 'red line' for the talks. For Germany an agreement would have been a breakthrough, as Bethmann Hollweg was all too aware.[65] Haldane stayed in Berlin for five days. The negotiations were intense, not only between the British and German sides, but also within the Wilhelmine government. The chancellor had to threaten the Kaiser with his resignation, in order to be allowed to negotiate a compromise with regard to naval strength, but Tirpitz was still able to insist on British neutrality as the sticking point. Only in return for this concession was he prepared to compromise on the most recent naval law, which foresaw a substantial rise of the number of ships in the active fleet.[66] But neutrality in the event of a war between Germany and France was too high a price for Asquith and Grey, who were fully aware that they had practically won the naval race.[67] Thus the Haldane mission failed.

The main reason why Britain and Germany did not come to an agreement in the two decades following the cession of Heligoland lay in the distance between the two countries' positions, as Haldane's visit had demonstrated once again. London was able to keep aloof, retaining the flexibility in Europe that was necessary to uphold its imperial position. The idea that Berlin could coerce Britain through the naval programme seemed fanciful now. After the Haldane mission Berlin faced a fundamental dilemma. Its position was clearly too weak to force Britain into making any far-reaching concessions. Yet most in the Wilhelmine leadership believed that the Reich was also too strong not to aim for a change in the status quo. While German foreign policy was flexible enough to respond to this dilemma, Tirpitz's doctrine was not.

The Haldane mission was the last time the admiral was able to impose his strategy on Germany's diplomacy. What dealt the lethal blow to the Tirpitz Plan was that the accelerated naval race with Britain coincided with a resurgence of French and, significantly, Russian military strength. In the wake of the Second Moroccan Crisis the German army pushed hard for more funds: in order to remain equal to the challenge of its Continental rivals it had to modernize urgently. In 1912 it got its way with an army law that allowed for an extraordinary programme of military armament. It also demonstrated that Germany's strategic priorities were on land, not at sea. The reversal back to traditional doctrine was complete by June 1913, when the Reichstag passed a new law, providing for an unprecedented increase of the army's peacetime strength and for a far-reaching modernization programme. Tirpitz, in contrast, failed to garner support for a new naval increase. Moreover, as he bitterly noted after his audience with Wilhelm II in September 1913, he had lost the Kaiser's all-important confidence.[68] The Anglo-German naval race was over. Britain had successfully defended its naval supremacy against the Kaiserreich.

The de facto abandonment of the Tirpitz Plan removed a key obstacle to Anglo-German détente. Bethmann Hollweg and his foreign secretary, Alfred

von Kiderlen-Wächter, now focused their efforts on the lessening of tensions.[69] As Kiderlen-Wächter told the Kaiser, 'practical co-operation with
England' was better than the choice between 'all or nothing', between
antagonism and alliance.[70] The two Balkan Wars of 1912 and 1913 (the first
between the Balkan League and Turkey was followed by the second, in
which Bulgaria fought Serbia, Greece, and Romania) remained localized
because London and Berlin worked together in holding back Austria and
Russia. The two governments collaborated similarly during the Liman von
Sanders crisis, provoked by the appointment of the Prussian general of that
name to the German military mission in Constantinople in October 1913.
German–Russian tensions could be defused by Britain restraining Russia
and by Berlin cooperating in finding a formula that was agreeable to all
sides.[71] All this showed that Britain and Germany were perfectly able to
work together efficiently to keep the peace in Europe when they wanted to.
Bethmann Hollweg was confident that 'an improvement of our relations
with England' was under way. London and Berlin had entered a 'transitory
stage', he thought—soon enough London would re-orientate its European
policy away from Paris and St Petersburg.[72] Grey did not go quite that far
when he penned a widely circulated dispatch about Anglo-German relations in March 1913. But he too was convinced that things had 'greatly
improved'.[73]

The Anglo-German détente of the years immediately before the war
drew on a wide range of shared interests which had continued to grow,
despite naval competition and diplomatic conflicts. While the image of
two hostile nations facing each other across the North Sea dominated
public discourse, Britain and Germany had in fact reached unprecedented
levels of mutual dependency. Nowhere was this more significant than in
the economic sphere. As Arthur von Gwinner, director of Deutsche Bank
and a member of the Prussian Upper House, put it in 1912: 'With no other
country in the world do we maintain such active and important commercial relations as with the British Empire'.[74] Britain imported more goods
from Germany than from any other nation. Germany bought more products from Britain than from anywhere else.[75] To be sure, there was competition, but even in those areas in which the Kaiserreich was overtaking
British production, the British profited financially. The majority of
German products that went overseas were exported in British ships, most
German shipping was insured in London, and most of the Kaiserreich's
imported raw materials were paid for through London banks. Even if

British exports to Germany were rising less significantly than German exports to Britain (the latter tripled, while the former only doubled between 1890 and 1914), the City's profits easily made up for the gap. In short, German and British prosperity were interlinked: it was by trading with the other country and by cooperating in global markets that both nations prospered. Sir Edward Grey, foreign secretary from 1905 to 1916, was acutely aware of this. In January 1906 he told his staff that 'German success in trade may stimulate us to fresh efforts, but will not cause political estrangement, and we want to see the commerce between the two countries grow'.[76]

To call this period a 'cold war' is therefore to fundamentally misunderstand the nature of this paradoxical relationship.[77] Britain and Germany became more interdependent at the very time when political conflict dominated between them. A dense web of mutual ties linked them not only economically, but also through a myriad of cultural and scientific activities. The two nations continued to be role models for and imitators of each other. Until the 1890s Germans formed the largest group of migrants coming to Britain.[78] Thousands of students went to the other country in the decades before the war—in 1914 there were 332 German students at Oxford alone.[79] They were part of an unusually intensive relationship in which a vast range of institutions and ideas flourished through cooperation. This was visible in education and social reform, in architecture and urban planning, in fashion and design, in sports and gardening, in religious affairs and industrial relations, in printing and publishing, in literature and music; in the whole range of sciences, arts, and humanities.[80] The Tirpitz Plan and the Dreadnought race may have established a new language of enmity between Britain and Germany. But this did little to alter the two countries' underlying interdependence. On the contrary: at the height of political conflict the two countries were more closely bound up with one another than ever before.

Heligoland, situated at the fault line between the two nations, encapsulated this paradox. In the popular imagination it flourished unabatedly as a dark rock threatening Britain from across the North Sea. Just weeks before the outbreak of war in August 1914 *The Sea-Girt Fortress* by Percy Westerman came out, a blatant imitation of Childers's *Riddle of the Sands*. Here too an innocent cruise in the North Sea ends in Anglo-German conflict. En route to Kiel two young sailors (Jack Hamerton and his American friend Oswald Detroit) are denied a visit to Heligoland:

It's forbidden ground now...The civil population had to clear out. It's a sort of second Kronstadt. Our Intelligence Department would dearly like to know a great deal more about it than they do at present.

Facing bad weather the duo anchor close to Heligoland and end up witnessing a full-scale German attack on Britain. Hamerton and Detroit are, predictably enough, instrumental in the counter-offensive, a combined Anglo-American effort that results in the capitulation of the island and the Imperial Navy. 'Heligoland, the mailed menace to Great Britain, had fallen', concludes the novel, with the British taking possession again of 'the fire-swept rock' that had for a short time been 'the pride of the Teutonic Empire'.[81]

Yet in reality Heligoland was never 'forbidden ground'. Throughout the naval race it continued to be a popular seaside resort, visited by hundreds of thousands. Some of them were British tourists—Austin Harrison came back from a visit in 1907 with colourful stories about the peculiar bathing habits of the Germans.[82] What was more, the island still functioned as an Anglo-German site of exchange and collaboration. It reminded Adolf Wermuth, the island's interim governor in 1890, of 'the countless threads which intersect the intellectual life of Germany and England in science, in art, in literature'.[83]

Two scientific institutions facilitated these links on the island. Both had their roots in the colonial period when British and German zoologists had begun to frequent Heligoland. The zoologist Anton Dohrn had mooted the idea of an international research station as early as 1869. Charles Darwin had been supportive, but not the government in London.[84] In 1893, after the German acquisition of Heligoland, the Royal Biological Institute was finally founded.[85] It became part of an international network of science organizations, first headed by a German, then a Briton.[86] William John Dakin, a zoologist, was one of the British who came to do research at the institute (whose director lived in a house known as 'Prince of Wales').[87] Another one was Alexander Bowman, the director of the Fishery Board for Scotland, who arrived in March 1911.[88] The Heligoland ornithological station, established in 1910, fulfilled a similar function as a node connecting different scientific cultures. Its beginnings, too, went back to the colonial period.[89] The Anglo-German links fostered by these institutions were to last well into the twentieth century.[90] Despite the imagery of enmity associated with Heligoland, the island continued to be a location, as Wermuth put it in 1912, for the 'common work' of the two countries.[91]

The Heligolanders themselves showed how much their outpost was bound up with both nations, if not in a way that was appreciated in

Berlin. For the German government the islanders never lost their status as go-betweens whose loyalty seemed at best divided. After the turn of the century Berlin declared Heligoland a focal point for counter-espionage and expanded the police presence on the island.[92] Hugo Emsmann, the commandant of the naval station, had a number of informants whom he paid for details about pro-British activities. On the basis of this information he kept a black list of suspects.[93] Amongst them were the post master, his assistant, and a number of locals who were 'unreliable' or had British contacts. Franz Schensky, the pioneering photographer whose pictures of the island were beginning to become well known, raised particular concerns. One of Emsmann's informants denounced Schensky as the illegitimate son of the former British governor Maxse, saying that he was in 'direct correspondence with England'.[94] The commandant suspected that Schensky had acted as a British agent ever since the handover of 1890. But the most dubious, in Emsmann's eyes, was Jasper Nickels, who had served in the Royal Navy before returning to the island in 1907. The commandant was adamant that Nickels (who, quite apart from everything else, had 'a foreign-looking beard') had to be watched 'constantly'.[95]

Figure 5.2 'Heligoland in Heavy Sea'. Photograph by Franz Schensky, 1912.

But keeping a tab on potential saboteurs and spies was tricky: too many of the islanders were suspects.[96] By November 1907 Emsmann was convinced that 'the vast majority' of Heligolanders 'cannot be trusted'. They had a 'deceitful and dishonest character'.[97] The Kaiser promptly sent his self-acclaimed master spy, Gustav Steinhauer, to keep an eye on the Heligolanders. Steinhauer, who mingled incognito with the islanders in pubs and cafés, confirmed that they were not trustworthy: they 'all spoke English' and 'had relatives in England and America'.[98] In October 1908 Emsmann reported again about the 'insecure situation in Heligoland'. There was a sense that the islanders were still, almost twenty years after their takeover, contesting German rule:

> My judgement of the Heligolanders gets less favourable day by day. I person-
> ally do not trust anyone... We need to intervene without making any allow-
> ances. The entire nest needs to be taken out in one hit... In the interest of our
> own security we must not refrain from violent measures, as long as the law
> allows for them.[99]

It was out of fear of the islanders and their affinity to Britain that German mobilization plans foresaw the deportation of all civilians. Already in March 1891 the Caprivi government decided that the inhabitants would be moved in the case of war.[100] In February 1892 it issued a secret decree which was to be the legal instrument for their deportation.[101] All details were minutely planned. By early February 1906 the navy had reached a confidential agreement with HAPAG, the shipping line, to ensure the speedy 'evacuation' of the island in the event of war. Should Germany mobilize, HAPAG would send enough steamers to Heligoland to remove the entire population.[102]

When the war came, it was not triggered by Anglo-German conflict, but nor was it prevented by cooperation between the two governments. On 28 June Archduke Franz Ferdinand, the successor to the Austrian throne, was assassinated in Sarajevo. Early on in the ensuing crisis, London and Berlin assured one another that they would work together to mediate between Vienna and St Petersburg. On 9 July 1914 Grey told Prince Lichnowsky, the German ambassador, that he would 'continue the same policy as I had pursued through the Balkan crisis, and do my utmost to prevent the outbreak of war between the Great Powers'.[103] Lichnowsky was optimistic that Berlin would be 'smoothing the Austrian intentions with regard to Serbia'.[104] But the kind of cooperation that the two governments had practised successfully during the recent Balkan Wars was lacking for almost the entire duration of the July crisis.[105] The Kaiser pledged Germany's unreserved support to the Austrians. Bethmann Hollweg did nothing to retract this 'blank cheque' or hold Vienna back otherwise. His main aim was to localize the conflict, avoiding a general European war while allowing Austria-Hungary to 'solve' its Balkan problems. This strategy depended in one crucial respect on London. Bethmann Hollweg and his foreign secretary, Gottlieb von Jagow, escalated the conflict by backing Vienna unconditionally. Yet they expected Britain to do the opposite: de-escalate it by leaning on Russia which, in supporting Serbia against Austria, was playing a high-stakes gamble that mirrored the German one. But Edward Grey, the foreign secretary, felt he had little leverage over Russia. He tried to steer a course of non-commitment, aimed at encouraging neither St Petersburg nor Berlin, telling his staff that the cooperation of Germany was 'essential' to prevent war.[106]

Only late in the crisis did Grey use a possible British entry into the war as a direct threat.[107] On 29 July, a day after Vienna had declared war on Serbia, he told Lichnowsky that Berlin should not 'be misled into thinking that we should stand aside'. It was wrong to suppose that 'we should not take action' if Germany attacked France.[108] Simultaneously Grey urged the ambassador to impress on his government that 'mediation was ready to come into operation by any method that Germany thought possible if only Germany would "press the button" in the interests of peace'.[109] In parallel to Grey's warning, Bethmann Hollweg launched an extraordinary, last-minute 'bid for neutrality': should Britain assure Germany of its neutrality, he told Goschen, Germany would not make any territorial acquisitions at the expense of France in the event of a victorious war. In addition, Belgium's integrity would be restored after the conclusion of the war.[110] But it seems unlikely that Bethmann seriously expected Britain to stand aside. Only weeks before the assassination of Franz Ferdinand he had predicted that in case of a German war against France even 'the last Englishman will march against us'. This, he was clear, would mean 'world war'.[111] Most in the German leadership, with the exception perhaps of the Kaiser, anticipated a similar scenario. Grey was well entitled to believe that 'Germany does not expect our neutrality'.[112]

When, late on 29 July, Bethmann Hollweg told Goschen that he was 'pressing the button for peace as hard as he could',[113] there was truth in this: the chancellor at this point finally intervened in Vienna, urging the Austrian government to negotiate with St Petersburg.[114] Pre-mobilization preparations went ahead, while for two days a last flurry of Anglo-German

exchanges took place. On 31 July St Petersburg ordered general mobilization. On the same day, Winston Churchill, the First Lord of the Admiralty,
was still assuring his wife: 'We are working to soothe Russia'.[115] A day later
the Kaiser signed the German mobilization order.

On 4 August German troops invaded Belgium, triggering the British
demand for a 'satisfactory explanation' by 11 p.m. Greenwich Mean Time.
Goschen now went to see Bethmann Hollweg for the last time. He found
the chancellor 'very agitated'. Bethmann Hollweg exclaimed that

> just for a word—'neutrality', a word which in war-time had so often been
> disregarded—just for a scrap of paper Great Britain was going to make war on
> a kindred nation who desired nothing better than to be friends with her.[116]

From the British point of view, Bethmann Hollweg's contempt for that
'scrap of paper' (the 1839 Treaty of London, in which Britain had guaran-
teed Belgium's neutrality) demonstrated that the Germans had never been
interested in moral or legal considerations—they were following a strategy
of 'might is right'. From the German point of view, the chancellor had
highlighted what seemed the climax of British hypocrisy: the true British
intention, namely to prevent Germany from victory over France, remained
hidden behind the moral argument about Belgium.

Bethmann Hollweg's remark was to become a central exhibit in the
twentieth-century repertoire of Anglo-German insults.[117] But, apart from
expressing the frustration and haplessness of the imperial chancellor on the
brink of war, the 'scrap of paper' offered a convenient myth for both sides.
Belgian neutrality was a red herring. The fact that the German army invaded
Belgium helped Grey and Asquith in their efforts to mobilize the cabinet,
Parliament, and public opinion, but the crucial point lay elsewhere. As Grey
put it in his speech in the Commons on 3 August, it was fundamentally in
Britain's national interest to prevent 'the whole of the West of Europe
opposite us . . . falling under the domination of a single power'.[118] It was for
this reason—the prevention of German hegemony on the European
Continent—that Britain went to war. Along with most members of the
German government, Bethmann Hollweg expected the Asquith government to do so. His emotional clamouring simply sought to shift responsibility for Britain's entry into the war. By suggesting that Britain could have
remained neutral and that she had declared war on Germany unexpectedly
at the last minute, and only to protect Belgium, the chancellor laid the
foundations of the myth of English 'betrayal' and 'deceit', endlessly repeated in

wartime propaganda and peddled later by the Nazis. The Kaiser had employed the same strategy a week earlier upon receiving Grey's warning that Britain would not stay neutral: 'That mean mob of shopkeepers has tried to trick us with dinners and speeches... England alone carries the burden of responsibility for war and peace, not us any longer!'[119]

In the evening of 4 August, when the British ultimatum had expired, Grey sent a short letter to Lichnowsky, the German ambassador in London, enclosing passports for him, his family, and his staff and informing him 'that a state of war exists between the two countries as from today at 11 o'clock pm'.[120] For the first time in modern history, Britons and Germans were to take up arms against each other.

The transition from peace to war was especially poignant in Heligoland, with its curious combination of seaside resort and naval fortress. The summer season had reached its peak, promising a new record in visitor numbers, when the preparations for war began. While tourists continued to arrive in droves, naval detachments were busy placing defences around the island. The batteries of heavy artillery on top of the island's red cliffs were manned, ammunition was stockpiled. The first and second U-boat flotillas arrived in the harbour, not officially mobilized, but visibly on a war footing. On 30 July the Foreign Office received intelligence about this activity on Heligoland. 'These are preparations for war against England', observed Eyre Crowe. 'Or for defence against an English attack', added Arthur Nicolson, the permanent under-secretary.[121]

While the July crisis was nearing its climax, the island's council was busy reassuring its visitors that the resort would remain open. On 28 July advertisements still appeared in the Hamburg newspapers enticing tourists to spend time on Germany's North Sea island.[122] Yet on 31 July the spa director announced abruptly that the entire resort would close by the end of the day. All visitors had to leave, and the employees were to be laid off.[123] In the early hours of 2 August 1914 the deportation of the islanders began.[124] Bethmann Hollweg, the chancellor in Berlin, called it the 'emptying of Heligoland'.[125] The islanders were allowed to take some food and a small amount of luggage with them, but had to leave everything else behind, with their houses open, keys in locks.[126] Two large HAPAG steamers brought them to the mainland. The majority of islanders were given temporary accommodation in Hamburg and the surrounding area. The British subjects amongst them were deported to the Ruhleben camp outside Berlin, the so-called

Engländerlager, in which most British nationals who happened to be in Germany at the outbreak of the war were interned.[127] Those Heligolanders who had been on the commandant's black list for having British contacts were promptly arrested. This included Jasper Nickels, the former Royal Navy petty officer with the un-German beard. No evidence was ever produced against him, but he remained under police surveillance throughout the war.[128]

By the afternoon of 2 August Heligoland had been emptied of civilians and was under military rule. Officers and crews arrived in large numbers from the mainland, anxious not to miss the great sea battle they confidently expected to take place in the days ahead. Heligoland, imagined for so long as the centre of Anglo-German conflict, was ready for war.

6

To Heligoland and Back

Early in the evening of 4 August 1914 a heavily laden steamer left Heligoland Bight on course for the Thames. The British ultimatum to Germany was to run out later at 11 p.m., but the German Imperial Admiralty Staff was not going to wait until then with the mission of the *Königin Louise*. Until recently, this had been one of the HAPAG ferries shuttling between Heligoland and Hamburg. The navy had requisitioned it on 1 August and converted it into a minelayer. Dockyard workers had then painted it in the colours of the British ferries connecting Harwich and Holland. Thus disguised, the *Königin Louise* sailed to the Thames estuary. She was discovered there laying mines in the morning of 5 August. The Admiralty sent HMS *Amphion*, a light cruiser, to engage her, together with a flotilla of destroyers. After a short chase, the *Königin Louise*, defenceless with its two small revolving canons, sank under heavy British fire. More than a hundred German men died. Amongst them was Commander Karl Biermann, who, realizing that there was no escape, had ordered the scuttling of the ship. Those who survived were pulled out of the water by British boats and taken on board by HMS *Amphion*. The light cruiser then continued with its original mission, patrolling the southern North Sea. On its return on 6 August the *Amphion* sailed into the minefield the *Königin Louise* had laid the day before. Hit twice, she sank within 20 minutes. As Winston Churchill, the First Lord of the Admiralty, told the House of Commons the next day, 130 of her crew died together with the 20 German prisoners on board. The wreck of the *Amphion* was to be their shared grave.[1]

The mutual destruction of the *Königin Louise* and the *Amphion* marked the moment when Britain and Germany entered battle over the North Sea in 1914. It foreshadowed the nature of the naval war that was to unfold over the next four years. While there had been much talk before about 'The Day' on which the two battle fleets would meet, there was little sign of a modern-day Trafalgar now. Instead, there were seemingly endless searches, patrols, and small engagements. Heligoland, built up over two decades as the fortress from where the German fleet would challenge the Royal Navy, epitomized the contrast between pre-war imagination and wartime realities. Rather than the epicentre of an all-out Anglo-German sea battle, it became the cornerstone of the defensive strategy followed by the German leadership throughout the war. On 4 August an advance picket line of submarines and destroyers was sent out into the Bight, describing a defensive arc around the island, guarding the approaches to Wilhelmshaven and the Kiel Canal. This floating chain, backed up by Heligoland's artillery, was the safety-net (*Sicherung*) behind which Germany's main fleet was to be hidden until the day it could attack the Royal Navy in 'favourable conditions'. But these conditions, as the Imperial Navy's war orders described them, were rarely met: the British Admiralty was hesitant to send its battle fleet into the Bight, where its numerical superiority could be outweighed by the proximity of Germany's naval strongholds. Instead, the Royal Navy set up a 'distant' blockade, guarding the entrance to the Channel and patrolling the North Sea between Scotland and Norway. With the Germans keeping their battle fleet locked up and the British unwilling to send theirs into the heavily guarded home waters of the Imperial Navy, an all-out confrontation seemed unlikely.

The Battle of Heligoland Bight on 28 August 1914 underlined this with some force.[2] This was the first of the three large battles puncturing the waiting game that was the war in the North Sea. The British plan was for two destroyer flotillas, commanded by Reginald Tyrwhitt, to enter the Bight at dawn and go close to Heligoland. Here they would intercept a part of the German destroyer force safeguarding the Bight, drawing out a larger numbers of German vessels in support, which could then be engaged by submarines and light cruisers. The plan worked, though coordination errors at the Admiralty hampered its execution. The decoy ships sent to approach the island 'played their part to perfection', noted one of the seamen on board Tyrwhitt's destroyers:

> They were attacked by a number of German destroyers and when they retreated they were followed until they came within sight of the *Arethusa* and *Fearless* and the encircling line of English destroyers to the north and south.[3]

The German light cruisers coming out to support their attacking destroyers were surprised by the nearing battle cruiser squadron commanded by David

Beatty. Heavily outgunned, the *Ariadne*, *Mainz*, and *Cöln* were destroyed in short order. Adolf Neumann, stoker on the *Cöln*, described the last minutes before he went overboard:

> Mutilated bodies lay in heaps amidst a jumble of smashed boats, davits, iron ladders, spars, wireless antennae, ammunition and shell fragments. The bridge had vanished; each of the three funnels was riddled through and through; shell holes of enormous diameter appeared in the superstructure.[4]

Neumann abandoned ship together with some 250 other men. He was the only one to survive.

While the battle had been short, the aftermath was prolonged. Those treating the wounded worked all night. Duncan Lorimer was a surgeon on board the cruiser HMS *Bacchante*, which had been ordered to pick up survivors:

> From 4.30 that evening, all night till 8 o'clock the following morning we were operating. Most of the wounds were so extensive that we had to anaesthetise a large number of cases even to dress them properly, and a number had to be operated on straight away…The wounds were mostly deep. Ragged, flesh wounds, full of dirt and fragments of metal. There were crushed limbs with bones absolutely shattered, hopeless to conserve. We retired at intervals for food, more especially for drink, while fresh cases were brought in. We lost four after being brought on board, two after operations, in spite of transfusions and all sorts of stimulants. The wounded were splendid and wonderfully patient. We took them in order of severity, making no respect of persons or nationality; the bulk of the wounded were naturally Germans, as they were the defeated side, but we had also a number of our own.[5]

There was no doubt that the Germans had been defeated. Three of their light cruisers, the *Mainz*, the *Cöln*, and the *Ariadne*, had been sunk, while no British vessels were destroyed. A total of 1,251 German officers and men had been killed, wounded, or captured. Only 35 British had been killed and 40 wounded. But to call this a 'victory' seemed out of place. Not only had there been serious problems with the coordination of the attack, prompting Beatty to write that 'Their Lordships' at the Admiralty 'would have hung me if there had been a disaster, as there very nearly was, owing to the extraordinary neglect of the most ordinary precautions on their [Lordships'] part'.[6] What was more, the forces pitted against each other at Heligoland were of such difference in size and character that the outcome was seen as inevitable. The British had a squadron of the most modern battle cruisers in place just at the right time, while the German naval staff was unable to commit any capital vessels at all. Its destroyers and light cruisers, surprised by the presence of Beatty's battle cruisers, had no chance. As Eugene Hollingworth, a seaman on board the destroyer *Laertes*, wrote: 'It can hardly be called a victory, as its issue was certain from the commencement owing to the very great disparity of the forces engaged'.[7]

While all of this was abundantly clear to the officers involved in the battle, the Admiralty was determined to present the battle as a major triumph. A key element in this strategy was to link the victory to the image of Heligoland as the 'German Gibraltar'. The battle had of course never been about the island: only a few of the British destroyers had temporarily come within range of Heligoland's battery, which, hampered by fog, had held its fire; nor had it been the Admiralty's intention to attack the island. But the symbolic value of the fortress was such that the navy's leadership was keen to have the battle associated with it. In its official communications, the Admiralty stressed the danger the fortress had posed to the British ships; and it made sure that the 'battle honours' would refer directly to the island. Each ship 'engaged in the recent action…whether damaged or not' was to display the words *Heligoland August 28th 1914* in a prominent place, using gold letters.[8] George V received the 'Heroes of Heligoland' at Buckingham Palace and handed out commemorative medals.[9] Most of the press followed the Admiralty's lead, calling the battle the 'Heligoland Sea-Fight' or the 'Heligoland Triumph'. *The Times* described the island as the 'scene of action' with details of its fortifications, armaments, and the 'enormous sums spent upon it to make it impregnable'.[10] The headline most cited was that of the *Daily Express*: 'We've Gone to Heligoland and Back; Please God, We'll Go Again!'[11]

What stuck in the public mind, then, was the image of the British fleet penetrating Heligoland Bight and threatening the red cliffs of Germany's island fortress. Poems, songs, and souvenirs commemorated the event. Photographs of the commanding officers were sold on London's streets. Special issues and official accounts appeared with lavish illustrations and the inevitable lines by Rudyard Kipling.[12] Churchill made a point of travelling to Sheerness and Chatham to receive the returning ships. As Tyrwhitt wrote to his wife, he 'fairly slobbered over me. Offered me any ship I liked and all the rest of it'.[13] Taking all this in, Roger Keyes, who had commanded the submarines in the battle, wrote on 5 September: 'I think an absurd fuss was made over that small affair'.[14]

The extent to which the engagement off Heligoland was celebrated in Britain reflected the paucity of naval success stories. At a time when the Expeditionary Force was suffering heavy losses on the Western Front, the navy was keen to be seen to be contributing to the war effort. The crews involved in the battle were told that the news of their victory at Heligoland 'greatly heartened our weary, hard-pressed troops' in France.[15] Beatty and other commanding officers emphasized privately that the Germans had been 'gallant' and 'indeed worthy foemen' during the battle.[16] But the official account issued by the government painted a radically different image: German officers had shot their own men in the water and hindered British boats from picking up the wounded and drowning. Broadsheets and tabloids alike repeated such stories in which 'German brutality' served to highlight 'British chivalry'. It was not only in Belgium, but also in the North Sea, they suggested, that the Germans behaved like 'Huns'.[17]

While the British government and the London press were busy making the most of the outcome of the battle, the German authorities were keen not to let the defeat provoke a negative public response. Early on, they decided that the casualty numbers should not be made public. Downplaying the impact the battle would have on the course of the war at sea, they stressed instead the heroic character of those fighting the overwhelming British forces. The Kaiser's officers and seamen had demonstrated their 'battle ardour' and 'indomitable will' to get at the enemy, the chief of the Admiralty Staff, Admiral von Ingenohl, told Wilhelm II in a widely publicized telegram.[18] Their heroism was encapsulated by Adolf Neumann, the only survivor of the *Cöln*, who had been rescued after floating in the North Sea for sixty-seven hours. His narrative as 'The Last Man of the *Cöln*' was one of the rhetorical exercises by which the German government attempted to turn the defeat into a moral victory.[19] It helped the construction of this myth that the bow of one of the *Cöln*'s lifeboats was found shortly after the battle, riddled with holes. The wreck, celebrated as an emblem of heroism, was given to the city of Cologne where it became part of a public memorial inaugurated in late September 1914.

The result of the Battle of Heligoland Bight was hardly as 'far-reaching' as Churchill suggested later—German morale had not been broken enduringly by the loss of three light cruisers.[20] Tirpitz thought of the engagement as a series of mere 'skirmishes', despite the fact that his son had been captured during the battle as a much-vaunted 'British trophy of the Bight'.[21] But nor was the effect of the battle insignificant. The Kaiser was adamant that from now on his battle fleet would sortie for enemy action only with his explicit permission. This policy was revised in January 1915, but the underlying rationale remained the same: the High Seas Fleet was to avoid a direct engagement with the Grand Fleet. The chief of the German Admiralty Staff had clear orders that only isolated units of the Royal Navy should be attacked. This policy remained in place until the end of the war, as did the British blockade. As a result there was no pitched engagement between the two battle fleets, no 'Trafalgar of the North Sea'. Instead, the new weapons that both sides had denounced as 'un-chivalrous' before the war became the prime focus: as Admiral John Jellicoe, the commander of the Grand Fleet, wrote to the Admiralty in October 1914: 'The Germans have shown that they rely to a very great extent on submarines, mines, and torpedoes'.[22]

With hindsight, the Battle of Heligoland Bight can be seen as setting the stage for the rest of the war. It cemented the strategic stalemate in which the Royal Navy commanded the North Sea, but was unable to translate its superiority into the defeat of the German fleet. On the Western Front millions of soldiers fought a long war of attrition that brought death and suffering on an unprecedented scale. But in the North Sea, the much-anticipated theatre of Anglo-German war, there was little all-out contact between the two sides. From early on naval officers complained about the 'waiting game' they were engaged in. 'It seems as if there is no conduct of war', wrote Walther Zaeschmar, the third artillery officer of the German battleship *Helgoland*, on 9 October 1914. A few weeks later he added: 'Nothing happens any longer in the North Sea. Only the U-boats are constantly moving'.[23] Ernst von Weizsäcker, then an officer at the Admiralty Staff, expressed widely held feelings when he wrote to his father in October 1914:

> It is impossible that one builds a fleet for billions [of Marks], in order to deter one's opponents, without the intention to risk using it...If we do not have the audacity and conviction to use the fleet, it would have been better had we not built it.[24]

But the German fleet was not to be risked—unless the British navy could first be reduced through mine-laying, submarines, and smaller engagements. Only when this 'equalization of forces' (*Kräfteausgleich*), as Reinhard Scheer, the commander of the High Seas Fleet, called it, had been achieved would the High Seas Fleet seek decisive battle with the Royal Navy.[25]

The two other significant battles in the North Sea—at the Dogger Bank and at Jutland—did not change this strategy. The first was triggered when the German battle cruisers under Franz von Hipper went on a routine sortie to clear the Dogger Bank of fishing craft and neutral vessels on 24 January 1915. The Admiralty decoded the wireless message that ordered the operation and promptly sent a force of battle cruisers and light cruisers to engage Hipper. Upon sighting the British, Hipper ordered his squadron to turn and run, aiming to reach Heligoland before Beatty's battle cruisers. After an intense chase, his ships were engaged by the British. Hipper lost the *Blücher*, but the rest of his squadron escaped and returned safely to harbour. The outcome was trumpeted as a British triumph, with pictures of the capsized *Blücher* going around the world. But if this was a victory, it was an inconclusive one. 'The disappointment of that day is more than I can bear to think of', Beatty wrote to Keyes. 'Everybody thinks it was a great success, when in reality it was a terrible failure'.[26] For the Kaiser and his naval staff the narrow escape confirmed just how important it was to risk the High Seas Fleet only under favourable circumstances.

The last major battle, at Jutland on 31 May and 1 June 1916, the most important of the war, was brought about when Scheer thought he would be able to create such circumstances. Hipper was to lure out the British battle cruisers under Beatty by cruising off the Norwegian coast. He would then draw them into the path of the main German fleet, with submarines in between preparing an ambush. But just as in the run-up to the Dogger Bank operation, the Admiralty intercepted German signals. As a result Jellicoe's Grand Fleet and Beatty's battle cruisers were on their way to Jutland much earlier than Scheer had expected. In a running battle, Hipper managed to lure Beatty towards Scheer's battle fleet, before Beatty turned back towards the Grand Fleet. In the evening of 31 May the High Seas Fleet and the superior Grand Fleet engaged twice, then the Germans escaped. Both sides claimed victory—London days later than Berlin. Britain had lost more ships and twice as many men, but Scheer's plan of destroying a substantial portion of the British fleet had failed. The Royal Navy remained in command of the North Sea, while the High Seas Fleet returned, largely intact, to its home waters.[27]

The Anglo-German stand-off over the North Sea continued, as did the waiting game, about which officers and crews on both sides complained so much. As Scheer concluded in his report to the Kaiser of 4 July 1916, Britain's command of the sea was unlikely to be broken after Jutland. Only a large-scale U-boat campaign could result in a 'victorious end to the war'.[28] On 1 February 1917 Berlin resumed the unrestricted submarine warfare abandoned in September 1915 as a consequence of the sinking of the *Lusitania* earlier that year.[29] The German U-boat force was now to play the main role in the war at sea, while the two surface fleets continued their waiting game. 'The naval officer corps sit around, eat, drink [and] talk politics', Ernst von Weizsäcker noted in his diary after Jutland.[30]

The continued stalemate made Heligoland a symbol of British frustration. The island fortress, with all its historical connotations, remained undefeated, despite British popular culture predicting confidently that the outpost would be taken. The most striking example was the song 'We'll knock the Heligo— into Heligo—out of Heligoland!' Written by Theodore Morse (music) and John O'Brien (words), it celebrated the entry of the United States into the war as much as the imagined fall of the Kaiser's citadel. Its chorus ('well marked and not fast') was:

> We're on our way to Heligoland
> To get the Kaiser's goat
> In a good old Yankee boat
> Up the Kiel canal we'll float
> I'm the son of a gun
> If I see a Hun
> I'll make him understand
> We'll knock the Heligo into Heligo
> Out of Heligoland[31]

Similar fantasies existed amongst the naval leadership. For Churchill, in charge of the navy until May 1915, the island represented not only unfinished business with the Germans, but also an opportunity to break the deadlock of the war at sea.[32] His thinking drew on a series of plans which the Admiralty had discussed in the decade before the war. Storming the island had first been envisaged in 1903 as part of a war plan that foresaw blockading Germany's main ports.[33] In 1906 John Fisher, then First Sea Lord, had set up a special committee to investigate such an operation in detail. It came, as one of the participants put it later, 'to the conclusion that—much as we should have liked to take Heligoland—the scheme was utterly impractical. It could not be done'.[34] When the idea of a close blockade was given up, most at the Admiralty thought that trying to capture the German fortress would be far too risky an operation. Not so, however, Arthur Wilson, who had succeeded Fisher as First Sea Lord in 1910. On 23 August 1911, at the height of the Agadir crisis, Britain's political and

Figure 6.1 Sheet music for voice and piano by Theodore Morse and John O'Brien, 1917.

military leaders came together to discuss what action to take if war with Germany broke out. Wilson outlined an assault on Heligoland, to be undertaken by Royal Marines supported by at least one army division. Few of the participants were convinced that this was a realistic scenario, but the First Sea Lord was adamant that Heligoland would be needed as an advance base for an attack on Germany.[35] Though most of the committee had been decidedly sceptical, Churchill took the idea up again two years later and instructed Lewis Bayly, the commander of the 3rd Battle Squadron, to work out a scheme for an offensive operation. Bayly, who apparently had a plaster model of Heligoland made to simulate the assault, consulted Wilson and Fisher before submitting a detailed scheme to Churchill. Though George Ballard, the director of operations, saw Bayly's scheme as unacceptably risky, Churchill sent the proposal to the prime minister on 31 July 1914.[36]

This was the fertile ground on which ideas about seizing Heligoland fell during the war. In early September 1914 a conference involving most of the Admiralty's leadership was held to discuss, amongst other plans, an attack on the island.[37] Admiral Jellicoe, who hosted the meeting at Loch Ewe on board his flagship HMS *Iron Duke*, was not surprised that his flag officers and the chief of staff were unanimously against such an operation. They had good reasons:

> Ships were no match for the heavy fortifications known to exist on Heligoland. Their fire would be largely ineffective against the well-placed, heavily protected and well-concealed land guns of the island. Even if a storming party were able to land and to capture the island, it would be quite impossible to hold it, situated as it was close to German naval bases.[38]

Jellicoe thought after the meeting 'that the idea would be abandoned', given the force of argument against it, but he was wrong.[39] In November 1914 Wilson urged again that Heligoland should be stormed. Churchill asked Fisher for his opinion. 'I think the scheme if carried out would result in a national disaster', was Fisher's response. 'Needless to say that if it is decided to make the attempt I am quite ready to do it'.[40]

The longer the frustrating deadlock over the North Sea continued, the more attractive did an operation against the Kaiser's fortress seem. In late December William Wordsworth Fisher, captain of the battleship *St Vincent*, submitted a detailed scheme for a raid, involving seventeen battleships and an armada of supporting vessels. The navy would destroy the island's artillery and create a smoke screen, allowing the troops to storm the fortress. This would lure the Kaiser's heavy ships from Wilhelmshaven and Cuxhaven out into the North Sea where they would be 'dealt with'.[41] Another plan foresaw an attack with poison gas. 'The capture of Heligoland by asphyxiating gases would appear to be thoroughly practical, given good weather conditions, a superabundance of the right gases, and landing parties of troops in perfect co-ordination', explained the officer who submitted the scheme to Fisher. Under cover of darkness, twelve vessels fitted with large gas tanks would be anchored close to the island. Teams of specially trained commandos in gas masks would then use chlorine to 'clear' the tunnels, shelters, and gun emplacements of German troops.[42] Numerous other schemes were devised in which the island was seized or destroyed. 'I hated all these projects but had to be careful what I said', wrote Henry Oliver, the head of naval operations at the Admiralty, after the war.[43]

In December 1915 British, Australian, and New Zealand forces retreated from Gallipoli. After eight months of heavy losses, they conceded defeat to the Ottoman Empire. In the wake of the disastrous campaign there was little enthusiasm at Westminster and Whitehall for similar 'wild projects' (Fisher)—Churchill was bitterly mocked in Parliament for his obsession with storming Germany's North Sea bastion.[44]

Yet Heligoland continued to be an *idée fixe* not only amongst politicians and officers, but also for the wider public. In September 1916 Arthur Balfour, who had succeeded Churchill as First Lord of the Admiralty, penned a cabinet memorandum entitled 'Questions on Heligoland'. 'The man in the street', he wrote,

> undoubtedly holds the view that the possession of Heligoland has been a great naval strength to Germany and that, whether Great Britain was right or wrong to cede it under the settlement made in 1890, modern developments both in sea and air power have proved that she made a very bad bargain.[45]

But would it be helpful if Britain got the island back? Balfour sent the memorandum to the navy's leading officers for comment. They all agreed that trying to seize the island would be suicidal. 'The case of Gallipoli', Jellicoe answered,

> will assist in appreciating the Heligoland case. At Gallipoli we held undisputed surface command of the sea: the distances were small, yet a few submarines deprived us of several battleships, and reduced us to communicating at night, and by trawlers, tugs and other small craft. We should never be as favourably placed as regards *supply* to Heligoland as we were at Gallipoli.[46]

Even if Britain managed to seize the fortress, having to hold it 'would be a great misfortune'. The fleet of vessels needed to supply the island with stores and munitions would be at constant risk of being attacked, with British losses likely to be much heavier than German ones, 'because the enemy's primary bases are within 30 miles and, lying round it in a semi-circle, *command* all approaches to it'.[47]

Despite the near unanimous opposition amongst commanding officers, the question of storming the island continued to be discussed in government circles. In July 1917 the French, American, and British naval leadership were asked to consider a coordinated Allied assault. According to Jellicoe, the plan was based on a scheme originally put forward by Churchill. The Allies concluded that the proposal was not practical. Neither the French nor the American authorities were prepared to commit the ships required. Getting the island back was a good idea, storming it while the German fleet was in a position to defend it, was not.[48]

The prominence attached to the island in official thinking and popular culture during the war seemed to vindicate those who had opposed its cession in 1890. Salisbury's 'gift' to the Kaiser seemed a tragic error now: it had allowed the Germans to prepare an advance position against which the Royal Navy seemed powerless. This was the 'Heligoland Mistake', a phrase coined by Percy Evans Lewin, a long-standing critic of Germany.[49] Britain was 'reaping the whirlwind' of the disastrous decision taken under Salisbury, he argued.[50] Numerous armchair admirals agreed, amongst them John St Loe Strachey, the editor and owner of The Spectator, who was 'anxious to retake Heligoland'.[51] Churchill continued to lament the 'surrender' of Heligoland after the war. 'With a complete detachment from strategic considerations, Lord Salisbury exchanged Zanzibar for Heligoland', he wrote in The World Crisis.[52] After the Second World War, he was even more caustic: 'A future German naval base was traded for a spice island'.[53] But this ignored the simple truth, reiterated by Jellicoe and others throughout the war, that holding the island against the Germans would have been near impossible. Giving up Heligoland had made a lot of sense, strategically, in 1890 and it still did during the war. Defending the island in August 1914 would have resulted in the very scenario the Royal Navy had been so keen to avoid: a drawn-out campaign being fought close to Germany's home bases.

While the 'Heligoland mistake' was read back into the British past as a fateful decision that had contributed to the North Sea stalemate, the opposite movement took place in Germany. Back in 1890 the Wilhelmine colonial lobby had fiercely opposed the island's acquisition, regarding the loss of the African protectorates as too high a price. With the outbreak of war this school of thought disappeared. 'The subject of Heligoland', wrote J. M. de Beaufort, a Dutch journalist who toured Germany extensively during the war, 'is one that today is very near to the heart of every German':

The mere mention of the name will bring delight to his face. More likely than not, he'll slap you on the back and, with a grin of satisfaction and a confidential, knowing air—as if he were personally responsible for the fact that the island is German now—will assure you that 'We certainly scored a point on old England that time'...

Heligoland has become the very apple of their eye, and I am certain the Germans would sooner return Alsace and Lorraine tomorrow, than give up that mile-long piece of rock. 'Heligoland *must and shall* always remain German soil'—so everybody in Germany will assure you.[54]

Most German commentators agreed that the war had revealed the true wisdom of the Kaiser's acquisition. An exaggerated relevance was now attached to the treaty of 1890. 'Without Heligoland, German world policy would not exist', declared Maximilian von Hagen in 1916, in his book-length account of the 1890 Heligoland agreement. The island was the 'bridgehead' for Germany's domination of the North Sea, without which the Fatherland would be defenceless.[55]

In popular culture and wartime propaganda Heligoland turned into the maritime equivalent of the 'Watch of the Rhine', the mythical idea of Germania guarding the nation's border with France.[56] Zdenko von Kraft's popular novel *Die Stimme von Helgoland* evoked this imagery at considerable length.[57] Written in the vein of the 'Boy's Own' genre, it portrays the island as an iron fortress menacing all who dare approach it. Thousands of soldiers hold the 'terrible guard at the batteries'. Without the slightest sound the artillery turrets swing round whenever a ship is sighted. 'Heligoland was on guard. Germany could go to work'.[58] Easily the most powerful visual depiction of this motif was the painting by Reinhold Max Eichler that appeared on the cover page of *Jugend* magazine in January 1915. Subsequently sold in postcard format and adopted by the military *Feldpost* service, it depicted the red cliffs of Heligoland as an allegory of Germany: surrounded by imperial eagles, the island resembled Germania, defiantly searching the horizon and guarding the Bight.[59] The German war loans campaign used a similar image in its advertising, though its portrayal of the island was by necessity more ambivalent. In order to underline the need for financial sacrifice, an image of both defiance and need had to be evoked. But here too, Heligoland was Germany: a metaphorical piece of *Heimat* that stood for all the other *Heimats* being threatened by the British.[60]

Heligoland thus played a key role in the process by which the two nations mobilized the past for the war effort. A conscious effort was made in the

Figure 6.2 *Helgoland*. Drawing by Reinhold Max Eichler, published in *Jugend*, 1915.

official and popular culture of both countries to purge the nation of any association with the other. In Britain this ranged from everyday food items to the royal family. OXO, originally a German invention, became now a 'genuinely British product'.[61] So did the House of Saxe-Coburg, swiftly renaming itself 'Windsor'. The myriad of mutual ties which had grown between the two countries in the long nineteenth century were thus severed. Heligoland was one of these links, now imagined as a site of battle, with the Royal Navy driving the Germans off in an attempt to exorcize the past that the two nations had in common. Soldiers on the Western Front, too, 'played Heligoland', naming German strongholds and trench systems after the naval fortress.

But while propaganda and popular culture made Heligoland into a symbol of deep division, the islanders themselves continued to be bound up with both nations. It was an expression of their peculiar position as Anglo-German go-betweens that Heligolanders were to be found on both sides of the war—in the trenches and in the camps for 'enemy aliens'. Men born in Heligoland volunteered in Britain, Australia, and the United States.[62] No islanders born before 1890 were meant to serve in the Kaiser's army, but the authorities did accept volunteers. When British forces stormed a position near St Julien in Flanders in July 1915 they took as prisoner a soldier in German uniform who claimed to be British. They thought he was joking, but he was serious, insisting that he had been born in a North Sea colony under the British flag.[63]

For the German government the Heligolanders never lost their status as an unreliable border population. It spoke volumes that the Prussian officials dealing with the islanders were also tasked with running the camps for 'enemy aliens' in Germany.[64] They were adamant that the Heligolanders should remain billeted on the mainland for the rest of the war—'i.e. probably for several months', an official predicted in 1914.[65] The islanders' forced exile was to last for four years, a time characterized by continuous mutual mistrust. In October 1914, August Kuchlenz, one of the most outspoken critics of German rule in Heligoland, wrote to the Prussian minister of the interior with a list of complaints. Trying to make his requests more palatable he stressed that the islanders 'owed the great German Fatherland so much'. The official dealing with the query in Berlin underlined the passage and wrote 'hypocrite' next to it.[66]

In August 1915, when the twenty-fifth anniversary of the island's cession was celebrated with a religious service, there was much public rhetoric about the Germanness of the islanders.[67] But behind this façade the cat-and-mouse game between the authorities and the islanders' representatives continued. While the Hamburg Political Police monitored the islanders' activities, the Heligolanders collected evidence for their maltreatment by the authorities.[68] The longer the war went on for, the more fraught did the relations between islanders and officials become. The ministries in Berlin,

Hamburg, and Altona agreed that 'any public discussion' of the Heligolanders' complaints had to be 'avoided under all circumstances' for propaganda reasons.[69] As it became more and more doubtful that Germany would be able to win the war, some of the islanders began to envisage a future in which Heligoland might be ruled by Britain again. In early August 1917 the Foreign Office in London received the first anonymous letter 'from the Heligolanders' urging annexation by Britain in the event of a German defeat.[70]

In Britain, too, the ambiguous status of the islanders made them suspect. Those who were British residents, but had German citizenship or were 'known to have German sympathies',[71] came under police surveillance at the outbreak of war. John Elias Dirks was one of them. Born in Heligoland on 13 March 1883, he had left the British colony as a young man to serve on British ships. After eighteen years spent mostly at sea, he had become resident in Newport, Wales. But since his parents had not opted for British nationality after 1890, the authorities there regarded him as German. Despite his protestations that he 'has always considered himself to be a British subject', he was arrested as an enemy alien in October 1914.[72] A month earlier a similar case had ended with the opposite result when another islander, Bernhardt Baron, had been prosecuted under the Aliens Restriction Act. The Act had been passed by Parliament in August 1914 in order to 'remove or restrain the movement of undesirable aliens'.[73] The prosecution argued that Baron, a former inhabitant of Heligoland, was German: he had not declared his wish to remain a British citizen after the island's cession, nor had he been naturalized since, while living in Britain. Yet in direct contradiction of the line taken by the Home Office in a number of similar cases, the government declared that Baron had 'not become a German'.[74] He was discharged and left the courtroom as a naturally born British subject.

Britain and Germany continued to be bound up in such personal histories. This was the case not only in Britain and the Kaiserreich, but also in the more distant locations where some of the islanders had settled, especially in Australia and the USA. Those of them who volunteered during the war had to realize that even here their nationality remained contested. Some of them succeeded in persuading the authorities to let them enlist. Theodor Lührs was a particularly intriguing case. Born in colonial Heligoland, he had left the island after its cession, 'not liking the German rule'. Having served on British ships, he had claimed residence in Australia in December 1910, found work, and married 'a Tasmanian girl'.[75] In February 1916, Lührs volunteered to fight in the Great War. It was time, he felt, that he did his bit. The Australian authorities were less convinced. Certainly, they desperately needed volunteers—two new infantry divisions were to be sent to Europe and their ranks had to be filled. But Lührs was German, or so the Department of Defence thought. For six months it discussed his case with other government departments, a case in which the terms 'nationality', 'loyalty', and 'empire' seemed frustratingly conflicted. As far as Lührs was concerned, he was a subject of the empire. The Australian Army disagreed. In its view, Lührs's parents had turned from natural-born British subjects into German nationals: he was of 'enemy alien parentage'. A number of local dignitaries wrote to protest that Lührs was 'a loyal subject of the Empire' and had 'no German leanings'. On the contrary, he had 'always been proud to have been born under the British flag'.[76] But the Department of External Affairs was clear: 'the enlistment in the Australian Imperial Force of men of enemy parentage is not permitted'.[77] Lührs, who found this to be 'an extremely awkward and unfortunate position', continued to insist that he was not German, but a British subject. In June 1916, the Intelligence Section of the General Staff put him on its Register of Aliens, but admitted him to serve in the Australian Imperial Force. They judged him to be 'of good character' and 'a loyal subject' after all.[78] On 10 August 1916, Lührs joined the 12th Battalion as part of its 22nd Reinforcements. Seven weeks later he embarked for Europe. Until the end of the war he fought on the Western Front against the country the Australians thought he somehow belonged to.[79]

Charles Bertholdt Nissen was another case. Rather than state his nationality directly as British or German, he described himself as 'Church of England' and 'born in Heligoland when under Great Britain'. The authorities at Blackboy Hill, the Western Australian training camp, accepted him on that basis as a subject of the empire. Aged 37, he enlisted and embarked for the Dardanelles on 6 June 1915. He joined his unit there on 4 August. Two days later he was shot in the opening phase of the Allies' August offensive. Badly injured with a stomach wound, he was transferred to a hospital ship where he died on the same day. He was buried at sea on 7 August 1915. For years after his death, the Australian Defence Department tried to find his relatives to whom personal belongings and posthumous decorations could be given, but could not locate any in Australia. This was hardly surprising: they were most likely in Germany.[80]

Neither in Imperial Germany nor in the United Kingdom and its empire was there a consistent standard by which the Heligolanders' status was treated during the war: too much was their island bound up with both the German and the British pasts. In the United States, too, the islanders remained orphans of both empire and nation state.[81] When Fred Kuchlenz, a resident of San Francisco, was drafted in 1917, the local military board rejected him on the grounds that he was German. Yet his brother, born like him in Heligoland, was accepted and sent to the army camp at American Lake, Washington. All the while, the Kuchlenzes had relatives in Germany who had been arrested, suspected of harbouring foreign sympathies.[82]

Several similar cases became known in Britain, Germany, Australia, and the United States during the war, linking distant locations with what had once been Britain's smallest colony. They all involved individuals born in Heligoland whose loyalty was mistrusted on both sides of the war. In Britain some of them eventually succeeded in claiming their status as British subjects, either through enlisting as volunteers or through registering as voters.[83] Others continued to live in a legal limbo, a situation which mirrored their island's position at the fault line between national and imperial histories.[84]

As the war neared its end in the autumn of 1918 the question of where Heligoland and the islanders belonged gained new significance. On 29 September Erich Ludendorff and Paul von Hindenburg, the two generals who led the Army Supreme Command, told the rest of the German government that the country faced imminent defeat on the Western Front. Having run Germany as a de facto military dictatorship for the past two years, they handed power over to a new imperial chancellor, the liberal-minded Prince Maximilian von Baden. The prince, who had the confidence of the majority of the Reichstag, enacted a raft of overdue political reforms and sued for peace.

Negotiations for an armistice had already begun when the Admiralty Staff, defying the chancellor, ordered the fleet to prepare for a last sortie against the Royal Navy.[85] On 29 October, with the fleet assembled off Wilhelmshaven, sailors refused to obey orders and weigh anchor for what they regarded as a senseless, suicidal mission. From here the mutiny spread to the navy's main bases. By 4 November soldiers' councils were in control of Wilhelmshaven and Kiel. Two days later the revolution arrived in Heligoland. The naval commander of the island recorded wryly how his authority was being undermined.[86] At first, troops and crews met secretly at night, then openly, defying their officers' orders. Demonstrating their power, they marched through the streets and voted for a council, which then took

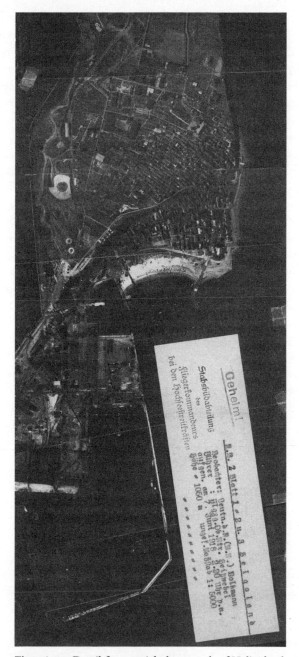

Figure 6.3 Detail from aerial photograph of Heligoland taken by the German Naval Air Service, 7 June 1918.

charge of the naval base. It was this council, effectively an improvised revolutionary government (complete with its own official stationery and seal), which organized the affairs of the island now.[87] With the red flag flying over Heligoland, the commander was a prisoner in his own fortress.

On 9 November, a republic was declared in Berlin. The Kaiser abdicated and Prince Maximilian handed the chancellorship to Friedrich Ebert, a Social Democrat. Two days later the new government signed the armistice, agreeing to the Allies' terms. Germany would have to hand over her fleet, internationalize the Kiel Canal, and demilitarize Heligoland. The Kaiser's navy had to be ready to sail into internment within a week, otherwise Heligoland would be occupied by the British. In the meantime, the Grand Fleet under Beatty maintained the naval blockade of Germany.

On 19 November 1918 the German High Seas Fleet left for Scapa Flow, where it was to be interned and eventually scuttled by its own officers in a vainglorious attempt to 'rescue' its honour.[88] Late in the afternoon of that day, the long line of battleships commanded by Vice-Admiral Ludwig von Reuter passed Heligoland. In Reuter's account, published three years later, the moment came to symbolize Germany's imperial sunset. The island was 'illuminated by the last rays of the autumn sun', he wrote. Heligoland was 'glowing in all colours' while Germany's fleet, built up over two decades, sailed past its North Sea fortress one last time, never to return. Scapa Flow was to be the navy's 'grave', Reuter wrote. At least, he consoled himself and his officers, Heligoland was still German.[89]

7

Disarming Germany

Early in December 1918 the Ebert government decided to move the Heligolanders back onto their island. It did so ostensibly to meet the demands of the islanders, who had lobbied for their return throughout the war. Most of all, though, Berlin was keen to create a fait accompli before negotiations for a peace treaty began: having its own subjects on the island could only help to underline Germany's claim to the outpost. It was a measure of how uncertain this claim was that Berlin had to ask the British for permission to re-settle the Heligolanders: the Grand Fleet, still blockading Germany, controlled the Bight and the North Sea. Admiral Beatty, its commander-in-chief, agreed to the transports, which were carried out in the first two weeks of December despite grim winter weather. But he insisted that the demilitarization, to be supervised by an Allied commission, begin in parallel. By 13 December 2,500 Heligolanders had returned to their island. Together with them arrived 1,000 labourers, the core of the work force that was to demolish the naval fortress.[1]

In Britain the pending demolition of the 'German Gibraltar', though not yet confirmed by a peace treaty, was greeted with thinly disguised triumph. Heligoland's demilitarization, wrote *The Times* under the headline 'Disarming Germany', would 'give the Germans a good object-lesson in the futility of their navalism'.[2] Numerous newspapers suggested that this was the historic moment at which to correct the 'Heligoland mistake'.[3] The long-standing opponents of the island's cession felt vindicated. Admiral Fisher (retired since 1915, but far from silent) had no doubt that Heligoland had to be 'delivered up' to Britain now.[4] The Navy League, still busy promoting a strong fleet, sent an appeal to Arthur Balfour, the foreign secretary. Signed by a string of admirals it demanded 'that, in any terms of peace, the restitution of Heligoland to Great Britain must be an integral article'.[5]

Many in the senior service agreed. During the war Jellicoe, Beatty's predecessor as commander of the Grand Fleet, had been sceptical about the
prospect of taking Heligoland by force. But possessing it in times of peace
would make sense, he had written in September 1916. As 'an unfortified
island which would be given up at once at the outbreak of war', Heligoland
would give Britain 'the advantage that the Germans could not make it
into an advanced base'.[6] Jellicoe's proposal addressed the impossibility of
defending Heligoland against Germany, highlighted in numerous wartime
memoranda. But he had conveniently forgotten about the islanders themselves: presumably they would have to be 'given up' too in case of war.

Jellicoe's assessment had reflected a wartime consensus amongst naval
officers: if Britain could not seize Heligoland by force, it would have to be
taken back from the Germans after the war. The armistice of 11 November
1918, however, left open the question of where Heligoland would ultimately belong. Leading officers, amongst them Beatty, saw this as a serious
mistake: Britain should have claimed its prize then rather than wait for a
peace treaty. Beatty complained bitterly about this point to Sir Rosslyn
Wemyss, the First Sea Lord who represented Britain at the armistice. Wemyss
wrote back from Compiègne Forest, where the armistice was about to be
signed by Matthias Erzberger on behalf of the German government: Lloyd
George, the prime minister, had opposed the inclusion of the island, but
Wemyss was sure that 'eventually the enemy would have to give it up. And
this is to be a matter for the Peace Conference'.[7]

In early January 1919 the delegates from more than thirty-two countries
came together in Paris for the peace negotiations. High on their agenda
stood the demilitarization of Germany and the re-drawing of its boundaries. Heligoland mattered in both respects.[8] In formulating the British position, Arthur Balfour, the foreign secretary, left little doubt that he thought
the island's cession had been a mistake:

> Heligoland was British up to the year 1890, and would have been British still had
> the development of the Submarine and Aeroplane been foreseen. As matters,
> however, then stood it was regarded by the British Government as of no use to
> Great Britain, while its sentimental value to Germany was considerable.

The war, however, had shown that the island 'fortified as it is at present, can
be made a most formidable naval base':

> This evidently concerns not merely Britain but the whole scheme of Western
> defence against Germany, which requires unimpeded communication between

Great Britain and the Continent in case of German aggression. It is of great importance, therefore, that the offensive value of Heligoland be destroyed.[9]

How was this to be done? Balfour set out three options. First, Germany could be forced to give Heligoland back to Britain. This, he wrote, 'would doubtless be agreeable to British public sentiment'. There were many voices advocating reannexation, not only in the press, but also in Parliament. Amongst them was Francis Channing, one of the MPs who had voted against the treaty in 1890, who was certain that 'that amazingly ill-judged surrender' would now be reversed.[10] But Balfour doubted the strategic wisdom of this option. In contrast to Jellicoe and Beatty, he had never been convinced that getting the island back was a good idea. Nor had Walter Long, since January 1919 the First Lord of the Admiralty, who felt strongly that the cession in 1890 had been a mistake. 'The history of Heligoland should be a warning to us', he wrote when proposals for the cession of Cyprus were being mooted in October.[11] But nor did Long want the burden of having to defend an outpost so close to the German coast. As Balfour noted, the Admiralty 'would strongly disapprove' of adding Heligoland to its responsibilities.[12]

The second option was to blow up the island altogether. 'This proposal has been seriously put forward, but I cannot say that in my opinion it is worth serious consideration', wrote Balfour. The plan (which was to be revived after the Second World War) addressed the dilemma Britain faced with Heligoland: how to deny it to the Germans without committing Britain to taking it on. As one of the officers in the Allied Armistice Commission put it after a visit to the island: 'it is a thundering nuisance to us if the Germans have it, and no good if we stick to it ourselves'.[13] Edward Grey, Balfour's predecessor, had this dilemma in mind when he suggested leaving the island as a no-man's land in between Britain and Germany, frequented only by birds. 'For some reason this, humanly speaking, unattractive and barren spot is a resting place for millions of birds on migration', he wrote to Edward House, Woodrow Wilson's chief negotiator. Would it not be best to make it a sanctuary for them, free of humans?[14] Ornithologists all over Europe were likely to agree, but Balfour showed no interest: it was hard to see how an outpost situated so close to Germany's main ports could remain uninhabited for long; and besides, Heligoland was not uninhabited: the islanders had just been allowed to move back.

Balfour's third option was to 'neutralize' the island under a League of Nations mandate. 'So far as Britain is concerned, this solution would be quite satisfactory', he thought: it would keep Heligoland out of Germany's hands, while not lumbering Britain with any direct responsibility.[15] The mandate system was a convenient formula which London advocated generally as a solution to the geopolitical changes brought about by the First World War. Applied especially as a framework of control for Germany's former colonies, it perpetuated the pre-war imperial order and favoured Britain's global position.[16] Hanging on to Heligoland as a mandate fitted into this framework perfectly, or so Balfour thought. But the Americans were none too keen to create a British-controlled enclave in the North Sea, which they clearly thought of as a de facto re-colonization. In the run-up to the conference Robert Lansing, the American secretary of state, had suggested that the island ought to be given back to Denmark, re-creating the state of 1807, before the British had taken the outpost by force.[17] This idea seemed outlandish to Balfour. Going into the talks on the Council of Four (in which the American, British, French, and Italian governments negotiated the terms of the peace treaty), he prepared a compromise as the fall-back option: London would agree to leave Heligoland in German possession on the condition that the outpost be comprehensively demilitarized.[18]

When the Council of Four met on 15 April 1919 it soon became clear that this was the lowest common denominator.[19] Woodrow Wilson, the American president, did not push the idea of giving Heligoland 'back' to the Danish. But nor were there any signs that he would accept a British-controlled mandate. For him Balfour's demands for demilitarization went too far and seemed vindictive. 'I think that the importance of Heligoland has been exaggerated', declared Wilson's naval adviser, Admiral Benson—to the dismay of Balfour, who did everything he could to explain its significance:

> I could invoke another argument, although I only wish to do it with discretion; it is that of public feeling in England. The island of Heligoland belonged to Great Britain until 1890. We would never have ceded it to Germany if we had known what uses she could make of it . . . Since then bitter reproaches about this cession have been made against [the Salisbury] government, of which I was a member, whilst forgetting the large transaction of which it was part. If today, with the left bank of the Rhine being disarmed, and even with the force reduction of the German army, Heligoland retains even a dismantled military port, English public opinion won't forgive us for it.[20]

'I fear I did not convince the President', Balfour wrote later that day, 'but he finally yielded'.[21] Supported throughout by Georges Clemenceau, the French prime minister, Balfour got the compromise he had aimed for:

Wilson accepted the comprehensive demolition of all military installations in Heligoland as a condition of the peace treaty. An Allied commission would control the demilitarization and all costs would be borne by Germany. With the French and Italian prime ministers' agreement, the terms were adopted as article 35 of the Naval, Military, and Air Conditions of Peace.[22]

On 28 June 1919, five years exactly after the assassination of Archduke Franz Ferdinand, Germany's foreign secretary, Hermann Müller, and colonial secretary, Johannes Bell, signed the Versailles Treaty. 'They do not appear as representatives of a brutal militarism', observed Harold Nicolson, attending as a junior member of the British delegation. 'The one is thin and pink-eyelidded [sic]', he noted in his diary. 'The other is moon-faced and suffering'.[23] If anything, Müller (a Social Democrat) and Bell (a member of the Catholic Centre Party) were representatives of a new Germany, which faced the legacy of militarism and war left by the old regime. But such niceties mattered little in June 1919. There was a strong need in Britain (and even more so in France) to see the Weimar Republic shoulder the responsibility for the war. In Germany there was outrage and disbelief when the terms of the Versailles Treaty were announced. Article 231, the 'war guilt clause', seemed particularly offensive. Clearly included to legitimize the stringent conditions imposed by the Allies, the article obliged the Germans to accept sole responsibility for the outbreak of war in 1914. To Philipp Scheidemann, the Social Democratic chancellor who resigned in protest against the treaty, it felt

> as if the bloody battlefield from the North Sea to the Swiss border has become alive again, as if ghosts are fighting a last battle of hate and desperation over mountains of dead bodies.[24]

It was against this background that Heligoland turned into a symbol of defeat. For decades it had been cultivated as Germany's bulwark in the North Sea, invested with dreams of world power. Now it signalled humiliation and loss. Supervised by British officers, an army of German workers was to systematically destroy the Kaiser's fortress. In late September the first members of the control commission arrived. Led by Admiral Andrew Cunningham, it was made up almost entirely of British officers, with one American accredited as observer.[25] They were the first Allied officials to inspect the fortress which had featured so prominently in the wartime imagination. 'The name Heligoland', wrote one of them, 'has meant so much to us since the war'.[26] It was thrilling to see the place at last. To Cunningham the island seemed like 'a ravelin of an old-time fortress'. The amount spent on the outpost, he thought, 'can be described only by the German adjective *kolossal*'.[27]

In August 1920 Walter Long, the First Lord of the Admiralty, went for an official inspection. Heligoland was 'a most remarkable instance of German preparation', he wrote to George V and the prime minister:

> It is like a miniature Gibraltar; precipitous cliffs of a sort of red sandstone, with occasional strata of, I think, chalky substance. As the cliffs show signs of decay, the Germans had built a really wonderful seawall in order to protect them. They had created a magnificent harbour capable of holding a great many destroyers; and during the war, not less than 60 submarines lay in the portion reserved for these vessels at one time. The harbour is the most complete thing of its kind I have ever seen. There are coal and oil stores, underground passages, and every arrangement to make the place secure. The main body of the island is fortified in a most remarkable way. There are subterranean galleries which go from one end of the island to the other, and which are approached by a tunnel which passes also right through the island. There are galleries, munition stores, gun emplacements—everything calculated to offer a determined defence. The whole of this marvellous structure is covered by concrete which is 8 feet deep, soil again being laid on top of it to a sufficient depth to enable grass of an excellent quality to grow.[28]

Long was so impressed with the Kaiser's fortress that he felt 'almost sorry' to see 'such fine work' being thrown into the sea:[29] 'Convinced as I am that demolition is right, and that so far as the Germans are concerned it is only a small punishment for all they did, yet one cannot help regretting that such splendid works should now be destroyed'.[30] He thought 'it a strange commentary upon all the money and labour expended upon these fortifications that during the whole of the war it is said that the big guns there were only fired twice'.[31]

There seemed a huge waste in all this. But Long was glad to be able to report to king and cabinet that the 'work of demolition is being most efficiently and steadily carried out under the supervision of British officers'. Heligoland, he concluded, had become a symbol of Germany's defeat:

> If some of those at home who complain of existing conditions could see what is going on at Heligoland, they would realise what is the difference between victory and defeat! The conditions regarding food, clothing, etc. are certainly much worse in Germany and its possessions, than they are in the United Kingdom; and added to this common suffering there is the horrible evidence

Figure 7.1 'The Demolition of the Sea Fortress Heligoland'. British press photograph, 1 June 1920.

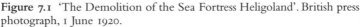

of defeat in the constant work which is being carried out by Germans, efficiently enough no doubt, though very sullenly, under the control and supervision of those who have conquered them. It was a sight, once seen, never to be forgotten![32]

For a quarter of a century the Germans had dug and drilled into the cliffs of Heligoland, building the most formidable fortress their naval engineers could conceive of. The pre-war transformation of the island had expressed their ambition to become a world power, their will to translate Germany's economic rise into global influence, if need be against the British. Now the fortress, admired even by its former enemies, was comprehensively destroyed. The German government sent film crews to the island to document the demolition works 'for propaganda purposes' and passed the footage on to newsreel companies.[33] German cinema audiences were treated to a government-sponsored *Helgoland-Film*, which showed the destruction of the fortress in full detail, further fanning the resentment against the Allies.[34] British newspapers and magazines, in the meantime, ran a series of triumphant articles. 'Before and after' pictures were particularly popular, showing the long-range guns cut into pieces, the bunkers blown apart, the

naval harbour sealed with debris and wrecks.[35] There was nothing dignified, British visitors observed, in the way in which the Germans were
demolishing the erstwhile symbol of their global ambitions. This was 'a
country that, brutal in war, has totally failed to preserve its dignity in
defeat'.[36] More than a thousand German workers were engaged in dis-
mantling the fortifications. They were portrayed as drab and humiliated,
working sullenly under the supervision of British officers, inclined 'neither to forget nor forgive'. 'Prussianism Ended' and 'Finis Germaniae'
were recurrent headlines. In making the most of the image of defeat, the
London press celebrated the Heligolanders as the liberated victims of
German militarism. Proud and dignified, they openly showed their
'hatred for Prussianism and sympathy with England'.[37] 'If the right of
self-determination were justly applied', observed a special correspondent, 'the Union Jack would float in the breeze' over the island once
again.[38]

The Lloyd George government, however, had little appetite for encouraging self-determination amongst former colonial subjects. As in 1890 a
plebiscite was out of the question. Once reannexation had been ruled out,
Whitehall was disinclined to reopen the question—to the great dismay of
those islanders who wanted to return to Britain. Led by August Kuchlenz
and Franz Schensky, they wrote to Lloyd George in January 1919: 'The
inhabitants of Heligoland continually remember the glorious times which
they were able to enjoy under the British flag'. The islanders 'were all
entirely of the opinion that we should now return again to our old flag'. It
had been an injustice when 'the British government exchanged us without
our approval' in 1890. Since it had not 'obtained the view of its faithful subjects' then, it should do so now.[39]

The same demand was at the heart of a petition which a group of
islanders handed to officers of HMS *Westcott* in June 1919—an incident
which underlined just how much the Heligolanders continued to be
caught up between Britain and Germany. 'We anchored off Heligoland
in the late evening', wrote Captain Brian de Courcy Ireland, the *Westcott's*
navigating officer, in his diary. 'Shortly after dark...we heard one of the
sentries challenge. We all went on deck'.[40] A boat of Heligolanders had
made it over to the destroyer. Led by Jasper Nickels, long suspected by
the German authorities of being a British agent, they were eager to demonstrate their pro-British sentiment. Nickels declared that he had served
in the Royal Navy before the war:

'I wish I could prove my service', he said, but if any proof were required it was forthcoming, for suddenly he remarked to the captain 'I've served with you Sir' and the captain replied 'You were M[aster] A[t] A[rms] in the *Glory* in 1907'... The old man was so affected that it was some minutes before he could go on.

Nickels handed over a petition which he 'begged us to forward' to the government.[41] Its gist was that the islanders had been treated exceedingly badly by the Germans and were keen to be taken back by the British.

There were several more occasions on which Heligolanders made similar appeals, but they all fell on deaf ears. In September 1919 Franz Schenksy, like Nickels on the black list of pro-British islanders before the war, wrote to a friend in Britain: 'We all confidently believed that Great Britain would take back our Island. We are very disappointed that this is not the case'.[42] There were good reasons why the islanders' committee (initially the '62er Commission', then the '25er Commission', both led by Kuchlenz) continued its lobbying nonetheless. The Heligolanders rightly sensed that by approaching London they could exert pressure on Berlin. As on other past occasions when their island had been in a power vacuum between the two nations, they engaged in their own Anglo-German diplomacy now, forcing the Weimar government to make unprecedented concessions.

Two key questions were in dispute. The first concerned German electoral law. All over Germany a new six-month residence franchise had come into practice in April 1919. For Heligoland this meant that a large part of the workers engaged in the demolition works (most of them from the mainland) would be allowed to vote. Local elections had been called for November 1919 and if the majority of workers were to opt for the SPD or other national parties, the socio-political hierarchy on the island, traditionally dominated by a few influential families, would be overthrown. Yet the islanders' wish for an exemption from the new electoral law stood in conflict with the Weimar constitution, which prescribed equal franchise rules for all constituencies.

The second question concerned the privileges which the islanders had enjoyed before the war. The Anglo-German treaty regulating the cession had stipulated that pre-existing laws and customs—above all the comprehensive absence of taxation—would be upheld 'as far as possible' by the German government.[43] But the Weimar government was decidedly sceptical that the treaty was still valid. The legal advice sought by Berlin, some of it made public, suggested that the Versailles Treaty had superseded the

Anglo–German agreement of 1890. The government had consequently begun to incorporate the island into its tax regime. The islanders commissioned a counter-exposé from Hans Helfritz, a law professor at Breslau University. Helfritz, who was an MP for the far-right German National People's Party (DNVP), promptly concluded that their claim for continued tax exemption and other privileges was valid.[44]

The islanders' political manoeuvres came at a time when questions concerning Germany's borders were at the centre of public debate. Few foreign policy issues dominated Weimar politics more than the loss of territory and the re-drawing of Germany's boundaries, evoked in metaphors such as the 'mutilated' or 'denuded' nation.[45] Both in domestic and international politics it was crucial for Berlin to show that it was able to exert control over its border regions. The government was especially concerned about particularist movements which could give the Allies justification to make further territorial demands. Some in the Weimar cabinet thought the Heligolanders' lobbying amounted to high treason, but the chancellor and the foreign secretary were adamant that the islanders had to be pacified, lest the British (who were going to have officers on the island for the next few years) use them as a pretext for their own agenda.[46] In late October 1919 the imperial cabinet agreed to postpone local elections on the island 'because of the fear of losing Heligoland'.[47]

This did little to quell the islanders' pro-British activities. By December 1919 the German Central Office for Domestic Propaganda warned the imperial chancellor that a 'separatist movement' existed in the island.[48] Talks between the Prussian authorities and the islanders continued through the first half of 1920, without any success. In early July 1920 Constantin Fehrenbach, the imperial chancellor, explained to his cabinet that the Heligolanders were 'considering separating themselves from the *Reich* and seeking annexation by Britain'.[49] The government now sent another delegation to the island, which came back suggesting a change of the electoral law towards a five years' residence franchise. This could only be achieved through an exemption from the imperial constitution. Within weeks the government introduced a constitutional amendment bill in the Reichstag.[50] Only the Independent Social Democrats (USPD) voted against it. There was no doubt for them, declared MP Alfred Henke in the Reichstag on 2 August 1920, that the demands of the islanders were 'directed against the interests of the workers'. The Heligolanders had 'without exception become propertied people' and the present law was designed to cement their privileged position on the island.[51] Hermann Müller, who had stepped down as imperial chancellor in June and was now the parliamentary leader of the Social Democrats (SPD), made clear that his party found it similarly difficult to vote for the law. Yet 'for international reasons' they were prepared to support the government.[52] This secured the necessary two-thirds majority.

The government had rushed an unprecedented change to the German constitution through the Reichstag, allowing the Heligoland council to exclude anyone from local elections who had not been resident on the island for a minimum of five years. (This led to the victory of the party of the traditional Heligolanders when elections were eventually held.)[53] But if Berlin had thought the exemption, unique in Germany, would pacify the islanders it was mistaken. There remained the taxes which the islanders were disinclined to pay. Back in January 1919 the German treasury minister had been adamant that the financial concessions made so far were 'the utmost that can be granted to the Heligolanders'.[54] In July 1920 the Weimar cabinet had agreed that no tax exemptions would be made.[55] So the islanders' committee continued with its separatist diplomacy. In early October 1920 a delegation went to the British ambassador in Berlin to urge London to consider annexing the island. Two weeks later a group of islanders conveyed yet another open letter to Downing Street and gave it to the London press, under the headline 'Appeal to the British Nation'. In it they asked 'for help in preservation of the rights accorded to us under the Anglo-German agreement of 1890':

> These rights have now been practically all abolished by the German authorities. The Prussian Government asserts that by international law all treaties between belligerents were terminated by the late war. The agreement has therefore become a scrap of paper and the rights, till then preserved to us by British signature, are declared to have passed.[56]

The well-crafted text invited British readers to identify with the Heligolanders as victims of German aggression. Just as the Germans had disregarded Belgian neutrality as a 'scrap of paper' in August 1914, they were now disregarding the islanders' rights.[57] Both had been safeguarded by the British. London was all the more obliged to help, the appeal continued, since it had turned a blind eye to the islanders' interests in 1890:

> We were transferred from Great Britain to Germany by a transaction to which we were not party and to which our consent was never asked. We would have preferred to remain under the British flag exercising our liberties under British justice. We would prefer it today.[58]

The appeal, widely published, caused a public debate in Britain. Did the British not have a historic responsibility to help the islanders, who had been wronged by the Germans ever since Salisbury had abandoned them? The government under Lloyd George did not think so. There was little it could do, since Britain had no legal claim after Versailles.[59]

But while the Foreign Office was at pains not to encourage the islanders any further, the British press was not interested in diplomatic niceties. In what was effectively a continuation of the 'press wars' from before 1914, British newspapers mobilized well-worn stereotypes and traded insults over the 'Heligoland question'.[60] Former British subjects had first been ruthlessly Germanized, now they were robbed of their freedom. This was what would have happened to the British had they lost the war. It was a tragic mistake that, despite Germany's defeat, the enclave in the North Sea had not been returned to Britain. Heligoland might be German in legal terms, but the islanders were British in their longing for freedom and justice. 'Is it right that the Heligolanders should suffer because the Germans lost the war which they forced upon the world?', asked Lord Sydenham in *The Times*.[61]

On the island itself the lines were drawn between victorious Britons and humiliated Germans, with the Heligolanders in between. The Prussian officials were under strict instruction to minimize all contact with the British. Any hint of fraternization had to be avoided. Even at Christmas no greetings were to be exchanged and no social functions to be shared between the two sides.[62] The islanders, in contrast, cultivated numerous contacts with the British officers. Cunningham, the admiral supervising the demolition, thought that they were 'very friendly'.[63] A Fleet Street reporter wrote:

> One is immediately struck by the frank and friendly attitude of the islanders, so different from the general attitude on the mainland. The Prussian weed cannot be said to have flourished in Heligoland... Hatred for Prussianism and sympathy with England show themselves in several ways—in the pleasure at being able to speak English, in the number of English newspapers procurable, and in the English greetings exchanged by the natives amongst each other.[64]

With the demolition works in full swing and British officers in charge of scores of German workers, it was easy to forget that the island was not in fact occupied by Britain. The Heligolanders became increasingly confident. They sang the British national anthem in public, spoke English in front of German officials, and openly refused to fly German flags.[65] In November 1920 a group of them presented an elaborate gift to a departing

British officer, explicitly thanking him and expressing the hope that he would 'always remember his time here'. The German press was aghast. It was as if the islanders had thanked the British for publicly humiliating Germany. The *Hamburger Nachrichten*, which had broken the story, thundered:

> As everyone knows Germany has been forced through the Versailles *Diktat* to dismantle its fortress in the North Sea. Thousands of workers, commanded by the marauding Allies [*Raubstaaten*], are engaged in its destruction…British naval officers are guarding German workers and are squandering vast sums of German money, which impoverished Germany has to pay them. For the time being we can do nothing against the destruction of the fortifications in Heligoland. Nor can we do much against the British minions who stand over the German worker. But one should expect that all those who have to collaborate in this work of destruction do so with disgust and abhorrence for our enemies.

It was therefore all the more shocking to learn that the 'British minions' had been treated with demonstrative courtesy on the island.[66] None of the newspapers surveyed at the Auswärtiges Amt, ranging from Socialist to arch-conservative, showed any understanding for the islanders. It was an unprecedented act of 'self-humiliation' and 'high treason'. No words could adequately describe the 'disgraceful boot licking', 'disgusting grovelling', and 'self-defilement' committed by the islanders.[67] The rage caused by the incident indicated the depth of German resentment against the Allies and the Versailles Treaty. It was additionally fanned by the London press, clearly relishing an opportunity to mobilize wartime stereotypes. The agitation reached such levels that the control commission worked out a plan for the occupation of the island by British forces, should the Germans turn against the islanders.[68]

The Berlin government, acutely aware of the negative international headlines, tried to influence the Heligolanders with an extended propaganda effort. Brochures, posters, and advertisements urged them to seek their future in Germany: they ought to abandon all false hope for British help.[69] But the campaign had little effect on the islanders, who had clearly judged the situation well. 'From the very beginning the Heligolanders have been keen to enlist Germany's enemies for their cause', concluded a crisis meeting at the German Foreign Office.[70] Given Weimar Germany's weak internal and external position, it was essential that the islanders be pacified and international attention be diverted. Otherwise similar issues might erupt in other border regions under Allied control or supervision. 'We are on the shortest route to having a "Heligoland Question" on our hands', wrote Carl von Schubert, the head of the Anglo-American department at the Auswärtiges Amt, in a memorandum that was circulated amongst the members of the cabinet:

> The dangers are clear. Perhaps we do not need to worry too much that Britain will try to repossess the island. But it would be particularly unpleasant to see an otherwise non-existent 'Heligoland Question' feed the claim that Germany does not understand how to govern people so different from themselves, as it has been alleged with regard to Poland and Alsace-Lorraine. How much it is in our interest to deny our enemies all such excuses is evident when we consider Upper Silesia, the Saar, German Austria, the former German protectorates etc.[71]

It was therefore 'desirable to accommodate the Heligolanders as far as possible, even if this is made difficult by their stubbornness and the widely held outrage in Germany that they went to our former enemies in search of support'.[72] 'The aim', Schubert added in another assessment, had to be to deny 'the Entente any excuse to get involved'.[73]

The chancellor and the foreign secretary agreed. Sweeping aside the objections of the Prussian minister of the interior, the cabinet signed off on far-reaching financial concessions. In March 1921 the Treasury advised the regional tax office to stop raising income tax from the islanders. All forms of direct taxation were also to be discontinued, including sales tax and stamp duty.[74] The decision to include the island in the German customs area was reversed too, effectively making Heligoland a duty-free zone. The exemptions were confirmed and extended in the following months.[75] In December 1921 all imperial taxes owing, including those on property and capital gains, were annulled.[76] As the chancellor explained to the treasurer this was 'for political reasons urgently necessary', in order that the Heligoland issue 'quietens down'. 'It would be extremely unfortunate if movements in the West that are detrimental to the unity of the Reich gained strength'.[77]

There was no precedent, the Weimar government concluded, for the financial and political concessions made to the Heligolanders. No other place in Germany had been granted 'even remotely similar' privileges.[78] All this confirmed the authorities in their long-held conviction that the Heligolanders had to be distrusted: these were *Halb-Engländer* who had only their own interests in mind. Since the mid-nineteenth century German officials had again and again attested that the islanders lacked national sentiment and were inherently disloyal to any larger state authority. This tendency was now reaching new heights. 'The mental state of the Heligolanders is boundlessly stubborn. Even the highest financial concessions will not satisfy them', noted a memorandum of the Prussian Ministry of the Interior in November 1920.[79] 'Their character is inflexible and tends towards dissent', wrote the chief negotiator sent to the island.[80] The islanders, declared Otto Braun, the Prussian minister president, with palpable frustration, 'are filled with the deepest distrust towards the imperial and state administration'.[81]

It was misleading to explain the Heligolanders' position, which caused so much outrage in Germany, as inherently pro-British. The islanders had insisted on their 'ancient rights' on every previous occasion when a transition from one rule to another had seemed imminent. They had used much the same tactic against the British, to whom they were now appealing as their historical guardians. Notably in the 1860s, when London had tried to introduce taxation in the colony, the Heligolanders had approached the Prussians for help against the 'despotic British'.[82] But rather than engage with the political tradition of the islanders, explained by their position at the edge of the Continent, the German press portrayed them as pawns in London's game. The British followed 'imperialist intentions', wrote the *Vossische Zeitung*.[83] It was time that they accepted that 'geographically and in national sentiment Heligoland belongs to Germany', thundered the *Hamburgischer Korrespondent*. Heligoland was 'the German rock in the German Sea'; every attempt to change this would amount to an 'act of violence and injustice'.[84] The denials issued by London were explained as part of the 'typically two-faced character' of the British.[85] Practically all newspapers, concluded the *Deutsche Allgemeine Zeitung* in August 1921, were agreed that 'London's scheming' over Heligoland had to be opposed. What the demolition of the island fortress expressed was the 'British will to exterminate Germany [*Vernichtungswille*]'. London was wilfully humiliating Germany by destroying its 'cultural monument' in the North Sea.[86]

Both in Britain and Germany the island thus continued to function as a metaphor of Anglo-German difference, a rhetorical tool that was ideally suited to mobilize well-established stereotypes. While the German press relished the opportunity to paint Britain as the aggressor, the newspapers in London portrayed the islanders as victims of 'Germanization'. The German Embassy in London noted in August 1921 that 'the Heligoland question is being followed here continuously in the press'.[87] Alarmed by the intensity

of the press coverage, the Berlin government continued to monitor the
'Heligoland question' closely. It was 'common knowledge', wrote the Office
for Domestic Propaganda in January 1923, 'that Heligoland belongs to the
very critical points' amongst those areas with particularist movements:

> It has to be assumed that the loosening of the overall structure of the Reich, as
> it is taking place on the Rhine and in Bavaria, will give those in Heligoland
> who want to get away from Germany additional material.

The authorities should therefore do everything in their power to work
against this tendency.[88] 'It is essential that the island be re-conquered morally', wrote the *Hamburger Echo*, a newspaper close to the SPD.[89]

Making Heligoland German was back on the agenda. Just as in the 1890s,
when the Kaiser's officials had employed much the same strategy, the Weimar
government was keen to foster links between Germany and the island. Thus
the 'Day of the Constitution', a public ritual invented to celebrate the new
republic, was staged on the island as an occasion to show solidarity with the
Fatherland.[90] Leading politicians made a point of invoking the Heligolanders'
Germanness. Chancellor Wilhelm Cuno expressly thanked them for their
'loyalty to the Reich and the Prussian state' in August 1923.[91] The Reich
Office for Domestic Propaganda did what it could to create pro-German
sentiment amongst the islanders.[92] The Foreign Office distributed photographs of the island to schools and universities as well as embassies and con-
sulates, advertising the island as a German 'natural monument'. Heligoland
was thus incorporated into the canon of 'German landscapes': just like the
Alps and the Rhine, it was a key example of 'nature in Germany'.[93]

In late May 1922 Sir Edward Charlton, the head of the Inter-Allied
Commission of Control, came to inspect the former naval base with a
group of engineers. 'They have made wonderful progress', he noted.[94] For
two and a half years scores of labourers had been demolishing the fortifications, using hundreds of tons of explosives. On 6 June Charlton confirmed
to the Allied governments that the demilitarization had been accomplished.
Germany's erstwhile naval fortress was 'a dreary waste' now, 'resembling a
ruined city, and is rapidly sinking into the Harbour'.[95]

With the demolition works finished, Heligoland could be rebuilt as a
holiday destination. Three weeks after the last British officers had left the island,
the HAPAG shipping line resumed a regular steamship service to the island.[96]
Within a year the tourist industry was back in full swing. By the summer of

1923 there were, according to tourist guides, 84 spa doctors on the island, looking after 1,800 resident patients.[97] Rising numbers of day trippers arrived daily, many of them on 'combined tickets', others as part of the notorious *Helgolandfahrten*, excursions organized by local clubs and societies throughout northern Germany.[98] Just as before the war, the participants in these trips took full advantage of the cheap, duty-free alcohol available on the island.

Heligoland's rebirth as a tourist destination mirrored the recovery of the Weimar economy in the mid-1920s, a period later depicted as 'golden'. Politically associated above all with Gustav Stresemann (chancellor in 1923 and foreign secretary from 1923 to 1929), this was a time of relative stability. Germany became part of the League of Nations. Radical parties both on the left and the right lost support. A majority in the Reichstag supported the new republic and Stresemann's course of international cooperation. Living standards rose, even if unemployment remained high. For Heligoland, in any case, the label 'golden' was apt. Already by 1924 the island had reached pre-war visitor numbers.[99] Guidebooks noted approvingly that most facilities had reopened. Even the 'English shops' had returned, offering whisky, cigarettes, jams, raincoats, scarves, and blankets made in Britain.[100]

One of the many pre-war regulars who came back in the mid-1920s was Aby Warburg, the Hamburg art historian, still suffering from hay fever. HAPAG, the shipping line, had to be reminded to give him the best cabin on board the Heligoland steamer and to disembark him ahead of other passengers.[101] But otherwise everything was back to the agreeable pre-war setup for Warburg, now in his fifth decade of Heligoland visits.[102] The outpost, associated with his youth and with the better health that accompanied it, continued to be a refuge for him.[103] He encouraged practically everyone in his extended family to spend time on the island. Many of them came, staying like him mostly in the hotel Empress of India.[104] He insisted that Gertrud Bing, his congenial assistant and later the director of the London Warburg Institute, take a holiday on the island, all expenses paid.[105] He even volunteered to pay for employees of the family's banking firm to recuperate on the island.[106] Warburg, who described himself as 'one of the oldest and best of Heligoland's friends', continued to visit at least once a year until his death in October 1929.[107]

Amongst the thousands of hay fever patients who flocked, like Aby Warburg, to Heligoland during the Weimar years was Werner Heisenberg, the physicist.[108] In June 1925 he arrived for what was to be a momentous visit. Apparently Niels Bohr, Heisenberg's mentor, had told him that infinity

Helgoland. Unterland

Zur Erinnerung 16, - 22. Sept, 1929.

Figure 7.2 'In memory, 16 to 22 Sept. 1929'. Postcard from Aby Warburg's last visit to Heligoland with annotation by Gertrud Bing, who accompanied him on the trip.

could be grasped only by those 'who look across the sea'.[109] Heisenberg took Bohr's advice to heart—or at least that is what he wanted his readers to believe when he wrote about the discovery of quantum mechanics years later. In keeping with the romantic tradition that had canonized the image of the solitary genius, Heisenberg styled his breakthrough in Heligoland as explained by the experience of nature. It was as if the great eureka moment of his career could only take place in isolation from others and through exposure to the elements:

> It was almost three o'clock in the morning before the final result of my computations lay before me. The energy principle had held for all the terms, and I could no longer doubt the mathematical consistency and coherence of the kind of quantum mechanics to which my calculations pointed. At first I was deeply alarmed. I had the feeling that, through the surface of atomic phenomena, I was looking at a strangely beautiful interior and felt almost giddy at the thought that I now had to probe this wealth of mathematical structures [that] nature had so generously spread out before me. I was far too excited to sleep, and so, as a new day dawned, I made for the southern tip of the island, where I had been longing to climb a rock jutting out into the sea. I now did so without too much trouble, and waited for the sun to rise.[110]

Thus, if this account is to be taken at face value, Heisenberg came to write his 'Quantum Theoretical Re-interpretation of Kinematic and Mechanical Relations', the first in a series of foundational contributions to modern physics for which he was awarded the Nobel Prize in 1932.[111] It is safe to assume that Heisenberg's epiphany had less to do with the mythical qualities of Heligoland than with his intelligence, training, and the inspiration he received from others. But the idea of the scientist discovering the laws of the universe through the experience of nature proved too attractive not to be perpetuated, and Heisenberg in Heligoland became a staple ingredient in the story of the quantum revolution.[112]

In July 1925, a few weeks after Heisenberg, a young Leni Riefenstahl arrived on the island. She complained about the 'scorching heat', but was determined to make the most of her stay.[113] While booked to give dance performances for the spa guests, she had mostly come for the filming of Arnold Fanck's *Holy Mountain*. Weimar's budding film industry had first taken note of Heligoland as a location when F. W. Murnau had shot his avant-garde *Nosferatu* (1922) on the island. Now Fanck was to use the imposing cliffs of this 'natural monument' as a backdrop for his Alpine epic. *Holy Mountain* was a melodrama about two mountaineers and their desire for the same woman, Diotima, played by Riefenstahl in her first screen appearance. When the film came out in late 1926 Siegfried Kracauer, one of Weimar's leading critics, panned its 'sun-drenched stupidity' in the *Frankfurter Zeitung*.[114] Later, after the rise and fall of Hitler, he saw *Holy Mountain* as 'rooted in a mentality kindred to [the] Nazi spirit'. The film's 'idolatry of glaciers and rocks', he thought, 'was symptomatic of an antirationalism on which the Nazis could capitalize'.[115] The critic Susan Sontag argued along the same lines a generation later in her landmark essay on 'Fascinating Fascism'. *Holy Mountain*, she wrote, was the first of 'Fanck's pop-Wagnerian vehicles for Riefenstahl'. While these 'were no doubt thought of as apolitical when they were made', they appeared in hindsight as 'an anthology of proto-Nazi sentiments'.[116] It is easy to see why the Nazis would have liked *Holy Mountain* and its monumental imagery. But epic films about nature and human willpower were not a Nazi monopoly. The 'mountain cult', which Kracauer saw as so dangerously close to the Hitler cult, was an international phenomenon.[117] Fanck's film was just as popular with audiences in Britain, France, and the United States as it was in Germany.

As monumental and melodramatic as *Holy Mountain* was, the filming on Heligoland had a strong comical side. For the opening scene Fanck was determined to have Riefenstahl perform a 'dance to the sea' to Beethoven's fifth symphony in front of the Heligoland cliffs. This was meant to express Diotima's 'stormy soul' and love for the sea. In order to provide the right musical inspiration Fanck had a violinist lowered from the cliff tops of the *Oberland*. While the musician stood precariously on a ledge above the sea and played Beethoven, Riefenstahl could not hear a note. Dancing her own choreography without music, she was repeatedly knocked over by the crashing waves.[118] In the film Fanck interspersed her ecstatic dance with dramatic footage of the sea and the Heligoland cliffs. Hitler told Riefenstahl later that her performance was the 'most beautiful thing I have ever seen in a film'.[119] *Holy Mountain* launched her career as an actress and film maker— Riefenstahl went on to shoot some of Hitler's most successful propaganda films.[120]

The renaissance of Heligoland in the Weimar years seemed complete when, in October 1925, a group of businessmen, politicians, and aristocrats founded the *Club von Helgoland*, a gentlemen's club.[121] Its members, some of whom owned property on the island, met regularly in Berlin and on Heligoland itself. Amongst them were Wilhelm Cuno, general director of the HAPAG shipping line and German chancellor from 1922 to 1923; Albert Südekum, a veteran SPD politician who had a reputation as a champagne socialist (hence Lenin's derogatory term 'Südekumism'); Ernst Wallach, the

Figure 7.3 The Sass brothers on Heligoland, *c.*1928.

director of the Berlin banking house Goldschmidt & Rothschild; and Hans
Albers, the Hamburg actor who was to become one of Germany's most
popular film stars. What brought them together was the consensus that
Heligoland was the place to see and be seen in.

If the *Club von Helgoland* made the island fashionable again amongst the
privileged classes, it was the Sass brothers who gave it currency in the under-
world. Franz and Erich Sass were Berlin's most famous professional criminals, equally adept at cracking safes as at playing the legal system. The police
suspected them of being behind a string of spectacular break-ins, but had to
let them go repeatedly due to lack of evidence. The brothers clearly relished
their notoriety, giving press conferences and showily distributing money
amongst the poor. The holidays in Heligoland which they enjoyed in
between their criminal hauls were part of this ostentatious lifestyle. Eager to
show off their affluence, they had their picture taken in full suits on deck
chairs at the beach.[122]

In August 1926 Heligoland celebrated its centenary as a spa town. Prussia
and Hamburg sent high-ranking delegations. The Weimar government was
to be represented by foreign secretary Gustav Stresemann.[123] To mark the
occasion, *Deutsche Luft Hansa* (later *Lufthansa*), the budding national airline,
put on its first flight to the island.[124] The spa management published the
inevitable souvenir picture book, celebrating one hundred years of island
tourism. It betrayed a sense of prosperous normality. The last season had
brought record visitor numbers. After the cataclysm of the war and the
humiliation at the hands of the Allies, the island outpost was on an even
keel again. 'Things have quietened down in Heligoland', the authorities
announced. 'The small island is again what it was before. It has withstood
these testing times and is looking towards a new, hopeful future'.[125]

8

Hitler's Island

On 17 July 1928 four tourists set off from Hamburg for a much anticipated trip to the 'German island': the Nazi party leader, Adolf Hitler,
his half-sister Angela Raubal, her 20-year-old daughter Angela 'Geli' Maria,
all of whom had arrived from Munich; and Joseph Goebbels, who had
joined them from Berlin, where he had just taken up his Reichstag seat as
one of twelve Nazi members elected to parliament. There was little, initially,
that distinguished their trip from the experience of the hundreds of thousands of other travellers who went to Heligoland in the late 1920s: the mon-
otonous journey down the River Elbe, the fog, the sudden, imposing sight
of Heligoland's cliffs. Upon arrival Hitler, Goebbels, and the Raubals went
on a guided tour around the island. Before visiting the aquarium (where
Goebbels was to witness some agreeably predatory behaviour amongst the
fish: 'Such is nature! It shows no mercy!'), they took a stroll on the island's
Oberland. It was at this point that it became obvious that this was more than
a mere private holiday: the group led by Hitler was on a pilgrimage to
Germany's vulnerable northern border. As they walked along the cliff tops
and enjoyed the sweeping views, Goebbels noted: 'Here stood the artillery
once. Over there lies England'.[1] It seemed to him a poignant reminder of
how Germany's fate had changed. Once the island had been a symbol of the
Reich's claim to world power. Now it was a metaphor for the Fatherland's
shameful humiliation by the Allies: 'Down below the broken fortifications.
That is Germany'.[2]

Hitler and Goebbels were not the first to discover Heligoland as a symbol
of the Reich's downfall. Numerous right-wing groups, ranging from paramilitary leagues to student associations, appreciated the island as a site where
they could act out their resentment against the Treaty of Versailles. Only a
few weeks before Hitler's and Goebbels's trip the *Stahlhelm*, Weimar's popular
right-wing veterans' league, had staged a rally on Heligoland. More than

6,000 of its members had made the five-hour trip from Hamburg with their deputy leader Theodor Duesterberg. After marching through the town, Duesterberg and his comrades laid a wreath of oak leaves at the memorial for the poet Hoffmann von Fallersleben. The rally culminated in a joint singing of the *Deutschlandlied*. Three generations earlier its author, Fallersleben, had dreamt of a better German future. Now the veterans were calling out for national renewal. Heligoland, the 'broken rock' in the North Sea, signified 'broken German might', wrote the *Stahlhelm*'s newspaper. The island's ruins 'reminded us of the past, showed us the vulnerability of the present and warned us for the future'. This was 'a demolished German fortress, an annihilated German outpost', turned into 'neutralized territory'. 'The chains of the shameful Treaty of Versailles: Heligoland showed them to us in immediate and devastating proximity'. The island urged them to right this wrong—in future the Germans would have 'to live as a free people, free from internal and external servitude'.[3]

Such trips to Germany's 'bleeding borders' were a popular phenomenon in Weimar Germany.[4] Their underlying aim was twofold: to agitate against the Treaty of Versailles and to mobilize support for right-wing organizations that were keen to undermine the new democratic order. Heligoland was an ideal destination: it evoked past imperial dreams as much as the present trauma of defeat. For decades it had been cultivated as the nation's bulwark in the North Sea. Now it symbolized victimhood and vulnerability. Importantly, its ruins represented not only defeat, but also territorial loss, both at home and abroad. Northern Schleswig, linked to the island through a long history of German–Danish conflict, came under Danish rule in March 1920 after a plebiscite granted at Versailles. This was especially galling for German nationalists as the province had been acquired in 1864 during the 'wars of unification': it stood for Bismarck's historic achievements, now undone by the Allies.

But Heligoland was also a poignant reminder of the overseas empire which Germany had lost in 1919. For years the *Kolonialverein*, Germany's main colonial lobby group, tried to have a statue of Carl Peters, the infamous colonialist, erected on the cliff tops of the island, symbolically gesturing over the sea towards Africa. The monument, more than six metres tall, had originally graced the German settlement in Dar es Salaam, where it had survived the First World War mothballed in a warehouse, only to be 'repatriated' in the 1920s. Now the colonial lobby wanted it to stand on top of the Heligoland cliffs, advertising Germany's claim to a future empire in which the lost colonies would be regained. The Weimar government intervened, but the monument was eventually set up in the *Unterland* on the promenade, where it was inaugurated with much fanfare in June 1931.[5]

The way in which German revanchist fantasies found a home in the ruins of Heligoland mirrored Weimar's politics of defeat more generally. There is little doubt that most Germans shared a profound feeling of injustice over the Versailles Treaty, but it is questionable whether they had one 'collective trauma' in common.[6] Rather, defeat resembled a process in which personal experiences, political allegiances, and public discourse intersected.[7] Most Germans had experienced the war in different and often contradictory ways. They reacted to the armistice and the peace treaty in a similarly varied fashion. In the political arena, the meanings of 'defeat' were heavily contested between parties, veterans' leagues, and paramilitary groups. The radical right's main interest in this struggle was to fan a sense of victimhood and instrumentalize it as a weapon against the Weimar Republic.

Heligoland was particularly well suited for this purpose. The naval fortress had remained 'undefeated' in November 1918: the Royal Navy had never dared to attack it. Just like the fleet and the army, it could be depicted as a victim of the home front, 'stabbed in the back' by mutinying sailors and left-wing civilians.[8] As a former icon of the Kaiserreich's naval aspirations, Heligoland not only mobilized ideas of humiliation and revenge, it also directed them against Britain. While Jews and Communists were marked as internal traitors, the British could be styled as external ones here. It was their 'betrayal' of 1914, having entered the war on the side of France and Russia, that had led to Germany's defeat. Heligoland, left 'unprotected' and 'vulnerable' by the demolition of the fortress, was a rare site at which this sense of injustice and humiliation could be acted out against the British.

Heligoland was thus well established as a symbol of revanchism when Hitler rose to power. In July 1932 the NSDAP won a landslide election victory, making it the strongest party in the Reichstag. Its success owed much to the dramatic economic crisis that engulfed Germany at the time. But it also reflected the weakness of the short-lived governments of the Weimar Republic in the early 1930s, ruling without the backing of a parliamentary majority. In January 1933 Hitler was appointed as chancellor. The Nazis now swept aside what was left of the republic, ruthlessly terrorizing their opponents and rallying their supporters. By August 1934 they had established a dictatorship that was in near-total control of Germany, led by Hitler as *Führer* and Reich chancellor.[9]

Hitler's rise and the Nazi consolidation of power followed similar patterns all over Germany, but there were significant local and regional differences.[10] As elsewhere in the Reich, the Nazis in Heligoland were initially politically isolated. The local NSDAP branch was only founded in 1928. When its activists started to display the Nazi flag prominently an alliance of local organizations, led by the tourist board, protested vehemently. In a letter to the Prussian authorities they wrote that the swastika should be forbidden during the tourist season.[11] This was economic opportunism rather than political opposition: the signatories were mostly worried about the impression the swastika would leave on well-heeled guests. Two months later 42.7 per cent of the island's electorate voted for the Nazi party in the Reichstag elections of July 1932. This was considerably above the national average of 37.3 per cent. The Heligolanders were clearly not 'immune' to the Nazis, as some of them were to argue after the war.[12] In March 1933 the NSDAP became the largest party in the island's council, though holding only a third of the seats. A number of local politicians were adamant that they represented the Heligolanders' interests better than Hitler's party. Their ideological background, though, was close to that of the Nazis, as their mouthpiece, the *Heimat-Bund*, readily acknowledged.[13] But the Nazi councillors were not interested in cooperating with what they saw as narrow-minded local traditionalists. Backed by SA troops, they ousted the leader of the council, Erwin Lange, and replaced him with a Nazi official from the mainland. The leader of the local NSDAP branch, Karl Meunier, became his deputy and soon thereafter his successor.

The Gestapo now targeted all islanders who were known to have opposed the rise of the Nazis: Communists and Social Democrats, but also 'separatists' like August Kuchlenz and Erich Friedrichs, who had openly appealed to the British to reannex Heligoland in the 1920s. Both were arrested and deported to a concentration camp. The Gestapo released them after they had signed documents in which they renounced all political activity. When Julius Blatzkowski, one of the more prominent Communists on the island, returned from his internment, Meunier, the Nazi party leader, told him that he would 'treat him sharply' if he relapsed.[14] This was part of the systematic intimidation that characterized the Nazi consolidation of power in the months after Hitler's rise to power. As Meunier explained in January 1934, this was a phase during which the party had to 'crack down hard' (*hart durchgreifen*) in order to achieve 'political unity'.[15]

The other key aim of Meunier's reign was to strengthen the link between
Heligoland and the Reich. This link, he claimed, had been destroyed by
Marxists and Jews during the Weimar years. Now the island would become
again what it had been in the past: an Aryan outpost, symbolizing the *Volk's*
origins, its rootedness and resilience. Seemingly endless public rituals
emphasized the unity between party, people, and the 'Germanic island'.[16]
Apart from Heligoland's allegedly pure racial character, the Nazis trumpeted
the fact that one of their earliest heroes had come from the island: Johann
'Hans' Rickmers, one of the 'martyrs' who had been shot during Hitler's
failed Munich putsch in November 1923. A number of places on the island
were named after him, as if to physically demonstrate the island's incorpor-
ation into the Nazi version of Germany's past.[17]

British visitors noted the ubiquitous Nazification with a combination of
bemusement and worry. Ronald Lockley, a Welsh zoologist who worked at
the Heligoland ornithological station, wrote in his diary in October 1936:

> Yesterday there had been a demonstration by some political organization—I
> did not know what—at which all young men had to attend. And almost every
> day a new 'thought' appears on the notice-boards on the staircase joining
> Upper and Lower Towns. I notice that 'Bolshevismus' and 'Return our
> Colonies' seem to be the two most burning themes. All this, and the 'Fly your
> Swastika' and other patriotic law and etiquette, combined with the swarms of
> people in the streets, is suggestive of the law, order, and communism of the
> ant-heap—warriors and workers complete.

In the cinema he noted more propaganda: 'road-making scenes, marching,
counter-marching, goose-stepping, and fierce speeches'.[18] Yet none of this
dented his liking for the iconic island and its 'once-upon-a-time town'. He
still loved Heligoland's 'assured air of old-fashioned charm'.[19]

It was difficult to detect much of that charm in the Nazi broadcasts that
styled the island as the nation's 'holy outpost in the sea'. A prominent
example was the *Stunde der Nation* ('Hour of the Nation'), a house production of the *Reichs-Rundfunk-Gesellschaft*, the German equivalent of the BBC
that was tightly controlled by Goebbels's Ministry of Propaganda. Heligoland
was 'a piece of holy soil' for every German, the programme declared in June
1933. It was impossible to resist its 'stubborn beauty', which reminded the
Germans about the origins of the 'most noble blood of our race'. The island
was 'the monument of the sea' that united the Germans in their unanimous will to restore the Fatherland's greatness. Once this had been the
'strongest fortress in the world'. The shameful Versailles Treaty had destroyed

it. Germany had been 'disarmed and dishonoured'. But now it was being re-born under Hitler. It was to be respected again in the world. Nothing symbolized this 'new Germany' better than Heligoland, where the Germanic race had worshipped its gods in the prehistoric past. Here, at the 'altar of Germany's eternal youth', all Germans came together. The programme closed with a series of obligatory 'Sieg Heils' and the national anthem.[20]

In May 1935 Hitler participated in the maiden voyage of the steamer *Scharnhorst* from Bremerhaven to Heligoland. The trip inaugurated an ambitious programme of state-sponsored tourism, run by the Nazi organization *Kraft durch Freude* (*KdF* or 'Strength Through Joy').[21] Heligoland fitted its aims perfectly. Here was a traditional seaside resort, well established in the canon of 'German natural beauty', laden with the right ideological meanings and close enough to the mainland to allow for large numbers of visitors. Formerly frequented by the wealthy and noble, it could now be paraded as accessible for everyone in the 'racial community'.[22] In the wake of Hitler's visit the first *KdF* steamers arrived, carrying crowds of tourists from all over Germany. They were followed by a steady stream of ships bringing record numbers of day trippers to the island. On-board magazines gave the visitors some background about Heligoland's past, but this remained light on outright propaganda: *KdF* was to offer cheap holidays, sunshine, and entertainment rather than long lectures about the Aryan race.[23] The standard programme involved a guided tour, followed by duty-free shopping and time out on the beach. Here the *KdF* travellers were to relax and enjoy themselves. Back on the mainland Hitler wanted them to 'work, work, work'.[24]

After the Second World War 'Strength through Joy' was blamed for having started the mass tourism that was to be the islanders' scourge (and main source of income) for the second half of the twentieth century. But *KdF* was hardly revolutionary. Day trips for low-budget travellers had started long before the First World War. As early as 1890, commentators had lamented the demise of Heligoland's *noblesse*. In the 1920s the first package tours had started. When visitor numbers had fallen by almost a quarter during the Great Depression the tourist board had introduced further discounts.[25] *KdF* pushed this trend to new extremes, negotiating cheap deals with the locals in return for an increase in visitor numbers. The Nazis thus accelerated the transformation from exclusive to mass tourism that had been notable for some time. A British holiday-maker who visited in the summer of 1936 observed that Heligoland consisted 'for the most part of hotels and lodging houses with shops to supply the needs of a cheap class of visitors'.[26] The *KdF* scheme caused some disgruntlement amongst

wealthy guests, but it did little to put off the middle-class travellers who traditionally dominated Heligoland tourism. In fact, the *KdF* tourists themselves
were rarely from underprivileged backgrounds. Observers noted mostly Nazi
officials, civil servants, and office employees amongst the crowds. As an agent
working for the Social Democratic Party's organization in exile (SOPADE)
wrote, there were plenty of Nazi bigwigs and 'their arrogant ladies' coming to
Heligoland on *KdF* tickets, but rarely a worker.[27]

KdF brought free nation-wide advertising for the 'Germanic Island'. On
its recommendation posters of Heligoland were put up in canteens and
offices, showcasing the island as a source of the nation's physical and psychological strength. The *KdF* office *Schönheit der Arbeit* ('Beauty of Work')
published photographs of employees happily eating their lunch under large
pictures of the sea-girt island.[28] This and the many well-advertised visits by
Nazi luminaries were hardly something Heligoland's tourist board was going
to discourage, busy as it was marketing 'Germany's rock in the sea'.[29] Visitor
numbers went up dramatically. From 1933 to 1934 they rose by almost 70
per cent, reaching record highs.[30] Trips organized by clubs, associations, and
schools increased too.[31] Large numbers of students and academics went to
the 'German Isle' every year with the *Helgolandfahrt* of the University of
Hamburg. In June 1937 so many of them wanted to go that an additional
vessel had to be chartered. All lectures and seminars were cancelled for the
day. Visiting students from Britain, the United States, China, Sweden,
Finland, Hungary, and Yugoslavia were allowed to come along, after being
reminded that photography would not be permitted.[32]

To the Nazis, the rise of Heligoland as a Germanic icon, frequented by party
functionaries and *KdF* crowds, represented the triumph of the German
Volk over the hated Jews. In Nazi parlance Heligoland had been one of the
Judeninseln, the 'Jew islands'.[33] This played on anti-Semitic stereotypes
which had accompanied the rise of the island as a tourist resort in the second
half of the nineteenth century.[34] But while such malicious sniggering had
been a recurrent feature, especially amongst the Kaiserreich's conservative
elite, it had never translated into political agitation, let alone official policy. It
was the Nazis who started to target Jewish holiday-makers in a blatant attempt
to scapegoat them. In the late 1920s, when Hitler was the leader of a fringe
movement with little political success, they had seized on every opportunity
to style Heligoland as a Jewish holiday enclave. Their favourite target was the
Club von Helgoland, the gentlemen's club co-founded by Ernst Wallach.[35]

Wallach, the director of a Berlin banking house, owned a villa on the island. He was also the vice-president of the *Centralverein deutscher Staatsbürger jüdischen Glaubens*, set up before the war to combat anti-Semitism.[36] The Social Democrat Albert Südekum, another prominent member of the club, was on the board of the *Verein zur Abwehr des Antisemtismus*, another association working against anti-Semitic tendencies in Germany.[37]

In targeting the *Club von Helgoland* the Nazis aimed to discredit their political opponents and mobilize their own supporters—at a time when the NSDAP was a marginal party with little electoral success. In 1928 the *Club von Helgoland* volunteered to raise capital to invest in the island's infrastructure. When this caused unease amongst some of the Heligolanders, the Nazis sensed a propaganda opportunity: rich holidaying Jews were scheming to take over the small community of hard-working fishermen in Germany's famous North Sea outpost. 'Heligoland's battle against Jewish big business', was a typical headline in Nazi-controlled newspapers.[38] The liberal press lambasted the campaign for what it was: an obvious attempt to create a scandal.[39] The island's council declared promptly that everyone was welcome on Heligoland; there was no prejudice against Jews.[40] But local Nazi members continued their agitation.[41] In July 1929 the *Centralverein* began to monitor the island. It noted the increasing activity of the local Nazi party, but acknowledged that there was no official policy against Jewish visitors.[42]

Aby Warburg, one of the most long-standing regular island visitors, was sure that the locals were 'impartial', as he stressed in a letter to the *Frankfurter Zeitung*.[43] Yet the 'apolitical character' of Heligoland seemed under threat. There were 'forces at work who want to set up a systematic anti-Semitic movement. So far, they are few and far between and have to count on a measure of resistance from Lange, the mayor'. But it was important to watch the 'deeply pernicious movement' carefully.[44] During his last visit to the island in September 1929 Warburg met with Lange to urge him to combat the anti-Semitic agitation. Should he fail to do so, he wrote to the mayor, it would be seen as 'a repulsive attack on the finest privilege of Heligoland: the conservation of social peace'.[45] Warburg died some weeks later in October 1929. In May 1931 the *Centralverein* warned its members that a number of establishments no longer welcomed Jewish guests.[46] A month later the regional Prussian authorities complained that the island's council had done too little against the 'incitement of hatred against the Jews, which has been driven by irresponsible local elements'.[47] Mayor

Lange promptly announced that Jewish guests were 'as always welcome on our island'.[48]

This remained the official line for another two years, during which the authorities were however unable to stop Nazi members carrying out anti-Semitic agitation.[49] In May 1933, four months after Hitler's appointment as chancellor, the council adopted an excruciatingly awkward resolution according to which 'there was unanimous agreement that a visit to Heligoland can be recommended to Jewish patients (*jüdische Kranke*)'.[50] The *Centralverein* duly passed on the message.[51] Jewish summer residents, amongst them Ernst Wallach, read the signs and sold their properties on the island. When *Der Stürmer*, the rampantly anti-Semitic Nazi newspaper, sent a correspondent to Heligoland in the summer of 1935, he found little to complain about. Occasionally, he wrote, the locals needed a reminder about the Jewish threat, such as 'He who accepts food from the Jew will die of it'. On the whole, however, he thought good progress was being made. The few Jewish visitors who were still arriving were immediately targeted by local activists. It was only a matter of time before Heligoland would be *judenfrei*, 'free of Jews'.[52]

Two months later, on 15 September 1935, the Nuremberg Laws were promulgated, prescribing systematic discrimination against Jews in German public life. 'One should not let them into every seaside resort', Goebbels told a meeting of propaganda officers in Nuremberg. Rather, the Jews of Germany would be given a ghetto-like retreat in the Baltic. This should be 'perhaps the worst that we have'. There they would 'have their waiters and their business directors and their bath directors and there they can read their Jewish newspapers, all of which we want to know nothing about'.[53] Goebbels's idea of a 'holiday ghetto' for Germany's Jews was a cynical euphemism for what the Nazis had in mind. Even in the summer of 1935, long before Hitler's bureaucrats were to discuss their murderous plans for a 'final solution', it was clear that there were to be no Jewish holiday retreats. A year later the Heligoland spa management declared that Jews would be well advised to stay away from the island: the vast majority of visitors were Aryan now. Non-Aryan visitors would be at risk of causing embarrassment.[54] By the summer of 1937, the *Centralverein* told its members categorically not to visit any seaside resort in Germany, be it on the North Sea or the Baltic: all of them had an official anti-Jewish policy now. This explicitly included Heligoland.[55] By 1938 tourist guides were writing about Jewish visitors in the past tense: in the trenchantly anti-Semitic tones of one travel writer, the island '*used* to be visited particularly often by rich Jews, who caused many quarrels during the time of the [Weimar] System'.[56]

One of the last Jewish visitors to come to the island was Philipp Manes. Manes, a businessman from Berlin, clearly loved Heligoland and the North Sea, as did his wife Gertrud. In the summer of 1934 he wrote sixty-four pages of a holiday diary during one of their trips. He dutifully listed the sights and noted the names of artists, writers, and scholars who had spent time on the island. He also recorded the increasing presence of soldiers and the 'militarization' of Heligoland. 'The exclusiveness of the island is gone for ever', he commented. But what had made Manes, husband and wife, come back time and again was the light and the sea. Heligoland was a 'dream of sun-air-waves-water'. His account ends with a wistful goodbye and the hope for a return to 'the red rock'.[57]

While his four children Rudolf, Walter, Eva, and Annemarie left Germany before the outbreak of the Second World War, Manes and his wife stayed in Berlin. In July 1942 the Gestapo deported them to Theresienstadt, the concentration-camp-like ghetto in which the SS held more than 50,000 Jews. Manes became a key figure in the cultural life of Theresienstadt, organizing lectures, readings, and literary competitions.[58] He kept a diary here too, in which he recorded meticulously what he experienced, hoping that his children would be able to read it one day. Amongst the deprivation and humiliation he documented is a touching ritual which he and his wife adhered to, especially in the summer months. Whenever they found time, they would walk up to the *Südberg* (also called *Bastei*), a hill with playing fields. Here it was possible, Manes wrote,

> to lose oneself in extensive dreams, which carry me to that far-away, rocky island, the beloved Heligoland. Many a year we lay there, my wife and I, in the small, sheltered dips of the cliff tops... There was always a strong wind and from below rose quietly the sound of the surging waves.

He would hold his wife's hand, close his eyes and feel 'connected with the past in wondrous ways'. It was 'a moment of mercy'.[59] On 28 October 1944 the SS forced Philipp and Gertrud Manes onto a freight train, together with more than 2,000 other men, women, and children. It was to be the last *Transport* from Theresienstadt to Auschwitz-Birkenau, the extermination camp.[60] Two days later they arrived at Birkenau. The SS murdered them on the same day in the gas chambers. Philipp Manes was 69 years old, Gertrud Manes 61.

While Hitler's regime was busy proclaiming Heligoland as a proud Nazi monument, 'cleansed' of decades of Jewish visits, it trusted the islanders as little as any German government had before. In May 1935 Martin Seidel, a high-ranking party official, went to the island to investigate complaints made by a party member against the island's Nazi leader. He came back with an assessment that was remarkable not only for its depiction of the Heligolanders, but also for what it said about the ideas held at the top of the Nazi party. 'The small, narrow alleys of the island, the spatially very concentrated circumstances' were, Seidel wrote, 'the best breeding ground for gossip and rumours'. The Heligolanders were mostly driven by their own interests, not by larger ideological beliefs: 'National Socialism has, for the time being, not been able to change this kind of interest-driven and materialist acting and thinking'. There were historical reasons for this:

> The privileges, the freedom from custom duties, tax incentives etc., which all governments have conceded to the Heligolanders, have always been at the centre of their political interests. Furthermore one needs to note that Heligoland was after the war, during the reign of the [Weimar] System, the Dorado of the Berlin Jews, the racketeers and Socialist bigwigs, who liked to take their spa holidays here. There was naturally a strong danger that these circles would infect the population with subversive ideas (*zersetzerisches Gedankengut*). One can conclude that National Socialism is facing considerable educational tasks in Heligoland, the solution of which will, for the given reasons, be significantly more difficult than on the mainland.

Seidel saw 'external dangers' in this deplorable state: tourists from the neighbouring countries were still visiting the island and could get the wrong ideas about the Third Reich. 'It is therefore urgently necessary that a strong hand establishes peace and order in this outpost'.[61]

So behind the façade of racial harmony the surveillance and persecution of dissenters continued, as it did across Nazi Germany. The Gestapo and the SS intelligence service, the *Sicherheitsdienst* (SD), kept a close eye on the Heligolanders until the very end of the Third Reich. In 1938 Nazi functionaries started a systematic campaign against 'homosexuals' on the island. This was part of the wider Nazi attack on gay men, which had started earlier on the mainland, but the 'fight against indecency' also served as a pretext for the brutal removal of suspects and rivals, targeted through denunciations and rumours.[62] More than two dozen 'suspects' were charged, some of whom were convicted and imprisoned. Two of the accused committed suicide, another died in a concentration camp.[63] Denunciation also played a key role in October 1943 when the Gestapo arrested Heinrich Prüß, a hairdresser who had been a little too open about his dislike of the Nazis. One of his regular customers had informed the Gestapo. Prüß was brought before the *Volksgerichtshof* in Berlin, the court set up by Hitler for particularly serious 'political crimes'.[64] After a short, perfunctory trial Prüß was sentenced to death. He was executed in the Brandenburg-Görden prison on 14 August 1944. His daughter recalled after the war the fear she had until the end of the Nazi years, the fear of being found out and deported, combined with the inability to trust anyone. 'We never knew, is this a friend or are they still persecuting us'.[65]

It was this climate of terror that lay at the heart of the attitude taken by most of the Heligolanders towards the Third Reich. Most of them belonged to the 'silent majority': they were neither dyed-in-the-wool Nazis nor outright opponents.[66] Only a few had entered the party before the Nazis' rise to power. Their ranks were swollen by the larger numbers who joined once Hitler's dictatorship had been established.[67] But this core of the Nazi constituency remained a minority that claimed to speak for the majority. Nazi rhetoric never tired of styling the German people as united by 'one will'. Yet the Heligolanders rarely spoke with 'one voice'. It was their public silence, if anything, which united them. This was brought out powerfully in August 1943 when the Heligolander Jakob Krüss was arrested for making illicit contact with prisoners of war. Rudolf Krebs, an electrician employed by the navy, had observed Krüss leaving small parcels of bread outside the *Kurhaus* for the forced labourers who were regularly marched past the building. Krebs stated that 'a Russian' had picked up one of the parcels. The Gestapo arrested Krüss and investigated his background. They could find nothing in his past that spoke against the 65-year-old. On the contrary, he was known to be 'reliable' and 'trustworthy'. Krüss had a severely ill wife, whom he looked after. His three sons were in the Wehrmacht on the Eastern Front.[68]

The court case produced little further evidence against Krüss, but it shone a stark light on the Heligolanders' attitude towards the many prisoners of war held on the island. Few could not have been aware of the inmates, ruthlessly exploited in the fortification works. Every day their columns were marched to the building sites, guarded by armed troops. Krüss was not the only one to show some compassion towards them. The local GP, who described the prisoners as 'poor, miserable wretches', treated some of them for free.[69] In leaving a few pieces of bread for them Krüss may have been thinking of his sons' uncertain fate in Russia—the Wehrmacht's disastrous defeat at Stalingrad six months earlier had underlined all too forcefully that

Germans too could become prisoners of war.[70] Whatever his motivation, his case had wider significance: it revealed that numerous Heligolanders had had contact with the forced labourers held on the island. As the solicitor representing Krüss discovered, it had become customary for 'the Russian prisoners of war to make toys for the local children'. Some of the children or their parents would 'pay' for the toys by giving bread to the forced labourers. This had been 'quietly tolerated by the guards'.[71]

Krüss was clearly not alone in breaching legal boundaries. Many Heligolanders routinely acquired foodstuffs outside the official channels and sent packets to relatives on the mainland or swapped goods on the black market.[72] Petty crime was, as everywhere in Germany, a regular occurrence. There was the cook who diverted meat and butter for his own purposes; the shopkeeper whose stores were larger than what was on record; the skipper who requested rations for more workers than he supervised; the adolescent who refused to go to Hitler Youth meetings.[73] The court cases brought against such offenders revealed a consistent pattern: many Heligolanders were prone to overstep laws and regulations in petty ways, but they were anxious not to be seen to challenge the Nazis' rule. Precisely because many of them had carved out a practice of circumventing the law in their daily lives not one of them was prepared to go on record to defend Krüss. Potentially implicated by his case, they were eager to protect their own minor secrets from the eyes of the Gestapo.[74]

Behind the propaganda image of the 'people's community' lurked the banal everyday compromises and conflicts that existed under the surface of the Heligolanders' daily life. What they had in common was not any ideological or political stance, but the fear of denunciation and deportation. Yet this climate of fear was not the only factor that explains the attitudes taken by the islanders towards the Nazi regime. Whether they thought of themselves as indifferent, dissenting, or supportive of the regime, they were part of a community which benefited economically from Nazi rule, at least until the war. After January 1933 the government had been quick to confirm the islanders' traditional privileges. Hitler intervened personally when the Treasury wanted to abolish a tax exemption in 1935.[75] He condoned, in contrast, the restoration of an older law, which allowed Heligoland to raise its own import tax on alcohol and tobacco. As the mayor and his councillors put it in a letter to Hitler, this was the restitution of a privilege which they had fought for ever since 'the Marxist system' had abolished it. The additional revenue would go into local infrastructure projects and support for the unemployed.[76]

The extensive building programme started by Hitler's regime brought another stream of income. Many of the islanders found new work or expanded their existing businesses. In addition, the council's budget received an unprecedented amount of tax revenue. For every worker whom they employed on the island the companies involved in the building works had to pay a trade tax to the island's authorities.[77] After much wrangling, the mayor accepted that a part of this income had to be passed on to the local councils on the mainland where the workers had their permanent residences, but this still left Heligoland with roughly a third of the tax revenue.[78] The money went into the island's infrastructure, welfare, housing, and public services. This propping up of the local economy and the expansion of Heligoland's financial privileges helped to feed the consent which the vast majority of islanders adhered to. Wherever this was not the case, the regime resorted to intimidation and outright terror, especially during the initial and final phases of the Third Reich.

While the Nazis' embrace of Heligoland consisted of the usual combination of coercion and consent, it had a particular ideological undertone. From the late nineteenth century onwards scholars had interpreted the North Sea enclave as the site of a prehistoric Germanic cult. The island's name, they argued mistakenly, indicated that it had once been the sacred home ('holy land') of Germanic gods.[79] Some authors went as far as identifying Heligoland with the mythical Atlantis. The most prolific amongst them was Heinrich Pudor, a virulent anti-Semite who had served a prison sentence for incitement of hatred in 1926.[80] He described himself as a 'pioneer of Germandom and anti-Semitism' and impressed Hitler enough to be granted a monthly 'honorary salary'.[81] Pudor founded a Society for Heligoland Research, published a journal of *Heligoland Studies*, and incessantly lobbied government officials.[82] In a string of publications he proclaimed that the island was the birthplace of the Germanic race, a mythical Aryan Atlantis.[83]

Given these potent connotations, it was hardly surprising that the Nazis were eager to cultivate Heligoland as a racial monument. Heinrich Himmler, leader of the SS and a keen devotee of Germanic mysticism, was determined to establish scientifically what Pudor had described speculatively: that the island was evidence of the prehistoric greatness of the Aryan race.[84] But while Pudor had impressed Hitler with his impeccably anti-Semitic credentials, Himmler did not trust him. Pudor had failed to toe the party line in the past and was seen as 'undisciplined' by Goebbels, who repeatedly censored his publications.[85] Himmler commissioned instead the *Ahnenerbe*,

the research organization he had co-founded and subsequently incorporated into the SS apparatus. Its aim was to explore the Germanic past and
provide evidence for the long-term ascendancy of the Nordic race.[86]
Herman Wirth, the *Ahnenerbe*'s director until 1937, had argued a similar
case to Pudor, proclaiming the North Sea island to be the Aryan Atlantis.[87]
In September 1938, after his latest visit to Heligoland, Himmler instructed
the *Ahnenerbe* to research the island's past. A number of specialists were to
demonstrate that a larger, prehistoric Heligoland had been a centre of
Germanic worship.[88] Himmler was enraged when the academics reported
back with vague and inconclusive evidence. 'I could have come up with that
myself', he told Wolfram Sievers, the *Ahnenerbe*'s general secretary: 'I don't
need a professor for that'.[89]

While Nazi Germany was gearing up for war in the summer of 1939
Himmler found, remarkably, the time to continue with his pet project.
Disappointed by the academics sent out to establish Heligoland as the Aryan
Atlantis he turned to Peter Wiepert, an amateur historian and author of
Germanic folk books.[90] Wiepert was a cousin of Lina Heydrich, the wife of
Reinhard Heydrich, head of the Gestapo. Himmler gave him the brief to
explore Heligoland's past. Wiepert was to document the oral traditions and
folk sagas that could be used as evidence of the island's past as a holy grail
of the Aryan race.[91] And he was to find all available evidence in Scandinavian
archives and museums that linked the island as a pan-Germanic site to
Denmark, Sweden, and Norway.[92] At the same time deep-sea divers were to
establish the prehistoric size of the island and provide evidence for the
Atlantis thesis. Heydrich met with Wiepert in July 1939 to assure him that
the SS would fund his activities generously.[93] Three months later, after
Germany's invasion of Poland, Himmler insisted that Wiepert's research
should continue, but eventually the war put an end to the project.[94] In April
1940 Himmler begrudgingly handed his charts of the island back to the
navy, which had more urgent uses for them. Himmler made sure the High
Command knew that he would need the charts back after the war, so that
the *Ahnenerbe* could complete its task.[95]

It came as no surprise, certainly not to British observers, that the Nazi
regime was keen to incorporate Heligoland not only ideologically, but also
militarily. As early as November 1920 George Clark (Lord Sydenham), an
authority on military fortifications, had warned in the House of Commons
that it would only be a matter of time before the Germans rebuilt their

North Sea base: 'I am very much afraid that in twenty-five years we shall find that Heligoland is a strongly fortified position again'.[96] It was to take the Nazi regime rather less time than that. Initial works were carried out in 1934. Tunnels and bunkers were excavated, the embedded positions on the cliff tops cleared. Soon, a *Time Magazine* reporter wrote, the Germans would 'thank Hitler for a brand new Heligoland'.[97] On 21 May 1935 Hitler repudiated the disarmament clause of the Treaty of Versailles. Now the rebuilding of the naval outpost, part of his ambitious plan to rearm Germany, began in earnest.[98] The 'May Programme' of 1935, publicly declared to consist merely of 'salvage works' (*Aufräumarbeiten*), foresaw a comprehensive list of measures designed to turn the island into a fortress again.[99]

The rearmament of Heligoland signalled the Nazis' determination to turn past defeat into future victory, but it left open the question what sort of a war Hitler was preparing for. Behind the bold front his attitude towards Britain remained ambivalent. He was keen to keep Britain at least initially out of a war in which he anticipated Germany would suppress Western Europe and conquer much of Eastern Europe. His belief in the possibility of an Anglo-German accommodation was premised on ideological and strategic assumptions about Britain and Germany which were shared not only amongst the Nazi leadership: ideas about cultural and racial affinities; fantasies about the division of the world between a land-based Nazi empire and a sea-based British empire.[100] The Anglo-German naval agreement, signed by Joachim von Ribbentrop and Sir Samuel Hoare on 18 June 1935, was welcomed by Hitler as an important step in that direction. This was little more than an arms limitation treaty, establishing that the German navy would not expand beyond 35 per cent of the Royal Navy's tonnage. Still, the agreement was hailed in the German press as putting to rest the historic rivalry between the two nations. According to Ribbentrop, Hitler called 18 June 'the happiest day of his life'.[101]

But behind the façade of Anglo-German harmony, Nazi Germany continued to arm against Britain, circumventing the restrictions of the agreement practically from the day it had been signed.[102] The rebuilding of the Heligoland fortress went ahead unabated. Goebbels instructed the German press to keep all details out of the papers, his Propaganda Ministry proclaiming in June 1936 that: 'It is strictly forbidden... to mention the problem of the re-fortification of Heligoland'.[103] However, British tourists, free to visit Heligoland until 1938, found it hard to escape the ubiquitous building activity. A visitor reported in October 1936:

Notices signed by the German military authorities are posted up all over the
island and in the steamers prohibiting photography outside the precincts of
the upper and lower towns. Police, posted along the bricked walk around the
top of the island, enforce the rule.[104]

Reactions in Britain to the rebuilding of Germany's naval fortress mirrored
the broader uncertainty about how to handle Hitler and Nazi expansionism.[105] In March 1936 German troops re-occupied the Rhineland, until
then demilitarized. The Conservative government under Stanley Baldwin
urged the French to show restraint (which they did). Harold Nicolson, now
an MP, having resigned from the diplomatic service, noted in his diary that
'the feeling in the House [of Commons] is terribly "pro-German", which
means afraid of war'.[106] Three months later reports appeared in the London
press about the rearmament of Heligoland, a clear violation of the Treaty
of Versailles, just like the re-militarization of the Rhineland. The opposition
pressed the government: if Heligoland was being re-fortified, should
Britain not intervene? The answer was that 'no useful purpose would be
served by taking up this matter with the German government'. Britain had
no right to inspect the island and questioning Hitler about it 'might prejudice negotiations'.[107] This remained the official line under Baldwin and
then Neville Chamberlain (who took over from Baldwin in May 1937). It
expressed their hope to contain Germany through diplomatic rather than
military means, an aim that was supported by a large part of British public
opinion.[108]

Studying the reports from London in the summer of 1936, a satisfied
Goebbels instructed the German press 'not to take any notice of the
Heligoland discussion' in Britain. 'The English government has, as is known,
given an evasive answer [to its critics], so that it is superfluous for the
German press to touch upon this topic'.[109] Emboldened by the British
response, Hitler instructed the navy to work out plans for the complete
military transformation of the island. In March 1937, Erich Raeder, the
commander-in-chief of the navy, discussed the first details of the project.[110]
In the summer of 1938, with international tensions running high over the
Sudeten Question, *Projekt Hummerschere* was unveiled to a circle of leading
Nazi functionaries: Heligoland was going to be turned into a German Scapa
Flow, a naval base big enough to house almost the entire High Seas Fleet.
Few reminders of the project remain today, but even they convey a sense of
its gigantic scale. Both Heligoland and Sandy Island were to be extended far
into the sea, more than tripling the land mass in size. A huge new harbour

was to be built, with a circumference of more than 10 km. In May 1939, with the works well under way, the navy calculated that they would take ten years to complete.[111] A labyrinth of tunnels and shelters was dug into the rocks, big enough to house both the civilian population and all military personnel during air raids. The subterranean system, five floors deep, included a hospital, several kitchens, and a bakery. Provisions and ammunition were stored to enable the troops to hold the island when cut off from the mainland. Extensive facilities for Germany's submarine fleet were constructed; an airfield and further fortifications were built on Sandy Island.

In the years before the war Heligoland resembled a gigantic building site, with thousands of workers constructing one of the Reich's most sophisticated systems of fortifications, bunkers, and U-boat pens. Whether any of this made sense strategically was just as debatable as it had been when the Kaiser's fortress had been built thirty years earlier, but the German navy was not going to miss out on the opportunity to rebuild its North Sea stronghold. *Projekt Hummerschere* was the symbolic resurrection of the Wilhelmine dream of sea power, on a scale that exceeded even the Kaiser's wildest fantasies. Just as Tirpitz had hoped to do before the First World War, Raeder aimed to build up Germany's capacity for war against Britain in secret. From the start of the project, foreigners were no longer allowed to visit the island. Photography was forbidden everywhere. German tourists, although still permitted to come, had to relinquish their cameras upon arrival. When Hitler visited the island with Hungary's regent, Admiral Horthy, in August 1938, there was much orchestrated media hype, but all photographs and films were carefully censored so as not to show any sensitive aspects of the fortifications. The press followed Goebbels's lead: Hitler and Horthy had met to see Germany's 'Jewel of the North Sea', admiring the 'greatness of nature' and celebrating their friendship. Not a single one of Germany's main newspapers alluded to the island as a site of possible future conflict.[112] When publications appeared that did portray Heligoland as a flash point of rivalry, the Propaganda Ministry was quick to act and had them censored.[113] Privately, however, Goebbels left little doubt about Heligoland's uses. The island posed 'a silent warning', he noted while he accompanied Hitler and Horthy on their visit. For Goebbels, the outpost remained a symbol of Germany's humiliation by the Allies, a humiliation which the Nazis had vowed to undo.[114]

On 29 September 1938 Hitler, Chamberlain, Mussolini, and Édouard Daladier, the French prime minister, signed the Munich agreement, which carved up Czechoslovakia in a desperate attempt to appease German aggression. Returning to London on the next day, Chamberlain announced that the agreement meant 'peace for our time'. Clement Attlee, the Labour leader, was more prescient. 'We all feel relief that war has not come this time', he declared in Parliament; 'we cannot, however, feel that peace has been established, but that we have nothing but an armistice in a state of war'.[115] Three months later, in January 1939, Hitler signed off on *Plan Z*, an ambitious naval programme aimed at rapidly increasing Germany's ability to challenge the Royal Navy. The programme was a blatant violation of the Anglo-German agreement of 1935. It showed with some force that Hitler had abandoned the idea of an Anglo-German alliance; and it expressed his expectation that Britain would not stand aside if he unleashed a European war.[116]

When the war came it made obvious how illusionary the British appeasement strategy had been: Nazi Germany was not pursuing a merely revanchist agenda that could be satisfied by the re-drawing of a handful of borders. Rather, it aimed for a new order in Europe, based on German military and racial supremacy.[117] On 1 September 1939 the German army invaded Poland. Britain and France issued a joint ultimatum, which Hitler ignored. On 3 September London and Paris declared war on Germany. As in the First World War Britain blockaded Germany, cutting it off from vital supplies. The German Navy was, as before, not in a position to challenge the Royal Navy in an all-out battle. So the U-boat fleet was to play the key role, aiming to counter-blockade Britain. While this conflict, the 'Battle of the Atlantic', was fought until the end of the war, Britain's war on the Continent came to a temporary end in early June 1940 with the withdrawal of its army from Dunkirk. Six weeks later, on 16 July 1940, Hitler gave a directive for the invasion of the British Isles. The date for *Operation 'Sea Lion'* was left open while the Naval High Command investigated the most promising locations for a landing.[118] But before an invasion attempt could be made, the Luftwaffe would need to gain air supremacy. Churchill, who had taken over as prime minister from Chamberlain in May 1940, rejected all German peace offers: Britain would fight to the end rather than give Hitler control of the Continent. 'If we can stand up to him, all Europe may be free', Churchill declared in Parliament.[119] On 1 August 1940 Hitler gave the order to launch air strikes on Britain. The 'Battle of Britain', which Germany was to lose within less than four months, had begun.

It was now that Goebbels began to project Heligoland as a symbol of Germany's struggle against Britain. On 10 August 1940 the fiftieth anniversary of the island's cession was celebrated as a re-affirmation of Anglo-German enmity. Heligoland, newspapers wrote, embodied a free and powerful Germany that could stand up to the 'most vengeful and envious of opponents, the English'. The 'great struggle against our most persistent enemy Albion' had to be won, otherwise Germany would face the same fate as the Heligolanders had in 1807 when 'the criminal Briton' had struck against their island and the Danish fleet.[120] The military, too, employed the island as a symbol of Germany's fighting prowess. A feature in *Signal*, the Wehrmacht's popular magazine sold all over Europe, showed German soldiers preparing the fortress for battle with Britain. There was little doubt about the island's purpose now: caricatures painted on anti-aircraft batteries showed a rotund Churchill, complete with cigar and the heading 'against England'.[121]

Heligoland as a bulwark against Britain was also the main theme of the painting that became the most prominent depiction of the island in official Nazi culture. This was *Die Wacht* (The Watch) by Michael Kiefer, completed in 1940 to mark the fiftieth anniversary of German rule over Heligoland. Kiefer (not related to Anselm Kiefer, one of the most influential artists of post-war Germany)[122] was a trusted exponent of Nazi traditionalism whose

Figure 8.1 'Against England'. German propaganda photograph, published in *Signal*, 1941.

Figure 8.2 *Die Wacht*. Oil painting by Michael Kiefer, 1940.

paintings featured repeatedly in the official art magazine *Die Kunst im deutschen Reich*. His landscape and maritime paintings were thoroughly conventional, though much more infused with an outright heroic meaning than the nineteenth-century tradition associated with Caspar David Friedrich. *Die Wacht*, a canvas of 2 m by 3.2 m, was a prime example. It played on a motif which had been popular during the First World War: eagles in full flight over the North Sea against the backdrop of the cliffs of Heligoland, a metaphor of Germany projecting its military might over the North Sea. The implied enemy was Britain, all too obviously in the summer of 1940. Kiefer's painting was chosen for the fourth *Große Deutsche Kunstausstellung* (Great German Art Exhibition) which opened at the Munich *Haus der Kunst* in July 1940.[123] This was the annual exhibition of Nazi-sanctioned high art, the most important showcase for the celebration of what Hitler and Goebbels thought of as 'German art'—the opposite of 'degenerate' modernism.[124] *Die Wacht* was positioned prominently in room 21 of the exhibition, framed by two neoclassical sculptures. Hitler liked it so much that he promptly bought the painting for 8,000 Reichsmark.

With the Battle of Britain raging in the skies over England, British propaganda and popular culture created the mirror image of Heligoland. In *Berlin or Bust*, a 'patriotic dexterity game', the island served as a stepping stone which had to be conquered before Germany would fall.[125] *Raid on Heligoland* by Arthur Catherall, first published in 1940, envisaged a combined naval and aerial attack. Yet another an adventure novel written in the style of Erskine Childers's *Riddle of the Sands*, Catherall's story centres on Dan Short, a 17-year-old civilian who gets involved in a 'mad, breath-taking exploit on Heligoland'. Through a number of unlikely coincidences, Short becomes part of a covert operation leading the way for an all-out assault on the island.

> We were to penetrate the Nazi defences, entering the south-eastern harbour of Heligoland. Under cover of darkness we were to do what damage we could and at the same time land a party.

Having succeeded, Short and his commandos alert the RAF, which promptly destroys the island's defences before the navy pounds the fortress. Luckily for the British, the civilian population had been evacuated a long time ago—no hint of moral ambiguity here. 'Britain rejoiced. The return of the men who had made possible the magnificent raid on Heligoland was the final touch to the victory'.[126]

Such dramatization of the German threat stood in stark contrast to the strategic role Heligoland actually played during the war. For the first two years the construction of the gigantic harbour continued. Thousands of prisoners of war were forced to work on the sites run by the infamous Organisation Todt (OT), the Nazi construction conglomerate, alongside some of Germany's biggest engineering companies. But when Hitler unleashed his war against Russia in June 1941 and shelved the invasion of Britain all building projects on Heligoland were stopped. The U-boat pens were completed, but only sporadically used—most German submarines operated from the French coast.[127] With *Operation 'Sea Lion'* abandoned after Germany had lost the Battle of Britain, there was little offensive use for the island fortress. Its role for the rest of the war became almost exclusively defensive. A novel radar system was set up on the *Oberland* to warn mainland Germany about approaching Allied planes. Rather than the stepping stone for an attack on Britain, Heligoland became Germany's 'Ear to the West'.

Demands for the bombing of Heligoland were made incessantly by British politicians and journalists, most of whom overestimated the threat posed by the outpost. As early as March 1940 Sir Archibald Southby declared in Parliament that Heligoland was a 'nest' that the RAF would have to 'smoke out'.[128] But it was not until the tides of aerial warfare had turned that Bomber Command devoted significant resources to an attack on the island. After a few minor raids which had proved too costly, the RAF flew two larger missions in May 1943, together with the US Air Force.[129] Encountering stiff resistance the bombers inflicted some damage, but none of any significance to the fortifications.[130] So the RAF turned to special operations. *Operation 'Aphrodite'* (September 1944) was designed to guide planes loaded with explosives into the fortress with the pilots parachuting out in advance. This too proved ineffective and the Allies returned to conventional bombing, targeting the U-boat base without success in October 1944, but destroying large parts of the *Unterland*.

It was out of frustration with this lack of success that Bomber Command selected Heligoland for strategic bombing. If targeted missions had repeatedly failed, a systematic raid would be needed to destroy the entire island. In contrast to its raids on Germany's cities the RAF decided not to use any incendiaries for the attack. Still, the blanket bombing of Heligoland was bound to have a devastating effect, given the concentrated character of the island's housing stock. As was the case with the strategic bombing of Germany more generally, public opinion in Britain saw the attacks as a necessary evil aimed at ending a war in which Germans had bombed Britons first.[131] As far as Bomber Command was concerned, it was only a matter of time now before the North Sea fortress ceased to exist.

While the Allies continued with their pin prick attacks, the Nazi regime tightened its grip on the island. Shortly after the outbreak of the war, Himmler had ordered that the island be declared a *Sicherheitsbereich*, prescribing tight controls.[132] From March 1940 any visit to the island for 'private purposes' was forbidden.[133] In June 1940 all civilian shipping to the island was stopped.[134] The trickle of tourism that had still been in evidence came to a complete standstill. Clearly not trusting the islanders, the Nazi regime repeatedly strengthened the Gestapo presence on the island, as well as that of the SD.[135] In November 1944 the Naval High Command assigned Heligoland the status of a *Festung*, making it a position which had to be defended at all costs. Promising more troops and ammunition, the chief of naval staff was adamant that the island 'must be held' even if it was cut off from the mainland and the Allies were to blockade it.[136]

Both German and British propaganda reflected this uncompromising attitude. When Germany's Overseas News Agency declared in early 1944 that Heligoland had been turned into 'a defence bastion surpassing everything else in strength', British newspapers commented that the Nazis were boasting.[137] 'This is their only natural bastion', they retorted, explaining that 'to the Germans the red cliffs are symbolic'.[138] While the strategic use of Heligoland continued to be minimal, most of the British press were adamant that the island would have to be taken eventually, however much the Germans fortified it. As one magazine put it in February 1944: 'It has been their island only 54 years. Before that it was ours'. Heligoland posed a stark reminder of everything that had gone wrong between the two nations. It had been a mistake to cede it to the Germans in 1890 and even more of a mistake not to have reannexed it in 1919. Now it would have to be taken against all resistance.[139]

While in propaganda and popular culture the two nations were preparing for a dogged fight over the North Sea fortress, some of the islanders continued their traditional role as Anglo-German go-betweens. As during the First World War, there were émigré Heligolanders who volunteered to fight against Germany. Robert Olendrowsky was one of them. Born on the island in 1906, he served in the Australian Imperial Force from April 1942 to the end of the war.[140] Otto Tolley, born in Heligoland in 1883, was another émigré supporting the Allies. He had served in the US Army during the First World War and was now, at the age of 57, enlisted as an interpreter in the Australian forces.[141]

The dead, too, linked Britain and Germany in Heligoland. From the very beginning of the war the islanders took on the role of recovering the bodies of those killed on both sides, especially airmen shot down over the North Sea. The first case was Sergeant Robert Leslie Ward, one of the very first British casualties of the war. Ward, a pilot from Emsworth in Hampshire, was reported missing on 4 September 1939. A day later his body was discovered by a German boat and brought to Heligoland, where it was identified and then buried on the Dune.[142] 'One gets to know the dead of the RAF intimately', noted Walter Kropatscheck in his diary in October 1942.[143] Kropatscheck, a doctor, was involved in most of these cases. He recorded painstakingly the objects found on British officers and speculated about their personal backgrounds. Occasionally, he noted, the bodies 'still smelt as if fresh from the East End'.[144] As part of a detailed routine, the dead were buried in the 'Cemetery of the Nameless' on Sandy Island or in a corner of the cemetery in the *Oberland*.[145] Dozens of cases were communicated to the Allies during the war, more afterwards.[146] Families in Britain, Australia, and the United States were told that their deceased had found a last resting-place on a small German island in the North Sea. Flight-Sergeant Scandos

Scouller of the Royal Australian Airforce was one of them. He was 27 years old when his plane was shot down over the North Sea. A year later his family began a tradition by which they put a notice in Sydney's newspapers on the day of his death, using invariably the same words: 'Killed in action, May 11th, 1942. Buried at Oberland Cemetery, Heligoland, Germany. Always remembered by his loving mother and sister'.[147]

Given their advance position in the North Sea, the Heligolanders can have had few doubts about the way in which the war was turning. From spring 1942 onwards Heligoland lay in the approach path used by the RAF for the 'area bombing' of northern German cities. The islanders became used to the sight of waves of bombers passing over the island, unmolested by what was left of Goering's Luftwaffe. In July 1943, Hamburg was devastated during *Operation 'Gomorrah'*, one of the heaviest assaults the Allies were to fly against Nazi Germany. The firestorm caused by the attack killed tens of thousands. More than a million people fled the city.[148] The news of Hamburg's destruction made it all too clear that Heligoland would become uninhabitable if it was targeted in the same way.

Could the fortress be surrendered to the Allies before it was too late? It was only in the dying days of the Third Reich that an active discussion about this question began amongst some of the Heligolanders. By late March 1945 the island belonged to the last northwestern corner of the Third Reich still controlled by German forces. The Allies had crossed the Rhine; the British were pushing towards the north coast. In many places civilians were trying to save their livelihoods by displaying white flags and pleading with the German troops not to fight on.[149] There was a similar sentiment amongst the Heligolanders, but their situation was different. The proximity in which civilians and soldiers lived here in a heavily fortified stronghold surrounded by the sea created its own dynamic. The naval commander, aided by the Gestapo, kept a close eye on the islanders.[150] Still, he could not prevent contacts from developing between his troops and the Heligolanders. In early April, a group of locals, led by Georg Braun and Erich Friedrichs, joined with a circle of low-ranking officers to hatch a plan for the surrender of the fortress. Friedrichs had been detained by the Gestapo in winter 1933–4, and one of the officers, Kurt Pester, had been active in the Social Democratic resistance during the initial phase of the Nazis' consolidation of power. Yet the Heligoland conspirators were hardly a 'resistance group' in the sense of an active political or moral opposition to Hitler's regime—and if so, this opposition came pitifully late in April 1945.[151] By the time they decided to act the British army was about to capture Bremen and had begun its attack on Hamburg. Hitler was holed up in his bunker, with Russian forces on the outskirts of Berlin. What the rebellious locals hoped to achieve was that Heligoland would be spared, now that the war was clearly coming to an end. Their plan kept to the islanders' traditional *raison d'être*. Approaching the British in the face of the Nazis' imminent demise made perfect sense in this tradition—certainly to Friedrichs, who had been prominently involved in the appeal to London and the League of Nations at the end of the First World War. Now, thirty years later, the aim was a similar one: to secure Heligoland's transition into a future in which the British were likely to be their rulers again.

In retrospect the idea of a handful of civilians and low-ranking officers taking over a naval base manned by 6,000 troops seems ambitious, to say the least. That they were betrayed by two of their co-conspirators indicates that not all of those involved were convinced that the plan could work. The commander-in-chief of the German Bight was contemptuous about the 'contemplated mutiny' when he was told of the scheme.[152] In the early hours of 18 April 1945 Gestapo and SS officers arrested ten soldiers and five civilians. They were brought to Cuxhaven, the navy's headquarters in the German Bight.[153] A brief military tribunal sentenced the ringleaders to death. On 21 April 1945, a fortnight before the end of the war, Georg Braun, Erich Friedrichs, Kurt Pester, Karl Fnouka, and Martin Wachtel were executed for treason.

The day on which the Heligoland conspirators were arrested was also the moment chosen by Sir Arthur Harris, commander-in-chief of the RAF's Bomber Command, for the last, conclusive air attack on the island. In the morning of 18 April 1945 more than a thousand aircraft left their bases in the east of England.[154] They were manned by crews who had been involved in the strategic bombing of German cities for some time. In their diaries and journals they showed little doubt that Heligoland was a target worth destroying. As one of the pilots put it, the attack was 'designed to cripple the island for all times'.[155] Four days earlier General Eisenhower, supreme commander of Allied forces in Western Europe, had warned the combined chiefs of staff that 'the Germans intend with every means in their power to prolong resistance to the bitter end'. Heligoland belonged to one of the 'inaccessible areas' in which he feared 'resistance may be continued after the general linking up of our forces with the Russian Armies'. This was one of the 'final citadels of Nazi resistance', the storming of which 'may well call for acts of endurance and heroism on the part of the forces engaged comparable to the peak battles of the war'.[156]

The first planes were spotted from Heligoland at 12.25. They were over the island three minutes later, dropping markers. Six waves of Lancasters and Halifaxes followed, 945 of them in total, carrying 5,000 tons of high explosives. They were escorted by Spitfire and Mosquito fighters, whose role was largely symbolic: there was no opposing air force and Heligoland's defences were powerless against the magnitude of the attack. 'The sky was cloudless and the waves of planes could clearly be seen many miles ahead and behind', noted R. E. Wannop, the 26-year-old pilot of one of the Lancasters:

> We did the bombing run as if we were on a practice range—no 'ack-ack' [anti-aircraft artillery] greeted us—and many skippers turned and did a second run. The island was soon hidden under a pall of smoke as tons of high explosives did their deadly work. The occasional bomb dropping short into the sea causing a huge fountain of water which settled to a boiling cauldron. Some small boats endeavoured to flee from the place of Hell but the fighter boys were waiting and swooped down like birds of prey—those boats never made the mainland.[157]

At 12.38 Bomber Command received the message that the 'target' was 'saturated'. The pilots noted 'an intense concentration of craters, bursts, fires and smoke, blotting out the greater part of the island'.[158] Heligoland was a smouldering wasteland of craters and ruins.[159] Practically the entire civilian population had fled into the shelters dug deep into the rock. When they re-emerged after the raid the island was changed beyond recognition. The German High Command recorded 95 per cent of housing as destroyed.[160] There was no electricity and hardly any water. Along with almost all buildings, the inferno had devastated the cemetery where Allied servicemen had been buried alongside the Heligolanders' dead. Their remains lay scattered around, indistinguishable. Only the U-boat pens and some of the gun emplacements had withstood the bombing, a vain triumph of military engineering.

Later that afternoon Hitler attended a military conference in his Berlin bunker, which downplayed the extent of the raid in routine fashion.[161] The next day, while the RAF returned to drop massive 'Tallboy' bombs on what was left of the fortifications, the evacuation of the island began.[162] The Heligolanders wound their way through the smouldering ruins to get onto the waiting ships. They were told to bring only light luggage and leave behind their pets. The *Volkssturm militiamen* took away all dogs and shot them. There was no space on board for the bodies of the soldiers who had died in the attack, so they were buried at sea, wrapped in blankets and weighed down with bricks. By the early hours of 22 April the last islanders had embarked. They left behind an island so devastated that it was difficult

Figure 8.3 Heligoland after the Allied aerial attack of 18 April 1945.

to imagine that anyone could ever live there again. 'You could not recognize anything', one of them remembered later: 'Bomb craters and smoke, ruins and a few solitary chimneys. A completely different, terrifying world'.[163]

As if to defy reality, the remaining troops and scores of forced labourers, amongst them Italian and Dutch prisoners, were ordered to repair the defences. A week later Alfred Roegglen, the naval commandant, congratulated his men on having 'largely restored' the fighting capability of the fortress. 'We stand as a strong rock in the sea again, in an advance position, facing the most fateful hour of our Fatherland', he told them.[164]

But there was nothing left to defend. Much of Germany was already occupied and the British had advanced as far north as Hamburg. On 30 April Hitler committed suicide in his bunker in Berlin. On 2 May Grand-Admiral Karl Dönitz, his successor, sent Hans-Georg von Friedeburg, the commander-in-chief of the German navy, to the British headquarters at Lüneburg Heath. On 4 May Friedeburg signed a partial capitulation on the terms dictated by Field Marshal Bernard Montgomery. At 8 a.m. the next day all German forces in north-west Germany were told to lay down their arms.[165] This

explicitly included Heligoland, where the British were not to arrive for
another six days.

For a brief period the island was in an eerie interim. In other remote
parts of Germany soldiers had withdrawn before the Allies' arrival, leaving
behind pockets of anarchy or improvised self-rule.[166] Not so here: Heligoland
remained controlled by German forces, despite the capitulation of 4 May.
Roegglen, the commandant, upheld strict discipline. The orders he had been
given reflected the trauma which the experience of mutiny and revolution in
November 1918 had left amongst the naval leadership. Even in the moment
of total capitulation in May 1945 the High Command was anxious to keep
control. ('Never will a November 1918 happen again', Hitler and Goebbels
had repeatedly declared.[167]) Roegglen told his troops that any political statements and any attempt at sabotage would be severely punished.[168] For an
entire week he took them through the usual routines, though he made one
concession: there were to be no more Nazi salutes. Anticipating the imminent arrival of the British, his men practised the traditional military salute
now. The locals were busy burning Nazi flags.[169] 'The day of reckoning is
approaching', wrote Walter Kropatscheck, the doctor in charge of the island's

Figure 8.4 Alfred Roegglen, commander of the naval fortress, capitulates, 11 May 1945.

hospital.[170] He watched as the forced labourers, for years enslaved in the fortification works, left the island. 'Now they are the ones who are free', he wrote.[171]

On 11 May 1945, Rear-Admiral Gerard Muirhead-Gould, the British naval commander in north-west Germany, arrived with a company of Scots Guards to occupy Heligoland. He found an island that 'had been completely destroyed'.[172] There was no need for another formal capitulation. The surrender of the German forces in north-west Germany signed on 4 May had explicitly included the island. It had been followed by the total German capitulation of 7 May and 8 May, leaving no ambiguities.[173] Still, Muirhead-Gould, who had been an intelligence officer at the British Embassy in Berlin before the war, was keen to have a symbolic act by which Heligoland capitulated. The island had been an icon of the German menace for generations, fought over in two world wars. There had to be a ceremony and a document by which it formally surrendered to the British. Muirhead-Gould had brought a *Times* correspondent and a military photographer for the purpose. They duly recorded how Roegglen, the German commandant, signed the surrender 'at once'.[174] Just as in September 1807, when the Danish governor had signed a similar document, the British had taken the island without encountering any resistance. After fifty-five years of German rule they had re-occupied their former colony. There was no reason to believe that they would give it back any time soon.

On 12 May 1945 all German troops were embarked as prisoners of war. Roegglen was arrested for obstruction. A number of other German officers had to be reprimanded for not following orders. It was embarrassing, thought Kropatscheck, the doctor, who found the British commanding officer to be 'very mild, like a missionary'.[175] A group of intelligence officers spent a few more days inspecting the ruins of the fortress. On 17 May they too left.

For the first time since antiquity Heligoland was entirely empty of humans. This was the state Edward Grey, the former foreign secretary, had envisaged when debating the island's future after the First World War. The 'unattractive and barren spot' ought to be left unoccupied, as a no-man's land, frequented only by birds, he had recommended.[176] Heligoland in May 1945 was just that. It lay between Britain and Germany as a deserted battlefield, a moon-like landscape of craters and ruins. The battered island was to be a temporary haven for seals and sea birds, undisturbed by the Anglo-German struggle for the North Sea.

9

Out of Ruins

'Blow the bloody place up'.[1] There was nothing ambiguous about the instructions which Commander F. T. Woosnam had been given. Woosnam was the naval engineer in charge of preparing Heligoland for Operation 'Big Bang', the destruction of all military installations on the island. Sir Harold Walker, the commander of Britain's naval forces in Germany, was sure that it would be 'by far the biggest demolition ever carried out by the Royal Navy'.[2] Preparations began in August 1946 when the first British officers returned to Heligoland since its evacuation a year earlier. They had, Woosnam wrote, 'little idea of how to tackle such a unique task'.[3] Experts from the UK were flown in to conduct tests. After extensive trials they decided to connect all the British and leftover German explosives through one gigantic network of wires.[4] Led by Woosnam's team, 120 German technicians and labourers worked on the project for eight months. By April 1947 they had wired up more than 6,700 tons of explosives, ready to be detonated simultaneously.

Operation 'Big Bang' was meant to solve a number of problems. A seemingly endless amount of ammunition and shells had been stored on the island, much of it now hidden under piles of debris. Demilitarizing the island involved technical problems that were 'without precedent', wrote the secretary of the Admiralty.[5] Blowing the whole place up seemed by far the easiest solution. Yet symbolic considerations were just as important. The island's demilitarization was not to be a cumbersome process involving international commissions and protracted negotiations with the Germans. That had been the approach after the First World War, when Balfour had explicitly dismissed plans to blow up Heligoland.[6] Not so now, after another war in which the Germans had shown even greater military potential and expansionist ambition than in 1914. Their threat to Britain had to come to a conclusive end, once and for all. The very command—'Blow the bloody place up'—seemed to carry the weight of generations of Anglo-German conflict, to be settled now in one symbolic act: 'No more Heligolands'.[7]

To drive the point home, the navy made an unprecedented public spectacle of the operation. Charles Gardener, the BBC's veteran war reporter, was given his own plane for a running radio commentary. A special transmitter was brought in to allow for live broadcasts. The Royal Navy's headquarters in Berlin made sure that the press would be given a chance to take 'before and after' pictures of the island.[8] Automatic cameras were set up on Sandy Island to capture the blast and the tidal wave caused by it. The vessel chosen for the reporters and cameramen was HMS *Dunkirk*, a detail that was not lost on British newspapers celebrating the operation as a thinly disguised act of vengeance.[9] Britain's top military brass in occupied Germany was keen to attend. 'There is nothing I would like to do better', wrote Air Marshal Sir Philip Wigglesworth. He had a tight schedule, but would make sure to 'fly round at some safe distance and watch the upheaval from a Dakota' together with General Sir Richard McCreery, the commander-in-chief of the British Army of the Rhine.[10]

There were critics in Britain who objected to the planned detonation, billed as the biggest non-nuclear explosion in history. Most of the objections focused not on German sentiment, but on the rare birds known to use the island as a breeding ground. Could nothing be done to save them? Woosnam's engineers promptly devised a mechanism by which a series of minor explosions would be triggered just before the big blast, thus scaring off the gannets and guillemots. There would only be minor disturbance to bird life, the air force assured worried ornithologists.[11] The government was less accommodating toward German objections. Once the press in occupied Germany had got hold of the details for 'Big Bang', there was an outcry across the political spectrum. Heligoland was 'a symbol', wrote the bishop of Holstein. Blowing it up two years after the end of the war was against the conscience of all Christians.[12] The regional government of Schleswig-Holstein begged London 'to refrain from blasting the island'.[13] There were plenty more petitions and appeals, but none of them washed with the British government. This was occupied territory, uninhabited and unsafe. The object of its demolition, the navy explained in a press release, 'is not to destroy the island, but to dispose of the extensive fortifications, which have made Heligoland one of the most heavily defended places in the world'.[14]

On 18 April 1947, on the fourth pip of the BBC's 1 o'clock time signal, E. C. Jellis, Woosnam's deputy, pressed the button.[15] After a bright flash,

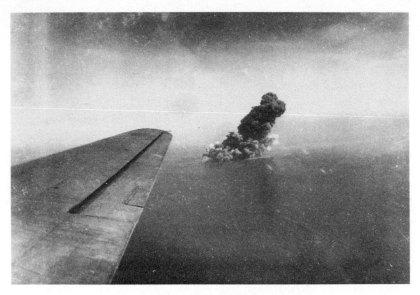

Figure 9.1 Operation 'Big Bang', 18 April 1947.

pillars of debris and dust rose up 'in almost frightening splendour', as one reporter had it.[16] The giant mushroom cloud reminded observers of a nuclear explosion. The shockwave was felt on the mainland, 70 km away.[17] At Kew, south-west of London, the seismographs of the Meteorological Office registered the impact.[18] The British press was jubilant. 'Biggest Bang since Bikini', 'A very reasonable way of celebrating Hitler's birthday' (which was on 20 April), 'Hitler's pride and joy, heavily fortified Heligoland, enveloped in mass of flames' were typical headlines.[19] The Admiralty produced a handsome souvenir book, complete with charts and photographs, praising the complete success of the operation.[20]

German reactions were predictably less enthusiastic. Most reports focused on the fact that the island seemed still intact. 'Der rote Felsen steht noch' ('the red cliffs are still standing'), ran one front-page headline—however many explosives the British threw at them, the cliffs would withstand them.[21] The expectations of the Allies, one commentator wrote, had been bitterly disappointed. Heligoland was like the rest of Germany. It remained what it had been, 'outwardly harmed and scarred by the visible marks of the detonations, but still in its erstwhile greatness and beauty'.[22] The narrative, adopted in countless articles and pamphlets that were to follow, was that the British had tried to eliminate the island. Yet the island had defied them. *Trotzen* ('to defy') and *trotzig* ('defiant') were the words the press used—perhaps unaware that Goebbels had used the same phrase in August 1938, writing about Heligoland 'defiantly' facing up to the British.[23]

The response to the demolition showed a marked willingness amongst Germans to portray themselves as victims.[24] There was little sign here of a general taboo about the recent past—the German media mentioned the war incessantly. But in doing so it focused overwhelmingly on the suffering endured by Germans. No doubt, this expressed a deeply felt psychological need; and after all, huge numbers of German civilians *had* become victims of Allied violence.[25] Still, the deafening public silence on the question of causation was striking in the post-war years. Even if many Germans addressed the link between their own roles during the war and the destruction of Germany privately, this was rarely discussed in public. In most of the press, responsibility for the past remained dissociated from suffering in the present.[26] Heligoland was part of a wider discourse which spoke eloquently about the ordeals of Germans and remained silent about the ordeals of others. The island was depicted as emblematic of the *Heimat* which so many Germans had lost: a small, peaceful community that had suffered a series of sudden, devastating blows towards the end of the war.[27]

Heligoland's currency as a metaphor of victimhood rose dramatically when the British announced after Operation 'Big Bang' that they would use the island as a bombing range. Throughout the war MPs and civil servants in Britain had raised questions about the future of Heligoland. The government's standard answer had been that the island would be dealt with in a peace treaty.[28] But with the beginning of the Cold War such a treaty seemed a distant possibility: too fundamental was the disagreement between western and eastern Allies about the future of Germany. Using the island as a bombing practice target, which the RAF was keen to do, seemed a good interim solution. It would keep the Germans away from their former naval fortress and reserve it for British use until the day of a general treaty. In December 1947 the RAF started its practice sorties with live ammunition.

The reaction in Germany could not have been worse. The British were continuing the bombing war as if Germany had not capitulated over two years previously. The RAF was out to annihilate the island for ever and with it Germany's self-respect. Had Germany not suffered enough? A number of initiatives began to document 'British atrocities' against 'the German island'.

They centred on two institutions set up by the governments of the West German states *Länder* to prepare the German position for an eventual negotiation of a peace treaty: the German Office for Peace Questions, in Stuttgart (*Deutsches Büro für Friedensfragen*), and the Peace Treaty Secretariat, in Hamburg (*Sekretariat Friedensvertrag*). Their staff collaborated in producing a bilingual pamphlet, *The Heligoland Issue*, aimed at influencing international opinion.[29] Most regional governments endorsed the pamphlet, which was backed by the churches and the vast majority of the press.[30] Its main author, Hans Peter Ipsen, a law professor, had been a high-ranking bureaucrat in the Justice Ministry under the Nazis.[31] He focused on two points. First, what the British were doing in Heligoland was a violation of international law and human rights. Second, the Germans had a special relationship with this 'monument of nature'. The millions who had visited the island in the past were demanding 'that their well-founded feelings and love to [*sic*] the home soil are respected'. Britain was 'deliberately denying due respect to a defeated nation's tradition and love to the home country'. This 'elementary injustice' had to stop.[32]

The displaced Heligolanders themselves were actively involved in cultivating this narrative of victimhood. Initially, their representatives had gone back to the long-held tradition of acting as Anglo-German go-betweens. In March 1948 they appealed to the UN. The islanders, they argued, were neither German nor British. They had detested the militarism of the Nazis. 'Why are we Heligolanders to pay for the sins and stupidity of German imperialism?', they asked in an open letter sent to British newspapers.[33] But when it became clear that there was a growing movement in Germany demanding the return of the island, the Heligolanders realigned their position swiftly. By the summer of 1949 their own publications focused almost entirely on their status as expellees, echoing the chorus of the *Heimatvertriebene*, the millions who had been forced to leave Germany's former eastern territories after the war.[34]

The Heligolanders' politics played skilfully on this dynamic. After their evacuation in April 1945 most of them had been resettled in cities and towns across northern Germany. They gained a voice through the *Helgoland* journal edited by James Krüss, later a popular children's book author.[35] Its political stance betrayed the same tunnel vision as most of the *Vertriebenen* literature of this period. The demand to return home and the accusation of Allied immorality was entirely de-coupled from any talk about the Nazi past. As in villages, towns, and cities all over Germany the implication was that the Heligolanders were not to be blamed for the Nazis and should not be made to pay for Hitler's war. This stance amounted to more than a mere 'keeping quiet' about the Third Reich—it involved actively constructing a version of the past which separated the Heligolanders' with the Nazi regime from their role as victims of the Allies. It was crucial for this narrative that the chronology of suffering began in 1945. 'Hitler', 'Nazis', 'invasion', or 'Battle of Britain' never featured in *Helgoland*, but no issue failed to mention the British 'atrocities' against the innocent North Sea island.[36]

The images shown in the journal, too, emphasized victimhood. They were mostly variations on two motifs: depictions of the senseless destruction caused by Allied bombers; and images of 'old Heligoland', showing the small town dominated by church tower and lighthouse, complete with picturesque harbour and beach. Numerous brochures and books appeared from the 1950s onwards which idealized 'das alte Helgoland' in an ahistorical pre-war state. Franz Schensky's famous pictures, taken between the turn of the century and the 1940s, served this purpose particularly well. Artistically the most impressive photographs that exist of Heligoland, they highlighted the picturesque and parochial: Schensky focused on the sea and the cliffs, the Heligolanders' traditional occupations, the relationship between nature and islanders. Hardly ever did his photographs hint at the military machine which Heligoland had resembled in 1914 and in 1939. Schensky offered a narrow, selective window on an evocative past, one that suited the politics of victimhood and *Heimat* idealization perfectly.[37]

The Heligolanders' attempts to style their island as a metaphor of German suffering reflected a broad political consensus, promoted by the new West German state. An entire government office was set up under Konrad Adenauer, the first post-war chancellor, to collect evidence for war damages. This led to the publication of the multi-part series *Dokumente deutscher Kriegsschäden*, a collaboration between the government and lobby groups representing those who had been bombed or expelled.[38] The *Dokumente* had two main aims: to acknowledge the suffering of millions of Germans and to prepare their claims for compensation. As Theodor Oberländer, the minister for expellees, refugees, and war injured, put it in the introduction to the series, the 'heavy human sacrifices' caused by the Allied bombing of Germany ought to be recorded 'as a warning for the future'.[39] Oberländer had served the Nazi regime in several military and intelligence roles during its genocidal war against Eastern Europe.[40] It was hardly surprising that his

ministry kept the Third Reich strictly out of the picture now. An entire
volume of the *Dokumente* was dedicated to Heligoland and Germany's 'battle'
for its 'liberation'.[41] Nowhere did the volume mention Hitler's war against
Britain. Anyone reading it could be forgiven for imagining that the Allies'
destruction of the island had come out of the blue. The fact that Britain continued to bomb the island years after the war was taken as evidence for London's
destructive intent, described as 'arbitrary' (*willkürlich*) and 'senseless' (*sinnlos*). For
once, Germans could claim the moral high ground against the Western Allies.

All this explains why the 'Heligoland Question' gained such currency in the
immediate post-war years. On 20 September 1949 the first West German government, led by Konrad Adenauer, was sworn in. Shortly after, the Bundestag,
the new West German parliament, unanimously passed a resolution which
called on the Allies to return the island. The speaker introducing the appeal,
Hans-Joachim von Merkatz (Deutsche Partei, later Christian Democrat), was
eager to demonstrate that the British were violating a string of international
laws. 'Every single bomb is hitting not only the Heligolanders, but every
German', he exclaimed. 'These are Germans who have been expelled from
their *Heimat*'.[42] Willy Max Rademacher, a leading Freie Demokratische
Partei (FDP) politician, rose in support: 'Heligoland is a German question'.
He reminded the Bundestag about the 'path of suffering and extermination'
the island had been forced on. It was a path every German knew: 'Heligoland
has a particular place in the heart of all Germans. It is a unique monument
of nature'. Every additional bomb would 'hurt the true national feeling of
every German'.

> I would like to ask the English nation: what would you say if your Isle of
> Wight was being systematically bombed three years after the cessation of all
> hostilities, with the aim of completely annihilating that island?[43]

The 'English nation', however, was not that worried. Too recent were the
memories of the war—giving up a barren rock half the size of Gibraltar
seemed hardly too big a price for the Germans to pay. Only a handful of
critics in the UK seized on the issue. The most prominent of these 'friends
of Heligoland', as the Foreign Office dubbed them, was Douglas Savory,
a professor of French and Ulster Unionist MP.[44] In his writing and lobbying
he continued the tradition (which had started in 1890 and has never ceased
since) of blaming the British for 'betraying' the Heligolanders.[45] Savory
raised question after question in the Commons. Why was the RAF still,
five years after the war, pounding a German island in the North Sea? The

Germans seemed to be rather sentimental about the island. Should it not be given back to them?[46]

The answer was a resounding 'no'. Returning Heligoland was impossible, explained Aidan Crawley, under-secretary of state for air, in July 1950. Crawley knew what he was talking about. He had flown around the island 'only a week or two ago'.

> At the moment it is the nearest thing to the Warsaw Ghetto I have seen in Western Europe. It is literally a rock sticking out of the sea, and just a mass of rubble, with two or three long spits on each side, one of which was used as the Germans' naval base. There is no question of anybody's home being on that island, nor can there possibly be any question of more than a handful of people—of fishermen—gaining their living there again. What were the industries there, or what sort of life was supported there? It had a fashionable seaside resort and a great naval base and arsenal. I do not think anybody can imagine that any Government…would spend money on making a seaside resort there amid a heap of rubble while Germany has so many other problems.

As for the Germans' sentimental feelings, Crawley was having none of it. He had been an intelligence officer and fighter pilot during the war. Shot down in July 1941, he had spent almost four years in the infamous Stalag Luft III camp, trying in vain to escape. He knew the Germans first hand and felt rather uncompromising about them:

> If it is a question of sentiment, I cannot believe the present German Government would want to make this a sentimental issue. Heligoland has not been in the possession of Germany for very long…and in so far as it has any sentimental value for the Germans it can only be as a great military base from which two terrible wars were waged against the people whom we all hope the Germans will now consider their friends and Allies. I should hope that if any tradition was worth breaking, and if any sentiment was worth changing, then the German sentiment about Heligoland was such a one.[47]

The North Sea island represented everything that had gone wrong with Germany since the nineteenth century. It stood, above all, for a long tradition of militarism which had only just come to an end. Giving Heligoland back would amount to repeating the mistakes of the past.

It looked as if this would be the Attlee government's position for the foreseeable future. Nor did the Tory opposition show any inclination to question it.[48] Churchill, its leader, never tired of invoking Heligoland as an icon of the German menace—in his post-war writing it featured as a monumental error made by his predecessors.[49] In November 1950 Ivone Kirkpatrick, Britain's highest representative in Germany, told Adenauer that

London had no intention of making the island available. Ernest Bevin, the foreign secretary, reiterated the position in the Commons.⁵⁰ Adenauer's advisers were dismayed. MPs, regional governments, and the press were pushing for the chancellor to reclaim Heligoland. An 'inestimable gain in prestige' was to be had if he could secure its release, wrote one editor.⁵¹ But the British, backed by the Americans and the French, rebuffed Adenauer—despite their stated policy of propping up the West German government. Here was an issue perfectly suited to promote reconciliation, but they refused to give way. 'It is one of the most astonishing stupidities of recent times', commented one of the senior staff in Adenauer's office liaising with the Allied High Commission.⁵²

With London and Bonn at an impasse, it was perhaps predictable that some of the Germans who felt so strongly about the island would take matters into their own hands. Still, the turn to popular nationalism which occurred towards the end of 1950 took both the Adenauer and Attlee governments by surprise. On 20 December Georg von Hatzfeld and René Leudesdorff, students at Heidelberg University, persuaded a fisherman in Cuxhaven to take them and two journalists to Heligoland. It was a rough crossing, but when they eventually landed on the island, they felt elated. Encouraged by the reporters, Hatzfeld and Leudesdorff raised a German flag and the flag of the European Movement. As Hatzfeld noted in his diary, they were not entirely sure about the message they wanted to send with their 'invasion'.⁵³ But the German press celebrated them as 'liberators'. In the name of Europe—a peaceful and democratic Europe, to be sure—the two students had reclaimed the island from the British. What was more, they were inspiring more 'conquerors' and 'occupiers' (terms which turned around the established roles of occupied Germans and occupying Allies). On 27 December a group of Heligolanders joined them and on 29 December the eccentric Prince Löwenstein arrived, keen to translate the 'occupation' into a larger international issue.

Hubertus Prinz zu Löwenstein-Wertheim-Freudenberg had been a youth leader in the *Reichsbanner* paramilitary organization, founded in the 1920s by Weimar's centre-left parties to oppose the rise of right- and left-wing extremism.⁵⁴ An outspoken opponent of the Nazis, he had been involved in an abortive coup against the von Papen government in 1932. Shortly afterwards Löwenstein left Germany for Britain, where he had relatives: his grandfather was Henry de Worms (Lord Pirbright), Conservative politician before the First World War; his mother, Constance Baroness

Alvensleben, had British citizenship, though she lived in Austria.[55] MI5 observed Löwenstein throughout his London years, never quite sure what to make of him. 'An Austro-German prince', noted a report in 1936:

> His mother... is said to be an English woman of good family but who was of half Jewish descent... In character he is very much the German Royal Prince and he has a complete contempt for the 'Petit Bourgeois' (in whose ranks he classifies Hitler).[56]

Though involved with the Comintern, Löwenstein was not classed as a Communist by MI5: 'We know this man as politically eccentric and somewhat unstable in character, but there is no doubt that he is a genuine anti-Nazi'.[57] Yet he was also a staunch German nationalist. His publications betrayed a similar bent, combining different political traditions in a way that seemed more mid-nineteenth than mid-twentieth century: national *and* liberal, democratic *and* imperial.[58] Vernon Kell, the director of MI5, was disdainful: 'He has an ardent faith in the future of Germany as the leader of Europe—provided it is led by a great personage such as himself'.[59]

In November 1946 Löwenstein went back to Germany, settled in a Bavarian castle, and took up a teaching position at Heidelberg University. He recruited Hatzfeld, one of his students, as his assistant and started a patriotic league, the *Deutsche Aktion*.[60] Whether Löwenstein himself had the idea of 'invading' Heligoland is unclear, but he knew what to do when the students had succeeded with their landing—he rushed to the island with a group of journalists and seized the initiative. On 29 December 1950 he issued a declaration:

> I landed this morning at 9 at Heligoland. The destruction exceeds anything one can imagine possible. In the name of the *Deutsche Aktion* I have taken possession of the island for the German Empire and the Western community (*Abendländische Gemeinschaft*). Long live the German Empire.[61]

The occupation of Heligoland, he explained, was to herald the rebirth of a democratic German *Reich*. Much of Löwenstein's busy activism smacked of megalomania and self-aggrandizement. 'He left an impression of just that kind of woolly German idealism which paves the way for the adventurer', commented the British commissioner in Kiel after meeting him.[62]

But precisely because of his idealism Löwenstein, later an MP in the Bundestag (first for the FDP, then the CDU), gained a huge amount of publicity, linking Heligoland to wider debates about the future of Germany.[63]

The influential *Bund der Heimatvertriebenen*, the lobby group representing German refugees and expellees, declared its solidarity and sent delegations to the island. Heligoland stood for Germany, it claimed. Just as the island would become part of the nation again, a greater Germany would be resurrected, defying the Allies and overcoming post-war division.[64] The support for the prince and his 'occupiers' ran across the entire political spectrum, wrote *Time Magazine*:

> All German political factions, including the Communists, cheered the news of the invasion. Fresh from Helgoland, where a century ago poet Hoffmann von Fallersleben had written *Deutschland, Deutschland über Alles*, invader Leudesdorff exulted: 'This is the first time since the war that all Germans are united'.[65]

Löwenstein and his *Deutsche Aktion* put London in an awkward position. Sir Ivone Kirkpatrick, Britain's high commissioner in Germany, issued an ordinance according to which any attempts to interrupt the RAF's use of Heligoland were 'not in the real interest of Germany'. Without written permission 'no person shall land or remain upon the island'.[66] West Germany's police was now obliged to keep all 'squatters' off the wind-swept rock. This was no easy task, and the authorities on the mainland, many of whom sympathized with the 'liberators', were less than enthusiastic about fulfilling it. British enforcers, so-called Public Safety Officers, had to supervise the regular German police. There were bizarre scenes when the occupiers were removed, with German officers openly congratulating Löwenstein and the students before arresting them.[67] Kirkpatrick noted with a sense of bitterness that Hermann Ehlers, the president of the Bundestag, made a point of publicly receiving the two students as soon as they were released.[68]

The 'Battle over Heligoland', as German newspapers dubbed it, put a spotlight on the Anglo-German relationship at a time of rapid change. London and Bonn had begun to move tentatively towards a new partnership, but post-war occupation was still very much a reality.[69] Kirkpatrick himself embodied the tension between these two poles. Both during the First and Second World Wars he had been an intelligence officer, running spies and orchestrating propaganda against Germany. At the British Embassy in Berlin from 1933 to 1938, he had watched the rise of the Nazis first hand. From September 1944 he had been in charge of organizing the British occupation of Germany. Made high commissioner in June 1950, he was now both Adenauer's opponent and partner. Together with his American and French counterparts he continued to exercise important aspects of sovereignty over

West Germany, especially with regard to foreign policy and military matters. At the same time he was instrumental in negotiating the road to West Germany regaining autonomy in return for its commitment to a defence structure dominated by the Western powers.[70]

In Heligoland, Kirkpatrick thought, the British seemed stuck in the war-time past, more interested in retribution than conciliation. In early January 1951 he recommended to Ernest Bevin that 'we should now review the whole position'.[71] He was not the only one who thought so. Heligoland was 'a political embarrassment', commented *The Times*, indicating that public opinion in Britain was beginning to shift.[72] In mid-January Sir Henry Vaughan Berry, who had been the regional commissioner for Hamburg until May 1949, wrote a widely quoted open letter, lamenting London's insensitivity. Heligoland was the 'perfect example of how not to deal with Germany', he argued.[73] But the Attlee government was not so easily swayed. Bevin told Kirkpatrick 'that we must deal firmly with current acts of defiance'.[74] It was undesirable, he wrote, to yield 'to popular German clamour'.[75] The chiefs of staff in particular were hesitant. Ever since the end of the war, they had assumed that Heligoland would remain under British control until a peace treaty. They had confidently assumed that in the eventual negotiations for such a treaty Britain would push for the annexation of the island.[76] They would not be dissuaded from that course by a few student squatters and a blustering Austro-German prince.

But this seriously underestimated the potency of the issue. In March Bevin was to summarize the UK's policy towards Germany in a secret cabinet memorandum. Since the inception of Adenauer's government, it had been Britain's policy

> gradually to build up the prestige and authority of that Government and to bring it and German public opinion to opt in favour of full association with the West.[77]

Over Heligoland that policy seemed to be failing abysmally.[78] There was a danger that the issue would mobilize German public opinion not only against Britain, but also against Adenauer, whose pro-Western policy was far from uncontested within Germany.

This point was lent urgency when it became clear that behind the scenes East Berlin was getting involved. The quarrel over the island must have seemed a heaven-sent gift to Walter Ulbricht's Socialist Unity Party (SED), which had ruled the German Democratic Republic since its foundation in October 1949. Here was a symbolic issue that united Germans across the

East–West divide in a patriotic stance against the Western Allies—at a time
when the geopolitical future of Germany was still in flux: the two German
states, founded in 1949, were yet to be formally integrated into the Western
and Eastern military alliances. On 4 January 1951 the West German branch
of the *Freie Deutsche Jugend* (FDJ), which was controlled by, though officially
independent from, the SED, decided to run its own 'covert invasion'.[79] A
few weeks later the East German leadership began to orchestrate a broader
'Heligoland movement'. By early February, the Bonn government assumed
rightly that East German organizations had begun to infiltrate the squatters
on the island.[80] The first posters and brochures appeared, styling Heligoland
as the site of an anti-imperialist struggle which united Germans on both
sides of the iron curtain in their opposition against the Western Allies.[81]

The involvement of East Germany, known in London by mid-February,
raised the stakes. Attlee leant heavily on his chiefs of staff now. 'The political
risks inherent in continuing to bomb the island', conceded the secretary of
state for air on 20 February, 'are considered wholly unacceptable'.[82] A day
later the Defence Committee acknowledged 'that we should have to give
up Heligoland sooner or later'.[83] The line agreed in cabinet was that Britain
would hand the island back within a year, but not before an alternative
bombing target had been found in Germany. Kirkpatrick told Adenauer as
much on 26 February. The chancellor agreed.[84] The decision, made public
on the same day, was meant to take the wind out of the sails of the Heligoland
occupiers. Löwenstein and his *Deutsche Aktion* promised to refrain from further provocations. So did the Heligolanders.

But the release of the island seemed far from secure. Nor did it help that the
RAF resumed its use of the outpost as a bombing range. East Berlin pulled all
levers to exploit the opportunity. On 28 February the FDJ leadership started a
large-scale 'Aktion Helgoland' directed against both Bonn and the Western
Allies.[85] A *Deutsche Bewegung Helgoland* (German Heligoland Movement) was
set up in Hamburg, representing 'all strata of society', as the East German
newspaper *Neues Deutschland*, the SED's mouthpiece, claimed.[86] The aim of
this 'movement' was, as its leader Albrecht Müller put it, nothing less than the
creation of 'a national resistance'. The struggle for the 'liberation of Heligoland'
would mobilize public opinion 'against the re-militarization and for the re-
unification of Germany', or so he hoped.[87] The West German government had
no doubts that the *Deutsche Bewegung* was an FDJ front—effectively the headquarters for the organization of a new string of 'invasions'.[88] Most of these
covert operations followed a similar pattern: young northern Germans, often

students, were recruited as 'invaders'. A 'guide' would bring them to a boat, give them equipment, and assure them that, if caught, they would get legal assistance from 'the movement'. On the island they would be met by other occupiers and set an example against the 'bombing terror' of the British.[89]

Practically all of these *Helgolandfahrer* were arrested by the West German police—as East Berlin had confidently assumed they would be. Amidst much publicity a series of court battles took place which ended with British judges sending young Germans to prison for having peacefully occupied an island which continued to be bombed by the RAF. The East German press had a field day, making martyrs of the 'liberators' and branding the British as 'imperialists', 'militarists', and 'terrorists'. The SED government sent well-publicized telegrams to Kirkpatrick, demanding the immediate release of the 'young patriots' who had given 'a shining example of the battle against re-militarization and for a united, independent and peace-loving Germany':

> The abduction of the brave German patriots which has taken place in accordance with your commands cannot be kept quiet and will cause a storm of protest and outrage amongst the entire German people, which will one day sweep aside all those who harm the peaceful interests of our people through violence and terror.[90]

Universities, schools, and factories all over the GDR declared their solidarity with the 'peace fighters' (*Friedenskämpfer*).[91] A wave of demonstrations, appeals, and declarations followed, betraying the efficient organization of the SED as much as the currency of the topic. Perhaps the most curious among the many instances of East German Heligomania was Peter Martin Lampel's play *Kampf um Helgoland* ('Struggle for Heligoland'), commissioned by the Ulbricht government.[92] This was a straightforward narrative of a typical 'invasion' succeeding despite bad weather and British bombers. The play culminated in a long court scene which pitted a ruthless British military judge and his obedient West German helpers against freedom-loving, patriotic students from all over Germany. As the GDR state news agency explained, the play 'showed mercilessly the true face' of Western imperialism and made the convicted students the 'real winners'.[93]

Much of this was aimed at uniting public opinion in East Germany behind the SED. Yet the campaign was clearly also designed to drive a wedge between West German voters and the Adenauer government. A petition against 're-militarization', begun by West German peace activists and heavily promoted by the FDJ in parallel to the Heligoland 'invasions', gained millions of signatures.[94] There was no doubt that the SED leadership had judged the situation exceedingly well. In May 1951 Walter Bartram, the minister president of Schleswig-Holstein, wrote to Adenauer:

> It cannot be denied that the propaganda of the Eastern Zone is making good use here of a situation that is psychologically extraordinarily favourable for it...I would summarize my impression as being that with every deportation of invaders from the island and their appearance in British courts, the West suffers a further defeat in the Cold War.[95]

The British commissioner in Schleswig-Holstein agreed. He warned Kirkpatrick about the 'violence of Eastern Zone propaganda on Heligoland'. It was especially worrying that the 'squatters' were 'receiving full support from that body of public opinion in the Eastern Zone which is otherwise unsympathetic to the GDR regime'. There was no doubt that the 'Communist infiltration to the island was centrally directed' and that 'special police operations' would be necessary to counter it.[96]

While the West German police did what it could to get a handle on the FDJ-led 'movement', the Adenauer government joined the propaganda battle. For this it relied heavily on the semi-official People's League for Peace and Freedom (*Volksbund für Frieden und Freiheit* or VFF), co-founded by Eberhard Taubert in August 1950. Taubert had been a leading official in the Nazi Propaganda Ministry under Goebbels. It was no exaggeration in his case when East Berlin accused Bonn of employing some of the worst representatives of the former Nazi elite. Taubert had written the script for the film *Der ewige Jude*, one of the most notorious anti-Semitic propaganda films of the Third Reich. Designed to prepare the German public for the 'Final Solution', it featured a language and imagery that was so abhorrent that one would have thought that the Allies would refrain from employing Taubert after the war.[97] But both the American and British governments sought his expertise. Under the cover name 'Erwin Kohl' he was recruited by the US Army's Counterintelligence Corps (CIC), had contacts with the British secret service, and served as adviser to the arch-conservative West German defence secretary Franz Josef Strauß.[98] Funded by Washington and Bonn, Taubert was instrumental in turning the VFF into West Germany's most important anti-Communist propaganda institution.[99]

Taubert clearly relished the opportunity to engage in the propaganda battle over Heligoland. For him the island was a symbol of an older Germany that needed to be defended against 'Bolshevism'. Even in the 1980s, when he had long since fallen from grace, he would meet with neo-Nazis and Holocaust deniers on the 'Aryan island' to celebrate its German past. But it was not only Taubert's involvement that highlighted how much the Nazi past reached into the Cold War present. His main opponent in East Berlin was Heinz Lippmann, a high-ranking SED official responsible for controlling the work of the FDJ in West Germany. Lippmann had survived twelve years of Nazi persecution. In January 1945, after three years in as many concentration camps, he had been liberated by the Red Army from Auschwitz. For him, as for so many Jewish Germans who worked for the GDR government in the 1950s, 'anti-fascism' was much more than rhetoric. The reliance of the Adenauer government on some of Hitler's leading bureaucrats seemed to indicate that the Nazi past was being rehabilitated rather than confronted in West Germany. It was as if the battle lines of the late Weimar Republic were being re-drawn: conservatives and former Nazis on one side, resisted by Communists and anti-fascists on the other.[100]

While Taubert continued to peddle anti-Communist slogans that echoed those he had spread under Hitler, Lippmann did everything he could to mobilize public opinion against the Adenauer government.[101] Working together with Dieter Schmotz on the FDJ's central council, he made sure that the 'Heligoland movement' was expanded. At the same time he was careful not to involve the FDJ directly. The groups landing on the island were led by the *Deutsche Bewegung Helgoland*, which avoided all association with the FDJ and the SED. The posters and brochures distributed by the 'movement' underlined its ostensibly pan-German character. 'Heligoland for the Germans, Heligoland for Peace! No German will take down this poster!' was a typical example. Nor were all 'occupiers' outspoken Communists or Socialists. A large number of them seem to have been naive and bored rather than highly politicized. Heligoland offered a sense of adventure and the trips there came with a generous supply of food (the *Bewegung*'s handlers often took the 'squatters' out for a pub lunch before sending them off). Some of those arrested played the role of the pacifist martyr in front of the British judge, but just as many denounced the East German involvement as well.[102] Most of them came from Hamburg and Bremen, rather than East Germany.

All this meant that Bonn's argument about 'Communist provocation' carried relatively little weight among the West German public. The FDJ involvement was seen as unfortunate or outrageous, but it did not change the underlying national narrative about 'the German island'. This line, taken by much of the West German press, showed that there was a broad consensus about the issue, defying Germany's Cold War division. The documentary

Figure 9.2 'Heligoland for the Germans, Heligoland for Peace!' Poster, *Deutsche Bewegung Helgoland*, 1951.

Insel der Entscheidung ('Island of Decision'), shown in cinemas in the summer of 1951, demonstrated this with some force. This was a West German production, but it could just as well have been from East Germany. 'The fate of our fatherland is mirrored in a small island', the dramatic voiceover declared. 'This is Germany: defeated, fragmented, desperate'. But just as the German nation would rise again, so would the island be free again and in German hands.[103]

For a large part of the German public Heligoland was clearly not an issue between West and East, but between the Germans and the Allies, between victims and occupiers. What most of the letters and petitions, sent by individuals to the governments in London, Bonn, and East Berlin, had in common was that they combined anti-British posturing with self-pity, irrespective of age and politics.[104] A typical poem, written by a Berliner, used words which suggested that the war was not over yet in 1951:

> Bombs and fire
> Are brought by this hand
> From England!
> Albion's sons in their planes
> Are mocking HUMANITY.
> . . .
> England wants to eliminate
> But God will right it!
> In God's Hand
> The Holy Land![105]

Note the prominence of vocabulary here that had been standard staple of propaganda in both world wars: the hypocritical British taking the moral high ground, but committing atrocities against the truthful Germans. Here as elsewhere the verbs used to describe what Britain was doing to Heligoland (that 'holy land') unwittingly betrayed the Nazi past: 'annihilate', 'eliminate', 'exterminate'. Bonn and London might succeed at building a Cold War partnership out of former enmity, but translating that partnership into popular sentiment was clearly going to be a longer process.

By November 1951 the two governments had finally agreed on an alternative archipelago which the RAF could bomb.[106] But since this choice (the uninhabited Großer Knechtsand in the Weser estuary) was also controversial it took until the New Year before the handover could be finalized.[107] In late February 1952 Kirkpatrick confirmed to Adenauer that London would 'relinquish control of Heligoland'.[108] Adenauer wanted a major state ceremony to mark the occasion. No expense would be spared. Around 1,500 official guests were to be invited. The highest representatives of West Germany would attend, including the president, the chancellor, and his cabinet. Three hundred press correspondents were to be present. Schools all over West Germany were to hold special assemblies; all public buildings to fly the national colours.[109] The celebrations, Adenauer told the cabinet, ought to 'express the thought that the return of Heligoland represents Germany's first success in gaining back lost territories through peaceful means'. It would be 'essential that this success be exploited for the strengthening of the national consciousness (*Staatsbewußtsein*)'.[110]

But in planning Heligoland's 'homecoming' Adenauer's staff had overlooked the fact that the island currently resembled an apocalyptic battlefield that was entirely unsafe for thousands of official guests. As the minister of transport had to remind them, only a handful of visitors could be accommodated in the small area that had been cleared.[111] In the end a brief, modest ritual was held amongst the craters and piles of rubble. On 1 March 1952 Friedrich-Wilhelm Lübke, the prime minister of Schleswig-Holstein, went to the island with a small delegation and gave the order to raise the German flag. His short address disavowed the tradition of militarism previously associated with the island. The Germans, he claimed, loved Heligoland not as a symbol of a glorious past, but as a 'natural monument' that stood for their *Heimat*. It would be rebuilt as a 'symbol of new hope' and national unity.[112]

The main message associated with the handover came from Adenauer, keen to claim the political prize in front of national and international audiences. In a prime-time radio broadcast he declared:

> From tomorrow Heligoland will be free again! That means that our people has finally been given back a piece of soil to which we Germans are attached with so much love [*mit ganz besonderer Liebe*], no matter whether we live on this or the other side of the iron curtain.

There had been much suffering, but the islanders would have their *Heimat* back. All Germans would join in the reconstruction, determined to resurrect the former 'island beauty'. The new Heligoland would allow everyone to forget the time when the island had been a threat 'bristling with guns'.

> We all carry in us the conviction that the time of the self-destruction [*Selbstzerfleischung*] of the Western world has to belong to the past once and for all. Peaceful Heligoland, set in the seas between Germany and Britain, will be in future a symbol of the will to peace and friendship of both nations.[113]

'Thus the post-war saga of Heligoland ends', Kirkpatrick reported to London. Adenauer's broadcast had been 'dignified'. 'Pleasure', 'gratitude', and 'friendship'

Figure 9.3 West Germany takes possession of Heligoland, 1 March 1952.

were the key words the high commissioner highlighted for government consumption.[114] He diplomatically skipped the passage in which Adenauer had talked about the war as the 'self-destruction of the Western world'—this was the sort of Cold War platitude behind which opposing German and British versions of the past would continue to coexist. Two months later

Kirkpatrick and Adenauer signed the Bonn Convention, together with the American and French high commissioners. The agreement, granting Bonn sovereignty over its territory except in a number of key matters concerning Berlin, the Allied forces, and an eventual peace treaty, paved the way for West German rearmament, eventually leading to NATO membership, while East Germany was to join the Warsaw Pact.[115]

West Germany's moral rehabilitation on the international stage, facilitated by the unfolding of the Cold War, required Bonn to demonstrate that it had overcome the Nazi past. The reconstruction of Heligoland was to create a showcase of the new, peaceful, prosperous West Germany. Even before the island's handover had taken place the government commissioned a Heligoland propaganda film, which would be distributed internationally.[116] The task, the director noted, was to make the island a symbol of 'Europe's tragedy'. 'Through the centuries one [sic] has fought over Heligoland', but now it was time to end the conflict. 'The first step is: no recriminations!' The island would be 'better and more beautiful' than before.[117]

British commentators were convinced that rebuilding the island was neither affordable nor desirable. But they underestimated how important the project was for the Germans. This was 'a national task', declared Adenauer when he opened the first meeting of the Heligoland Board, set up to bring together all institutions involved in the reconstruction.[118] The government would pledge large sums, but everyone was asked to help.[119] An appeal signed by the federal president, the Adenauer cabinet, and the *Länder* governments addressed 'all Germans':

> The small island shall become a symbol of the German people's readiness to make sacrifices and its will to live (*Lebenswille*) as well as its unanimous desire for equal partnership in a united Europe.

Germany would 'turn Heligoland into a monument of peace, a symbol of European understanding and reconciliation'.[120] The charity set up for the purpose, the *Helgoland-Stiftung*, was backed by the West German political establishment as well as the Protestant and Catholic churches. There were street collections, Heligoland books, memorabilia, and special stamps. Particularly generous donors received a piece of the island's rock. Payments came in not only from all over Germany, but also from Sweden, Austria, Turkey, the USA, and Southern America.[121]

Would the British contribute? Many Germans thought they should. The Auswärtiges Amt helped to draft an appeal 'to the British people' and there was some support from members of the Bundestag, but the idea was dropped: Bonn was not going to risk a new debate about the 'German Gibraltar' in Britain.[122] Feelings about the war and reparation for it were still raw in both countries. In March 1952, just days after the handover of the island, Ernst Helmers, a teacher, wrote to the British commissioner in Hamburg, John K. Dunlop. Helmers wanted to see if Dunlop would consider giving something for the reconstruction of Heligoland. He himself had recently sent his daughter to Britain as part of an initiative to improve Anglo-German understanding.[123] It would make a big impression on the German public if the occupying British made similar gestures of reconciliation by funding the rebuilding of a church or school in Heligoland.

Dunlop was clearly taken aback by the naive-friendly tone of the teacher's letter. Helmers seemed to be implying that Germans and Britons were engaged in an equal relationship—as if both sides were called upon to make an effort at reconciliation. Dunlop's reply was curt. Of course he knew about 'the emotional appeal' for the reconstruction of Heligoland. But he believed 'that many of those who now write to the newspapers think of the island as it was twenty years ago or so'. They forgot what lay between that idyllic past and the present: the war, a war in which Germany had attacked Britain, a war which would not disappear, however much the Germans might wish. It seemed to Dunlop that the whole idea of reconstructing Heligoland was 'exaggerated': 'One should think carefully before investing large sums there'.[124] Helmers, replying by return of post, disagreed: 'This is not a question of money, but of feeling'. The British ought to understand the 'sentimental feeling that we Germans happen to have'.[125]

Ever since the 1830s German commentators had argued this line. British observers from Salisbury to Churchill, too, had claimed that there was a peculiar, German sentiment about Heligoland. But what did that mean? That the Germans had a liking for a picturesque North Sea island seemed harmless enough. Nor did the woolly talk about *Heimat* and nature have to have any political implications. Or did it? German discourse about Heligoland had, since Heinrich Heine's days, never failed to invoke the idea of the 'natural monument'. Every German generation had used that term in order to define its feeling for the island, yet they had meant radically different things. There was no 'natural' or 'nature-given' meaning. Politics and culture, not nature, had conditioned its metaphorical use.[126] At the core of this island of the mind lay its association with German nationhood and Germany's relationship with the sea. From the second half of the nineteenth century onwards, the latter had inevitably involved thinking about Britain.

From Bismarck to Wilhelm II to Hitler to Adenauer, German senti-ment about Heligoland had again and again been a sentiment about Britain. The island had stood for the Anglo-German relationship and the German need to be equal and to be recognized as equal by the British. That was cer-tainly what Adenauer had in mind when he made his radio broadcast in March 1952:

> From now on, we shall act in the same spirit by which 62 years ago Heligoland became, by friendly agreement between the then German Reich and Great Britain, a part of the German soil, in exchange for German rights and claims in Africa. How much misery the world would have been spared, if this policy of mutual recognition and mutual balance of claims had been made the guiding principle underlying the treatment of European problems. But it is not yet too late to steer this course.[127]

It seemed best, in March 1952, to go back to the nineteenth century, to Bismarck and the time when a 'mutual balance' had existed between the two nations. Adenauer's broadcast, no doubt reflecting his voters' feelings, sounded harmless and agreeable. But it betrayed an underlying assumption that seems both brazen and naive in hindsight: that after all that had taken place the Germans could simply forget about the Nazi past, rebuild the island, and go back to where Bismarck had left things off.

That is not, of course, what happened. It was impossible to go on as before—the history of Germany in the second half of the twentieth century demonstrates how hardly any aspect of public or private life remained untouched by the violent decades between 1914 and 1945. Whatever the interpretative frame used to make sense of that period, the Nazi past grad-ually moved towards the centre of Germany's self-understanding, certainly from the late 1960s onwards.[128]

The Heligoland that was eventually built out of the ruins of the war reflected Germany's relationship with the past directly. Even before the island was handed over, the regional government had started an architec-tural competition for its reconstruction. The successful plan, the guidelines suggested, would need to respect the 'peculiarity of Heligoland' so beloved by 'all Germans'. At the same time it would provide for a 'new Heligoland'.[129] The composition of the jury prefigured a compromise between these two notions. Bureaucrats and politicians were in the majority, but the chairman was a prominent modernist architect. Otto Bartning, since 1950 president of the Federation of German Architects, was known for an influential essay in which he had argued against a return to tradition in public architecture after

1945. *Wiederaufbau*, reconstruction, was impossible, he had written. The very word *wieder* was wrong. It suggested a repetition, a going back to the past.[130]

Bartning's advocacy of a break with tradition would have to be brought into line with the planners and politicians who favoured a return to the town's traditional structures and dimensions. For them the stress was not on the dangers of the '*Wieder*', but on the functioning of '*Aufbau*'. By the competition's deadline in March 1952, 119 designs had been submitted. The jury shortlisted seven submissions, amongst them one by Hans Scharoun, later famous for the design of the Philharmonic concert hall and State Library in West Berlin. Two schemes were selected as joint winners, the first by Georg Wellhausen and Helmut Bunje, the second by Wolfram Vogel. Rejecting imposing avant-garde designs and clunky traditionalist schemes, the commission in charge of the reconstruction went with the sensitive modernism suggested by Wellhausen and Bunje.[131]

It was easy to dismiss this compromise as an uninspiring fudge that lacked ambition, but, when completed in the mid-1960s, the new Heligoland stood as a rare achievement in West German architecture: an entire town had been rebuilt in a new style while respecting pre-war dimensions.[132] This was a modest, unspectacular modernism, tempered by frequent breaks in lines and levels. It followed the island's topography rather than imposing itself upon it. The gable roofs used throughout the new town suggested tradition. Yet their asymmetrical shapes provided a clear departure. The colour scheme, drawn up by the painter Johannes Ufer, also signalled a new aesthetic beginning. It was these striking colours (dark red, blue, and yellow hues, combined with green and black) which most critics saw as paradigmatic for the new Heligoland and its 'Scandinavian influences'. In fact, Ufer's colour scheme referenced the Weimar modernism of Bruno Taut and Walter Gropius more than anything else, but that was not the point.[133] The new Heligoland was meant to look like the Denmark or Sweden of the present rather than the Germany of the past.

The reconstructed island signalled a clear break, the understated character of its modernism notwithstanding. Hardly anywhere in the new town was there a reference to the nineteenth century. With the exception of the resurrected Fallersleben memorial and a few gravestones in the cemetery, there was nothing that reminded visitors of the Georgian, Victorian, Wilhelmine, or Nazi eras. Rather than follow the nostalgic impulse which Adenauer was so keen to serve, the island was rebuilt as something which more closely resembled an antidote to the past. Its emphasis on 'democratic planning' and social housing foreshadowed the Social Democratic consensus which was to be at the heart of West Germany's political culture. There was ample opportunity to deride this as parochial utopianism or escapism from the past. British commentators saw in the 'Scandinavian' design a deliberate attempt to disguise the history of Anglo-German conflict—just as the constant talk about 'Europe' seemed to hide 'Germany'.[134]

It felt like a big lie to some, but it was to serve the Bonn Republic exceedingly well. With the reopening of the island for tourism (a process completed with its official re-designation as 'North Sea Spa' in 1962), the West German government sent films to its embassies around the world, to be generously distributed amongst the foreign media.[135] These low-level propaganda products praised the new Heligoland, 'visited by nearly a million tourists every year', as a showcase of West Germany: economically powerful and internationally uncontroversial.

In April 1954, after nine years of exile on the mainland, the first Heligolanders returned to the island. Not all of them liked what they found. During the consultation on the masterplan for the reconstruction it had become obvious that many amongst them favoured the very opposite of what the architects and town planners were drawing up. Most islanders had wanted a return to 'old Heligoland' rather than a radical departure from tradition. As they settled into their brand new modernist houses, they shared a sense of alienation. Very little in the new town reminded them of the Heligoland they had known. Even the iconic St Nicolai church which had once towered over the *Oberland* was subjected to the modernist vision of the town planners. An appeal to reconstruct the church according to the original drawings was turned down—to the dismay of most Heligolanders.[136]

Yet the resentment that this created amongst the islanders did not translate into political activism. At no point during or after the resettlement was there an attempt to return to the Heligolanders' traditional *raison d'être* as Anglo-German go-betweens. Throughout the Kaiserreich and the Weimar Republic they had been seen as disloyal and pro-British. Under the Nazis they had been mistrusted as a narrow-minded border population that had never quite been incorporated into the German *Volk*. It was, paradoxically, the British who convinced the Heligolanders that their future lay in Germany. The repeated destruction of their island and London's refusal to let them return pushed them into an alliance with the

Bonn government. In the spring of 1954 a long tradition of stubborn separatism seemed to come to a conclusive end. The Heligolanders had finally arrived in Germany—at the very moment when, for the first time since Bismarck, the Germans no longer had any strategic use for the cliff-bound isle in the North Sea.

Epilogue

No More Heligolands

In the late 1970s the German painter and sculptor Anselm Kiefer began to work on a series of monumental paintings which were to establish his reputation as one of the foremost artists of his generation: vast canvases of scorched earth and barren fields in which the recent past merged with the myths that Kiefer saw at the heart of German culture and identity. These were history paintings not in the sense that they depicted key moments in the German past, but in that they deconstructed central metaphors of that past: battles, heroes, myths, and, most of all, landscapes.

Heligoland was one of these totemic sites. Kiefer first adopted it as a subject in a book of grainy black-and-white photographs entitled *Hoffmann von Fallersleben auf Helgoland* which he exhibited at the Venice Biennale in 1980.[1] The pictures formed a loosely connected narrative, leading the spectator into a dimly lit room and towards a zinc bathtub, the sort that would have been standard issue in Nazi Germany. The tub revealed a fleet of model-sized U-boats and battleships capsized in between rocks and shelves of ice. The reference to Caspar David Friedrich's famous painting *Sea of Ice*, depicting a shipwreck buried in the Arctic ice, was obvious.[2] But the pictures also recalled memories of Anglo-German conflict. In particular, they seemed to re-enact *Operation 'Sea Lion'*, the Nazis' planned invasion of Britain, which Kiefer had previously evoked in a number of artworks.[3] An obscene sense of historic futility was on display in these photographs: what seemed to have come to an end in this 'wreck of hope' was both the Nazi dream of conquering Britain and the romantic tradition associated with Fallersleben and Friedrich, a tradition which the Third Reich's 'blood and soil' ideology had claimed as part of its pedigree.

Six years later Kiefer completed an oil painting to which he gave the same title and which spoke to the same leitmotif. *Hoffmann von Fallersleben auf Helgoland*, on permanent display at the Berlin National Gallery, is a vast canvas, stretched out over 5.6 by 3.8 metres. A dark horizon divides it into a narrow stretch of glowering, leaden sky, and a much larger seascape of floating debris beneath it. There is the illusion of moonshine on water, a dirty, seeping moon, giving the painting depth. But the spectator is drawn in less by these compositional lines than by the texture of the painting. The sea is dominated by thick, furrow-like waves, covered with a flotsam of burnt wood: ash and paint coagulated in the bulging surface of the canvas, the encrusted remains of Germany's past and its conflict with Britain. Where horizon and waves meet Kiefer has fixed a model warship, mummified in corrosion, abandoned and irrelevant.[4]

This, the title suggests, is what has become of the view from Heligoland which Fallersleben had been so impressed with in the summer of 1841, when he penned the *Lied der Deutschen*, while wandering 'in solitude along the cliffs, with nothing but the sky and the sea around me'.[5] Kiefer refracted this view through the past that followed Fallersleben. His painting, a seascape of memory, forces together two different periods during which Heligoland became an icon of German nationalism: the *Vormärz* before the 1848

Figure 10.1 *Hoffmann von Fallersleben auf Helgoland*. Oil painting by Anselm Kiefer, 1980. Nationalgalerie im Hamburger Bahnhof, Berlin.

revolution, associated with the romantic nationalism of Fallersleben and Friedrich; and the Third Reich's genocidal war against Europe. Kiefer does not suggest that there is a direct, causal relation between the two periods: the dream of a unified Germany did not have to lead to Bismarck, Wilhelm II, the First World War, and Hitler, just as the wars between Britain and Germany were not the direct consequence of German nationalism and the rise of the Prussian-dominated Kaiserreich. But nor does Kiefer allow for the nineteenth century to be neatly separated from the twentieth. In his art, described by himself as 'stratigraphic', the different layers of the past are merged materially in encrusted paint and corroding lead.[6]

All this stood in stark contrast to the generation of artists who had rediscovered Heligoland in the immediate aftermath of the Second World War. Alfred Mahlau, professor at the Hamburg Academy of Arts, was the first, beginning to paint scenes of the island in the 1950s. He was followed by a group of artists, some of whom he had taught, including Horst Janssen, Rolf Meyn, and Rüdiger Pauli. While they developed their own styles and interests—Janssen perhaps the most intriguing amongst them—they all continued the tradition of landscape painting which had embraced the North Sea outpost ever since Johann Joachim Faber, Eduard Schmidt, and Christian Morgenstern had established it as a *sujet* in the first half of the nineteenth century. Here was Heligoland again as a 'natural monument', its imposing cliffs and picturesque harbour scenes, a miniature German *Heimat* at the edge of the Continent.[7]

Kiefer demolished that tradition comprehensively. The German past had made a monster out of nature—there were no more innocent landscapes. It was impossible, he suggested, to reclaim morally a time before the 'German catastrophe'. The widely shared impulse in post-war Germany, expressed by Adenauer when he announced the 'liberation' of Heligoland in March 1952, had been just that: to go back to the romantic idea of Germany as a small, innocent home set in its 'natural' environment untainted by Nazism. Kiefer's generation revolted against this mentality. Holding up a mirror to West German society required symbols which the public recognized, loaded with historical meaning. Fallersleben, the *Deutschlandlied*, and the 'German island' provided such a trope.[8] Behind the harmless façade of the reconstructed Heligoland, and behind the new-found West German prosperity that it epitomized, lurked the Nazi past. By working that past into the present Kiefer's art gave a compelling expression to a broader shift in German culture and society, a shift which put the Third Reich and the Holocaust at the centre of the country's self-understanding.[9]

Anselm Kiefer's work on Heligoland as a site of German memory marks the end point of the arc of two centuries that had given this small place in the North Sea its historical role. For generations the island had served as a symbol of Germany's troubled relationship with Britain. By the 1960s the legacy of Anglo-German conflict had lost much of its political potency: West Germany had been integrated into NATO and the European Economic Community, East Germany into the Warsaw Pact. But culturally the conflicted past associated with Heligoland continued to matter. For much of the second half of the twentieth century there remained a need to foster Anglo-German understanding. In 1965 both governments were keen to stage the seventy-fifth anniversary of Heligoland's cession as a moment of reconciliation. Ludwig Erhard, the West German chancellor, gave a widely reported speech claiming that the island was a 'beacon of peace and freedom'. Once 'the symbol of unhealthy opposition to England', Heligoland was no longer 'a bulwark against a supposed trad-itional enemy'. 'The ghosts of the past', Erhard exclaimed, 'no longer sep-arate Germany from England'.[10] Frank Roberts, the British ambassador in Bonn, went to the island with a delegation, London sent a warship to participate in the celebration, and the Public Record Office in Kew put together an exhibition of historical documents showcasing the Anglo-German character of the island.[11] Roberts reported back that the celebra-tions had shown a 'spirit of friendship and goodwill'.[12] All levels of government, 'from the Federal Chancellor and the Minister President of Schleswig-Holstein down to the Mayor and local authorities', had done their best to turn the occasion 'into a very striking manifestation of Anglo-German friendship'. Roberts himself gave a speech in which he repeated what the queen had declared during her visit to West Germany three months earlier: 'For fifty years we have heard too much about the things which have divided us. Let us now make a great effort to remember the things which united us'.[13]

Heligoland continued to be wheeled out whenever West German gov-ernments felt they had to convince the world that they had overcome Germany's militarist past. Pressed by the USA to make a contribution to the Vietnam War, Willy Brandt's cabinet sent the hospital ship *Helgoland* to Saigon. As the West German press noted with satisfaction, the name of the North Sea island stood for humanitarian help, not aggression and war.[14] This still held true in the summer of 1990, when the centenary of Heligoland's cession was celebrated. Helmut Kohl's government was keen to invoke

Anglo-German friendship, not least since Margaret Thatcher, in her final year as prime minister, had been less than discreet about her opposition to German re-unification (which came into effect in October that year). So Kohl declared publicly that the former British colony would remain an icon of Anglo-German friendship and cooperation for the new, united Germany: 'This is the peaceful mission which Heligoland shall have in future'.[15] As with most official Anglo-German rituals of this period, Kohl's words betrayed a sense of wishful thinking. The less that public and political sentiment could in reality be taken for granted, the more it had to be talked up. Thatcher dragging her feet over unification was one thing, the Germanophobia thriving in British popular culture quite another. Successive German ambassadors to London criticized the British for still failing to 'understand' the Germans.[16] But that missed the point. The tabloid culture of the 1980s and 1990s was mostly self-referential: it said a lot about contemporary Britain (or, more precisely, England) and increasingly little about the Anglo-German past.[17]

By May 2015, when Elizabeth II visited Germany, the cacophony of tabloid clichés had largely faded. The queen told the German president that the two nations had reached a state of 'complete reconciliation'.[18] The two countries were engaged in unprecedented levels of strategic and economic interdependence. What was more, the press felt little need to talk about it—the Anglo-German relationship was becoming reassuringly boring. Heligoland had fulfilled its historical role: it was no longer required as a marker of difference, or as a symbol of friendship. When the 125th anniversary of its handover loomed in August 2015, no one in Berlin or London saw any need for a public ritual. There were no official statements or visits. Not even regional politicians were present at the low-key festivities on the island.[19] It was a striking contrast to fifty years before when the official Anglo-German celebrations had been so elaborate that the British ambassador likened them to a royal visit.[20]

From the turn of the century, the island took on an increasingly obscure and exotic role in the British imagination. There were Heligoland-themed pop albums and songs, dances, and re-enactments. A number of plays and historical novels used the outpost as a dramatic backdrop. But most of these styled the former colony as a metaphor of distance and isolation—an island of the mind more than a geographical reality. In Shena Mackay's 2003 novel *Heligoland*, the outpost is 'a hazy, faraway, indefinable place of solace and reunion'.[21] Rowena, the book's heroine, listens in vain to the Shipping Forecast for a mention of the island ('Heligoland' had been renamed 'German Bight' by the Meteorological Office in 1956):

> Heligoland was never mentioned now. Political and meteorological maps had been redrawn. Heligoland, or Helgoland, did exist, she knew, from checking an atlas, a small island in the North Sea belonging to Germany, off the mouth of the River Elbe, but the Heligoland of her heart was, as the imagination makes possible, both an island over unnavigable seas and a fairground roundabout.[22]

'No more Heligolands', concludes Rowena, a century after Admiral Fisher had first coined the phrase.

While the island was slowly sliding back into the obscurity it had enjoyed at the beginning of the Napoleonic Wars, it continued to wear the scars of the twentieth century. To visit Heligoland today is to walk through an archaeology of the Anglo-German past. Tourists can take a 'historical path' along the craters left behind by the RAF. They can go on a guided tour of what is left of Nazi Germany's naval fortress: a subterranean maze of air raid shelters, shafts, and tunnels. And they can buy historical souvenirs in the island's museum. Heligoland has turned into a memorial, like so many other German sites once dedicated to national glory and then destroyed by war.[23]

But Heligoland serves also as a reminder of how fortunate Britons and Germans have been since the end of the Second World War. For generations this island was a site of conflict. It expressed the German will to bully Britain and wage war to unseat her; and it mirrored the British determination to prevent Germany from establishing hegemony on the Continent. By the end of the twentieth century both strategies were defunct. The two nations had become second-rank partners in a global alliance dominated by the USA. Both played crucial, if different, roles in a larger and increasingly unpredictable Europe, a continent which neither of them could control or escape.

Coexistence seemed so much of an everyday fact that those growing up at the beginning of the twenty-first century could be forgiven if they struggled to appreciate just how conflict-ridden and violent the Anglo-German past had been. Yet they would be wrong to take this state for granted. Viewed from the longer perspective of the two centuries covered by this book, the uncontentious relationship of our present looks like a relatively recent construct. Politically, economically, and culturally Britain and Germany are more closely bound up with one another today than at any point since the late nineteenth century. But none of this is irreversible.

List of Abbreviations

AA	Auswärtiges Amt
ADM	Admiralty
AHR	*American Historical Review*
AWM	Australian War Memorial, Canberra
BA	Bundesarchiv
BA-FA	Bundesarchiv-Filmarchiv, Berlin
BA-MA	Bundesarchiv-Militärarchiv, Freiburg
BD	*British Documents on the Origins of the War*
BDC	Berlin Document Center
BFI	British Film Institute, London
BL	British Library
BStU	Behörde des Bundesbeauftragten für die Unterlagen des Staatssicherheitsdienstes der ehemaligen Deutschen Demokratischen Republik, Berlin
CAC	Churchill Archives Centre, Churchill College, Cambridge
CDU	Christlich Demokratische Union
CIC	Counterintelligence Corps
CO	Colonial Office
CSU	Christian Social Union
CUL	Cambridge University Library
CV	Centralverein deutscher Staatsbürger jüdischen Glaubens
DD	*Die deutschen Dokumente zum Kriegsausbruch*
DHM	Deutsches Historisches Museum, Berlin
DNB	*Dictionary of National Biography*
DRA	Deutsches Rundfunkarchiv, Frankfurt
EHQ	*European History Quarterly*
EHR	*English Historical Review*
FDJ	Freie Deutsche Jugend
FDP	Freie Demokratische Partei
FO	Foreign Office

GDR	German Democratic Republic
GhStA PK	Geheimes Staatsarchiv Preußischer Kulturbesitz, Berlin
GP	*Die Große Politik der Europäischen Kabinette, 1871–1914*
Hansard	Hansard Parliamentary Debates
HAPAG	Hamburg-Amerikanische Packetfahrt-Actien-Gesellschaft, Hamburg
HC	House of Commons
HJ	*Historical Journal*
HL	House of Lords
HO	Home Office
HStA	Hauptstaatsarchiv
HZ	*Historische Zeitschrift*
IHR	*International History Review*
IWM	Imperial War Museum, London
JCH	*Journal of Contemporary History*
JMH	*Journal of Modern History*
KdF	Kraft durch Freude
KPD	Kommunistische Partei Deutschlands
LA	Landesarchiv
LBI	Leo Baeck Institute
LHR	*Law and History Review*
MGZ	*Militärgeschichtliche Zeitschrift*
NAA	National Archives of Australia, Canberra
NARA	National Archives and Records Administration, Washington
NAS	National Archives Scotland, Edinburgh
NBA	Niels Bohr Archive, Copenhagen
NGS	National Galleries of Scotland, Edinburgh
NMM	National Maritime Museum, Greenwich
NORAG	Nordische Rundfunk AG
NSDAP	Nationalsozialistische Deutsche Arbeiterpartei
OKM	Oberkommando der Marine
ÖNB	Österreichische Nationalbibliothek, Vienna
OPG	Oberstes Parteigericht
OT	Organisation Todt
PA	Parliamentary Archives, London
PA-AA	Politisches Archiv des Auswärtigen Amts, Berlin
P&P	*Past & Present*
PRONI	Public Record Office of Northern Ireland, Belfast

RA	Royal Archives, Windsor
RAL	Rothschild Archive, London
RCMS	Royal Commonwealth Society
RT	Reichstag
SA-RA	Statens Arkiver, Rigsarkivet, Copenhagen
SD	Sicherheitsdienst
SED	Sozialistische Einheitspartei Deutschlands
SLNSW	State Library of New South Wales, Sydney
SPD	Sozialdemokratische Partei Deutschlands
StA	Staatsarchiv
Sten. Ber.	*Stenographische Berichte über die Verhandlungen des Reichstages*
TNA	The National Archives, Kew
V&A	Victoria and Albert Museum, London
VFF	Volksbund für Frieden und Freiheit
WIA	Warburg Institute Archive, London
WL	Wiener Library, London
WLP	Ward Library, Peterhouse, Cambridge
WO	War Office

Notes

PROLOGUE

1. Hansard, HC, 28 July 1950, 912.
2. Charles Prestwood Lucas, *A Historical Geography of the British Colonies*, vol. 1 (Oxford, 1888), 6.
3. John R. Gillis, *Islands of the Mind: How the Human Imagination Created the Atlantic World* (London and New York, 2004).
4. *Die Tagebücher von Joseph Goebbels*, ed. Elke Fröhlich, part 1, vol. 6 (Munich, 1998), 56.
5. BA, B 136/20694, Rundfunkansprache des Bundeskanzlers anläßlich der Übergabe von Helgoland, 29 Feb. 1952.
6. Austin Harrison, *England and Germany* (London, 1907), 180.
7. See Fanny A. Barkly, *From the Tropics to the North Sea* (Westminster, 1897), 141, for Heligoland as the 'gem of the North Sea'.
8. H. G. Wells, *The War in the Air* (London, 1908), 99; Erskine Childers, *The Riddle of the Sands: A Record of Secret Service* (London, 1903), 105. See Chapter 5 for a more detailed discussion.
9. Arthur J. Marder (ed.), *Fear God and Dread Nought: The Correspondence of Admiral of the Fleet Lord Fisher of Kilverstone*, vol. 2 (London, 1956), 435, Fisher to Churchill, 5 Mar. 1912.
10. Paul M. Kennedy, *The Rise of the Anglo-German Antagonism, 1860–1914* (London, 1980) is by far the most important study. See also Robert K. Massie, *Dreadnought: Britain, Germany, and the Coming of the War* (New York and London, 1991); Ian Kershaw, *Making Friends with Hitler: Lord Londonderry and Britain's Road to War* (London, 2004). For a detailed discussion of the historiography see Jan Rüger, 'Revisiting the Anglo-German Antagonism', *JMH*, 83 (2011), 579–617.
11. PA-AA, R 2496, Rudolf Lindau to Marschall von Bieberstein, 23 June 1890.
12. Sebastian Conrad, *Globalisierung und Nation im deutschen Kaiserreich* (Munich, 2006); Andrew Zimmerman, 'Race and World Politics: Germany in the Age of Imperialism, 1878–1914', in Helmut Walser Smith (ed.), *Oxford Handbook of Modern German History* (Oxford, 2011), 359–77.
13. C. A. Bayly, *The Birth of the Modern World 1780–1914* (Oxford, 2004), ch. 6; Jürgen Osterhammel, *Die Verwandlung der Welt: Eine Geschichte des 19. Jahrhunderts* (Munich, 2009), 1010–55; Jane Burbank and Frederick Cooper, *Empires in World History: Power and the Politics of Difference* (Princeton, NJ, 2010), ch. 11.

14. Medievalists and early modernists were the pioneers of such microhistories; see especially Emmanuel Le Roy Ladurie, *Montaillou* (London, 1978); Carlo Ginzburg, *The Cheese and the Worms: The Cosmos of a Sixteenth Century Miller* (Baltimore, MD, 1980); Natalie Zemon Davis, *The Return of Martin Guerre* (London, 1983). But modern historians too have followed this approach. For notable examples in German history see William Sheridan Allen, *The Nazi Seizure of Power: The Experience of a Single German Town, 1922–1945* (New York, 1984); David Blackbourn, *Marpingen: Apparitions of the Virgin Mary in Nineteenth-Century Germany* (Oxford, 1993); Mary Fulbrook, *A Small Town near Auschwitz: Ordinary Nazis and the Holocaust* (Oxford, 2012). For methodological discussions see Carlo Ginzburg, *Clues, Myths, and the Historical Method* (Baltimore, MD, 1989); Guido Ruggiero (ed.), *Microhistory and the Lost Peoples of Europe* (Baltimore, MD, 1991); Giovanni Levi, 'On Microhistory', in Peter Burke (ed.), *New Perspectives in Historical Writing* (Cambridge, 1991), 97–119; John Brewer, 'Microhistory and the Histories of Everyday Life', *Cultural and Social History*, 7 (2010), 87–109.

15. Robert Montgomery Martin, *History of the Colonies of the British Empire in the West Indies, South America, North America, Asia, Austral-Asia, Africa, and Europe* (London, 1843), 601–2; *Colonial Office List* (London, 1871), 57–8.

16. Frederic Hamilton, *The Days before Yesterday* (London, 1920), 194.

17. R. M. Lockley, *I Know an Island* (London, 1938), 160.

18. Linda Colley, *The Ordeal of Elizabeth Marsh: A Woman in World History* (London and New York, 2007), 300, makes this point persuasively. See also Antoinette Burton, 'Not Even Remotely Global? Method and Scale in World History', *History Workshop Journal*, 64 (2007), 323–8; Bernhard Struck, Kate Ferris, and Jacques Revel, 'Introduction: Space and Scale in Transnational History', *IHR*, 33 (2011), 573–84.

19. It is precisely the absence of any larger context that is disappointing about the many local histories of Heligoland. Two are notable amongst the few which use some archival sources: Michael Herms, *Flaggenwechsel auf Helgoland: Der Kampf um einen militärischen Vorposten in der Nordsee* (Berlin, 2002) and Eckhard Wallmann, *Eine Kolonie wird deutsch: Helgoland zwischen den Weltkriegen* (Bredstedt, 2012). The recent all-too-brief survey by Martin Krieger, *Die Geschichte Helgolands* (Kiel, 2015), is inferior to these earlier publications.

20. Fernand Braudel, *The Mediterranean and the Mediterranean World in the Age of Philip II*, vol. 1 (New York, 1972), 154.

21. Paul Carter, *Living in a New Country: History, Travelling and Language* (London, 1992), 123.

CHAPTER 1: EDGE OF EUROPE

1. For the background see N. A. M. Rodger, *The Command of the Ocean: A Naval History of Britain, 1649–1815* (London, 2004), chs 34, 35 and Paul W. Schroeder, *The Transformation of European Politics 1763–1848* (Oxford, 1994), ch. 5.

2. *The Later Correspondence of George III*, ed. Arthur Aspinall, vol. 4 (Cambridge, 1968), 493–4, Cabinet Minute, Downing Street, 9 Dec. 1806 (doc. 3340).

3. Ibid.

4. BL, Add. MS 49497, 2, Sontag to Willoughby Gordon, 29 July 1807. For the report see ibid., Remarks relative Heligoland, 29 July 1807.

5. TNA, FO 33/38, Thornton to Canning, 11 Aug. 1807. Compare TNA, FO 933/24, Thornton to Falkland, 10 Aug. 1807 and TNA, FO 95/145, entry for 11 Aug. 1807.

6. BL, Add. MS 49497, 2.

7. TNA, FO 933/22, Bagot to Thornton, 30 Aug. 1807.

8. On Copenhagen see Schroeder, *Transformation*, 327–31; A. N. Ryan, 'The Causes of the British Attack on Copenhagen in 1807', *EHR*, 68 (1953), 37–55; Ole Feldbaek, 'Denmark and the Baltic, 1720–1864', in Göran Rystad, Klaus-Richard Böhme, and Wilhelm M. Carlgren (eds), *In Quest of Trade and Security: The Baltic in Power Politics, 1500–1990*, vol. 1 (Lund, 1994), 257–93.

9. All quotes from TNA, FO 933/21, Thornton to Bagot, 31 Aug. 1807. Thornton's assessment echoed the earlier report by Sontag mentioned in n. 4. See BL, Add. MS 49497, 2, Remarks relative Heligoland, 29 July 1807 and, for the Admiralty's copy, TNA, ADM 1/5121/22, Attack on the Danish Island of Heligoland.

10. TNA, ADM 1/557, Pole to Russell, 31 Aug. 1807. Compare ibid., Russell to Admiralty, 7 Sept. 1807.

11. *London Gazette*, 12 Sept. 1807, 1192.

12. For the reaction of the Danish minister of foreign affairs see SA-RA, Departementet for de Udenlandske Anliggender, England, 1919, Bernstorff to Dreyer, 9 Sept. 1807. For the background see Ole Feldbaek, 'Denmark in the Napoleonic Wars', *Scandinavian Journal of History*, 26 (2001), 89–101.

13. TNA, ADM 1/557, Articles of Capitulation, 5 Sept. 1807.

14. Ibid., Russell to d'Auvergne, 6 Sept. 1807.

15. Ibid., Russell to Admiralty, 7 Sept. 1807.

16. Manuel Borutta and Sakis Gekas, 'A Colonial Sea: The Mediterranean, 1798–1956', *European Review of History*, 19 (2012), 1–13; Robert Holland, *Blue-Water Empire: The British in the Mediterranean since 1800* (London, 2012); Desmond Gregory, *Malta, Britain, and the European Powers, 1793–1815* (Madison, NJ, 1996); George Hills, *Rock of Contention: A History of Gibraltar* (London, 1974); Stephen Constantine, *Community and Identity: The Making of Modern Gibraltar Since 1704* (Manchester, 2009); E. G. Archer, *Gibraltar: Identity and Empire* (New York and London, 2006); Desmond Gregory, *Sicily: The Insecure Base: A History of the British Occupation of Sicily, 1806–1815* (London and Toronto, 1988); Lucy Riall, *Under the Volcano: Revolution in a Sicilian Town* (Oxford, 2013).

17. Gould Francis Leckie, *An Historical Survey of the Foreign Affairs of Great Britain* (London, 1808). See also Diletta d'Andrea, 'The "Insular" Strategy of Gould Francis Leckie in the Mediterranean during the Napoleonic Wars', *Journal of Mediterranean Studies*, 16 (2006), 79–89; Maurizio Isabella, 'Italian Revolutionaries and the Making of a Colonial Sea, 1800–1830', in Maurizio Isabella and Konstantina Zanou (eds), *Mediterranean Diasporas: Politics and Ideas in the Long 19th Century* (London, 2015), ch. 4.

18. For a classic formulation of this 'blue water' strategy see the 'Memorandum for the Consideration of His Majesty's Ministers' by Henry Dundas, 31 Mar. 1800 in TNA, FO 30/8/243, printed in *British Naval Documents, 1204–1960*, ed. John B. Hattendorf, R.J.B. Knight, A.W.H. Pearsall, N.A.M. Rodger, and Geoffrey Till (Aldershot, 1993), 344–50. Dundas was secretary of war under Pitt from 1794 to 1801. For the background see John Ehrman, *The Younger Pitt*, vol. 3 (Palo Alto, CA, 1996), 353–6 and, for the broader debate, Brendan Simms, 'Britain and Napoleon', in Philip G. Dwyer (ed.), *Napoleon and Europe* (Harlow, 2001), 195–200.

19. Torsten Riotte, *Hannover in der britischen Politik 1792–1815: Dynastische Verbindung als Element außenpolitischer Entscheidungsprozesse* (Münster, 2005); Nick Harding, *Hanover and the British Empire 1700–1837* (Woodbridge, 2007); Brendan Simms and Torsten Riotte (eds), *The Hanoverian Dimension in British History, 1714–1837* (Cambridge, 2007).

20. Charles Pasley, *Essay on the Military Policy and Institutions of the British Empire* (London, 1810), 159. Pasley had been sent to Heligoland to report on its defences. In the diary which he kept throughout the war he wrote about the islanders: 'They are a sober, orderly and moral race, which may be ascribed in a great measure to their excellent establishment of a public school ... owing to which all on the island male and female can read and write'. See BL, Add. MS 41976, vol. 16, 6.

21. Pasley, *Essay*, 159.

22. Ibid., 176.

23. John M. Sherwig, *Guineas and Gunpowder: British and Foreign Aid in the War with France, 1793–1815* (Cambridge, MA, 1969). See also Roger Knight, *Britain against Napoleon: The Organisation of Victory, 1793–1815* (London, 2013), ch. 10.

24. For a comprehensive description of the island's role during the war see BL, Add. MS 38246, vol. 57, Nicholas to Wellesley, 20 Oct. 1811.

25. HStA Hanover, Dep. 110, A, Nr 109, Schultz to Münster, 3 Oct. 1807.

26. TNA, FO 33/39, d'Auvergne to Broughton, 29 Oct. 1807.

27. TNA, CO 118/1, Canning to Castlereagh, 7 Jan. 1808.

28. TNA, FO 33/36, Nicholas to Howie, 4 Nov. 1806.

29. TNA, CO 118/1, Canning to Castlereagh, 7 Jan. 1808.

30. *The Later Correspondence of George III*, vol. 5 (Cambridge, 1968), 317, Taylor to Canning, 25 July 1809 (doc. 3926n).

31. TNA, FO 36/8, memorandum respecting Mr Nicholas, n.d.

32. TNA, CO 118/1, Canning to Castlereagh, 7 Jan. 1808.

33. TNA, FO 36/1, Nicholas to Hamilton, 23 May 1808.

34. TNA, CO 118/1, Nicholas to Hamilton, 23 May 1808.

35. TNA, FO 36/10, Nicholas to Hamilton, 10 Dec. 1814.

36. TNA, FO 36/7, Wellesley to Nicholas, 22 Jan. 1811.

37. TNA, CO 118/1, Hamilton to Castlereagh, 15 Feb. 1808. See also ibid., Hamilton to Castlereagh, 26 Mar. 1808.

38. TNA, FO 36/1, Nicholas to Canning, 17 May 1808. See also FO 36/5, Nicholas to Wellesley, 8 Mar. 1810.

39. TNA, FO 36/8, Nicholas to Hamilton, 6 Aug. 1813.

40. On Parish see StA Hamburg, 622–1, B 1; Richard Ehrenberg, *Das Haus Parish in Hamburg* (Jena, 1925) and Otto Beneke, 'Parish, John', in *Allgemeine Deutsche Biographie*, vol. 25 (Leipzig, 1887), 172–3.

41. Niall Ferguson, *The World's Banker: A History of the House of Rothschild* (London, 2000), ch. 3. Compare the correspondence between Rothschild and Parish kept in RAL, XI/112/4–16.

42. TNA, FO 36/8, Nicholas to Cooke, 26 Sept. 1812.

43. Ibid. The conversion is based on the rate given by Nicholas, which is corroborated by Markus A. Denzel, *Handbook of World Exchange Rates, 1590–1914* (Farnham, 2010), 25.

44. TNA, FO 36/8, Nicholas to Hamilton, 14 Aug. 1813. The overall expenditure caused by his mission is difficult to calculate. The documented payments amount to £36,348, which equated to roughly 15% of the annual budget of Britain's colonial and foreign departments together. This calculation is based on the lists of disbursements and remittances contained in TNA, CO 36/1–8. It does not include transactions in kind such as deliveries of weapons and ammunition. The total sum would have been significantly higher as many payments made by Nicholas to governments and insurgents on the Continent are undocumented. The annual national budget for foreign and colonial services is given in B. R. Mitchell, *British Historical Statistics* (Cambridge, 1988), 587.

45. 'Extraordinary Anglo-German symbiosis' is from Brendan Simms, *The Longest Afternoon: The 400 Men Who Decided the Battle of Waterloo* (London, 2014), 70.

46. On the Legion see Jasper Heinzen, 'Die Königlich Deutsche Legion: Waffenbrüderschaft als Medium des transnationalen Gesellschaftsdialogs, 1803–1850', in Ronald G. Asch (ed.), *Hannover, Großbritannien und Europa: Erfahrungsraum Personalunion 1714–1837* (Göttingen, 2014), 310–34; Jens Mastnak, 'Werbung und Ersatzwesen der Königlich Deutschen Legion 1803 bis 1813', *MGZ*, 60 (2001), 119–42. For a case study of one of the Legion's leading officers who came to Britain via Heligoland see Jasper Heinzen and Mark Wishon, 'A Patriotic Mercenary? Sir Julius von Hartmann as a Hanoverian Officer in British Service (1803–16)', *Comparativ*, 23 (2013), 13–26. See also Bernhard Schwertfeger, *Geschichte der königlich deutschen Legion*, 2 vols (Hanover and Leipzig, 1907) and Adolf Pfannkuche, *Die königlich deutsche Legion 1803–1816* (Hanover, 1926).

47. Friedrich von der Decken, *Philosophisch-historisch-geographische Untersuchungen über die Insel Helgoland oder Heiligenland und ihre Bewohner* (Hanover, 1826).

48. See also HStA Hanover, Dep. 110, A, Nr 120, Cambridge to Münster, 25 June 1813.

49. TNA, TS 25/4, Opinion of Law Officers respecting the conduct of Major Kentzinger stationed at Heligoland, employed in raising and procuring recruits from the Continent for His Majesty's service, 2 Mar. 1811.

50. Those who had served with the French or their allies and could not demonstrate that they were 'natives of Germany' were normally treated as prisoners of war. In this respect too Heligoland functioned as a forward clearing station. Small numbers of prisoners were exchanged directly with Denmark or Sweden, larger numbers were transported to Britain. See TNA, CO 118/1, Bagot to Stewart, 16 Jan. 1808.

51. StA Hamburg, 331–2, 1821, Nr 287, Untersuchungsakten betr. englische Werbungen auf Helgoland; StA Oldenburg, Best. 82, Nr 362, Aufruf und Bekanntmachung zur Gemeinschaft mit den Feinden (Handel mit Engländern über Helgoland).

52. Simms, *Longest Afternoon*.

53. For 'short, stout, merry little monk' see Thompson Cooper, 'James Robertson', *DNB*, vol. 48 (London, 1896), 410, quoting James Augustine Stothert.

54. TNA FO 36/2, Wellesley to Robertson, 3 June 1808.

55. On Mackenzie see John Holland Rose, 'A British Agent at Tilsit', *EHR*, 16 (1901), 712–16 and Thomas Munch-Petersen, 'Colin Alexander Mackenzie: A British Agent at Tilsit', *Northern Studies*, 37 (2003), 9–16.

56. The account given here is based on TNA, FO 36/2, where most of Robertson's mission is documented. James Robertson, *Narrative of a Secret Mission to the Danish Islands in 1808* (London, 1863), published posthumously, is at pains to give Robertson as much credit as possible for the success of the mission. Frank Lynder, *Spione in Hamburg und auf Helgoland* (Hamburg, 1964), ch. 3, is by and large reliable, but cites relevant documents only in German translation and without giving the sources.

57. Robertson, *Narrative*, 16.

58. It took Robertson rather longer to get back to Britain. The route back to Heligoland was too risky; Holstein and Hamburg were swarming with French agents and police. He went to Erfurt in Prussia instead, where Benedictine monks hid him. From there he made it to his old monastery in Regensburg in Bavaria. Only during the next summer did he judge it safe to return to Heligoland via Hamburg and Cuxhaven. On 24 July 1809 he arrived on the island again, was debriefed by Nicholas, and eventually took a boat back to England. Convinced that his success had not been acknowledged sufficiently, he wrote repeatedly to Canning and Wellington, asking in vain for more money or 'any employment not dishonourable to the cloth' (TNA, FO 36/2, Robertson to Canning, 16 Aug. 1809). In 1815 Robertson returned to his Bavarian monastery, where he died five years later.

59. For the distribution of anti-French pamphlets see TNA, FO 36/11, Memorandum, 21 Dec. 1815.

60. For the following see especially TNA, FO 64/80, FO 36/4, and FO 36/5.

61. On Schill see Sam Mustafa, *The Long Ride of Major von Schill* (Boulder, CO, 2008).

62. TNA, FO 64/80, Supplement à la Note du 13 Mars 1809.

63. Maimburg accompanied Ludwig von Kleist, who had negotiated with Canning on behalf of one of the Prussian networks. See TNA, FO 64/80, Kleist to Canning, 13 Mar. 1809; Kleist to Canning, 11 Apr. 1809; Canning to Maimburg, 24 Apr. 1809. Compare Sherwig, *Guineas and Gunpowder*, 209–11. For a similar mission in May 1809, independent from Kleist's and aborted after Schill's defeat, see Christian Ompteda, *In the King's German Legion* (London, 1894), 227–34.

64. *The Later Correspondence of George III*, vol. 5, 222–3, doc 3831.

65. TNA, FO 36/3, Nicholas to Canning, 28 May 1809.

66. Ibid., Nicholas to Canning, 10 June 1809.

67. The main sources for the following are in HStA Hanover, Dep. 110, A, Nr 50; TNA FO 36/3; and TNA, CO 118/2. Compare Friedrich Thimme, 'Die hannoverschen Aufstandspläne im Jahre 1809 und England', *Zeitschrift des historischen Vereins für Niedersachsen*, 62 (1897), 278–381 and Torsten Riotte, *Hannover in der britischen Politik 1792–1815: Dynastische Verbindung als Element außenpolitischer Entscheidungsprozesse* (Münster, 2005), 176–83. For other planned insurrections which Heligoland was to supply with arms see TNA, FO 36/3, Nicholas to Canning, 10 May 1809.

68. TNA, CO 118/2, Hamilton to Castlereagh, 2 July 1809; HStA Hanover, Dep. 110, A, Nr 50, Nicholas to Münster, 2 July 1809; ibid., Canning to Münster, 14 July 1809; TNA, FO 36/2, Canning to Castlereagh, 7 July 1809; TNA, FO 36/4, Canning to Nicholas, 7 July 1809; ibid., Canning to Nicholas, 14 July 1809. See also TNA, FO 36/2, List of Transports at Heligoland.

69. TNA, FO 36/11, Memorandum, Johan Sanders, 15 Dec. 1815. See also ibid., Memorial of John Sanders, 14 Feb. 1815 and Memorandum, Joseph Mellish, 20 Dec. 1811.

70. The expedition began on 30 July when combined British forces sailed across the Channel and landed on Walcheren. They had two objectives: to destroy the French fleet thought to be at Flushing (Vlissingen) near Antwerp and to open a second front in support of the Austrians, who had been fighting the French since April 1809. Led by General John Pitt, the Second Earl of Chatham, the British failed abysmally at both tasks. By early September, with the troops plagued by fever, the expedition had to be called off.

71. TNA, FO 36/4, Nicholas to Canning, 10 Aug. 1809.

72. The evacuation of the Duke of Brunswick is documented in TNA, CO 118/2 and FO 36/4. Castlereagh wanted the duke's troops to join the British expedition to Walcheren, but his dispatch arrived in Heligoland too late, see TNA, CO 118/2, Castlereagh to Hamilton, 12 Aug. 1809.

73. TNA, FO 36/1, Nicholas to Canning, 25 May 1808.

74. Ompteda, *In the King's German Legion*, 233. Ompteda was on a secret mission from Berlin to London, on behalf of Count von der Goltz, the Prussian minister of foreign affairs. Nicholas had him released as soon as he heard of the mistake.

75. TNA, FO 36/4, Hammond to Nicholas, 1 Sept. 1809. See also ibid., Nicholas to Hammond, 27 Aug. 1809 and Nicholas to Hammond, 10 Sept. 1809.

76. Ibid., Nicholas to Hammond, 23 Sept. 1809.

77. TNA, FO 36/6.

78. TNA, CO 118/3, Stuart to Admiralty, 2 Nov. 1810. See also TNA, FO 36/5, Nicholas to Wellesley, 1 Nov. 1810.

79. See TNA, FO 36/5, Nicholas to Smith, 8 Nov. 1810, for his payments to the secretary of the Hamburg post master.

80. TNA, FO 36/8, Nicholas to Cooke, 15 Feb. 1813.

81. TNA, FO 36/11, Nicholas to Cooke, 20 Apr. 1814.

82. TNA, FO 36/8, Nicholas to Cooke, 15 Feb. 1813.

83. See TNA, FO 36/5, Nicholas to Foreign Office, 13 Aug. 1810, for an example.

84. TNA, FO 36/11, Nicholas to Cooke, 20 Apr. 1814.

85. HStA Hanover, Dep. 110, A, Nr 114, Memorandum, Friedrich von der Decken, 2 Dec. 1811. See also TNA, FO 36/9, Hamilton to Cooke, 22 Feb. 1813: 'From all the accounts received, it appears that the disposition of the people in Holstein, as well as Hanover, East Friesland and particularly all along the coast is most favourable'.

86. On smuggling see Katherine B. Aaslestad, 'Lost Neutrality and Economic Warfare: Napoleonic Warfare in Northern Europe, 1795–1815', in Roger Chickering and Stig Förster (eds), *War in an Age of Revolution, 1775–1815* (Cambridge, 2010), 373–94; Gavin Daly, 'English Smugglers, the Channel, and the Napoleonic Wars, 1800–1814', *Journal of British Studies*, 46 (2007), 30–46; Rodger, *Command of the Ocean*, 558.

87. RAL, XI/112/5, Cohen to Rothschild, 22 Oct. 1807.

88. Ibid., Cohen to Rothschild, 23 Oct. 1807. See also RAL, XI/112/5, Cohen to Rothschild, 16 Nov. 1807.

89. TNA, FO 36/1, Canning to Nicholas, 17 May 1808. See also ibid., Nicholas to Canning, 25 May 1808.

90. TNA, CO 118/3, Hamilton to Colonial Office, 26 Apr. 1810.

91. The Chamber's activities are documented in TNA, CO 118/1-9. See especially CO 118/2, Constitution, Chamber of Commerce, 19 Sept. 1808 and ibid., Report of the Chamber of Commerce, 29 Jan. 1809.

92. TNA, CO 118/2, Constitution, Chamber of Commerce, 19 Sept. 1808.

93. By the spring of 1809 Nathaniel Rothschild was sending three to four ships a day from Hull to Heligoland. On his trade via Heligoland see Margrit Schulte Beerbühl, 'Trading Networks across the Blockades', in Katherine B. Aaslestad and Johan Joor (eds), *Revisiting Napoleon's Continental System: Local, Regional and European Experiences* (Basingstoke, 2014); Margrit Schulte Beerbühl, 'Crossing the Channel: Nathan Mayer Rothschild and his Trade with the Continent during the Early Years of the Blockades (1803–1808)', *The Rothschild Archive Annual Review* (London, 2008), 41–8; and Ferguson, *World's Banker*, 60–2.

94. LA Schleswig, Abt. 174, 207, Listen englischer und ausländischer Kaufleute auf Helgoland, 1810; TNA, CO 118/2, Petition, Chamber of Commerce, 20 May

1809. Compare Wernher Mohrhenn, *Helgoland zur Zeit der Kontinentalsperre* (Berlin, 1926), 42–3.

95. TNA, CO 118/1, Schmiding to Nicholas, 10 Oct. 1808.

96. Nicholas describes the system in detail in TNA, FO 36/10, Nicholas to Hamilton, 3 June 1814.

97. TNA, CO 118/8, Chetwynd to Peel, 30 Sept. 1811 with enclosures; TNA, CO 118/6, Order in Council, 13 Oct. 1812.

98. For an example see NMM, WHW/1/7, James Whitworth to his wife, 6 June 1812, writing from HMS *Portia*, a brig-sloop frequently on convoy service to Heligoland.

99. Ompteda, *In the King's German Legion*, 231.

100. TNA, CO 118/3, Hamilton to Jenkinson, 21 Apr. 1808.

101. TNA, CO 118/1, Hamilton to Colonial Office, 29 Oct. 1808.

102. Ibid., Minutes, Chamber of Commerce, 20 Nov. 1808.

103. TNA, CO 118/3, Hamilton to Colonial Office, 26 Mar. 1810.

104. Ibid., Hamilton to Colonial Office, 26 Apr. 1810.

105. Michela d'Angelo, *Mercanti inglesi a Malta 1800–1825* (Milan, 1990); Desmond Gregory, *Malta, Britain and the European Powers, 1793–1815* (London, 1996).

106. TNA, CO 118/4, Note of Receipts. The Chamber stopped raising the levy after 1811 in response to the legal dispute with the merchant John W. Anderson, on which see n. 124.

107. D'Angelo, *Mercanti inglesi*, ch. 8.

108. TNA, CO 118/1, Minutes, Chamber of Commerce, 20 Nov. 1808.

109. Heinrich von Kleist, 'Geographische Nachricht von der Insel Helgoland', *Berliner Abendblätter,* 4 Dec. 1810. Kleist's only slightly exaggerated account was based on information supplied to him by officers who had been to Heligoland, including Christian von Ompteda. See Ompteda, *In the King's German Legion*, 251 and John Hibberd, 'Heinrich Von Kleist's Report on Heligoland', *German Life and Letters*, 51 (1998), 431–42.

110. StA Oldenburg, Best. 82, Nr 362, Aufruf und Bekanntmachung zur Gemeinschaft mit den Feinden (Handel mit den Engländern über Helgoland).

111. TNA, CO 118/1, Hamilton to Castlereagh, 15 July 1808.

112. BL, Add. MS 41345, Rennie to Melville, 16 Apr. 1814. On the risk the weather posed to these vessels see TNA, FO 36/7, Nicholas to Smith, 17 Oct. 1811.

113. TNA, CO 118/6, Return of quantity and description of colonial produce and British manufacture, 20 July 1812. See also NMM, HNL/56/10 and HNL/56/11, Accounts, Captain James Hillary of *The Fame*, 1810–11 and LA Schleswig, Abt. 174, 166, Rechnungsbuch der Firma Geller & Co, Helgoland, 1809–11.

114. TNA, CO 118/9, Total of Goods Exported and Imported from and to this Island from 1 Jan. 1813 to 1 Jan. 1814. The precise figure was 11,595,176 pounds of coffee, followed by 9,616,946 pounds of sugar and 588,347 pounds of tobacco. Compare TNA, CO 118/7, Statement of the Articles Exported and Imported from and to this Island, 11 May 1813 and Patrick Colquhoun,

A Treatise on the Wealth, Power, and Resources of the British Empire (London, 1814), 378.

115. Colquhoun, *Treatise*, 331.

116. Karl Marx and Friedrich Engels, *Werke*, vol. 3 (Berlin, 1969), 46.

117. LA Schleswig-Holstein, Abt. 174, Nr 191, Charles Graumann, 22 Nov. 1809. See also John Holland Rose, 'British West Indian Commerce as a Factor in the Napoleonic War', *HJ*, 3 (1929), 34–46.

118. TNA, CO 118/1, Hamilton to Castlereagh, 26 Mar. 1808.

119. Ibid., Minutes, Chamber of Commerce, 20 Nov. 1808.

120. TNA, CO 118/5, Memorandum, 16 Apr. 1811.

121. Ibid., Anderson to Hamilton, 5 Nov. 1810; CO 118/4 Liverpool to Hamilton, 2 May 1811. Compare CO 118/11, King to Colonial Office, 17 Oct. 1816, where the Heligolanders are described as 'not intelligent enough to do justice'.

122. TNA, CO 118/2, Robinson to Liverpool, 4 Nov. 1809. Compare CO 118/5, Heligoland Laws, 16 Apr. 1811 and CO 118/8 Plumer to Bathurst, 12 Dec. 1812 where Thomas Plumer, the attorney general, confirms 'that, the capitulation having been silent on the subject of the system of law by which Heligoland was to be governed after the conquest, we apprehend the Danish law before in force continues to be the law of the island until His Majesty should think fit to promulgate a new code of laws for its government. This not having been as yet done the Danish law must be considered to be the rule by which all persons residing in the island must be governed'.

123. TNA, FO 933/21, Thornton to Bagot, 31 Aug. 1807.

124. For the most important of these see the case of John W. Anderson, documented in TNA, CO 118/4 and 118/5. Anderson, a London merchant, was arrested in 1810, having refused to pay the levy raised by the Chamber of Commerce. He was confined to prison until July 1811 when his case was heard in London. Anderson eventually gained compensation for wrongful imprisonment, but the underlying doctrine that British laws did not apply in the island remained unchallenged. See also NAS, GD51/6/1787, Anderson to Melville, 19 July 1811 and *Facts Relating to the Trial which Took Place in the Court of King's Bench, 23 February 1816, in which Mr John Anderson was Plaintiff and Sir William Hamilton was Defendant* (London, 1816).

125. TNA, CO 118/4, Hamilton to Liverpool, 23 Feb. 1811; CO 118/5, Hamilton to Colonial Office, 4 May 1811. Compare CO 118/2, Opinion of the Committee appointed by the Merchants of this Island, 29 Nov. 1809.

126. TNA, CO 118/4, Liverpool to Hamilton, 15 May 1811.

127. TNA, CO 118/5, Nicholas to Smith, 10 May 1811.

128. Ibid., Solicitor General to Colonial Office, 19 Aug. 1811.

129. Mohrhenn, *Helgoland*, 47–9.

130. Apart from the correspondence of the Chamber of Commerce contained in TNA, CO 118/2–5, Ellerman's life is documented in the unpublished biography written by his son, William Alexander Ellerman, in 1861 and held by the

Ellerman family, Canberra. Ellerman left Heligoland in 1814 and moved with his family to Antwerp, where he continued his Anglo-German business while also acting as consul general for Hanover and agent of the underwriters at Lloyd's. He died there in 1831. See TNA, PROB 11/1798/183.

131. This is based on the levies he paid to the Chamber of Commerce for those years, recorded in TNA, CO 118/4, Note of Receipts.

132. William Alexander Ellerman, 'Abraham Daniel Frederick Ellerman', unpublished manuscript, 1861. I am indebted to John Ellerman for providing copies of this manuscript.

133. RAL, XI/112/5, Cohen to Rothschild, 22 Oct. 1807.

134. RAL, T3/395, Kohn Brothers & Co, Heligoland, to N. M. Rothschild, London, 7 Jan. 1812.

135. TNA, CO 118/1, Minutes, Chamber of Commerce, 20 Nov. 1808. For an example see HStA Hanover, Hann. 51, Nr 1406, Beschlagnahme eines nach Helgoland bestimmten Schmugglers durch französische Douaniers, 1808.

136. NAS, CS96/3985, Bodan and Skirving. Compare *The Tradesman*, 7 (1811), 438. See also NAS, CS96/3419, Alexander Livingston.

137. NAS, CS96/3430, James Forrest; NAS, CS96/3431, William Miller junior.

138. TNA, CO 118/7, List of Transports at Heligoland, 9 June 1813.

139. TNA, CO 118/9, Thornton to Hamilton, 20 Dec. 1813. For arms deliveries to Hanover see HStA Hanover, Hann. 47 III, Nr 470.

140. TNA, CO 118/8, Council Office to Goulburn, 2 Dec. 1813.

141. This is how Eliza Hughes, Abraham Ellerman's wife, described the island's expat community, according to William Alexander Ellerman, 'Abraham Daniel Frederick Ellerman', unpublished manuscript, 1861.

142. SA-RA, Departementet for de Udenlandske Anliggender, England, 1920, Dépêche circulaire aux mission du Roi à Vienna, Madrid, La Hague, Dresde, Hambourg, 19 Oct. 1807.

143. SA-RA, 302, 1929, Königliche Urkunde betreffend die Abtretung Helgolands an Großbrittannien, 26 Aug. 1814.

144. TNA, FO 93/29/2, Treaty of Peace, signed at Kiel, 14 Jan. 1814, art. 3.

145. SA-RA, 302, 1929, Königliche Urkunde betreffend die Abtretung Helgolands an Großbrittannien, 26 Aug. 1814.

CHAPTER 2: NATION AND EMPIRE

1. State Library of South Australia, Adelaide, PRG 536/9, Sir John Hindmarsh, journal extract covering a journey to Heligoland, June–Aug. 1843. Compare TNA, CO 118/23, Hindmarsh to Russell, 13 Oct. 1840. Some material used in this chapter was previously published in Jan Rüger, 'Sovereignty and Empire in the North Sea, 1807–1918', *AHR*, 119 (2014), 313–38.

2. TNA, CO 118/29, Blue Book for 1845, Governor's Report, 26 Feb. 1846. See also TNA, CO 118/27, Hindmarsh to Stanley, 9 Feb. 1844.

3. TNA, CO 118/24, The Constitution of Heligoland, Observations, 7 Oct. 1842.

4. Ludolf Wienbarg, *Tagebuch von Helgoland* (Hamburg, 1838), viii.

5. Ibid., x. On the exile literature of Heligoland see Günter Häntzschel, 'Das literarische Helgoland: Eine Insel zwischen Utopie und Apologie', in Jürgen Barkhoff, Gilbert Carr, and Roger Paulin (eds), *Das schwierige neunzehnte Jahrhundert: Festschrift für Eda Sagarra* (Tübingen, 2000), 27–40.

6. Heinrich Heine, *Historisch-kritische Gesamtausgabe der Werke*, vol. 11, *Ludwig Börne: Eine Denkschrift* (Hamburg, 1978), 35 (1 July 1830).

7. Ibid., 46.

8. The *Helgoländer Briefe* are assumed by most scholars to be based on a diary which Heine kept during this period, but which does not survive. Rather than publish them separately, as he seems to have intended in the autumn of 1830, Heine included the letters in his polemic against Ludwig Börne, which came out in 1840. See Helmut Koopmann, 'Die Helgoländer Briefe', in Heine, *Historisch-kritische Gesamtausgabe*, vol. 11, 251–67 and E. M. Butler, 'Heine and the Saint-Simonians: The Date of the Letters from Heligoland', *Modern Language Review*, 18 (1923), 68–85.

9. Heine, *Historisch-kritische Gesamtausgabe*, vol. 11, 46. Compare Heinrich Heine, *Ludwig Börne: A Memorial*, translated with commentary and an introduction by Jeffrey L. Sammons (Rochester, NY, 2006), 40.

10. Heine, *Historisch-kritische Gesamtausgabe*, vol. 11, 50–1.

11. All quotes in this paragraph from Heine, *Historisch-kritische Gesamtausgabe*, vol. 11, 36.

12. Ibid., 38.

13. Theodor von Kobbe, *Briefe über Helgoland* (Bremen, 1840), 40.

14. Harro Harring, *Die Passions-Möwe: Psalmen eines Verbannten* (London, 1838), 16.

15. Ibid.

16. Ibid., 16.

17. Ibid., 43.

18. TNA, CO 118/22, Law Officers to Lord Glenelg, 18 Aug. 1838.

19. TNA, CO 118/31, Hindmarsh to Grey, 31 Jan. 1851. Harring eventually returned to London, where he continued to publish. Hindmarsh, who rebutted all attempts by Harring to be given residence on the island, called it 'self-glorifying poetry', but Harring's writings found considerable attention on the Continent. Harring, who later suffered increasingly from mental illness, took his own life in his London flat in 1870. On the context see Sabine Sundermann, *Deutscher Nationalismus im englischen Exil: Zum sozialen und politischen Innenleben der deutschen Kolonie in London 1848–1871* (Paderborn, 1997); Christine Lattek, *Revolutionary Refugees: German Socialism in Britain, 1840–1860* (London, 2006).

20. TNA, CO 118/22, Magistrates to Lord Glenelg, 11 Sept. 1838.

21. See the police reports in HStA Hanover, Hann. 80, Nr 650 and StA Stade, Rep. 80, Nr 1231.

22. HStA Hanover, Hann. 80, Nr 650, Zusammenkunft Hannoverscher Oppositionsmitglieder auf Helgoland am 21. und 22. August 1841.

23. August Heinrich Hoffmann von Fallersleben, *Unpolitische Lieder*, 2 vols (Hamburg, 1840–1). By 1843 the *Lieder* had sold 90,000 copies.

24. Compare August Heinrich Hoffmann von Fallersleben, *Mein Leben: Aufzeichnungen und Erinnerungen*, vol. 3 (Hanover, 1868), 155. In August 1840 Campe and Fallersleben agreed a second edition of the *Unpolitische Lieder* and the publication of a sequel, which was to be more direct in its revolutionary tendencies. In parallel Fallersleben continued to write folksongs and poems, amongst them the *Helgolander Lieder*, a collection of love songs.

25. Fallersleben, *Mein Leben*, 210–11.

26. Ibid., 154.

27. On 'singing the nation' see Ryan Minor, *Choral Fantasies: Music, Festivity, and Nationhood in Nineteenth-Century Germany* (Cambridge, 2013).

28. *Das Lied der Deutschen von Hoffmann von Fallersleben. Melodie nach Joseph Haydn's 'Gott erhalte Franz den Kaiser, Unsern guten Kaiser Franz!' Arrangirt für die Singstimme mit Begleitung des Pianoforte oder der Guitarre* (Hamburg, 1841).

29. It makes no sense to blame Fallersleben for the violent expansionism that became associated with his song later, but the twentieth-century uses of the *Deutschlandlied* do highlight the ambivalence which had always been at the heart of the anthem. The first time it was played at an official ceremony was during the takeover of Heligoland in August 1890. It took on a prominent role during the First World War, before the Weimar government established it as Germany's official anthem. The Nazis continued to use it, though Hitler insisted that only the first verse ('Germany, Germany above all else') should be sung. After 1945 the Bonn government enacted the third verse ('Unity and justice and freedom') as West Germany's official anthem, while East Germany adopted a new song (lyrics Johannes R. Becher, music Hanns Eichler) as its official anthem. See Jost Hermand, 'On the History of the *Deutschlandlied*', in Celia Applegate and Pamela Potter (eds), *Music and German National Identity* (Chicago, IL, 2002), 251–68; Michael Jeismann, 'Die Nationalhymne', in Étienne François and Hagen Schulze (eds), *Deutsche Erinnerungsorte*, vol. 3 (Munich, 2001), 661–4; Roland Schlink, *Hoffmann von Fallerslebens vaterländische und gesellschaftskritische Lyrik* (Stuttgart, 1981), 53–60.

30. LA Schleswig, Abt. 174, 142, Metternich to Neumann, 8 Feb. 1844. See also ibid., Canning to Stephen, 21 Feb. 1844 and TNA, CO 118/27, Stanley to Canning, 11 Apr. 1844.

31. TNA, CO 118/27, Stanley to Canning, 7 Mar. 1844.

32. Ibid., Hindmarsh to Stanley, 23 Mar. 1844.

33. Ibid.

34. Ibid.

35. Ibid., Stanley to Hindmarsh, 27 Apr. 1844.

36. *Fraser's Magazine for Town and Country*, 37 (1848), 544.

37. TNA, CO 118/18, Siemens to Bathurst, received 25 Aug. 1826. See also TNA, CO 118/16, Siemens to Bathurst, 28 Dec. 1824.

38. Martin, *History of the Colonies*, 602. See also TNA, CO 118/23, Hindmarsh to Stanley, 20 Sept. 1841.

39. TNA, CO 118/29, Blue Book for 1845, Governor's Report, 26 Feb. 1846. See also TNA, CO 118/33, Pattinson to Labouchere, 12 Apr. 1858.

40. Kobbe, *Briefe*, 65, 106–22. See also Feodor Wehl, *Der kleine illustrirte Fremdenführer nach und auf Helgoland* (Hamburg, 1848), 8–9.

41. Gotthold Salomon, *Erinnerungen an das Seebad auf Helgoland im Jahr 1834* (Hamburg, 1835), 10.

42. Wehl, *Fremdenführer*, 7.

43. Stendhal, *Vie de Rossini* (Paris, 1824), 3. English and German translations had come out in the same year.

44. TNA, CO 118/34 contains a selection of *Verzeichnisse*.

45. TNA, CO 118/33, Pattinson to Colonial Office, 25 June 1858.

46. TNA, CO 118/29, Pattinson to Stanley, 27 Apr. 1858.

47. Ibid., Pattinson to Colonial Office, 2 Aug. 1858.

48. Ibid., Minutes on Pattinson to Stanley, 25 June 1858.

49. TNA, CO 118/33, Attestation, 31 July 1859.

50. TNA, CO 118/23, Hindmarsh to Stanley, 20 Sept. 1841.

51. *Der Freischütz*, 31 July 1856. See also *Bremer Tageblatt*, 7 July 1857.

52. *The Times*, 26 Aug. 1856, Letter to the Editor.

53. TNA, CO 118/33, Newcastle to Pattinson, 25 July 1859.

54. Ibid., Pattinson to Newcastle, 1 Aug. 1859.

55. TNA, CO 118/34, Hoffmann to Colonial Office, 30 Aug. 1859.

56. David Blackbourn, '"Taking the Waters": Meeting Places of the Fashionable World', in Martin H. Geyer and Johannes Paulmann (eds), *The Mechanics of Internationalism* (Oxford, 2001), 435–57; Alain Corbin, *The Lure of the Sea: Discovery of the Seaside 1750–1840* (Berkeley, CA, 1994).

57. Kobbe, *Briefe*, 65.

58. Ibid.

59. Karl Reinhardt, *Von Hamburg nach Helgoland* (Leipzig, 1856), 103–4; Kobbe, *Briefe*, 67. On the solitude of the traveller in nature see Eric Leed, *The Mind of the Traveller: From Gilgamesh to Global Tourism* (New York, 1991), 73–82, 289.

60. See the following in the Hamburg Kunsthalle: Christian Morgenstern, *Helgoland im Mondlicht* (HK-1130); Christian Morgenstern, *Düne bei Helgoland* (HK-2205); Eduard Schmidt, *Helgoland* (HK-3280); Ernst Willers, *Blick aus dem Fenster auf Helgoland* (HK-1336); Johann Joachim Faber, *Die Düne von Helgoland* (HK-2065). See Jenns E. Howoldt and Andreas Baur (eds), *Die Gemälde des 19. Jahrhunderts in der Hamburger Kunsthalle* (Hamburg 1993), 39, 145, 188, 230. For

more examples see the Heligoland Collection at the Altonaer Museum für Kunst und Kulturgeschichte, Hamburg.

61. *The Poetical Works of Thomas Campbell* (London, 1837), 237. The original is in the National Gallery of Scotland.

62. Clarkson Stanfield, *A Skirmish off Heligoland*, private collection. The painting was displayed at the Royal Academy in May 1867. See also the Heligoland paintings in the Royal Collection, especially those by John T. Macallum and John Christian Schetky: Delia Millar, *The Victorian Watercolours in the Collection of H.M. The Queen* (London, 1995), cat. 3726, 4906.

63. David Blackbourn, *The Conquest of Nature: Water, Landscape and the Making of Modern Germany* (London, 2006); Thomas M. Lekan, *Imagining the Nation in Nature: Landscape Preservation and German Identity, 1885–1945* (Cambridge, MA, 2004); Christof Mauch (ed.), *Nature in German History* (New York, 2004); Joachim Radkau, *Natur und Macht: Eine Weltgeschichte der Umwelt* (Munich, 2000), 260–73; Simon Schama, *Landscape and Memory* (New York, 1995), ch. 2.

64. Johann Peter Eckermann, *Gespräche mit Goethe in den letzten Jahren seines Lebens* (Zurich, 1948), 455, entry for 19 Feb. 1831.

65. Johann Wolfgang Goethe, *Briefe der Jahre 1814–1832* (Zurich, 1951), 742, Goethe to Christian Dietrich von Buttel, 3 May 1827.

66. Ibid., 767, Goethe to Karl Friedrich Zelter, 24 Oct. 1827.

67. Sternberg had sent Goethe a long description of his excursion to the island in October 1830; see Claudia Schweizer, *Johann Wolfgang Goethe und Kaspar Maria von Sternberg: Naturforscher und Gleichgesinnte* (Vienna, 2004), 115, 327. See also Johann Martin Lappenberg, *Über den ehemaligen Umfang und die alte Geschichte Helgolands: Ein Vortrag bei der Versammlung der deutschen Naturforscher im September 1830* (Hamburg, 1831).

68. Goethe, *Briefe*, 742, Goethe to Christian Dietrich von Buttel, 3 May 1827.

69. Ibid., 741, Goethe to Christian Dietrich von Buttel, 3 May 1827.

70. Ibid., 958, Goethe to Kaspar von Sternberg, 4 Jan. 1831. The island, Goethe wrote, provided 'evidence for the continued workings of the world spirit (*Weltgeist*)'. See also ibid., 767, Goethe to Karl Friedrich Zelter, 24 Oct. 1827.

71. Ibid., 958, Goethe to Kaspar von Sternberg, 4 Jan. 1831.

72. Wienbarg, *Tagebuch von Helgoland*, 102–3.

73. Celia Applegate, *A Nation of Provincials: The German Idea of Heimat* (Berkeley, CA, 1990); Alon Confino, *The Nation as a Local Metaphor: Württemberg, Imperial Germany, and National Memory, 1871–1918* (Chapel Hill, NC, 1997); Jost Hermand and James Steakley (eds), *Heimat, Nation, Fatherland: The German Sense of Belonging* (New York, 1997); Peter Blickle, *Heimat: A Critical Theory of the German Idea of Homeland* (Rochester, NY, 2002).

74. Heine, *Historisch-kritische Gesamtausgabe*, vol. 11, 36.

75. For 'Germanic utopias' see George L. Mosse, *The Crisis of German Ideology: Intellectual Origins of the Third Reich* (London, 1966), ch. 6.

76. Wehl, *Fremdenführer*, 45.

77. NAS, GD45/8/163, Notes on the Island of Heligoland, 1854.
78. TNA, CO 118/50, Maxse to Carnavaron, 19 June 1875, with enclosed copy of *Owen's College Magazine* for May 1875.
79. TNA, CO 118/29, Blue Book for 1845, Governor's Report, 26 Feb. 1846.
80. Karl Reinhardt, *Von Hamburg nach Helgoland* (Leipzig, 1856), 8.
81. TNA, CO 118/30, Hindmarsh to Grey, 10 May 1848. Compare TNA, CO 118/30, Foreign Office to Colonial Office, 27 May 1848.
82. The Anglo-German confusion is documented in BA, DB 52/12; BA, DB 59/20 and BA, DB 53/36, see esp. in the latter Cowley to Wittgenstein, 7 July 1849.
83. TNA, CO 118/31, Hindmarsh to Colonial Office, 4 June 1849.
84. Holger Hjelholt, *British Mediation in the Danish–German Conflict*, 2 vols (Copenhagen, 1965–6); Holger Hjelholt, *Great Britain, the Danish–German Conflict and the Danish Succession, 1850–1852* (Copenhagen, 1971); Anselm Doering-Manteuffel, *Vom Wiener Kongress zur Pariser Konferenz: England, die deutsche Frage und das Mächtesystem, 1815–1856* (Göttingen, 1991).
85. Hansard, HC, 19 Apr. 1848, 521.
86. Frank Lorenz Müller, *Britain and the German Question: Perceptions of Nationalism and Political Reform, 1830–63* (Basingstoke, 2002); Günther Gillessen, *Lord Palmerston und die Einigung Deutschlands: Die englische Politik von der Paulskirche bis zu den Dresdner Konferenzen, 1848–1851* (Lübeck, 1961).
87. Alexa Geisthövel, *Eigentümlichkeit und Macht: Deutscher Nationalismus 1830–1851. Der Fall Schleswig-Holstein* (Stuttgart, 2003); Peter Thaler, *Of Mind and Matter: The Duality of National Identity in the German–Danish Borderlands* (Lafayette, IN, 2009).
88. *Household Words*, 12 (1855), 145.
89. Ibid.
90. Ibid., 148.
91. BL, Add. MS 41976, vol. 16, 6. The linguistic peculiarities of Heligoland were analysed in detail by Theodor Siebs, *Helgoland und seine Sprache: Beiträge zur Volks- und Sprachkunde* (Cuxhaven, 1909). See also Nils Århammar, 'Historisch-soziolinguistische Aspekte der nordfriesischen Mehrsprachigkeit', *Zeitschrift für Dialektologie und Linguistik*, 42 (1975), 129–45.
92. TNA, CO 118/28, Hindmarsh to Stanley, 3 Sept. 1845.
93. TNA, CO 118/29, Barrow to Stephen, 5 Dec. 1846.
94. TNA, CO 118/28, Metropolitan Police to Colonial Office, 20 Nov. 1845; Minute by Barrow, 5 Dec. 1845.
95. TNA, CO 118/31, Hindmarsh to Pakington, 8 Nov. 1852.
96. Ibid.
97. Ibid., Hindmarsh to Newcastle, 14 Feb. 1853.
98. TNA, CO 118/30, Hindmarsh to Magrath, 4 Mar. 1848.
99. Ibid., Declaration, James Joseph Kelly, 21 Dec. 1847.
100. Ibid., Magrath to Hindmarsh, 9 Jan. 1848.

101. On the islanders' tradition as wreckers see TNA, CO 118/31, Hindmarsh to Pakington, 30 Apr. 1851: 'The business of wrecking is carried on with all the secrecy and cunning that smuggling is elsewhere while it moreover meets with general sympathy and assistance for all or nearly all here consider it natural to steal from wrecks while very great facilities are afforded for the concealment of stolen goods'.

102. TNA, CO 118/30, Magistrates to Hindmarsh, 4 Apr. 1848.

103. TNA, CO 118/30, Cumming, on behalf of underwriters Lloyd's, to Grey, 22 June 1848.

104. On imperial careers and family networks see David Lambert and Alan Lester (eds), *Colonial Lives across the British Empire: Imperial Careering in the Long Nineteenth Century* (Cambridge, 2000); Catherine Hall, *Civilising Subjects: Metropole and Colony in the English Imagination 1830–67* (Cambridge, 2002); Colley, *The Ordeal of Elizabeth Marsh*; Emma Rothschild, *The Inner Life of Empires* (Princeton, NJ, 2011).

105. On Stephen see TNA, CO 118/28, Hindmarsh to Stanley, 7 Jan. 1845 and SLNSW, A 1694, George Milner Stephen, diary and papers.

106. CUL, RCMS 59/4, Heligoland Report, General Edward Charles Frome, c.1858.

107. TNA, CO 118/30, Colonial Land and Emigration Office, 28 May 1847.

108. Ibid., Harrington to Grey, 14 Oct. 1847.

109. TNA, CO 118/34, War Office to Colonial Office, 2 Jan. 1855; ibid., War Office to Colonial Office, 24 Jan. 1855; Wiltshire and Swindon Archives, 2057/F8/ III/B/385, Hindmarsh to Grey, 11 Jan. 1855.

110. TNA, 118/32, Hindmarsh to Grey, 2 Apr. 1855.

111. W. B. Tyler, 'The British German Legion, 1854–1862', *Journal of the Society of Army Historical Research*, 54 (1976), 14–29; Charles Calvert Bayley, *Mercenaries for the Crimea: The German, Swiss, and Italian Legions in British Service, 1854–1856* (Montreal, 1977).

112. StA Oldenburg, Best. 31-13, Nr 66-146, Englische Werbungen für die Fremdenlegion in Helgoland.

113. *Oldenburgische Anzeigen*, 20 Jan. 1855.

114. StA Wolfenbüttel, 27 Neu 1, Nr 648, Untersuchung gegen den Soldaten Carl Wilhelm Schönian; ibid., Nr 666, Untersuchung gegen den Jäger Johann Georg Heinrich Wilhelm Knigge; ibid., Nr 135, Untersuchung gegen den Kanonier Theodor Charles Friedrich August Schmidt. See also PA-AA, R 19552, Bericht über die gegenwärtige Beschaffenheit und Benutzung der Insel Helgoland, 16 Sept. 1855.

115. *Bremer Tageblatt*, 7 July 1857.

116. William Westphal, *Ten Years in South Africa: Only Complete and Authentic History of the British German Legion in South Africa and the East Indies* (Chicago, IL, 1892); *The Letters and Journal of Gustav Steinbart, German Military Colonist to British Kaffraria, Cape Province, South Africa*, 2 vols (Port Elizabeth, 1975–8). The

Legion's settlement in South Africa is documented in TNA, WO 3/98, WO 6/196 and WO 15. See also John Laband, 'From Mercenaries to Military Settlers: The British German Legion, 1854–1861', in Stephen M. Miller (ed.), *Soldiers and Settlers in Africa, 1850–1918* (Leiden, 2009), 85–122. I am indebted to Jasper Heinzen for his advice on this point.

117. TNA, CO 118/26, Minute, 15 Mar. 1843, on Hindmarsh to Stanley, 7 Mar. 1843. On the pluralistic character of colonial rule see Peter Burroughs, 'Imperial Institutions and the Government of Empire', in Andrew Porter (ed.), *The Oxford History of the British Empire*, vol. 3 (Oxford, 1999), ch. 9 and John W. Cell, 'Colonial Rule', in Judith Brown and W. Roger Louis (eds), *The Oxford History of the British Empire*, vol. 4 (Oxford, 1999), 232–54.

118. TNA, CO 118/33, Address to the Queen, subscribed at Government House, 16 Feb. 1859.

CHAPTER 3: A MATTER OF SENTIMENT

1. PA-AA, R 19552, Bericht über die gegenwärtige Beschaffenheit und Benutzung der Insel Helgoland, 16 Sept. 1855; Promemoria, 16 Sept. 1855; Gaertner to War Department, 22 Sept. 1855.

2. PA-AA, R 19552, Promemoria, 16 Sept. 1855.

3. Klaus Hildebrand, *No Intervention: Die Pax Britannica und Preußen, 1865/66–1869/70* (Munich, 1997); Scott W. Murray, *Liberal Diplomacy and German Unification: The Early Career of Robert Morier* (Westport, CT, 2000); Jonathan Parry, *The Politics of Patriotism: English Liberalism, National Identity and Europe, 1830–1886* (Cambridge, 2006), ch. 6.

4. Kennedy, *Rise of the Anglo-German Antagonism*. For the historiographical context see Rüger, 'Revisiting the Anglo-German Antagonism'.

5. Paul M. Kennedy, 'Idealists and Realists: British Views of Germany, 1864–1939', *Transactions of the Royal Historical Society*, 5th ser., 24 (1975), 137–56.

6. TNA, CO 118/38, Minute by Elliot, 18 Mar. 1865, on Maxse to Cardwell, 6 Mar. 1865.

7. PA-AA, R 19552, Richthofen to Bismarck, 22 Sept. 1863.

8. TNA, CO 118/36, Minute on Pattinson to Newcastle, 4 Sept. 1862; ibid., Minute on Pattinson to Newcastle, 28 Sept. 1862; ibid., Minute by Newcastle, 27 Mar. 1863, on Pattinson to Newcastle, 13 Mar. 1863. On Pattinson see also CO 118/33, Official Memorandum Showing the Services of Major Richard Pattinson. When Pattinson finally left in April 1863, he bemoaned his fate in a valedictory dispatch: 'I came here poor, I go away poorer; I came here well and I go away sick'. See TNA, CO 118/36, Pattinson to Newcastle, 14 Apr. 1863.

9. TNA, CO 118/38, Minute by Elliot, 18 Mar. 1865, on Maxse to Cardwell, 6 Mar. 1865.

10. PA-AA, R 19552, Richthofen to Bismarck, 22 Sept. 1863.

11. TNA, CO 118/38, Minute by Elliot, 18 Mar. 1865, on Maxse to Cardwell, 6 Mar. 1865, commenting on Maxse's 'thorough knowledge of the German language and manners'.

12. TNA, CO 118/37, Maxse to Newcastle, 7 Feb. 1864.

13. RA, VIC/MAIN/QVJ (W), 24 Jan. 1883. A summary of Lady Maxse's career can be found in V&A, THM/37/7/31, Augusta Maxse to Henry Irving, 20 July [1890]. On the couple's trips to Vienna and Berlin see TNA, FO 918/54, Maxse to Russell, 12 Nov. 1881.

14. William George Black, *Heligoland and the Islands of the North Sea* (London, 1888), 31.

15. Hamilton, *Days before Yesterday*, 197. See also TNA, FO 918/54, Maxse to Russell, 18 Mar. 1880.

16. *Prince Bismarck's Letters to his Wife, his Sister, and Others, from 1844 to 1870*, translated from the German by Henry Fitzhardinge Berkeley Maxse (London, 1878).

17. PA-AA, R 19552, Bismarck to Münster, 19 Mar. 1876. On Russell see Karina Urbach, *Bismarck's Favourite Englishman: Lord Odo Russell's Mission to Berlin* (London, 1999). His correspondence with Maxse is in TNA, FO 918/54. The governor's nephew Leopold Maxse, editor of the *National Review* from 1893 to 1932, was decidedly less Germanophile. See Leopold Maxse, *'Germany on the Brain', or, the Obsession of 'A Crank': Gleanings from The National Review, 1899–1914* (London, 1915) for a sample of his pre-war articles which tended to combine Germanophobia with anti-Semitism.

18. Hamilton, *Days before Yesterday*, 196.

19. For the following see Linda Colley, 'Empires of Writing: Britain, America and Constitutions, 1776–1848', *LHR*, 32 (2014), 237–66 and her forthcoming study of constitution making and empire building.

20. Hugh Edward Egerton, *The Origin and Growth of the English Colonies and of their System of Government* (Oxford, 1903), ch. 9; John Darwin, 'A Third British Empire? The Dominion Idea in Imperial Politics', in Brown and Louis (eds), *The Oxford History of the British Empire*, vol. 4 (Oxford, 1999), 64–87; Duncan Bell, *Building Greater Britain: Empire, Ideology, and the Future of World Order, 1860–1900* (Princeton, NJ, 2007), ch. 7; Theodore Koditschek, *Liberalism, Imperialism, and the Historical Imagination: Nineteenth-Century Visions of a Greater Britain* (Cambridge, 2011), ch. 5.

21. Jennifer Pitts, *A Turn to Empire: The Rise of Imperial Liberalism in Britain and France* (Princeton, NJ, 2005); Andrew Sartori, 'The British Empire and its Liberal Mission', *JMH*, 78 (2006), 623–42.

22. TNA, CO 118/36, Draft of an Order in Council making provision for the Government of Heligoland, 4 Nov. 1863. See also TNA, 118/37, Maxse to Newcastle, 4 Feb. 1864; 7 Feb. 1864; 9 Feb. 1864.

23. Ibid., Maxse to Newcastle, 22 Feb. 1864 and 2 Apr. 1864.

24. TNA, CO 119/2, Colonial Office to Maxse, 8 and 18 Jan. 1864.

25. Lauren Benton, *Law and Colonial Cultures: Legal Regimes in World History, 1400–1900* (Cambridge, 2002), 170–83; Timothy Keegan, *Colonial South Africa and the Origins of the Racial Order* (Charlottesville, VA, 1996).

26. Fred D. Schneider, 'Deadlock on the Rock: Constitutionalism and Counteraction in Heligoland 1864–1868', *Canadian Journal of History*, 8 (1973), 23–35.

27. TNA, CO 118/36, Maxse to Newcastle, 10 June 1863; ibid., minute by Rogers, 19 June 1863. For the text of the constitution see *Return of the Orders in Council of 7 June 1864, and 29 February 1868, as to the Government of Heligoland* (London, 1890).

28. TNA, CO 118/36, Maxse to Newcastle, 19 Dec. 1863.

29. TNA, CO 118/37, Maxse to Cardwell, 26 Sept. 1864.

30. TNA, CO 118/24, The Constitution of Heligoland, Observations, 7 Oct. 1842; TNA, CO 118/30, Heligoland, 14 July 1847; TNA, CO 118/34, Memorandum and Minutes, 27 Feb. 1858.

31. TNA, CO 118/36, Maxse to Newcastle, 19 Dec. 1863.

32. See Chapter 2.

33. TNA, CO 118/37, Maxse to Newcastle, 7 Feb. 1864.

34. TNA, CO 118/36, Minute by Newcastle, 31 Dec. 1863, on Maxse to Newcastle, 19 Dec. 1863.

35. TNA, CO 118/37, Maxse to Cardwell, 9 May 1864; Hansard, HC, 6 May 1864, 103–4. In German–Danish counting, this was the Second Battle of Heligoland, the first having taken place on 4 June 1849 between the Danish navy and the unified German fleet commanded by Karl Rudolf Brommy. See Chapter 2.

36. LA Schleswig-Holstein, Abt. 174, Nr 114, Address by the Governor on new constitution, 1864. The address was read out to the assembled Heligolanders on 11 Apr. 1864. See TNA, CO 118/37, Maxse to Newcastle, 13 Apr. 1864.

37. TNA, CO 118/38, Maxse to Elliot, 30 Dec. 1865.

38. *Beschwerdeschrift der Helgolander Bürgerschaft wider den Gouverneur Maxse wegen Verletzung der der Insel Helgoland garantirten Rechte und Privilegien* (Husum, 1866).

39. For some of the legal advice they got see WLP, 951.1.4.

40. TNA, CO 118/40, Minute by T. F. Elliot on Maxse to Cardwell, 7 July 1866.

41. TNA, CO 118/38, Maxse to Cardwell, 6 Mar. 1865.

42. TNA, CO 118/40, Appeal to representatives, Government House, 11 Mar. 1866.

43. TNA, CO 118/41, Chief Judge of Court of Sessions and Chairman of Combined Courts to Maxse, 16 Oct. 1866.

44. TNA, CO 118/43, Stanley to Ward, 26 Dec. 1866.

45. Ibid., Minute by T. F. Elliot, 11 Jan. 1867.

46. TNA, CO 119/6, Rogers to Admiralty, 6 July 1867. See also TNA, CO 118/44, Heligoland, 14 Dec. 1867.

47. TNA, CO 118/44, Minute, Elliot, on Maxse to Buckingham, 10 Mar. 1868.

48. Ibid., Order of the Queen in Council, 29 Feb. 1868. See also TNA, CO 118/51, Memorandum on the Coast Guard establishment at Heligoland, 10 Oct. 1876.

49. Theodor Fontane, 'Helgoland und sein Gouverneur', *Kreuzzeitung*, 3 Oct. 1866.

50. On imperial liberalism see Pitts, *Turn to Empire*; Sartori, 'British Empire', 623–42. On the 'civilizing mission' of law see Nasser Hussain, *Jurisprudence of Emergency: Colonialism and the Rule of Law* (Ann Arbor, MI, 2003), ch. 2.

51. Hansard, HL, 13 Mar. 1876, 1852–3.

52. Sedley Taylor, 'British Despotism in Heligoland', *Pall Mall Gazette*, 14 Jan. 1876.

53. TNA, CO 118/51, Abolition of Old Constitution, minutes, 14 Jan. 1876; TNA, CO 118/52, Heligoland and Mr Sedley Taylor, memorandum by Maxse, received 23 Apr. 1879.

54. Ibid.

55. *The Collected Papers of Sir Adolphus William Ward*, vol. 5 (Cambridge, 1921), 89.

56. WLP, 951.1.4, John Ward, 'Heligoland', n.d.

57. WLP, 951.1.4, Maxse to Ward, 4 Jan. 1867.

58. CUL, MS Add. 6256/66, Maxse to Sedley Taylor, 24 Apr. 1876.

59. CUL, MS Add. 6256/47, 6256/64 and 6256/67.

60. CUL, MS Add. 6256/71, Notes on Dr Oetker's pamphlet published in German and English and entitled 'Constitution and Right in Heligoland', 18 Sept. 1878.

61. Friedrich Oetker, *Helgoland: Schilderungen und Erörterungen* (Berlin, 1855), 311. See also Ernst von Moeller, *Rechtsgeschichte der Insel Helgoland* (Weimar, 1905) and Lorenz Petersen, 'Zur Geschichte der Verfassung und Verwaltung auf Helgoland', *Zeitschrift der Gesellschaft für Schleswig-Holsteinische Geschichte*, 67 (1939), 29–190.

62. Oetker, *Helgoland*, 311.

63. TNA, CO 118/38, Minute by Elliot, 24 Mar. 1865.

64. TNA, CO 118/43, Stanley to Ward, 26 Dec. 1866. Compare LA Schleswig, Abt. 174, Nr 416, O'Brien to Justizrat Schleswig, 6 Sept. 1883, continuing the tradition of asking the Schleswig administration for legal advice. In some areas, notably medicine, Prussian law applied exclusively. When the Heligoland apothecary challenged a prescription made by Dr von Aschen, the colony's chief medical officer, in July 1869, Maxse told him 'that the Prussian medical code was that of this colony' and that the dispute would be settled by obtaining the opinion of the relevant authorities in Berlin (TNA, CO 118/45, Maxse to Granville, 26 July 1869).

65. For similar readings of colonial law in other parts of the empire see Lauren Benton, *A Search for Sovereignty: Law and Geography in European Empires, 1400–1900* (Cambridge, 2010); Benton, *Law and Colonial Cultures*; Elizabeth Kolsky, *Colonial Justice in British India: White Violence and the Rule of Law* (Cambridge, 2010); Jonathan Saha, 'A Mockery of Justice? Colonial Law, the Everyday State and Village Justice in the Burma Delta, c.1890–1910', *P&P*, 217 (2012), 187–212.

66. Renaud Morieux, 'Diplomacy from Below and Belonging: Fishermen and Cross-Channel Relations in the Eighteenth Century', *P&P*, 202 (2009), 83–125.

67. James C. Scott, *The Art of Not Being Governed: An Anarchist History of Southeast Asia* (New Haven, CT, 2009).

68. Maxse himself explained the 'state of anarchy' as an exception, caused by the introduction of taxation. It stood in contrast to the order which had existed before 1864 and had returned after 1868. See TNA, CO 118/51 Memorandum, 10 Oct. 1876.

69. TNA, CO 118/49, Gambling, Question in House of Commons, 13 May 1873. In the years to come the governor's men occasionally surprised secret gambling rings, arresting the players and seizing the money on the table. See ibid., Maxse to Kimberley, 28 Aug. 1873.

70. For examples see LA Schleswig-Holstein, Abt. 174, Nr 416, O'Brien to Governor of Gibraltar, 25 June 1883; ibid., Nr 110, Maxse to Governor of Jamaica, 22 Apr. 1884; TNA, CO 118/56, Articles of Agreement, 26 Mar. 1883; TNA, CO 118/60, Order for the removal of Fritz Ewald Albrecht alias Köhler and Hermann Ludwig Bernhard Johannes Moritz Horn alias Knoll under the Colonial Prisoners Removal Act 1884; TNA, CO 121/1, Draft of an ordinance framed in accordance with that of Newfoundland, 30 July 1887.

71. RA, VIC/ADD A15/2915, Arthur to Victoria, 20 Aug. 1872, emphasis in the original. See also LA Schleswig-Holstein, Abt. 174, Nr 110, Public Declaration, 9 Sept. 1858 and *Morning Post*, 21 Sept. 1858 on Prince Alfred's visit in 1858. The colony's public rituals honouring royal birthdays are documented in LA Schleswig, Abt. 174, Nr 110.

72. LA Schleswig, Abt. 174, 416, Tod des Sohns der Königin, 3 Apr. 1884. For loyal presentations by the Heligolanders see also *1887, The Royal Year: Chronicle of our Good Queen's Jubilee* (London, 1889), 100–1.

73. TNA, CO 118/56, Descriptive Roll of Boy P. J. Wenn and Declaration of Parent, 3 Apr. 1883; ibid., Admiralty to Colonial Office, 19 Apr. 1883. See also the service records in TNA, ADM 118/162/123709; ADM 118/170/127810; ADM 139/946/14567; ADM 188/70/79516; ADM 188/162/123710.

74. LA Schleswig, Abt. 174, Nr 110, Public Announcement, 15 Nov. 1884.

75. TNA, CO 118/55, Minute by C. A. Harris, 3 Mar. 1882; Minute by Kimberley, 7 Mar. 1882; both on O'Brien to Kimberley, 27 Feb. 1882. See also Jan Rüger, *The Great Naval Game: Britain and Germany in the Age of Empire* (Cambridge, 2007), 175–82.

76. TNA, CO 118/49, Maxse to Kimberley, 8 Feb. 1873; ibid., Convention between the Colonial Government of Heligoland and the Post Office of the German Empire for the Regulation of their Mutual Postal Relations, 5 June 1873. Letters sent between the island and Germany cost the same as those sent within the Kaiserreich. Letters to Britain were more than twice as much.

77. TNA, CO 118/50, Public Announcement, Colonial Postmaster, 15 June 1873.

78. Ibid., Maxse to Carnarvon, 10 Nov. 1874. For philatelic obsessions with Heligoland see G. Bryant, *The Postage Stamps of Heligoland and their History*

(Swansea, 1895); Jean-Baptiste Moens, *Heligoland, et ses timbres: Étude suivie du catalogue général de toutes les émissions postales* (Brussels, 1897); Ewald Müller-Mark, *Alt-Deutschland unter der Lupe*, vol. 5: *Helgoland*, 2nd edn (Berlin, 1940) and D. J. Gadsby, *Heligoland: Originals and Reprints* (London, 1947).

79. TNA, CO 118/50, Maxse to Carnarvon, 13 July 1874.

80. Ibid., Minute by Carnarvon on Maxse to Carnarvon, 13 July 1874.

81. Ibid., Introduction of new German currency, 13 Nov 1874.

82. Ibid., Minute, 3 Dec. 1874, on Derby to Carnarvon, 2 Dec. 1874.

83. Ibid., Maxse to Carnarvon, 10 Aug. 1875 with enclosed Ordinance Enacting Amendments to the Strand Ordinances of Heligoland; ibid., Maxse to Carnarvon, 22 May 1875; ibid., Foreign Office to Count Münster, 10 June 1875.

84. TNA, CO 118/52, Maxse to Carnarvon, 15 June 1878. (The Earl of Carnarvon had handed over the post of colonial secretary to Michael Hicks Beach in February 1878, but no one seems to have told Maxse.)

85. Ibid., Admiralty to Colonial Office, 22 June 1878. See ibid., Expected meeting of German Socialists, minutes, n.d.; ibid., Maxse to Hicks Beach, 25 June 1878; TNA, CO 118/62, Minutes, Hicks Beach, 10 June 1878.

86. TNA, CO 118/49, Agreement between the Government of the Colony of Heligoland and the United Telegraph Company at Berlin, 9 Apr. 1873. The negotiations are documented in TNA, CO 118/48; see especially Odo Russell to Granville, 12 June 1872 and The Projected Telegraph Line to Heligoland, Minutes, 13 July 1872. See also NMM, TCM/6/28, Telegraph Construction and Maintenance Company Limited.

87. TNA, CO 118/48, Proposed Submarine Cable, Minute, 8 Oct. 1872; Kimberley to Treasury, 26 Oct. 1872; TNA, CO 118/60, Hatzfeldt to Salisbury, 4 June 1888; ibid., General Post Office to Foreign Office, 22 June 1888; ibid., Knutsford to Salisbury, 3 July 1888. See LA Schleswig-Holstein, Abt. 174, Nr 145, Staatssekretär Reichspostamt to Governor Heligoland, 13 Mar. 1889.

88. TNA, CO 118/57, O'Brien to Derby, 19 Sept. 1884, with enclosed draft contract with Mr Lindner of Berlin.

89. TNA, CO 118/50, Treasury to Colonial Office, 31 Aug. 1874.

90. TNA, CO 118/58, O'Brien to Stanhope, 10 Sept. 1886.

91. Ibid., Minute, 23 Sept. 1884.

92. TNA, CO 118/45, Memorandum, Alfred Greene, 18 Sept. 1869.

93. TNA, CO 118/46, Maxse to Granville, 19 July 1870; ibid., Maxse to Kimberley, 13 Sept. 1870. See also Geoffrey Wawro, *The Franco-Prussian War: The German Conquest of France in 1870–1871* (Cambridge, 2003), 188–92.

94. TNA, CO 118/46, Maxse to Kimberley, 22 Sept. 1870.

95. TNA, CO 118/49, Russell to Granville, 17 May 1873.

96. *Sten. Ber.*, 29 (1873), no. 50, 'Denkschrift betreffend die Entwicklung der Kaiserlichen Marine und die sich daraus ergebenden materiellen und finanziellen Forderungen', 236–46. See Lawrence Sondhaus, *Preparing for Weltpolitik: German Sea Power before the Tirpitz Era* (Annapolis, MD, 1997), 109–11

and Ivo Lambi, *The Navy and German Power Politics, 1862–1914* (Boston, MA, 1984), 5. The Foreign Office became aware of plans drawn up by the German Admiralty for the fortification of Heligoland for the first time in 1875. See TNA, CO 118/50, Ward to Foreign Office, 7 June 1875, with minutes.

97. TNA, CO 118/52, Maxse to Hicks Beach, 25 June 1878.

98. TNA, CO 118/54, Maxse to Kimberley, 9 Sept. 1881.

99. Ibid.

100. Ibid., Maxse to Kimberley, 1 July 1881. See also TNA, CO 118/44, Minute by Elliot on Maxse to Buckingham, 10 Mar. 1868, commenting that Gätke's 'head is rather too much filled with German despotic notions'.

101. Theodor Fontane, 'Rudolf Lindau: Ein Besuch', in Theodor Fontane, *Werke, Schriften und Briefe*, ed. Walter Keitel and Helmuth Nürnberger, 3. Abteilung, vol. 1 (Munich, 1969), 555; Fontane to his daughter Martha, 25 July 1891, in Theodor Fontane, *Werke, Schriften und Briefe*, series 4, vol. 4, ed. Walter Keitel and Helmuth Nürnberger (Munich, 1982) 138. Compare Roland Berbig (ed.), *Fontane als Biograph* (Berlin and New York, 2010), 153–6.

102. TNA, CO 118/54, Maxse to Kimberley, 15 Sept. 1881.

103. From Newfoundland Maxse wrote to Odo Russell, Britain's ambassador in Berlin: 'I miss Heligoland and the easy trips to Berlin and Vienna and very much indeed also the immense advantage with boys at school and of being with one's family... Indeed for my personal comfort I would a million times sooner have remained at Heligoland, but this is a government it could have been madness to refuse if one wanted to remain in the line' (TNA, FO 918/54, Maxse to Russell, 12 Nov. 1881).

104. TNA, CO 118/54, Germany and Heligoland, Minute by C. A. Harris, 21 Dec. 1881.

105. For the earliest example see PA-AA, R 19552, Bernstorff to Bismarck, 2 Dec. 1870.

106. Ibid., Bismarck to Münster, 19 Mar. 1876.

107. Ibid., Memorandum, Herbert Bismarck, 20 June 1876.

108. TNA, CO 118/55, Strachey to Granville, 24 Dec. 1881.

109. Ibid.

110. Ibid., Fleischer to Strachey, 30 Dec. 1881.

111. *Allgemeine Zeitung*, 22 Dec. 1881; *Dresdner Anzeiger*, 9 Dec. 1881.

112. TNA, CO 118/55, Strachey to Granville, 31 Jan. 1882.

113. PA-AA, R 19553, Bismarck to Stosch, 8 Feb. 1882; Stosch to Bismarck, 10 Feb. 1882.

114. *Norddeutsche Allgemeine Zeitung*, 8 Feb. 1882.

115. TNA, CO 118/55, Russell to Granville, 8 Feb. 1882.

116. PA-AA, R 19553, Bismarck to Stosch, 8 Feb. 1882; TNA, CO 118/55, Strachey to Granville, 31 Jan. 1882.

117. Ibid., Bismarck to Münster, 5 May 1884. See also ibid., Bismarck to Münster, 11 May 1884.

118. Ibid., Münster to Bismarck, 8 May 1884.

119. Ibid., Münster to Bismarck, 26 May 1884.

120. Ibid., Bismarck to Münster, 25 May 1884.
121. Ibid., Bismarck to Münster, 1 June 1884.
122. *GP*, vol. 4, 67, marginalia by Otto von Bismarck on Herbert Bismarck to Otto von Bismarck, 16 June 1884 (doc. 745). There is a long tradition of interpreting Bismarck's turn to colonies as motivated by domestic considerations; see especially Hans-Ulrich Wehler, *Bismarck und der Imperialismus* (Cologne, 1969) and Matthew Fitzpatrick, *Liberal Imperialism in Germany: Expansionism and Nationalism, 1848–1884* (New York and Oxford, 2008), ch. 5. Bismarck's reaction to the abortive Heligoland talks with Britain in 1884 suggest that foreign policy considerations played just as great a role.
123. TNA, CO 118/57, Minute by Lord Derby, 26 Mar. 1885, on Strachey to Granville, 8 Mar. 1885. This stands in contrast to the German ambassador's recollection of a conversation he had with Derby about Heligoland in the winter of 1883: the colonial secretary had told him that 'one could talk about it one day' (PA-AA, R 19553, Münster to Bismarck, 8 May 1884).
124. Hansard, HC, 30 Mar. 1885, 1013.
125. PA-AA, R 19553, *The Times*, 31 Mar. 1885.
126. Hansard, HC, 30 Mar. 1885, 1012.
127. Hansard, HL, 10 July 1890, 1259–62.
128. Hansard, HC, 24 July 1890, 745–6. See also ibid., 801.
129. TNA, CO 118/52, Maxse to Hicks Beach, 25 June 1878.
130. Wilhelm Müller, *Politische Geschichte der Gegenwart: Das Jahr 1890* (Berlin, 1891), 105.
131. British diplomats observed as early as 1875 that the Germans were discussing the colony, the canal, and the fleet in one context; see TNA, CO 118/50, Ward to Foreign Office, 7 June 1875.
132. TNA, CO 118/59, O'Brien to Holland, 8 Nov. 1887.
133. Ibid.
134. PA-AA, R 19553, Münster to Bismarck, 8 May 1884.
135. TNA, CO 118/45, Strategic Value of Heligoland in the Event of Hostilities with a German Power, George Henry Richards, 23 Sept. 1869; ibid., Memorandum, W. Monsell, 11 Oct. 1869. This assessment was confirmed by discussions during the 1870s. See TNA, CO 118/50, War Office to Colonial Office, 26 Oct. 1875.
136. TNA, CO 118/62, Secretary, Admiralty, to Under Secretary, Colonial Office, 14 Nov. 1887.
137. TNA, CO 118/59, O'Brien to Holland, 8 Nov. 1887.
138. For discussions within British colonial circles see NAS, GD268/646, Henry Brougham Loch to Robert Herbert, 8 Jan. 1885.
139. On Hatzfeldt as the 'best horse' see Hermann von Eckardstein, *Lebenserinnerungen und politische Denkwürdigkeiten* (Leipzig, 1919), 174.
140. *Die politischen Reden des Fürsten Bismarck*, ed. Horst Kohl, vol. 12 (Stuttgart, 1894), 575 (26 Jan. 1889).

141. PA-AA, R 6115, Herbert Bismarck to Otto von Bismarck, 22 Mar. 1889. Compare *GP*, vol. 4, 404–19 (docs 945–54) on the following.

142. Ibid., Herbert Bismarck to Otto von Bismarck, 27 Mar. 1889.

143. Ibid., Hatzfeldt to Bismarck, 13 Apr. 1889.

144. Ibid., Marginalia by Bismarck on Hatzfeldt to Bismarck, 13 Apr. 1889.

145. Ibid., Herbert Bismarck to Berchem, 21 June 1889.

146. Ibid., Berchem to Bismarck, 21 June 1889.

147. Ibid., Herbert Bismarck to Berchem, 21 June 1889.

148. Ibid., Marginalia by Bismarck on Herbert Bismarck to Berchem, 21 June 1889, emphases in the original.

149. Ibid., Bismarck to Foreign Office Berlin, 23 June 1889.

150. Ibid., Berchem to Bismarck, 24 June 1889.

151. On Wilhelm II's ideas about 'personal rule' see John C. G. Röhl, *The Kaiser's Personal Monarchy, 1888–1900* (Cambridge, 2004) and Röhl, *The Kaiser and his Court: Wilhelm II and the Government of Germany* (Cambridge, 1994). For the realities of monarchical rule in Wilhelmine Germany which restricted the Kaiser's ambitions: Geoff Eley, 'The View from the Throne: The Personal Rule of Kaiser Wilhelm II', *HJ*, 28 (1985), 469–85 and Christopher Clark, *Kaiser Wilhelm II: A Life in Power* (London, 2009).

152. PA-AA, R 6115, Herbert Bismarck to Berchem, 21 June 1889.

153. *The Times*, 20 Mar. 1890.

154. *Die Reden Kaiser Wilhelms II.*, ed. Johannes Penzler, vol. 1 (Leipzig, 1913), 123 (9 Aug. 1890).

155. PA-AA, R 2490, Marschall to Hatzfeldt, 29 May 1890.

156. Salisbury's motivation for the 'Heligoland offer' has been the subject of debate, fuelled by the fact that there are few sources documenting his aims. For the different positions see D. R. Gillard, 'Salisbury's African Policy and the Heligoland Offer of 1890', *EHR*, 75 (1960), 631–53; G. N. Sanderson, 'The Anglo-German Agreement of 1890 and the Upper Nile', *EHR*, 78 (1963), 49–72; D. R. Gillard, 'Salisbury's Heligoland Offer: The Case Against the "Witu Thesis"', *EHR*, 80 (1965), 538–52; and Robert Collins, 'Origins of the Nile Struggle: Anglo-German Negotiations and the Mackinnon Agreement of 1890', in Prosser Gifford and W. Roger Louis (eds), *Britain and Germany in Africa: Imperial Rivalry and Colonial Rule* (New Haven, CT, 1967), 119–51. John Darwin, 'Imperialism and the Victorians: The Dynamics of Territorial Expansion', *EHR*, 112 (1997), 614–42, esp. 634–40, offers a convincing synthesis, stressing the value of Zanzibar and the protection of British commercial interests.

157. TNA, CO 118/62, Importance of Heligoland and Question of Exchange, Memorandum by C. A. Harris, 2 June 1890.

158. PA-AA, R 2490, Hatzfeldt to Marschall, 14 May 1890.

159. Ibid., Marschall to Hatzfeldt, 29 May 1890. Compare *GP*, vol. 8, 17–19 (doc. 1681).

160. PA-AA, R 2490, Marschall to Hatzfeldt, 29 May 1890.

161. Ibid., Marschall to Hatzfeldt, 25 May 1890 and Marschall to Hatzfeldt, 29 May 1890. Compare *GP*, vol. 8, 16–19 (docs 1680-1).

162. *The Letters of Queen Victoria*, ed. George Earl Buckle, third series, vol. 1 (London, 1930), 612, emphasis in the original.

163. Ibid., 614, Victoria to Salisbury, 11 June 1890.

164. Ibid., 614–15, Salisbury to Victoria, 12 June 1890.

165. Ibid., 615, Victoria to Salisbury, 12 June 1890.

166. For a poignant example see the map of the Nyassa Tanganyika Plateau included in the agreement (TNA, FO 93/36/24).

167. The handwritten original, with English and German texts running in parallel, is in TNA, FO 93/36/24. Compare TNA, FO 881/6146, Malet to Salisbury, 1 July 1890.

168. Qtd in T. G. Otte, *The Foreign Office Mind: The Making of British Foreign Policy, 1865–1914* (Cambridge, 2011), 183.

169. The draft agreement was published in the official *Reichsanzeiger* on 17 June. See also Manfred Sell, 'Die deutsche öffentliche Meinung und das Helgolandabkommen im Jahre 1890' (Diss., University of Cologne, 1926), 6–8.

170. Sell, 'Deutsche öffentliche Meinung'; TNA, FO 881/6146, Malet to Salisbury, 20 June 1890: public opinion 'may be said to have declared itself in favour of the agreement'.

171. Sell, 'Deutsche öffentliche Meinung', 39; Carl Peters, *Die Gründung von Deutsch-Ostafrika: Kolonialpolitische Erinnerungen und Betrachtungen* (Berlin, 1906), 61.

172. Arne Perras, *Carl Peters and German Imperialism, 1856–1918* (Oxford, 2004), 168–79; Roger Chickering, *We Men Who Feel Most German: A Cultural Study of the Pan-German League, 1886–1914* (London, 1984); Geoff Eley, *Reshaping the German Right: Radical Nationalism and Political Change after Bismarck* (New Haven, CT, and London, 1980).

173. *Casseler Stadtanzeiger*, 24 June 1890; *Reichsbote*, 1 July 1890; *Frankfurter Journal*, 11 July 1890. On Bismarck's motivation see Steinberg, *Bismarck: A Life* (Oxford, 2011), 452–3.

174. Caprivi responded to Bismarck's criticism in a Reichstag speech on 5 Feb. 1891, quoting liberally from internal memoranda which showed how much continuity there had been between Bismarck's approach and his own. See *Die Reden des Grafen von Caprivi im deutschen Reichstage, Preußischen Landtage und bei besonderen Anlässen*, ed. Rudolf Arndt (Berlin, 1894), 97–108. For Bismarck's reaction see Otto von Bismarck, *Gedanken und Erinnerungen*, vol. 3 (Stuttgart, 1920), 147–52.

175. Qtd in Robinson and Gallagher, *Africa and the Victorians: The Official Mind of Imperialism* (London, 1961), 299, Fergusson to Salisbury, 4 July 1890.

176. Hansard, HC, 24 July 1890, 749. See also Hansard, HL, 10 July 1890, 1258–92; Hansard, HC, 25 July 1890, 917–83; Hansard, HC, 28 July 1890, 1077–108.

177. Hansard, HL, 10 July 1890, 1290.

178. TNA, CO 118/62, Importance of Heligoland and Question of Exchange, memorandum by C. A. Harris, 2 June 1890. Compare TNA, CO 537/17, Barkly to Knutsford, 10 July 1890. Salisbury had taken a similarly insincere line in responding to the queen's criticism, telling her that 'the information available to the Cabinet is that the population…would readily come under the German Empire'. See *Letters of Queen Victoria*, vol. 1, 613, Salisbury to Victoria, 10 June 1890.

179. Hansard, HL, 10 July 1890, 1289.

180. Ibid.

181. *Neueste Mittheilungen*, 29 July 1890. See also 'Denkschrift über die Beweggründe zu dem deutsch-englischen Abkommen', *Das Staatsarchiv*, 51 (1891), 170.

182. *Standard*, 11 Aug. 1890.

CHAPTER 4: MAKING GERMANS

1. TNA, FO 84/2032, Anderson to Malet, 18 June 1890.

2. *Die politische und literarische Korrespondenz Rudolf Lindaus*, ed. Rainer Hillenbrand, vol. 1 (Frankfurt, 2007), 819–27; Heinrich Spiero, *Rudolf Lindau* (Berlin, 1909); Eberhard Naujoks, 'Rudolf Lindau und die Neuorientierung der auswärtigen Pressepolitik Bismarcks (1871/78)', *HZ*, 215 (1972), 299–344.

3. PA-AA, R 2496, Lindau to Marschall, 23 June 1890.

4. *Pall Mall Gazette*, 25 June 1890; PA-AA, R 2496, London Embassy to Caprivi, 25 June 1890; ibid., Lindau to Marschall, 29 June 1890.

5. Ibid., Lindau to Marschall, 23 June 1890.

6. 'Denkschrift über die Beweggründe', 186–7.

7. *Die fünfte allgemeine Versammlung der deutschen Gesellschaft für Anthropologie, Ethnologie und Urgeschichte zu Dresden vom 14. bis 16. September 1874* (Brunswick, 1875), 19. See also Rudolf Virchow, *Beiträge zur physischen Anthropologie der Deutschen mit besonderer Berücksichtigung der Friesen* (Berlin, 1876), 26, 361–2; Otto Bremer, *Ethnographie der germanischen Stämme* (Strassburg, 1904), 348–9.

8. Karl Reinhardt, *Von Hamburg nach Helgoland* (Leipzig, 1856), 8.

9. Siebs, *Helgoland und seine Sprache*, 41, 170.

10. Adolf Wermuth, *Ein Beamtenleben: Erinnerungen* (Berlin, 1922), 123.

11. TNA, CO 537/17, Barkly to Knutsford, 21 July 1890.

12. Ibid., Barkly to Knutsford, 10 July 1890.

13. TNA, CO 537/17, Proposed Arrangement for the Transfer of Heligoland.

14. Wermuth, *Beamtenleben*, 124.

15. PA-AA, R 2498, Telegram Boetticher to Auswärtiges Amt, 9 Aug. 1890.

16. TNA, CO 537/17, Report of Proceedings of HMS *Calypso* on the occasion of Heligoland being transferred to Germany on 9 Aug. 1890; ibid., Colonial Office to Governor, 7 Aug. 1890.

17. PA-AA, R2498, Allerhöchste Bestimmungen für den Besuch der Insel Helgoland, 10 Aug. 1890; BA-MA, RM3/8474, Übernahme der Insel Helgoland; *Reichs- und Staats-Anzeiger*, 11 Aug. 1890.

18. *Münchner Neueste Nachrichten*, 12 Aug. 1890.

19. *Reichs- und Staats-Anzeiger*, 11 Aug. 1890. See also TNA, CO 537/17, Proclamation by Kaiser Wilhelm II, 10 Aug. 1890; *Die Reden Kaiser Wilhelms II.*, 121–4.

20. Wermuth, *Beamtenleben*, 126.

21. Ibid., 127. See also *Reichs- und Staats-Anzeiger*, 11 Aug. 1890.

22. Decken, *Philosophisch-historisch-geographische Untersuchungen*, 144.

23. *Sten. Ber.*, 9 Dec. 1890, 813.

24. TNA, FO 881/6146, 97, art. 12, 2.

25. Alfred Wahl, *L'option et l'émigration des Alsaciens-Lorrains, 1871–1872* (Paris, 1972); Matthew P. Fitzpatrick, *Purging the Empire: Mass Expulsions in Germany, 1871–1914* (Oxford, 2015), chs 6, 8.

26. *Sten. Ber.*, 2 Dec. 1890, 751.

27. The Kaiser's gifts to the island are documented in GhStA PK, I. HA Rep. 151, IB Nr 2573.

28. TNA, FO 64/1321, Natives of Heligoland Electing to Remain British Subjects. See also TNA, CO 537/17, Marschall to Malet, 9 Aug. 1890.

29. TNA, FO 64/1321, Black to Rosebery, 28 Oct. 1892.

30. Ibid., Dundas to Malet, Feb. 1893.

31. *Sten. Ber.*, 9 Dec. 1890, 814.

32. TNA, CO 537/17, Treatment of Persons Opting for British Nationality, Minute, H. C. M. Lambert, 20 Feb. 1893.

33. Thaler, *Of Mind and Matter*; James E. Bjork, *Neither German nor Pole: Catholicism and National Indifference in a Central European Borderland* (Ann Arbor, MI, 2008); Elizabeth Vlossak, *Marianne or Germania? Nationalizing Women in Alsace, 1870–1946* (Oxford, 2010); Fitzpatrick, *Purging the Empire*.

34. TNA, CO 537/17, Treatment of Persons Opting for British Nationality, Minute, Harris, 21 Feb. 1893.

35. Ibid.

36. Ibid., Grievances of Islanders which have opted for British Nationality, Minute, Harris, 23 Nov. 1892.

37. Ibid., Wingfield, 23 Nov. 1892.

38. Ibid., Foreign Secretary to Secretary of State, CO, 17 Feb. 1893.

39. Ibid., Holstein to Malet, 21 July 1890; ibid., Malet to Foreign Office, 22 July 1890.

40. Ibid., Marschall to Malet, 9 Aug. 1890.

41. TNA, FO 64/1321, Verbalnote, Auswärtiges Amt, 30 Nov. 1891.

42. Ibid.

43. TNA, CO 537/17, Malet to Salisbury, 1 Dec. 1891.

44. Ibid., Minute, Wingfield, 23 Feb. 1893.
45. TNA, FO 64/1321, Malet to Rosebery, 11 Feb. 1893.
46. TNA, CO 537/17, Foreign Secretary to Secretary of State, CO, 17 Feb. 1893; FO 64/1321, Wingfield to Under-Secretary of State, FO, 25 Feb. 1893.
47. Ibid., John Franz to Dundas, 10 June 1892.
48. Ibid.
49. TNA, CO 537/17, Dundas for Jacob Botter, 29 Oct. 1891.
50. TNA, HO 144/609/B32890, Foreign Office to Secretary of State, Home Office, 30 Jan. 1901.
51. See TNA, HO 45/10732/255947.
52. GhStA PK, I. HA Rep. 77, Tit. 50 Nr 89, Vereinigung der Insel Helgoland mit dem preussischen Staat; ibid., Nr 90, Einführung von Reichsgesetzten und preussischen Landesgesetzen auf der Insel Helgoland.
53. Ernst von Moeller, *Die Rechtsgeschichte der Insel Helgoland* (Weimar, 1904), 265.
54. *Correspondence Respecting the Negotiations between Great Britain and Germany Relating to Africa* (London, 1891), 97, art. 12.4.
55. Wermuth, *Beamtenleben*, 134.
56. Wilfried Schroeder, *Ich reiste wie ein Buschmann: Zum Leben und Wirken des Australienforschers Erhard Eylmann* (Darmstadt, 2002), 25. See also Wermuth, *Beamtenleben*, 131.
57. Frida Strindberg, *Marriage with Genius* (London, 1937), 155–73; Eckhard Wallmann, *Strindbergs Hochzeit auf Helgoland* (Helgoland, 2000). The Strindbergs were divorced two years later. Frida Strindberg went on to live with a series of other famous writers, including Frank Wedekind and Werner von Oesteren. In 1912 she opened the Cave of the Golden Calf, a London club known for its avant-garde patrons. See Monica J. Strauss, *Cruel Banquet: The Life and Loves of Frida Strindberg* (New York, 2000).
58. Strindberg, *Marriage with Genius*, 162.
59. 'Smoke and enthusiasm' is from *Punch*, 16 Aug. 1890, 8. The Kaiser visited the island twenty-two times between 1890 and 1914.
60. *Die Gartenlaube* (1891), 668.
61. CUL, MS Add. 7949, C. Sever, The North Sea and the Baltic in 1895: Journal of a Pleasure Cruise, 53–4. Sever was part of a group of eighty British tourists who had chartered their own steamer. For an example of the new, Wilhelmine architecture see *Das neue Posthaus auf Helgoland: Eröffnung im September 1895* (Hamburg, 1895).
62. Adolf Lipsius, *Helgoland: Beschreibung der Insel und des Badelebens*, 2nd edn (Leipzig, 1895); Ludwig Salvator, *Helgoland: Eine Reise-Skizze* (Leipzig, 1901); Paul Kuckuck, *Der Nordseelotse: Lehrreiches und lustiges Vademekum für Helgoländer Badegäste und Besucher der Nordsee* (Hamburg, 1908).
63. Ernst Hallier, *Helgoland unter deutscher Flagge* (Hamburg, 1892); Friedrich von Dincklage-Campe, *Helgoland: Unsere Reichsinsel* (Berlin, 1894); Badedirektion Helgoland (ed.), *Der deutschen Nordsee Kronjuwel: Helgoland. Kleiner Führer*

(Cuxhaven, 1910); Emil Lindemann, *Das deutsche Helgoland* (Berlin, 1913); Jakob Bödewadt, 'Helgoland', in Hermann Krumm and Fritz Stoltenberg (eds), *Unsere meerumschlungene Nordmark*, vol. 1 (Kiel, 1914).

64. DHM, N 97/43, Medaille auf die Erwerbung der Insel Helgoland, 1890. See also the list of products advertised in *Wilhelmshavener Tageblatt*, 26 Nov. 1899.

65. William George Black, 'From Heligoland to Helgoland', *National Review*, 58 (1911), 320.

66. StA Hamburg, 331–3, SA 217, Club Helgoland 1893.

67. For an example see the 'Sängerfahrt des Kölner Männerchors, Peter und Paul 1907', documented in Manfred Wedemeyer (ed.), *Grüsse aus Helgoland: Ein historischer Spaziergang über die Insel mit 100 alten Ansichtskarten* (Borkum, 1988), 83. See also Georg Lang, *Mit Ränzel und Wanderstab: Schülerwanderungen durch deutsches Land*, 2nd edn (Munich, 1907).

68. *Jugend*, 2 (1904), 832.

69. *Sten. Ber.*, 2 Dec. 1890, 753.

70. StA Hamburg, 111–11, 4001, Auszug aus dem Protokoll des Senates, Hamburg, 9 Aug. 1895; ibid., Badecommissariat Helgoland to Burgomaster Lehmann, 14 Aug. 1895.

71. Emil Lindemann, *Helgoländer Badeplauderei* (Stuttgart, 1920), 54–5. For the background see Richard J. Evans, *Death in Hamburg: Society and Politics in the Cholera Years, 1830–1910* (Oxford, 1987).

72. Gisela Schütte, 'Helgolandfahrten und Seebäderdienst', in Volker Plagemann (ed.), *Übersee: Seefahrt und Seemacht im deutschen Kaiserreich* (Munich, 1988), 186–8.

73. For a good example see Ernst Robert Pietsch, *Reise nach Helgoland über Berlin und Bremen im Jahre 1912*, ed. Stefan Wolter (Göttingen, 2001).

74. Black, 'From Heligoland to Helgoland', 320.

75. On Fontane see *Werke, Schriften und Briefe*, 138, Fontane to his daughter Martha, 25 July 1891; Emilie and Theodor Fontane, *Der Ehebriefwechsel 1873–1898*, ed. Gotthard Erler, vol. 3 (Berlin, 1998), 541. On Kafka: Klaus Wagenbach, *Franzk Kafka: Eine Biographie seiner Jugend, 1883–1912* (Berlin, 2006), 99, 130; Brigitte and Helmut Heintel, 'Franz Kafka: 1901 allein auf Norderney und Helgoland?', *Freibeuter*, 17 (1983), 20–5. For other writers' correspondence from Heligoland see Wellcome Library, MS 6909, 55 (Leopold von Sacher-Masoch); ÖNB, Autogr. 210/56–2 (Hugo Thimig); ÖNB, Autogr. 638/12–16 (Alexander Conze).

76. *Politische und literarische Korrespondenz*, 824.

77. Ibid., 819–20.

78. See his obituary in *Berliner Lokal-Anzeiger*, 14 Oct. 1910.

79. On Warburg, founder of the *Kulturwissenschaftliche Bibliothek Warburg*, which was to become the London Warburg Institute after 1933, see Ernst H. Gombrich, *Aby Warburg: An Intellectual Biography* (Chicago, IL, 1986); Mark Russell, *Aby Warburg and the Public Purposes of Art in Hamburg* (Oxford and New York, 2007). On his role in the *Heufieberbund* see WIA, GC, Otto Schultz to Aby Warburg, 25 July 1906.

80. WIA, FC, Aby Warburg to Mary Warburg, 1 July 1911. On hay fever and Heligoland see also ibid., GC, Aby Warburg to Heinrich Brockhaus, 29 July 1898; ibid., Otto Hertmann to Aby Warburg, 24 June 1905.
81. WIA, FC, Aby Warburg to Mary Warburg, 2 July 1906; ibid., Aby Warburg to Mary Warburg, 4 July 1906.
82. WIA, FC, Aby Warburg to Moritz and Charlotte Warburg, 6 Jan. 1896; ibid., Mary Warburg to Aby Warburg, 24 Sept. 1929; Aby Warburg, *Images from the Region of the Pueblo Indians of North America*, translated with an interpretive essay by Michael P. Steinberg (Ithaca, NY, and London, 1995), 11.
83. Christine Knupp, 'Walter Leistikow (1865–1908): Helgoland, 1890', *Jahrbuch Altonaer Museum*, 12/13 (1974/75), 228; Margrit Bröhan, *Walter Leistikow* (Berlin, 1988).
84. Anton Bruckner, *Sämtliche Werke*, vol. 22/8, *Helgoland* (Vienna, 1993). For the full score see *Helgoland: Gedicht von Dr August Silberstein für Männerchor und großes Orchester von Dr Anton Bruckner* (Leipzig, 1893). On the contemporary context of the composition see August Göllerich and Max Auer, *Anton Bruckner: Ein Lebens- und Schaffensbild*, vol. 4/3 (Regensburg, 1922), 355ff. and Crawford Howie, *Anton Bruckner: A Documentary Biography*, vol. 2 (Lewiston, NY, 2002) 671–2.
85. Alexander Rehding, *Music and Monumentality: Commemoration and Wonderment in Nineteenth-Century Germany* (Oxford, 2009), 35. See also Barbara Eichner, *History in Mighty Sounds: Musical Constructions of German National Identity, 1848–1914* (Woodbridge, 2012), chs 5, 6.
86. Alexander L. Ringer, '*Germanenzug* bis *Helgoland*: Zu Bruckners Deutschtum', in Albrecht Riethmüller (ed.), *Bruckner-Probleme: Beiheft zum Archiv für Musikwissenschaft*, 45 (Stuttgart, 1999), 25–34.
87. Edmund Robert Fremantle, *The Navy as I Have Known It* (London, 1904), 376. See also Chapter 3.
88. TNA, FO 881/6146, 93, art. 2.
89. TNA, FO 84/2032, Trench (on behalf of Malet) to Salisbury, 13 Sept. 1890.
90. For an acknowledgement see *Frankfurter Zeitung*, 6 Oct. 1890.
91. Hansard, HC, 27 Nov. 1890, 128.
92. The following is based on the telegrams, dispatches, and memoranda contained in BA, R1001/959 and R 1001/8875–81.
93. *Sten. Ber.*, 6. Legislaturperiode, II. Session 1885/86, vol. 4 (Berlin, 1886), no. 44, 'Denkschrift über die deutschen Schutzgebiete', 137.
94. BA, R1001/959, Michahelles to Caprivi, 10 Oct. 1890, received in Berlin on 3 November.
95. Ibid., Marschall to Metternich, 8 Oct. 1890.
96. Ibid., Marschall to Metternich, 3 Oct. 1890.
97. Ibid., Michahelles to Caprivi, 18 Oct. 1890.
98. Ibid., Michahelles to Caprivi, 10 Oct. 1890.
99. Ibid., Marschall to Metternich, 3 Oct. 1890.
100. Ibid., Marschall to Michahelles, 12 Oct. 1890.
101. Ibid., Memorandum, British Embassy Berlin, 11 Oct. 1890.

102. Fremantle, *The Navy*, 387.

103. Ibid., 384. See also BA, R1001/959, Michahelles to AA, 29 Oct. 1890.

104. Fremantle, *The Navy*, 385.

105. *Neueste Mittheilungen*, 31 Oct. 1890.

106. Hansard, HC, 27 Nov. 1890, 128. Anglo-German cooperation over Witu is documented in BA, R 1001/959 and BA, R 1001/8875-81.

CHAPTER 5: ISLAND FORTRESS

1. 'Denkschrift über die Beweggründe, 170.

2. *Berliner Politische Nachrichten*, 30 July 1890.

3. *Deutsches Tagesblatt*, 18 June 1890. For similar sentiments see *Kölner Tageblatt*, 21 June 1890; *Nationalzeitung*, 18 June 1890; *Rheinisch-Westfälische Zeitung*, 22 June 1890; *Kreuzzeitung*, 30 July 1890.

4. *Standard*, 11 Aug. 1890. See also *Morning Post*, 11 Aug. 1890.

5. *Germania*, 19 June 1890; *Glasgow Herald*, 14 Aug. 1890; PA-AA, R 2495. See also Christopher Clark, *The Sleepwalkers: How Europe Went to War in 1914* (London, 2012), 129.

6. *Pall Mall Gazette*, 11 Aug. 1890. See also Fanny A. Barkly, *From the Tropics to the North Sea* (Westminster, 1897): 'the gem of the North Sea'; and C. Emma Cheney, 'A Crown Jewel: Heligoland', *Scribner's Magazine*, 8 (1890), 377–88: 'the jewel of the North Sea'.

7. H. G. Wells, *The War in the Air* (London, 1908), 99.

8. Erskine Childers, *The Riddle of the Sands: A Record of Secret Service* (London, 1903), 105. Childers based large parts of the book on a cruise he had made in 1897; see the logs of the *Vixen* in NMM, RCC2. On Childers, see Jim Ring, *Erskine Childers: A Biography* (London, 1996).

9. TNA, CO 118/35, Report on the Military Defences of the Island of Heligoland, 10 Jan. 1860; TNA, CO 118/36, Pattinson to Newcastle, 30 June 1862; Annie Brassey, 'Heligoland', *Macmillan's Magazine*, 37 (1878), 171; Martin, *History of the Colonies*, 601–2; WLP, 951.1.4, John Ward, 'Heligoland'. See also Richard Scully, *British Images of Germany: Admiration, Antagonism and Ambivalence, 1860–1914* (Basingstoke, 2012), ch. 2.

10. Dienstschrift IX, June 1894, qtd in Lambi, *The Navy and German Power Politics*, 75. On Tirpitz see Patrick J. Kelly, *Tirpitz and the Imperial German Navy* (Bloomington, IN, 2011); Rolf Hobson, *Imperialism at Sea: Naval Strategic Thought, the Ideology of Sea Power and the Tirpitz Plan, 1875–1914* (Boston, MA 2002); Michael Salewski, *Tirpitz: Aufstieg, Macht, Scheitern* (Göttingen, 1979); Volker Berghahn, *Der Tirpitz-Plan: Genesis und Verfall einer innenpolitischen Krisenstrategie unter Wilhelm II.* (Düsseldorf, 1971).

11. BA-MA, RM 3/1, Notizen des Staatssekretärs des Reichsmarineamts, Kontre-Admiral Tirpitz, zum Immediatvortrag am 28. September 1899 über die Vorbereitung und Zielsetzung der Novelle zum Flottengesetz. See also Volker

R. Berghahn and Wilhelm Deist (eds), *Rüstung im Zeichen der wilhelminischen Weltpolitik: Grundlegende Dokumente 1890–1914* (Düsseldorf, 1988), 159–62 and compare Alfred von Tirpitz, *Erinnerungen* (Leipzig, 1919), 107.

12. Allgemeine Gesichtspunkte bei der Feststellung unserer Flotte nach Schiffsklassen und Schiffstypen, sehr geheim, June 1897 (the 'Tirpitz Memorandum'), transcribed and translated in Jonathan Steinberg, *Yesterday's Deterrent: Tirpitz and the Birth of the German Battle Fleet* (London, 1965), 208–23.

13. Alfred von Tirpitz, *Politische Dokumente: Der Aufbau der deutschen Weltmacht* (Stuttgart and Berlin, 1924), 16, 1.

14. *Sten. Ber.*, 6 Dec. 1897, 60. On Bülow see Peter Winzen, *Bülows Weltmachtkonzept: Untersuchungen zur Frühphase seiner Außenpolitik, 1897–1901* (Boppard, 1977) and Gerd Fesser, *Reichskanzler von Bülow: Architekt der deutschen Weltpolitik* (Leipzig, 2003).

15. *The Times*, 30 Nov. 1899, reporting from Chamberlain's speech at the Unionist conference at Leicester. See also J. L. Garvin, *The Life of Joseph Chamberlain*, vol. 3 (London, 1934), 259–76.

16. *BD*, vol. 2, 68, Memorandum by Salisbury, 29 May 1901 (doc. 86).

17. PA-AA, Deutschland 148 secr., vol. 3, marginalia by Bülow to entry by Mühlberg, 27 Dec. 1901. On the talks, with hindsight often interpreted as a missed opportunity, but never intended to lead to a comprehensive treaty by either side, see Friedrich Meinecke, *Geschichte des deutsch–englischen Bündnisproblems 1890–1901* (Munich, 1927); Paul M. Kennedy, 'German World Policy and the Alliance Negotiations with England, 1897–1900', *JMH*, 45 (1973), 605–25.

18. Qtd in Walter Hubatsch, *Die Ära Tirpitz: Studien zur deutschen Marinepolitik 1890–1918* (Göttingen, 1955), 92.

19. Qtd in Richard Hough, *First Sea Lord: An Authorized Biography of Admiral Lord Fisher* (London, 1969), 308.

20. Varnbüler to Mittnacht, 5 Nov. 1897, qtd in Kennedy, *Rise of the Anglo-German Antagonism*, 224. Compare Lambi, *Navy and German Power Politics*, 35–6.

21. For examples see ibid., 119, 123, 144, 250, 256, 333, 345, 350, 354.

22. 'Allgemeine Gesichtspunkte', in Steinberg, *Yesterday's Deterrent*, 208.

23. GhStA PK, I. HA Rep. 151, IB Nr 2571, Imperial Chancellor to Prussian State Ministry, secret, 8 Oct. 1890.

24. The building plans are documented in GhStA PK, I. HA Rep. 77, Tit. 1278, Nr 1 and in BA-MA RM 2/v. 1788, 1789; RM 3/v. 4341, 5514; RM 33/v. 137–45; RM 43/v. 847; RM 43/v. 1291–5. For an exhaustive description of the fortifications see Claude Fröhle and Hans-Jürgen Kühn, *Hochseefestung Helgoland* (Herbolzheim, 2003).

25. Black, 'From Heligoland to Helgoland', 317.

26. Ibid., 319.

27. Jonathan Steinberg, 'The Copenhagen Complex', *JCH*, 1 (1966), 23–46.

28. BA-MA, RM 3/11679, Tirpitz to Hollweg, 16 Oct. 1902. See also Berghahn and Deist, *Rüstung*, 211–12.

29. The cases of those who were found out are documented in BA-MA, RM 43/844, RM 43/845, RM 43/865, and RM 43/866.
30. BA-MA, RM 43/845, Tapken to Schröder, 17 Sept. 1910. The notes and sketches Trench and Brandon had made while on Heligoland are enclosed in ibid., Tapken to Schröder, 19 Oct. 1910.
31. Stewart, Trench, and Brandon were pardoned and released in May 1913. See PA-AA, Botschaft London, 1319, Jagow to Embassy London, 19 May 1913. Two similar cases were brought against German nationals: Leopold Eilers and Olga Kling were sentenced for espionage in Heligoland in July 1912. In March 1914 the Berlin engineer Gaertner was sentenced for stealing a plan of the Heligoland fortifications. See RM 43/844 and compare *Evening Post*, 24 Aug. 1912 and *The Times*, 27 Mar. 1914.
32. PA-AA, Botschaft London, 1319, Metternich to Bülow, 3 Jan. 1911, reporting a conversation with Arthur Nicolson. The 'spy fever' in Britain had much the same function, fanned as it was by naval agitation. See Rüger, *Great Naval Game*, ch. 2 and David French, 'Spy Fever in Britain, 1900–1915', *HJ*, 21 (1978), 355–70.
33. *Ulk*, no. 37, Sept. 1911, 'Englische Annäherung'. The title was a pun—it implied that the English had no interest in a diplomatic rapprochement, but wanted to get closer to the Germans only in order to spy on their navy
34. Keith Neilson, *Britain and the Last Tsar: British Policy and Russia, 1894–1917* (Oxford, 1995), ch. 7; Andreas Rose, *Zwischen Empire und Kontinent* (Munich, 2011), ch. 1.
35. T. G. Otte, *The Foreign Office Mind: The Making of British Foreign Policy, 1865–1914* (Cambridge, 2013); John Darwin, *The Empire Project: The Rise and Fall of the British World-System, 1830–1970* (Cambridge, 2009); Christel Gade, *Gleichgewichtspolitik oder Bündnispflege? Maximen britischer Außenpolitik 1909–1914* (Göttingen, 1997).
36. See especially T. G. Otte, 'The Fragmenting of the Old World Order: Britain, the Great Powers and the War', in Rotem Kowner (ed.), *The Impact of the Russo-Japanese War* (London, 2007), 91–108 and Keith Neilson, 'The Russo-Japanese War and British Strategic Foreign Policy', in Rotem Kowner (ed.), *Rethinking the Russo-Japanese War, 1904–5*, vol. 1 (Folkestone, 2007), 307–17.
37. William Mulligan, 'From Case to Narrative: The Marquess of Lansdowne, Sir Edward Grey, and the Threat from Germany, 1900–1906', *IHR*, 30 (2008), 273–302. Compare T. G. Otte, *The China Question: Great Power Rivalry and British Isolation, 1894–1905* (Oxford, 2007), 3–12.
38. Mulligan, 'From Case to Narrative'; Frank McDonough, *The Conservative Party and Anglo-German Relations, 1905–1914* (Basingstoke, 2007).
39. P. M. H. Bell, *France and Britain 1900–1940: Entente and Estrangement* (London and New York, 1996), 30; P. J. V. Rolo, *Entente Cordiale: The Origins and Negotiations of the Anglo-French Agreements of 8 April 1904* (London, 1969); Christopher Andrew, *Théophile Delcassé and the Making of the Entente Cordiale: A Reappraisal of French Foreign Policy, 1898–1905* (London, 1968).
40. *GP*, vol. 20/2, 636, Metternich to Auswärtiges Amt, 28 June 1905 (doc. 6860). When Grey took over at the Foreign Office he repeated the warning, see *BD*, vol. 3, 209, Grey to Lascelles, 9 Jan. 1906 (doc. 229), summarizing his conversation with

Metternich on 3 Jan. 1906. Compare ibid., 180, Grey to Bertie, 31 Jan. 1906, reporting on his conversation with Cambon on the same day.

41. *Die geheimen Papiere Friedrich von Holsteins,* ed. Werner Frauendienst, vol. 4 (Göttingen, 1963), 298, Holstein to Radolin, 11 Apr. 1905.

42. *BD*, vol. 3, 174, Minute by Grey, 13 Jan. 1906, on Cambon to Rouvier, 11 Jan 1906 (doc. 212).

43. *BD*, vol. 3, 397–420, Memorandum on the Present State of British Relations with France and Germany, 1 Jan. 1907. On Crowe see T. G. Otte, 'Eyre Crowe and British Foreign Policy: A Cognitive Map', in T. G. Otte and Constantine A. Pagedas (eds), *Personalities, War and Diplomacy: Essays in International History* (London, 1997), 14–37.

44. *BD*, vol. 3, 409.

45. Ibid.

46. Paul M. Kennedy, 'The Tradition of Appeasement in British Foreign Policy 1865–1939', *British Journal of International Studies*, 2 (1976), 195–215.

47. Harrison, *England and Germany*, 180–1. Harrison's book was based on a series of articles which had appeared in the *Observer* earlier that year.

48. Robert Blatchford, *Germany and England* (London, 1909), 8, 9. The book was reissued in 1914 as *The War That Was Foretold: Germany and England*, selling more than a million copies.

49. Black, 'From Heligoland to Helgoland'; Horace Waller, *Heligoland for Zanzibar, or One Island Full of Free Men to Two Full of Slaves* (London, 1893); Robert Heron-Fermor, *Speech in Condemnation of the Cession of Heligoland* (Brighton, 1890).

50. Qtd in Frederic William Wile, *News Is Where You Find It: Forty Years Reporting at Home and Abroad* (Indianapolis, IN, 1939), 209. See also Dominik Geppert and Robert Gerwarth, 'Introduction', in Dominik Geppert and Robert Gerwarth (eds), *Wilhelmine Germany and Edwardian Britain: Cultural Contacts and Transfers* (Oxford, 2008), 7.

51. TNA, FO 800/349, Nicolson to Goschen, 18 July 1911.

52. *BD*, vol. 7, 602, Nicolson to Grey, 2 Nov. 1911, with minute by Grey, 16 Nov. 1911 (doc. 617).

53. Arthur J. Marder (ed.), *Fear God and Dread Nought: The Correspondence of Admiral of the Fleet Lord Fisher of Kilverstone*, vol. 2 (London, 1956), 435, Fisher to Churchill, 5 Mar. 1912.

54. *BD*, vol. 10/2, 614–15, Grey to Cambon, 22 Nov. 1912 (doc. 416).

55. 'Real isolation of Germany', Grey cautioned in February 1909, at the height of the naval race, 'would mean war'. TNA, FO 371/599/6296, Minute by Grey on Rodd to Grey, 10 Feb. 1909.

56. This was how Lansdowne had described the effect he thought press agitation over the issue of the South African War would have on Anglo-German relations: Lansdowne to Lascelles, 17 Jan. 1901, qtd in Mulligan, 'From Case to Narrative', 280.

57. T. G. Otte, 'Grey Ambassadors: The Dreadnought Revolution and British Diplomacy, 1906–1914', in Robert Blyth, Andrew Lambert, and Jan Rüger (eds), *The Dreadnought and the Edwardian Age* (Farnham, 2011), 51–78; Jon

Tetsuro Sumida, *In Defence of Naval Supremacy: Finance, Technology and British Naval Policy, 1889–1914* (Boston, MA, 1989); Nicholas A. Lambert, *Sir John Fisher's Naval Revolution* (Columbia, SC, 1999).

58. Marder (ed.), *Fear God and Dread Nought*, vol. 2, 51, Fisher to unknown recipient, 22 Feb. 1905. On the role of deterrence see Andrew Lambert, 'The Royal Navy 1856–1914: Deterrence and the Strategy of World Power', in Keith Neilson and Elizabeth Jane Errington (eds), *Navies and Global Defense: Theories and Strategy* (Westport, CT., 1995).

59. Tirpitz, *Erinnerungen*, 173–5. See also Michael Epkenhans, '*Dreadnought*: A "Golden Opportunity" for Germany's Naval Aspirations?', in Blyth, Lambert, and Rüger, *Dreadnought*, ch. 5.

60. Martin Daunton, ' "The Greatest and Richest Sacrifice Ever Made on the Altar of Militarism": The Finance of Naval Expansion, *c.*1890–1914', in Blyth, Lambert, and Rüger, *Dreadnought*, ch. 3.

61. See especially PA-AA, England, Nr 71b, vol. 77, Müller to Tirpitz, 9 Nov. 1913.

62. Michael Epkenhans, 'Was a Peaceful Outcome Thinkable? The Naval Race before 1914', in Holger Afflerbach and David Stevenson (eds), *An Improbable War? The Outbreak of World War I and European Political Culture before 1914* (New York and Oxford, 2007), 121.

63. Alfred von Tirpitz, *Politische Dokumente*, vol. 1, *Der Aufbau der deutschen Weltmacht* (Stuttgart and Berlin, 1924), 184, Aufzeichnungen für den Immediatvortrag beim Kaiser am 24. Oktober 1910.

64. On the Haldane mission see TNA, CAB 37/109/16; *BD*, vol. 6, 670–86 (docs 499–507); *GP*, vol. 31, 97–130 (docs 11347–70). See also John C. G. Röhl, *Wilhelm II: Into the Abyss of War and Exile, 1900–1941* (Cambridge, 2014), ch. 32; Konrad Canis, *Der Weg in den Abgrund: Deutsche Außenpolitik 1902–1914* (Paderborn, 2011), 459–79; Jonathan Steinberg, 'Diplomatie als Wille und Vorstellung: Die Berliner Mission Lord Haldanes im February 1912', in Herbert Schottelius and Wilhelm Deist (eds), *Marine und Marinepolitik im kaiserlichen Deutschland, 1871–1914* (Düsseldorf, 1972), 263–82; Stephen E. Koss, *Lord Haldane: Scapegoat for Liberalism* (New York, 1969), 71-86.

65. Konrad H. Jarausch, *The Enigmatic Chancellor: Bethmann Hollweg and the Hubris of Imperial Germany* (New Haven, CT, 1973), 126.

66. *GP*, vol. 31, 189, Bethmann Hollweg to Metternich, 18 Mar. 1912 (doc. 11406).

67. TNA, FO 800/61, Asquith to Grey, 10 Apr. 1912.

68. Albert Hopman, *Das ereignisreiche Leben eines 'Wilhelminers': Tagebücher, Briefe, Aufzeichnungen 1901 bis 1920*, ed. Michael Epkenhans (Munich, 2004), 336 (28 Sept. 1913).

69. Clark, *Sleepwalkers*, ch. 6; Friedrich Kießling, *Gegen den 'großen Krieg'? Entspannung in den internationalen Beziehungen 1911–1914* (Munich, 2002); Friedrich Kießling, 'Unfought Wars: The Effect of Détente before World War I', in Afflerbach and Stevenson (eds), *An Improbable War?* ch. 10; Jost Dülffer, Martin Kroger, and Rolf-Harald Wippich, *Vermiedene Kriege: Deeskalation von Konflikten der Großmächte zwischen Krimkrieg und Erstem*

Weltkrieg 1865–1914 (Munich, 1997), chs 32, 33; Sean M. Lynn-Jones, 'Détente and Deterrence: Anglo-German Relations, 1911–1914', *International Security*, 11 (1986), 121–50.

70. Ernst Jäckh (ed.), *Kiderlen-Wächter der Staatsmann und Mensch: Briefwechsel und Nachlaß*, vol. 2 (Berlin and Leipzig, 1921), 226.

71. William Mulligan, 'We Can't be More Russian than the Russians: British Policy in the Liman von Sanders Crisis, 1913–14', *Diplomacy & Statecraft*, 17 (2006), 261–82.

72. PA-AA, Botschaft London, 1208, Bethmann Hollweg to Lichnowsky, 19 Feb. 1913. On popular sentiment see Martin Schramm, *Das Deutschlandbild in der britischen Presse 1912–1919* (Berlin, 2007) and Scully, *British Images of Germany*, ch. 16.

73. *BD*, vol. 10/2, 563, Grey to Goschen, 3 Mar. 1914 (doc. 366). The dispatch was forwarded to the king and the prime minister, amongst others.

74. Arthur von Gwinner, 'English and German Economics', in Ludwig Stein (ed.), *England and Germany: By Leaders of Public Opinion in Both Empires* (London, 1912), 112.

75. *Statistisches Jahrbuch für das Deutsche Reich*, 32 (1911), 204–304. For a discussion of the statistical source material see Kennedy, *Rise of the Anglo-German Antagonism*, 471–4.

76. TNA, FO 800/61, Grey to Lascelles, 1 Jan. 1906. Compare TNA, FO 800/11, Grey to Lascelles, 13 Jan. 1906.

77. For book titles evoking the idea of a 'cold war', see Steinberg, *Yesterday's Deterrent* and Volker R. Berghahn, *Rüstung und Machtpolitik: Zur Anatomie des 'kalten Krieges' vor 1914* (Düsseldorf, 1973).

78. For a concise survey see David Blackbourn, '"As Dependent on Each Other as Man and Wife": Cultural Contacts and Transfers', in Geppert and Gerwarth, *Wilhelmine Germany and Edwardian Britain*, 15–37, here 22–5. See also Panikos Panayi, *German Immigrants in Britain during the Nineteenth Century, 1815–1914* (Oxford and New York, 1995); Panikos Panayi (ed.), *Germans in Britain since 1500* (London, 1996); Stefan Manz, *Migranten und Internierte: Deutsche in Glasgow 1864–1918* (Stuttgart, 2003); Rosemary Ashton, *Little Germany: Exile and Asylum in Victorian England* (Oxford, 1986).

79. Thomas Weber, '"Cosmopolitan Nationalists": German Students in Britain–British Students in Germany', in Geppert and Gerwarth, *Wilhelmine Germany and Edwardian Britain*, 249–70, here 252.

80. For a survey see Rüger, 'Revisiting the Anglo-German Antagonism', 3–7.

81. Percy Francis Westerman, *The Sea-Girt Fortress: A Story of Heligoland* (London, 1914), 296.

82. Harrison, *England and Germany*, 180.

83. Adolf Wermuth, 'Anglo-German Relations', in Stein (ed.), *England and Germany*, 118. See Chapter 4 on Wermuth, who was secretary of state for the Treasury from 1909 to 1912 and mayor of Berlin from 1912 to 1920.

84. Christiane Groeben (ed.), *Charles Darwin–Anton Dohrn Correspondence* (Naples, 1982), 26; Anton Dohrn, 'Der gegenwärtige Stand der Zoologie und die Gründung zoologischer Stationen', *Preussische Jahrbücher*, 30 (1872), 137–61. See LA Schleswig, Abt. 174, 161 for the early history of the Biological Institute.

85. Petra Werner, 'Die Gründung der Königlichen Biologischen Anstalt auf Helgoland und ihre Geschichte bis 1945', *Helgoländer Meeresuntersuchungen*, supplement, 47 (1993). See also GStA PK, Rep. 89 H Tit. XI Geheimes Civilkabinet, Nr 21326, Kultusminister to Wilhelm II, 12 June 1892 and 10 Mar. 1902.

86. Helen M. Rozwadowski, *The Sea Knows No Boundaries: A Century of Marine Science under ICES* (Seattle, WA, 2002).

87. Werner, 'Gründung', 68; W. J. Dakin, 'Variations in the Osmotic Concentration of the Blood and Coelomic Fluids of Aquatic Animals, caused by Changes in the External Medium', *Biochemical Journal*, 3 (1908), 473–80. The article duly acknowledges Dakin's debt to the *Anstalt*. Dakin returned to Britain in 1910 and taught at Belfast and at London, before taking up the chair of biology at the new University of Western Australia in 1913. See Ursula Bygott and K. J. Cable, 'William John Dakin', in *Australian Dictionary of Biography* (Melbourne, 1981), 190–1. For the background see Tamson Pietsch, *Empire of Scholars: Universities, Networks and the British Academic World, 1850–1939* (Manchester, 2013).

88. BA-MA, RM 43/845, Kuckuck to Schröder, 30 Mar. 1911.

89. Heinrich Gätke, *Die Vogelwarte Helgoland* (Braunschweig, 1891).

90. R. M. Lockley, *I Know an Island* (London, 1938), ch. 6. On the efforts of the international scientific community to save Heligoland from destruction after the First and the Second World Wars see GStA PK, I. HA Rep. 77, Tit. 311 a Nr 147 and PA-AA, R 22574. See also TNA, ADM 116/1981, Danish Embassy to Naval Inter-Allied Commissions of Control, 1 Apr. 1920; ibid., Note Relative to the Biological Station at Heligoland, British Embassy, Paris, 25 Feb. 1920; and BL, Add. MS 52583A, President Heligoland Sub-Commission to President Naval Inter-Allied Commission of Control, 3 Mar. 1920 on a similar Swedish initiative.

91. Wermuth, 'Anglo-German Relations', 118.

92. GStA PK, I. HA Rep. 77, Titel 872, Nr 12, Beiheft 10, Spionageabwehr auf Helgoland; LA Schleswig, Abt. 320.22, 44; BA-MA, RM 43/845 and RM 43/865.

93. BA-MA, RM 43/844.

94. BA-MA, RM 43/845, Kommandantur Helgoland to Kaiserliches Kommando der Marinestation der Nordsee, 18 Nov. 1907. On Schenksy see *Das alte Helgoland photographiert von Franz Schenksy*, ed. Evelin Schultheiß, 2nd edn (Helgoland, 2001); Wilhelm Rösing, *Franz Schenksy: Der Fotograf und das Meer* (Kiel and Hamburg, 2015).

95. BA-MA, RM 43/845, Emsmann to Tapken, 1 May 1907. On Nickels's record in the Royal Navy see TNA, ADM 188/170/127811.

96. BA-MA, RM 43/845, Kommandantur Helgoland to Kaiserliches Kommando der Marinestation der Nordsee, 13 July 1907.

97. BA-MA, RM 43/845, Verdächtige Helgoländer, Ganz Geheim, 16 Nov. 1907. See ibid., Bericht über die Verhältnisse auf Helgoland, a secret police report warning about the 'anti-German sentiment' amongst the Heligolanders.

98. Gustav Steinhauer, *Der Meisterspion des Kaisers: Was der Detektiv Wilhelms II. in seiner Praxis erlebte* (Berlin, 1930), 137. See also BA-MA, RM 43/845, Steinhauer to Emsmann, 13 Sept. 1908.

99. BA-MA, RM 43/845, Kommandantur Helgoland to Kaiserliches Kommando der Marinestation der Nordsee, 24 Oct. 1908.

100. GStA PK, I. HA Rep. 77, Tit. 332 r Nr 95, vol. 1, State Secretary of the Interior to State Secretary, Imperial Navy Office, secret, 9 Mar. 1891; ibid., Imperial Chancellor to Prussian State Minister and Minister of the Interior, secret, 23 Oct. 1891.

101. GStA PK, I. HA Rep. 151, HB Nr 1177, Magistrat Altona to Stellvertretende Intendantur des IX. Armeekorps, Altona, 2 Oct. 1914.

102. StA Hamburg, 621-1/95, 1105, Schiffsbesichtigungskommission to Direktion Hamburg-Amerika Linie, no date, but referring to Memorandum of Understanding of 5 Feb. 1906. See also BA-MA, RM 5/1880, Tirpitz to Büchsel, 10 Dec. 1905; BA-MA, RM 43/843, Mobilmachungs-Angelegenheiten, Ganz Geheim, 28 Nov. 1912.

103. *BD*, vol. 11, 33–4, Grey to Rumbold, 9 July 1914 (doc. 41).

104. Ibid.

105. For a fuller appreciation of the July crisis see Clark, *Sleepwalkers* and T. G. Otte, *July Crisis: The World's Descent into War, Summer 1914* (Cambridge, 2014).

106. *BD*, vol. 11, 87, Grey to Buchanan, 25 July 1914 (doc. 112).

107. On earlier, less explicit warnings by Grey see Otte, *July Crisis*, 142–9.

108. *BD*, vol. 11, 182–3, Grey to Goschen, 29 July 1914 (doc. 286). See *DD*, vol. 2, 86–8 for Lichnowsky's report of the conversation (doc. 368).

109. *BD*, vol. 11, 171, Grey to Goschen, 29 July 1914 (doc. 263).

110. *DD*, vol. 2, 95 (doc. 373); *BD*, vol. 11, 185–6 (doc. 293).

111. Qtd in Egmont Zechlin, *Krieg und Kriegsrisiko: Zur deutschen Politik im Ersten Weltkrieg* (Düsseldorf, 1979), 61 (Bethmann Hollweg to Ernst Bassermann, 6 June 1914).

112. *BD*, vol. 11, 220, Grey to Bertie, 31 July 1914 (doc. 352).

113. *BD*, vol. 11, 211, Goschen to Grey, 30 July 1914 (doc. 329).

114. *DD*, vol. 2, 125–6, Bethmann Hollweg to Tschirschky, 30 July 1914 (doc. 396); ibid., 159–60, Tschirschky to Bethmann Hollweg, 30 July 1914 (doc. 433).

115. Mary Soames (ed.), *Speaking for Themselves: The Personal Letters of Sir Winston and Lady Churchill* (London, 1999), 97 (Winston to Clementine Churchill, 31 July 1914).

116. *BD*, vol. 11, 351, Goschen to Grey, 4 Aug. 1914 (doc. 671).

117. T. G. Otte, 'A "German Paperchase": The "Scrap of Paper" Controversy and the Problem of Myth and Memory in International History', *Diplomacy &*

Statecraft, 18 (2007), 53–87; Isabel V. Hull, *A Scrap of Paper: Breaking and Making International Law during the Great War* (Ithaca, NY, 2014).

118. Hansard, HC, 3 Aug. 1914, 1809–32.

119. *DD,* vol. 2, 80, Minute by Wilhelm II (doc. 368).

120. *BD*, vol. 11, 330, Grey to Lichnowsky, 4 Aug. 1914 (doc. 643). For the last-minute confusion about this letter see Otte, *July Crisis*, 503–4.

121. *BD*, vol. 11, 188, Minutes by Crowe and Nicolson, 30 July 1914 (doc. 298).

122. *Hamburger Nachrichten*, 28 July 1914.

123. LA Schleswig, Abt. 320.22, 83, Landgemeinde Helgoland, Tagesordnung, 31 July 1914, Vermerk.

124. BA-MA, RM 43/830, Kaiserliche Kommandantur Helgoland, Kriegstagebuch, 2 Aug. 1914.

125. GStA PK, I. HA Rep. 151, HB Nr 1177, Reichskanzler to Minister of Interior, 16 Sept. 1914.

126. The Heligolanders' complaints about their wartime treatment are documented in LA Schleswig, Abt. 131, 10. See also NMM, WHI/68, Schensky to Black, 24 Sept. 1919.

127. BA-MA, RM 43/866, Kommandantur Helgoland to Station Wilhelmshaven, 11 Apr. 1916; *Vorschrift zur Behandlung von Angehörigen feindlicher Staaten* (Berlin, 1915), 11. See also Matthew Stibbe, *British Civilian Internees in Germany: The Ruhleben Camp, 1914–1918* (Manchester, 2008).

128. BA-MA, RM 43/866, Kommandantur Helgoland to Station Wilhelmshaven, 11 Apr. 1916; NMM, WHI/68, Schensky to Black, 24 Sept. 1919.

CHAPTER 6: TO HELIGOLAND AND BACK

1. Hansard, HC, 7 Aug. 1914, 2154; *The Times*, 7 Aug. 1914; *The Times*, 8 Aug. 1914.

2. For a detailed account of the battle see Eric W. Osborne, *The Battle of Heligoland Bight* (Bloomington, IN, 2006). See also Robert K. Massie, *Castles of Steel: Britain, Germany and the Winning of the War at Sea* (London, 2003), ch. 6; Arthur J. Marder, *From the Dreadnought to Scapa Flow*, vol. 2 (Oxford, 1965), 50–4 and the contemporary accounts in Archibald Hurd and H. C. Bywater, *From Heligoland to Keeling Island: One Hundred Days of Naval War* (London, 1914) and L. Cecil Jane, *The Action off Heligoland, August 1914* (London, 1915).

3. NMM, MSS/79/141, Eugene Hollingworth, 28 Aug. 1914.

4. Qtd in Osborne, *Battle*, 98.

5. IWM, 78/47/1, Journal of Duncan Lorimer, 10.

6. *The Beatty Papers: Selections from the Private and Official Correspondence of Admiral of the Fleet Earl Beatty*, ed. Bryan Ranft, vol. 1 (Aldershot, 1989), 132, Beatty to his wife, 2 Sept. 1914.

7. NMM, MSS/79/141, Eugene Hollingworth, 28 Aug. 1914.

8. NMM, BTY/3/1, Secretary of the Admiralty to Beatty, 22 Sept. 1914. See also TNA, ADM 1/8391/286.

9. BFI, 512441, Pathé, 'Heroes of Heligoland Leaving Buckingham Palace after Being Decorated by the King'. For the medals see NMM, E3427 and E4274.

10. *Illustrated London News*, 5 Sept. 1914; *The Times*, 29 Aug. 1914; 31 Aug. 1914.

11. *Daily Express*, 29 Aug. 1914.

12. *Battle of the Bight: Being the Official Narrative of the Naval Engagement between the British and German Fleets in the Heligoland Bight on Friday, August 28th, 1914* (London, 1914); William Watson, 'The Battle of the Bight', *The Times*, 31 Aug. 1914; J. Edgar Middleton, 'Off Heligoland', in George Herbert Clarke (ed.), *A Treasury of War Poetry: British and American Poems of the World War, 1914–1917* (New York, 1917).

13. Qtd in Marder, *From the Dreadnought to Scapa Flow*, vol. 2, 54.

14. *The Keyes Papers: Selections from the Private and Official Correspondence of Admiral of the Fleet Baron Keyes of Zeebrugge*, ed. Paul G. Halpern, vol. 1 (London, 1972), 19, Keyes to Goodenough, 5 Sept. 1914.

15. Roger Keyes, *The Naval Memoirs of Admiral of the Fleet Sir Roger Keyes: The Narrow Seas to the Dardanelles, 1910–1918* (London, 1936), 97.

16. W. S. Chalmers, *The Life and Letters of David Earl Beatty* (London, 1951), 153, Beatty to his wife, 30 Aug. 1914. For similar depictions see Nicolas Wolz, *Das lange Warten: Kriegserfahrungen deutscher und britischer Seeoffiziere 1914–1918* (Paderborn, 2008), 414.

17. *Illustrated London News*, 5 Sept. 1914, 'British Chivalry Towards a Defeated Enemy: Rescuing German Crews off Heligoland under Fire'; *The Times*, 31 Aug. 1914, 'German Officers' Brutality', 'German Sailors Shot by their Officers'. For the controversy over German atrocities in Belgium see John Horne and Alan Kramer, *German Atrocities, 1914: A History of Denial* (London and New Haven, CT, 2001).

18. Qtd in Otto Groos, *Der Krieg in der Nordsee*, vol. 1 (Berlin, 1920), 210.

19. Ibid., 218. Neumann continued to be celebrated in the Second World War, when Nazi propaganda had an acute need for role models that embodied individual sacrifice and heroism against all odds. See Wolfgang Loeff, *Der letzte Mann der 'Köln': Nach 76 Stunden hilflosen Herumtreibens in der Nordsee gerettet. Erzählung aus dem Gefecht bei Helgoland am 28. August 1914* (Gütersloh, 1939).

20. Winston Churchill, *The World Crisis*, vol. 1 (London, 1923), 309. For a corrective see Robin Prior, *Churchill's 'World Crisis' as History* (London, 1983), 17-19. The official view was encapsulated by *Naval Staff Monographs*, vol. 3, *The Battle of Heligoland Bight 28 Aug 1914* (London, 1921), 148, which suggests that the battle constituted a direct contribution to 'the final consummation' of the German fleet.

21. Frederic William Wile, *Who's Who in Hunland* (London, 1916), 73.

22. *Jellicoe Papers*, vol. 1, 75, Jellicoe to Secretary of the Admiralty, 30 Oct. 1914.

23. Qtd in Wolz, *Langes Warten*, 100.

24. *Die Weizsäcker-Papiere 1900–1932*, ed. Leonidas E. Hill (Berlin, 1974), 153, Weizsäcker to his father, 28 Oct. 1914.

25. Reinhard Scheer, *Deutschlands Hochseeflotte im Weltkrieg: Persönliche Erinnerungen* (Berlin, 1920), 52.

26. Keyes, *Memoirs*, vol. 1, 163.

27. Andrew Gordon, *The Rules of the Game: Jutland and British Naval Command* (London, 2005); N. J. M. Campbell, *Jutland* (New York, 2000).

28. BA-MA, RM 47/34, Immediatbericht Scheer, 4 July 1916.

29. Joachim Schröder, *Die U-Boote des Kaisers: Die Geschichte des deutschen U-Boot-Krieges gegen Großbritannien im Ersten Weltkrieg* (Bonn, 2003); Matthew Stibbe, 'Germany's "Last Card": Wilhelm II and the Decision in Favour of Unrestricted Submarine Warfare in January 1917', in Annika Mombauer and Wilhelm Deist (eds), *The Kaiser: New Research on Wilhelm II's Role in Imperial Germany* (Cambridge, 2003), ch. 9.

30. *Weizsäcker-Papiere*, 215.

31. *We'll Knock the Heligo—Into Heligo—out of Heligoland* (London and New York, 1917).

32. On the background see Christopher M. Bell, *Churchill and Sea Power* (Oxford, 2013), ch. 1.

33. TNA, CAB 38/4/9, Memorandum on the Military Policy to Be Adopted in a War With Germany, 10 Feb. 1903, 8.

34. TNA, CAB 17/8, Ottley to Churchill, 2 Nov. 1911.

35. TNA, CAB 2/2/2, Minutes of the 114th meeting of the C.I.D. on 23 Aug. 1911 (Sir Arthur Wilson). Fisher, who had not attended the meeting, was quietly supportive of the idea. See Ruddock F. Mackay, *Fisher of Kilverstone* (Oxford, 1973), 431.

36. Marder, *From Dreadnought to Scapa Flow*, vol. 2, 182–4; Lambert, *Sir John Fisher's Naval Revolution*, 179–80, 204–6; Osborne, *Battle of Heligoland Bight*, 42–6.

37. *Jellicoe Papers*, vol. 1, 68–9.

38. Admiral Viscount Jellicoe of Scapa, *The Grand Fleet 1914–1916: Its Creation, Development and Work* (London, 1919), 129.

39. Ibid.

40. CAC, FISR 1/16, Fisher to Churchill, 8 Nov 1914. See CAC, MCKN 3/22, Jellicoe to McKenna, 23 May 1915 for Jellicoe's response.

41. NMM, FHR/2, Scheme for an Offensive into Heligoland Bight, 30 Dec. 1914.

42. CAC, FISR 5/22, Attack on Helgoland.

43. William James, *A Great Seaman: The Life of Admiral of the Fleet Sir Henry F. Oliver* (London, 1956), 138.

44. Hansard, HC, 7 Mar. 1916, 1401–46. In his narrative of the war, published in 1923, Churchill was careful to distance himself from the 'hazardous . . . enterprise of bombarding and storming Heligoland'. See Winston S. Churchill, *The World Crisis*, vol. 2 (London, 1923), 41. For 'wild projects' see Marder (ed.), *Fear God and Dread Nought*, vol. 3, 241–2, Fisher to Asquith, 19 May 1915.

45. TNA, CAB 37/155/21, Questions on Heligoland, Arthur J. Balfour, 16 Sept. 1916. Copy with responses in CAC, AMEL 1/3/49.

46. BL, Add. MSS 48992, Jellicoe to Balfour, 10 Oct 1916, emphasis in original. Printed version in *Jellicoe Papers*, vol. 2, 86.

47. Ibid., emphasis in original.

48. *Jellicoe Papers*, vol. 2 174–6; BL, Add. MSS 48992, 97–106, 'Naval War Policy'.

49. Evans Lewin, 'The Heligoland Mistake', *Contemporary Review*, 110 (1916), 68–77. Lewin was librarian of the Royal Empire Society (later the Royal Commonwealth Society) from 1910 to 1946. See also Percy Evans Lewin, *The Germans in Africa* (Oxford, 1914) and *German Road to the East: Account of the 'Drang nach Osten' and of Teutonic Aims in the Near and Middle East* (London, 1916).

50. Lewin, 'Heligoland Mistake', 69.

51. PA, STR/18/2/9, Strachey to Edward Lyttleton, 31 Mar. 1915.

52. Churchill, *World Crisis*, vol. 1, 18.

53. Winston S. Churchill, *A History of the English-Speaking Peoples*, vol. 4 (London, 1958), 282.

54. J. M. Beaufort, 'A Voyage of Discovery in Germany', *Quarterly Review*, 226 (1916), 84–5, emphasis in original. See also his *Behind the German Veil: A Record of a Journalistic War Pilgrimage*, 2nd edn (London, 1917), 229–38.

55. Maximilian von Hagen, *Geschichte und Bedeutung des Helgolandvertrages* (Munich, 1916), 57–8.

56. On 'the Watch of the Rhine', the patriotic song popularized in the second half of the nineteenth century, see Georg Scherer and Franz Lipperheide (eds), *Die Wacht am Rhein* (Berlin, 1871) and Lucien Febvre, *Der Rhein und seine Geschichte*, ed. Peter Schöttler (Frankfurt, 2006).

57. Zdenko von Kraft, *Die Stimme von Helgoland* (Leipzig, 1916). See also Oskar Höcker's *Der Seekadett von Helgoland*, which had reached eleven editions by 1916 (Leipzig, 1916).

58. Kraft, *Stimme von Helgoland*, 271–2.

59. Reinhold Max Eichler, *Helgoland*, published in *Jugend*, 21 Jan. 1915. Eichler had been a member of the Munich *Scholle* before the war, a group of avant-garde artists, most of them former members of the Munich *Sezession* and students of the Bavarian Academy of Art. See Siegfried Unterberger, Felix Billeter, and Ute Strimmer (eds), *Die Scholle: Eine Künstlergruppe zwischen Sezession und Blauer Reiter* (Munich, 2007).

60. See *Jugend*, 23 (1918), back cover.

61. Jan Rüger, 'OXO: or, The Challenges of Transnational History', *EHQ*, 40 (2010), 656–68.

62. For Britain see especially TNA, BT 351/1 (James Temple) and TNA, ADM 188/548 (Harry Styles). For Australia and the USA see below.

63. *The Times*, 9 Oct. 1939, letters to the editor. For Heligolanders serving in the Royal Navy during the war see TNA, ADM 188/170/127810.

64. GStA PK, I. HA Rep. 151, HB Nr 1177.

65. LA Schleswig, Abt. 131, 10, Zur Frage der Unterbringung der Helgoländer.

66. GStA PK, I. HA Rep. 197 A, I h Nr 50 Beiheft 2, August Kuchlenz to Minister of the Interior, 5 Oct. 1914.

67. LA Schleswig, Abt. 131, 10, Festpredigt im Dank- und Erinnerungsgottesdienst der Gemeinde Helgoland, 10 Aug. 1915.

68. StA Hamburg, PP, Helgoländer Akten, 580/17; ibid., 5960/16. The files of the Hamburg Political Police to which these call numbers refer no longer exist, but they leave no doubt that the Hamburg police kept files on the Heligolanders' political activities. The islanders' complaints are documented in GStA PK, I. HA Rep. 77, Tit. 332 r Nr 95, vols 1–3 and LA Schleswig, Abt. 131, 10.

69. GStA PK, I. HA Rep. 77, Tit. 332 r Nr 95, vol. 3, Magistrat Stadt Altona to Imperial Chancellor, 18 June 1917.

70. TNA, FO 608/141, 182.

71. TNA, HO 45/10732/255947, Chief Constable of Newport to Under Secretary of State, Home Office, 22 Oct. 1914.

72. Ibid., T. S. Gower, Newport Liberal Association, to Home Office, 11 Aug. 1914; Chief Constable of Newport to Under Secretary of State, Home Office, 22 Oct. 1914; Under Secretary of State, Home Office, to Gower, 8 Sept. 1914. Dirks was transferred to the Queensferry internment camp, but later released on the condition that he report every morning at Newport police station. For the background see Panikos Panayi, *Prisoners of Britain: German Civilian and Combatant Internees during the First World War* (Manchester, 2012).

73. As Reginald McKenna, the home secretary, had announced. See Hansard, HC, 5 Aug. 1914, 1986. On the act see J. C. Bird, *Control of Enemy Alien Civilians in Great Britain 1914–1918* (London and New York, 1986), 14–44.

74. *Observer*, 19 Sept. 1915; Durham County Record Office, PS/CE 9, 101, 111.

75. NAA, A1, 1916/10522, H. B. Atkinson to Minister of Defence, 27 Mar. 1916.

76. Ibid., Warden, Devonport Municipal Council, Tasmania, to Secretary, Department of External Affairs, 17 Feb. 1916; ibid., H. B. Atkinson to Minister of Defence, 27 Mar. 1916.

77. Ibid., Secretary, Department External Affairs to H. B. Atkinson, 12 Apr. 1916; ibid., Secretary, Department External Affairs to Warden Devonport Municipality, Devonport, Tasmania, 13 Mar. 1916.

78. NAA, A401, Luhrs, Record of Aliens, Intelligence Section, 6th Military District.

79. Lührs returned to Tasmania in August 1919. On his wartime record see NAA, B2455, Luhrs, Theo.

80. NAA, B2455, Charles Bertholdt Nissen. For another example see NAA, B2455, Peter Nordenson, who enlisted as a 'natural born British subject' in September 1915 and embarked for Europe on 17 Jan. 1916. He fought at the Western Front until he developed a severe case of 'trench foot' and was hospitalized. He eventually returned to Australia in October 1917 and was discharged.

81. John Darwin, 'Orphans of Empire', in Robert Bickers (ed.), *Settlers and Expatriates: Britons over the Seas* (Oxford, 2010), 329–45.

82. TNA, FO 371/5967, 154, excerpt from *San Francisco Examiner,* 'Drafted Man is Very Certain He is Not German'.
83. *Daily Chronicle,* 27 Aug. 1918, 'Vote for a Man Born at Heligoland'.
84. *The Observer,* 19 Sept. 1915, 'A Native of Heligoland: Is He a British or a German Subject?'; TNA, FO 371/5967. For the context see Rieko Karatani, *Defining British Citizenship: Empire, Commonwealth and Modern Britain* (London, 2003); Ann Dummett and Andrew Nicol, *Subjects, Citizens, Aliens and Others: Nationality and Immigration Law* (London, 1990); Bird, *Control of Enemy Alien Civilians.*
85. Gerhard P. Groß, 'Eine Frage der Ehre? Die Marineführung und der letzte Flottenvorstoß 1918', in Hansjörg Duppler and Gerhard P. Groß (eds), *Kriegsende 1918* (Munich, 1999).
86. BA-MA, RM 43/842, Kaiserliche Kommandantur Helgoland, Kriegstagebuch, 6 to 10 Nov. 1918.
87. For its activities see GStA PK, I. HA Rep. 197 A, I h Nr 50 Beiheft 2.
88. Andreas Krause, *Scapa Flow: Die Selbstversenkung der wilhelminischen Flotte* (Berlin, 1999).
89. Ludwig von Reuter, *Scapa Flow: Das Grab der deutschen Flotte* (Leipzig, 1921), 24.

CHAPTER 7: DISARMING GERMANY

1. GStA PK, I. HA Rep. 197 A, I h Nr 50 Beiheft 2, Landrat to Staatskommissar, 13 Dec. 1918; BA-MA, RM 43/842, Kriegstagebuch, 6 to 17 Dec. 1918. For the demolition plans see BA-MA, RM 43/1292.
2. *The Times,* 19 Feb. 1919.
3. *Financial News,* 16 Oct. 1918; *The Times,* 6 Nov. 1918.
4. John Arbuthnot Fisher, *Records by the Admiral of the Fleet, Lord Fisher* (London, 1919), 244, Fisher to Hankey, 21 Oct. 1918.
5. TNA, CAB 24/66/97, Restitution of Heligoland to Great Britain, 3 Oct. 1918.
6. *Jellicoe Papers,* vol. 2, 87.
7. *The Life and Letters of Lord Wester Wemyss* (London, 1935), 397–8, Wemyss to Beatty, 10 Nov. 1918.
8. On the following see Margaret Macmillan, *Peacemakers: The Paris Conference of 1919 and Its Attempt to End War* (London, 2001), ch. 7; Zara Steiner, *The Lights that Failed: European International History 1919–1933* (Oxford, 2007), ch. 1; Heinrich Stocks, *Helgoland im Versailler Friedensvertrag* (Leipzig, 1927).
9. NAS, GD 40/17/65, Frontier Questions, Notes on Heligoland, 14 Apr. 1919.
10. *The Times,* 21 Feb. 1919, letter to the editor by Baron Channing of Wellingborough.
11. TNA, CAB 24/89/62, Proposal to Cede Cyprus to Greece, 3 Oct. 1919.
12. NAS, GD 40/17/65, Frontier Questions, Notes on Heligoland, 14 Apr. 1919.
13. N.C.M., 'Some German Ports after the Armistice', *The Brisbane,* 4 (1919), 27.
14. Grey to House, 3 June 1919, qtd in Macmillan, *Peacemakers,* 187.
15. NAS, GD 40/17/65, Frontier Questions, Notes on Heligoland, 14 Apr. 1919.

16. Susan Pedersen, *The Guardians: The League of Nations and the Crisis of Empire* (Oxford, 2015).

17. Robert Lansing, *The Peace Negotiations: A Personal Narrative* (Boston, MA, and New York, 1921), 196.

18. NAS, GD 40/17/65, Frontier Questions, Notes on Heligoland, 14 Apr. 1919.

19. Paul Mantoux, *The Deliberations of the Council of Four*, ed. and trans. A. S. Link, vol. 1 (Princeton, NJ, 1992), 252–6.

20. Ibid., 254.

21. NAS, GD 40/17/1175, Memorandum by Balfour, 15 Apr. 1919.

22. *Papers Relating to the Foreign Relations of the United States, 1919: The Paris Peace Conference*, vol. 4 (Washington, DC, 1943), 396. The Allies handed the conditions regarding Heligoland to the German delegation on 7 May 1919. See BA, R 43 I/1349, 83–6 for discussions by the cabinet in Berlin.

23. Harold Nicolson, *Peacemaking, 1919* (London, 1933), 368.

24. Philipp Scheidemann, 'Gegen die Annahme des Versailler Vertrages', 12 May 1919, in *Politische Reden 1914–1945*, ed. Peter Wende (Frankfurt, 1994), 254–62. On Versailles and German public opinion see Ulrich Heinemann, *Die verdrängte Niederlage: Politische Öffentlichkeit und Kriegsschuldfrage in der Weimarer Republik* (Göttingen, 1983); Richard Bessel, *Germany after the First World War* (Oxford, 1993), ch. 9; Wolfgang Schivelbusch, *Die Kultur der Niederlage: Der amerikanische Süden 1865, Frankreich 1871, Deutschland 1918* (Berlin, 2001), ch. 3.

25. The Heligoland control commission was a branch of the Naval Inter-Allied Commission of Control (NIACC), resident in Berlin and headed by Admiral Sir Edward Charlton. The commission's records are in TNA, ADM 116/1981, with additional papers in BL, Add. MS 52583A–L; those of its German counterpart (the *Unterausschuss für Helgoland*) in PA-AA, R 22574 and R 77407–9. On Cunningham see Michael Simpson, *A Life of Admiral of the Fleet Andrew Cunningham: A Twentieth Century Naval Leader* (London, 2004) and Andrew Cunningham, *A Sailor's Odyssey: The Autobiography of Admiral of the Fleet, Viscount Cunningham of Hyndhope* (London, 1951).

26. N.C.M., 'Some German Ports', 27.

27. BL, Add. MS 52583A, Heligoland Defences, Mar. 1920.

28. TNA, CAB 24/111/10, Memorandum, Walter Long, 24 Aug. 1920. Copy in TNA, LG/F/34/1/40. See also Wiltshire and Swindon Archives, 947/702/1.

29. Wiltshire and Swindon Archives, 947/712, Long to Zaharoff, 20 Aug. 1920.

30. TNA, CAB 24/111/10, Memorandum, Walter Long, 24 Aug. 1920.

31. Ibid.

32. Ibid.

33. BA, R 901/72196, Reichsschatzminister to Reichsministerium des Äußeren, 22 July 1920; ibid., Presseabteilung der Reichsregierung to Dr Cürlis, 19 Aug. 1920.

34. Ibid., Aufzeichnung, Presseabteilung der Reichsregierung, 11 Sept. 1920.

35. See especially *Illustrated London News*, 10 Jan. 1920; 15 May 1920; 22 Oct. 1921.

36. N.C.M., 'Some German Ports', 31. A similar contrast is evoked in Reuter, *Scapa Flow*, 139.
37. *The Times*, 12 Sept. 1919.
38. *The Times*, 24 Nov. 1919.
39. TNA, FO 608/141, Letter by Heligolanders, 19 Jan. 1919. For the roles played by Kuchlenz and Schensky before and during the war see Chapters 5 and 6.
40. NMM, NOT/13, Visit to Heligoland, 1919.
41. Ibid.
42. NMM, WHI/68, Schensky to Black, 24 Sept. 1919.
43. TNA, FO 93/36/24, Agreement: Africa and Heligoland, article 12.4.
44. Hans Helfritz, *Rechtsgutachten über den Fortbestand der der Gemeinde Helgoland gewährleisteten Gesetze und Gewohnheiten* (Berlin, 1929). Compare Arno Schreiber-Loetzenburg, *Das Finanzrecht der Gemeinde Helgoland* (Steglitz, 1931) and Lorenz Petersen, 'Zur Geschichte der Verfassung und Verwaltung auf Helgoland', *Zeitschrift der Gesellschaft für Schleswig-Holsteinische Geschichte*, 67 (1939), 29–190, both of whom stress the peculiarity of the island's legal position.
45. Vanessa Conze, 'Die Grenzen der Niederlage: Kriegsniederlagen und territoriale Verluste im Grenz-Diskurs in Deutschland (1918–1970)', in Horst Carl, Hans-Henning Kortüm, Dieter Langewiesche, and Friedrich Lenger (eds), *Kriegsniederlagen: Erfahrungen und Erinnerungen* (Berlin, 2004), 163–84.
46. BA, R 43 I/1351, Protokoll der Kabinettssitzung vom 29. Oktober 1919; ibid., Gemeinsame Sitzung des Reichskabinetts mit dem Preussischen Staatsministerium vom 31. Oktober 1919.
47. Ibid., Kabinettssitzung vom 28. Oktober 1919, Wahlen in Helgoland.
48. BA, R 43 I/1843, Reichszentrale für den Heimatdienst to Reichkanzlei, 23 Dec. 1919. On the role of the *Reichszentrale* see Wolfgang Wippermann, *Politische Propaganda und staatsbürgerliche Erziehung: Die Reichszentrale für Heimatdienst in der Weimarer Republik* (Bonn, 1976).
49. BA, R 43 I/1357, Kabinettssitzung vom 8. Juli 1920.
50. *Sten. Ber.*, 31 July 1920, 500.
51. Ibid., 555.
52. Ibid., 556.
53. *Hamburger Nachrichten*, 14 Feb. 1921. The 'Old Heligoland' party (the predecessor to the *Heimatbund* party which dominated from 1926 to 1933) got twice as many seats as all national parties (including the SPD) together.
54. PA-AA, R 22574, Reichsschatzminister to Abteilungspräsident, Landesfinanzamt, Abteilung III, Wilhelmshaven, 13 Jan. 1920.
55. BA, R 43 I/1357, Kabinettssitzung vom 12. Juli 1920; BA, R 43 I/1843, Auszug aus dem Protokoll der Sitzung des Reichsministeriums vom 12. Juli 1920.
56. TNA, ADM 116/1981, Letter to the Editor, 20 Oct. 1920, enclosed in Cunningham to Charlton, 25 Oct. 1920.
57. For the 'scrap of paper' controversy see Chapter 5 and Otte, 'A "German Paperchase"'.

58. TNA, ADM 116/1981, Letter to the Editor, 20 Oct. 1920, enclosed in Cunningham to Charlton, 25 Oct. 1920.

59. Hansard, HL, 10 Nov. 1920, 238–43. See also *The Times*, 22 Jan. 1921, 'The Heligolanders'.

60. On the 'press wars' see Dominik Geppert, *Pressekriege: Öffentlichkeit und Diplomatie in den deutsch-britischen Beziehungen 1896–1912* (Munich, 2007).

61. *The Times*, 22 Jan. 1921, 'The Heligolanders'. See also *Morning Post*, 22 Feb. 1921 and the cuttings in PA-AA, R 77408 and R 77409.

62. PA-AA, R 77408, Tagesbericht Nr 35. See also PA-AA, R 77407, Reichsschatzminister to Auswärtiges Amt, 1 Apr. 1920.

63. Cunningham, *A Sailor's Odyssey*, 109.

64. *The Times*, 12 Sept. 1919.

65. This was reported not only by German and British correspondents, but also by the neutral press, as the *Hamburger Fremdenblatt*, 1 Nov. 1920, and *The Times*, 24 Nov. 1919, acknowledged. See also *Basler Nachrichten*, 5 May 1920.

66. *Hamburger Nachrichten*, 12 Nov. 1920.

67. See the cuttings in PA-AA, R 77407 and R 77408.

68. TNA, ADM 116/1981, Military Occupation of Heligoland, Jan. 1921.

69. PA-AA, R 77409, Reichszentrale für Heimatdienst, *Was will Helgoland?*

70. PA-AA, R 77408, Besprechung über die Helgolandfrage am 17. November im Auswärtigen Amt.

71. Ibid., 'Helgoland', 25 Nov. 1920.

72. Ibid.

73. Ibid., Aufzeichnung, 16 Nov. 1920.

74. BA, R 43 I/1843, Imperial Finance Minister to Landesfinanzamt Schleswig-Holstein, 4 Mar. 1921. Copy in PA-AA, R 77408.

75. Ibid., Niederschrift über die Chefbesprechung am Montag, den 2. Mai 1921. See also ibid., Helgoländer Rechtszustand am 1. Januar 1927.

76. Ibid., State Secretary, Imperial Chancellery to Imperial Finance Minister, 16 Dec. 1921; ibid., Imperial Finance Minister to Prussian Minister of the Interior, 23 Dec. 1921; PA-AA, R 77409, Imperial Treasurer to Prussian Minister of the Interior, 8 Dec. 1921 ('Helgoländer Fragen').

77. Ibid., Imperial Chancellor to Imperial Treasurer, 8 Dec. 1921.

78. Ibid., Helgoländer Rechtszustand am 1. Januar 1927, 28.

79. PA-AA, R 77407, Stand der Helgoländer Frage, 5 Nov. 1920.

80. Ibid., Tagesbericht Nr 33, 16 Nov. 1920. See also BA, R 43 I/1843, Präsident Staatsministerium to Reichsregierung, 7 July 1920; LA Schleswig, Abt. 320.22, 83, Regierungs-Kommissar, Helgoland, 12 Nov. 1921; HStA Hanover, Hann. 122a, Nr 32, Landrat Helgoland, 10 Apr. 1931.

81. BA, R 43 I/1843, Präsident Staatsministerium to Reichsregierung, 7 July 1920.

82. See Chapter 3.

83. *Vossische Zeitung*, 23 July 1921.

84. *Hamburgischer Korrespondent*, 9 Aug. 1921.

85. *Neue Hamburger Zeitung*, 9 Aug. 1921; *Magdeburgische Zeitung*, 10 Aug. 1921; *Weser Zeitung*, 9 Aug. 1921. Compare cuttings in PA-AA, R 77409.
86. *Deutsche Allgemeine Zeitung*, 11 Aug. 1921.
87. PA-AA, R 77409, Deutsche Botschaft to Auswärtiges Amt, 23 Aug. 1921.
88. LA Schleswig, Abt. 320.22, 34, Reichszentrale für den Heimatdienst to Landrat des Kreises Helgoland, 22 Jan. 1923.
89. *Hamburger Echo*, 3 Aug. 1921.
90. LA Schleswig, Abt. 320.22, Nr 107, Landrat to Geschäftsführung des Kurhauses, 30 July 1923. On the *Verfassungstag* see Manuela Achilles, 'With a Passion for Reason: Celebrating the Constitution in Weimar Germany', *Central European History*, 43 (2010), 666–89; Manuela Achilles, 'Reforming the Reich: Democratic Symbols and Rituals in the Weimar Republic', in Kathleen Canning, Kerstin Barndt, and Kirsten McGuire (eds), *Weimar Publics/Weimar Subjects: Rethinking the Political Culture of Germany in the 1920s* (New York and Oxford, 2010), 175–91. See also Detlef Lehnert and Klaus Megerle (eds), *Politische Identität und nationale Gedenktage: Zur politischen Kultur der Weimarer Republik* (Opladen, 1989); Robert Gerwarth, 'The Past in Weimar History', *Contemporary European History*, 15 (2006), 1–22; Benjamin Ziemann, *Contested Commemorations: Republican War Veterans and Weimar Political Culture* (Cambridge, 2013).
91. BA, R 43 I/1843, Cuno to Gemeindevorsteher Lührs, 9 Aug. 1923.
92. LA Schleswig, Abt. 320.22, 34, Landrat Helgoland to Reichszentrale für Heimatdienst, Landesabteilung Hamburg-Lübeck, 13 Oct. 1923.
93. BA, BILD 111/030-06, Ausland-Abteilung des Lichtbild-Dienstes, Formen der Deutschen Landschaft, Helgoland Westküste, 1931. On the nationalization of nature in German history see David Blackbourn, *The Conquest of Nature: Water, Landscape and the Making of Modern Germany* (London, 2006) and Lekan, *Imagining the Nation*.
94. Frank Urban, *Ned's Navy: The Private Letters of Edward Charlton from Cadet to Admiral* (Shrewsbury, 1995), 158 (30 May 1920). See the progress reports in TNA, ADM 116/1981 and BL, Add. MS 52583A-C.
95. TNA, ADM 116/1981, Charlton to French, Italian, and Japanese delegations, 7 June 1922. See also ibid., Report, Civil Engineer in Chief, 6 June 1922; Leopold Savile, 'The Demolition of the Harbour and Defence Works of Heligoland', *Minutes of Proceedings of The Institution of Civil Engineers*, 220 (1924–5), 55–96; and Cunningham, *A Sailor's Odyssey*, 110.
96. *Helgoländer Zeitung*, 21 June 1922. When the shipping line threatened to interrupt the link during the winter, the government was quick to step in. Under no circumstances could Heligoland be cut off from the mainland. This, wrote Adolf Georg von Maltzahn, the state secretary of the Auswärtiges Amt, would cause a flare up of the 'particularist tendencies' that had found such an 'echo in the British press in the past'. The imperial and Prussian governments agreed to subsidize the connection and cover HAPAG's losses. See BA, R 43 I/1843,

Maltzahn to State Secretary at the Imperial Chancellery, 3 Jan. 1923. See also ibid., Imperial Minister of the Interior to State Secretary at the Imperial Chancellery, 6 Jan. 1923.

97. *Griebens Reiseführer*, vol. 107, *Helgoland* (Berlin, 1925), 38.

98. StA Oldenburg, Best. 262–4, Nr 11426; *Helgoländer Zeitung*, 1 Aug. 1928.

99. LA Schleswig, Abt. 320.22, Nr 83.

100. Ibid.; Emil Lindemann, *Helgoland-Führer* (Cuxhaven, 1925); *Führer des Nordseebades Helgoland* (Leipzig, 1928); *Helgoländer Zeitung*, 6 June 1928. On the role of guidebooks see Rudy Koshar, *German Travel Cultures* (Oxford, 2000).

101. WIA, GC, Warburg to Thomsen, 29 July 1927. See also ibid., Warburg to Thomsen, 4 July 1927.

102. WIA, GC, Warburg to Frankfurter Zeitung, 11 Sept. 1929. See also ibid., Warburg to Berliner Tageblatt, 19 Sept. 1929.

103. WIA, GC, Warburg to Saxl, 1 Aug. 1927; ibid., FC, Aby Warburg to Marietta Warburg, 17 June 1925; ibid., Mary Warburg to Marietta Warburg, 15 June 1925.

104. WIA, FC, Mary Warburg to Marietta Warburg, 23 May 1925; ibid., GC, Ruth Warburg to Empress of India Hotel, 31 Aug. 1929.

105. WIA, GC, Warburg to Bing, 23 May 1925.

106. WIA, FC, Mary Warburg to Marietta Warburg, 15 June 1925.

107. WIA, GC, Warburg to Lange, 24 Sept. 1929.

108. NBA, Heisenberg to Bohr, 8 June 1925.

109. Werner Heisenberg, *Physics and Beyond: Encounters and Conversations* (London, 1971), 60.

110. Ibid., 61.

111. Werner Heisenberg, 'Über quantentheoretische Umdeutung kinematischer und mechanischer Beziehungen', *Zeitschrift für Physik*, 33 (1925), 879–93.

112. Gerd W. Buschhorn and Helmut Rechenberg, *Werner Heisenberg auf Helgoland: Zur 75jährigen Wiederkehr der Entdeckung der Quantenmechanik durch Werner Heisenberg im Juni 1925* (Munich, 2000); Gino Segrè, *Faust in Copenhagen: A Struggle for the Soul of Physics* (London, 2007), 131–2; David C. Cassidy, *Uncertainty: The Life and Science of Werner Heisenberg* (New York, 1992), 201; Jagdish Mehra and Helmut Rechenberg, *The Historical Development of Quantum Theory*, vol. 1, *The Discovery of Quantum Mechanics, 1925* (New York and Heidelberg, 1982), 248–60.

113. ÖNB, Autogr. 1255/14-2 Han, Riefenstahl to Franz Servaes, 22 July 1925.

114. *Frankfurter Zeitung*, 4 Mar. 1927.

115. Siegfried Kracauer, *From Caligari to Hitler: A Psychological History of the German Film* (Princeton, NJ, 1947), 112.

116. *New York Review of Books*, 6 Feb. 1975.

117. Robert Macfarlane, *Mountains of the Mind: A History of a Fascination* (London, 2008); Tom Neuhaus, *Tibet in the Western Imagination* (Basingstoke, 2012). See

Kracauer, *From Caligari to Hitler*, 258 for 'the fusion of the mountain cult and the Hitler cult'.

118. Leni Riefenstahl, *Memoiren* (Munich, 1987), 87.

119. Ibid., 157.

120. On Riefenstahl, whose *Triumph of the Will* (1935) Sontag saw as 'the most successfully, most purely propagandistic film ever made', see Jürgen Trimborn, *Riefenstahl: Eine deutsche Karriere* (Berlin, 2002) and Steven Bach, *Leni—The Life and Work of Leni Riefenstahl* (New York, 2007).

121. *Vossische Zeitung*, 21 Oct. 1925. On the club see Wallmann, *Kolonie*, ch. 6.

122. On the Sass brothers see Ekkehard Schwerk, *Die Meisterdiebe von Berlin: Die goldenen Zwanziger der Gebrüder Sass* (Berlin, 1984) and Patrick Wagner, *Volksgemeinschaft ohne Verbrecher: Konzeptionen und Praxis der Kriminalpolizei in der Zeit der Weimarer Republik und des Nationalsozialismus* (Hamburg, 1996), 164–79. On their end at the hands of Rudolf Höß see Nikolaus Wachsmann, *Hitler's Prisons: Legal Terror in Nazi Germany* (New Haven, CT, and London, 2004), 207–8.

123. *Hamburger Correspondent*, 7 Aug. 1926.

124. Two years later *Luft Hansa* established a regular service; see *Helgoländer Zeitung*, 31 July 1928.

125. *Jubiläumsjahr des Nordseebades Helgoland: 1826–1926* (Helgoland, 1926), n.p. See also *Die Entwicklung der Gemeinde und des Bades Helgoland im Jahre 1928* (Helgoland, 1928); *Die Entwicklung der Gemeinde und des Bades Helgoland im Jahre 1929* (Helgoland, 1929).

CHAPTER 8: HITLER'S ISLAND

1. *Die Tagebücher von Joseph Goebbels*, ed. Elke Fröhlich, part 1, vol. 1/iii (Munich, 2004), 54.

2. Ibid., 55.

3. *Der Stahlhelm*, 24 June 1928.

4. Elizabeth Harvey, 'Pilgrimages to the "Bleeding Border": Gender and Rituals of Nationalist Protest in Germany, 1919–39', *Women's History Review*, 9 (2000), 201–29.

5. BA, R 32/374, Vize-Präsident Deutscher Kolonialverein to Reichskunstwart, 30 June 1930; ibid., Reichskunstwart to Reichsminister des Innern, 14 Aug. 1930; BA, R 1001/6516, Franz von Epp to Auswärtiges Amt, 23 Apr. 1929; LA Schleswig, Abt. 320.22, 84, Kolonial-Tagung und Werbewochen des Deutschen Kolonialvereins; *Helgoländer Heimat-Bund*, July 1931. See also Arne Perras, *Carl Peters and German Imperialism 1856–1918* (Oxford, 2004), 243–6.

6. 'Collective trauma' is from Schivelbusch, *Kultur der Niederlage*, 244. For more convincing assessments see Heinemann, *Verdrängte Niederlage*; Bessel, *Germany after the First World War*, ch. 9; Peter Fritzsche, *Germans into Nazis* (Cambridge, MA, 1998), 83–136; Tim Mason, 'The Legacy of 1918 for National Socialism',

in Anthony Nicholls and Erich Matthias (eds), *German Democracy and the Triumph of Hitler* (London, 1971), 215–39.

7. John Horne, 'Defeat and Memory in Modern History', in Jenny Macleod (ed.), *Defeat and Memory: Cultural Histories of Defeat in the Modern Era* (London, 2008), 11–29.

8. Schivelbusch, *Kultur der Niederlage*, ch. 3; Richard Bessel, '1918–1919 in der deutschen Geschichte', in Dieter Papenfuß and Wolfgang Schieder (eds), *Deutsche Umbrüche im 20. Jahrhundert* (Cologne, 2000); Boris Barth, *Dolchstoßlegenden und politische Desintegration: Das Trauma der deutschen Niederlage im ersten Weltkrieg 1914–1933* (Düsseldorf, 2003); Joachim Petzold, *Die Dolchstoßlegende* (Berlin, 1963); Friedrich Freiherr Hiller von Gaertringen, '"Dolchstoss"-Diskussion und "Dolchstosslegende" im Wandel von vier Jahrzehnten', in Waldemar Besson and Friedrich Freiherr Hiller von Gaertringen (eds), *Geschichte und Gegenwartsbewußtsein* (Göttingen, 1963), 122–60; Gerd Krumeich, 'Die Dolchstoß-Legende', in Étienne François and Hagen Schulze (eds), *Deutsche Erinnerungsorte*, vol. 1 (Munich, 2000), 585–99.

9. Ian Kershaw, *Hitler, 1889–1936: Hubris* (London, 1998), ch. 12; Richard J. Evans, *The Coming of the Third Reich* (London, 2003), ch. 5; Peter Fritzsche, 'The NSDAP 1919–1934: From Fringe Politics to Seizure of Power', in Jane Caplan (ed.), *Short Oxford History of Germany: Nazi Germany* (Oxford, 2008), 48–72; Martin Broszat, *Die Machtergreifung: Der Aufstieg der NSDAP und die Zerstörung der Weimarer Republik* (Munich, 1984); Karl Dietrich Bracher, Wolfgang Sauer, and Gerhard Schulz, *Die nationalsozialistische Machtergreifung: Studien zur Errichtung des totalitären Herrschaftssystems in Deutschland 1933/34* (Cologne and Opladen, 1960).

10. Jeremy Noakes, *The Nazi Party in Lower Saxony, 1921–1933* (Oxford, 1971); William Sheridan Allen, *The Nazi Seizure of Power: The Experience of a Single German Town, 1922–1945*, 2nd, rev. edn (New York, 1984); Martin Broszat et al. (eds), *Bayern in der NS-Zeit*, 6 vols (Munich, 1977–83); Horst Möller, Andreas Wirsching, and Walter Ziegler (eds), *Nationalsozialismus in der Region: Beiträge zur regionalen und lokalen Forschung und zum internationalen Vergleich* (Munich, 1996); Jill Stephenson, *Hitler's Home Front: Württemberg under the Nazis* (London, 2006).

11. LA Schleswig, Abt. 320.22, Nr 84, Verkehrsverein and Gastwirteverein to Landrat, 8 May 1932.

12. Kurt Friedrichs, *Umkämpftes Helgoland* (Helgoland, 1988), 54–68.

13. *Helgoländer Heimat-Bund*, Mar./Apr. 1933, 'Programm der Aufbauarbeit der Nationalsozialisten'.

14. BA, OPG (formerly BDC), Georg Friedrichs, Aussage des Zeugen Blatzkowski. See Chapter 7 for pro-British 'separatism' in the aftermath of the First World War.

15. *Nathurn*, 30 Jan. 1934.

16. For an example see Hitler's visit in 1938 recorded on film: NARA, 200 MTT 503 A.

17. *Nathurn*, 27 Feb. 1934 and 30 June 1934.

18. R. M. Lockley, *I Know an Island* (London, 1938), 176–7.

19. Ibid., 167.

20. DRA, 2743221, 'Helgoland: Das Bild einer Insel im deutschen Meer', broadcast on 14 June 1933; NORAG, 11 June 1933.

21. *Berliner Tageblatt*, 2 May 1935; *Berliner Lokal-Anzeiger*, 6 May 1935; Gabriele Toepser-Ziegert (ed.), *NS-Presseanweisungen der Vorkriegszeit*, vol. 3/1 (Munich, 1987), 258.

22. Shelley Baranowski, *Strength through Joy: Consumerism and Mass Tourism in the Third Reich* (Cambridge, 2004); Kristin Semmens, *Seeing Hitler's Germany: Tourism in the Third Reich* (Basingstoke, 2005); Koshar, *German Travel Cultures*. On the *Volksgemeinschaft* see Frank Bajohr and Michael Wildt (eds), *Volksgemeinschaft: Neue Forschungen zur Gesellschaft des Nationalsozialismus* (Frankfurt, 2009); Martina Steber and Bernhard Gotto (eds), *Visions of Community in Nazi Germany: Social Engineering and Private Lives* (Oxford, 2014).

23. *Bord-Zeitung der NS-Gemeinschaft Kraft durch Freude*, no. 1 (1937).

24. NS-Gemeinschaft 'Kraft durch Freude', *Dein Urlaub 1939* (1939), n.p.

25. LA Schleswig, Abt. 320.22, 84, Jahresrückblick 1930.

26. *Daily Telegraph*, 17 Oct. 1936.

27. Klaus Behnken (ed.), *Deutschland-Berichte der Sozialdemokratischen Partei Deutschlands (Sopade) 1934–1940*, 2. Jahrgang, 1935 (Frankfurt, 1980), 1458.

28. Baranowski, *Strength through Joy*, 84.

29. Badeverwaltung Helgoland, *Helgoland, Deutschlands Fels im Meer* (Hamburg, 1935). See also Fritz Otto Busch, *Das Buch von Helgoland* (Braunschweig, 1935).

30. *Nathurn*, June 1935, 'Die Badesaison der Sommer 1933 und 1934'.

31. On school visits see StA Hamburg, 362-2/5, 29 and Jörg Fligge, *Lübecker Schulen im 'Dritten Reich': Eine Studie zum Bildungswesen in der NS-Zeit im Kontext der Entwicklung im Reichsgebiet* (Lübeck, 2014), 287.

32. StA Hamburg, 364–5 I, M 90.16, Akademische Auslandstelle Hamburg to Quästur Hansische Universität Hamburg, 31 May 1937; Studentenführung der Hansischen Universität Hamburg to Geschäftstelle Universität Hamburg, 2 June 1937; Studentenwerk Hamburg to Rektor der Hansischen Universität, 26 May 1937; Svens-Tyska Föreningen to Akademische Auslandstelle Hamburg, 26 May 1937.

33. Frank Bajohr, *Unser Hotel ist judenfrei: Bäder-Antisemitismus im 19. und 20. Jahrhundert* (Frankfurt, 2003); Michael Wildt, '"Der muß hinaus! Der muß hinaus!" Antisemitismus in deutschen Nord- und Ostseebädern 1920–1935', *Mittelweg*, 36 (2001), 3–25.

34. See Theodor von Rodowicz-Oświęcimsky, *Unter Englands Fahnen zur Zeit des Krimkrieges: Humoristisch-satyrische Reminiscenzen,* vol. 1 (Hanover, 1875), 20, who wrote in 1875 that Heligoland was frequented 'especially by the rich of the tribe of Judah'.

35. See Chapter 7.

36. Avraham Barkai, '*Wehr dich!*' *Der Centralverein deutscher Staatsbürger jüdischen Glaubens (C. V.) 1893–1938* (Munich, 2002), 155.

37. Auguste Zeiß-Horbach, *Der Verein zur Abwehr des Antisemitismus: Zum Verhältnis von Protestantismus und Judentum im Kaiserreich und in der Weimarer Republik* (Leipzig, 2008); Barbara Suchy, 'The Verein zur Abwehr des Antisemitismus', *LBI Year Book*, 28 (1983), 205–39 and *LBI Year Book*, 30 (1985), 67–100. For Südekum's role in the Club see Chapter 7.

38. *Hamburger Volksblatt*, Beiblatt, Nr 45, Nov. 1928, 'Helgolands Kampf gegen das jüdische Großkapital'.

39. *Berliner Tageblatt*, 29 June 1929; *Frankfurter Zeitung*, 14 July 1929.

40. WL, 55/69/2344, Auszug aus dem Protokoll der öffentlichen Sitzung der Gemeindevertretung am 3. Juli 1929.

41. Particularly active was Carl Timm, a councillor and self-declared National Socialist. See *Helgoländer Zeitung*, 20 Sept. 1929; WL, 55/69/2344, Edgar Friede to CV, 5 Nov. 1929; ibid., CV to Edgar Friede, 12 Nov. 1929. See also ibid., Israelitisches Familienblatt to Edgar Friede, 5 Nov. 1929: it was common knowledge on the island that 'the brothers Timm are anti-Semites'.

42. WL, 55/69/2344, CV to Henry Rothschild, 11 July 1929; ibid., Memo 'Helgoland', 12 Aug. 1929.

43. WIA, GC, Warburg to Frankfurter Zeitung, 11 Sept. 1929. See also ibid., Warburg to Berliner Tageblatt, 19 Sept. 1929.

44. WIA, GC, Warburg to H. G. Pauls, Frankfurter Zeitung, 24 Sept. 1929. On Warburg and anti-Semitism see Russell, *Aby Warburg*, 202–4.

45. WIA, GC, Warburg to Lange, 24 Sept. 1929.

46. WL, 55/69/2344, CV to Villa Mohr, Villa Atlantik, and Villa Kronprinz, Mar. 1931; CV to Gemeindevorsteher Helgoland, 17 June 1931; Memo, 9 July 1931: 'Trotz zweier Vorkommnisse in letzter Zeit ist gegen den Besuch von Helgoland nichts einzuwenden'. ('Despite two recent incidents there is nothing to be said against visiting Heligoland'.) Cf. *Central-Vereins-Zeitung*, 8 May 1931 and Bajohr, *Unser Hotel*, 187. The establishments mentioned most often as anti-Semitic were Pension Georg Friedrichs, Villa Kronprinz, and Villa Mohr.

47. LA Schleswig, Abt. 320.22, 84, Landratsamt Helgoland to Landrat Pinneberg, 26 June 1931.

48. WL, 55/69/2344, Landgemeinde Helgoland to Reisedienst CV, 20 June 1931.

49. Ibid., Nordseebad Helgoland to CV, 2 Aug. 1932.

50. LA Schleswig, Abt. 131, 5, Abschrift des Protokolls der öffentlichen Sitzung der Gemeindevertretung am Montag, den 15. Mai 1933.

51. WL, 55/72/2418, CV to Josef Astruck, 11 June 1934; ibid., CV to Else Hähnlein, 24 July 1934; WL, 55/72/2420, CV Landesverband Nordwestdeutschland to CV Berlin, 29 May 1935.

52. *Der Stürmer*, no. 32 (Aug. 1935). Compare Mirjam Zadoff, *Next Year in Marienbad: The Lost Worlds of Jewish Spa Culture* (Philadelphia, PA, 2012), 211–14, for similar cases.

53. Helmut Heiber (ed.), *Goebbels-Reden*, vol. 1 (Düsseldorf, 1971), 246.

54. WL, 55/72/2421, Schwierigkeiten beim Besuch von Bädern durch Juden, 1936. Compare Wildt, ' "Der muß hinaus" ', 19.

55. WL, 55/72/2422, Leserdienst CV-Zeitung to Siegfrid Haas, 4 Aug. 1937.

56. Hartmuth Merleker, *Helgoland* (Hamburg, 1938), 8, emphasis added.

57. WL, 1346, 5/8, 'Helgoland', 48, 58, 64.

58. H. G. Adler, *Theresienstadt 1941–1945: Das Antlitz einer Zwangsgemeinschaft* (Göttingen, 2005), 602–3, 775; Philipp Manes, *Als ob's ein Leben wär: Tatsachenbericht Theresienstadt 1942 bis 1944*, ed. Ben Barkow and Klaus Leist (Berlin, 2005), 358.

59. Manes, *Als ob's ein Leben wär*, 407.

60. Nikolaus Wachsmann, *KL: A History of the Nazi Concentration Camps* (London and New York, 2015), 540.

61. BA, OPG (formerly BDC), Georg Friedrichs, Untersuchungsbericht, 8 May 1935. Two years later the Nazi party court of Schleswig-Holstein came to a similar conclusion: 'The circumstances in Heligoland are still difficult'. More than anything this was caused 'by the peculiarity of the local inhabitants, a large part of whom are more reserved about idealistic thoughts than the comrades (*Volksgenossen*) on the mainland'. See BA, OPG (formerly BDC), Wilhelm Behrens, Stellvertretender Vorsitzender, Gaugericht Schleswig-Holstein to Oberstes Parteigericht, 2 Apr. 1937.

62. Burkhard Jellonnek, *Homosexuelle unter dem Hakenkreuz: Die Verfolgung von Homosexuellen im Dritten Reich* (Paderborn, 1990), ch. 6; Burkhard Jellonnek, 'Staatspolizeiliche Fahndungs- und Ermittlungsmethoden gegen Homosexuelle', in Burkhard Jellonnek and Rüdiger Lautmann (eds), *Nationalsozialistischer Terror gegen Homosexuelle* (Paderborn, 2002), 149–61; Stefan Micheler, 'Homophobic Propaganda and the Denunciation of Same-Sex-Desiring Men under National Socialism', in Dagmar Herzog (ed.), *Sexuality and German Fascism* (Oxford and New York, 2004), 95–130; Robert Gellately, *The Gestapo and German Society: Enforcing Racial Policy 1933–1945* (Oxford, 1991), 202.

63. BA, OPG (formerly BDC), Alfred Wulff; *Cuxhavener Zeitung*, 19 Jan. 1939; 20 Jan. 1939; 21 Jan. 1939. See also the report 'Kriminalität und Gefährdung der Jugend. Lagebericht bis zum Stande vom 1. Januar 1941' by W. Knopp, reprinted in Arno Klönne (ed.), *Jugendkriminalität und Jugendopposition im NS-Staat: Ein sozialgeschichtliches Dokument* (Münster, 1981), 202.

64. Klaus Marxen, *Das Volk und sein Gerichtshof: Eine Studie zum nationalsozialistischen Volksgerichtshof* (Frankfurt, 1994).

65. Margot Prueß, 'Vergessen Nie!', in Elisabeth Wallmann (ed.), *Die Zerstörung Helgolands* (Helgoland, 1996), 10.

66. For a contemporary source stressing this see Walter Kropatscheck, *Nächte und Tage auf Helgoland: Aufzeichnungen des Inselarztes* (Pfullingen, 1972), 96. See also Detlev Peukert, *Inside Nazi Germany: Conformity, Opposition, and Racism in Everyday Life* (New Haven, CT, and London, 1989); Geoff Eley, 'Hitler's Silent

Majority? Conformity and Resistance Under the Third Reich', *Michigan Quarterly Review*, 42 (2003), 389–425, 550–83; Richard J. Evans, 'Coercion and Consent in Nazi Germany', *Proceedings of the British Academy*, 151 (2007), 57–74.

67. See the list of local Nazi functionaries with dates of party membership given in BA, OPG (formerly BDC), Georg Friedrichs, Zur Person der vernommenen politischen Leiter der Ortsgruppe Helgoland, n.d. For expressions of Nazi enthusiasm on the island see Henrik Eberle (ed.), *Briefe an Hitler: Ein Volk schreibt seinem Führer* (Bergisch Gladbach, 2007), 299–300.

68. StA Stade, Rep. 72/172, Nr 398.

69. Kropatscheck, *Nächte und Tage*, 45.

70. On the effect of Stalingrad see Nicholas Stargardt, *The German War: A Nation under Arms, 1939–1945* (London, 2015), 322–37.

71. StA Stade, Rep. 72/172, Nr 398, Rechtsanwalt Köhler to Amtsgericht Cuxhaven, 27 Jan. 1944. See also Kropatscheck, *Nächte und Tage*, 72–3.

72. StA Stade, Rep. 72/172, Nr 57.

73. Ibid., Nr 363; Nr 57; Nr 393; Nr 425. On petty crime during the war see Stargardt, *German War*, ch. 3; on non-conformist behaviour Peukert, *Inside Nazi Germany*.

74. Krüss was given a suspended sentence of two months' prison and a fine of 200 Reichsmark, to be paid in monthly instalments. He went missing in the spring of 1945 under circumstances that are unclear: he was presumed dead, but his body was never found. In 1950 his sentence was annulled.

75. See also BA, R43I/1843, Reichsminister der Finanzen to Chief of Imperial Chancellory, 29 May 1935 and ibid., Memorandum, 4 July 1935.

76. BA R43II/131, Landgemeinde Helgoland to Reichsregierung Berlin, 12 Jan. 1935. See also *Nathurn*, 24 Feb. 1935.

77. LA Schleswig, Abt. 131, Nr 13, Gewerbesteuerausgleich zwischen Helgoland und anderen Stellen in deutschen Städten, 1938–1942.

78. Ibid., NSDAP Reichsleitung (Hauptamt für Kommunalpolitik) to Bürgermeister Helgoland, 27 Nov. 1941.

79. Willy Norbert, *Die deutsche Nordsee* (Bielefeld and Leipzig, 1925), ch. 10; Paul Schulze-Berghof, *Das letzte Nerthusfest auf Helgoland* (Leipzig, 1935); Willy Krogmann, *Die heilige Insel: Ein Beitrag zur altfriesischen Religionsgeschichte* (Assen, 1942).

80. BA, R 3003/12J327/25; BA, R1507/2028. See also Uwe Schneider, 'Heinrich Pudor', in Uwe Puschner, Walter Schmitz, and Justus H. Ulbricht (eds), *Handbuch zur 'Völkischen Bewegung' 1871–1918* (Munich, 1996), 921–2.

81. BA (formerly BDC), RK, Heinrich Pudor, NSDAP Gauleitung Sachsen to Reichsministerium für Volksaufklärung, 15 May 1940; Heinrich Pudor, *Mein Leben: Kampf gegen Juda und für die arische Rasse* (Leipzig, 1940); *Heinrich Pudor: Ein Vorkämpfer des Deutschtums und des Antisemitismus* (Leipzig, 1934).

82. For Pudor's correspondence with various ministries see BA, R 4901/2646. See also BA, R 43I/1843, Pudor to Imperial Chancellor, 29 Dec. 1930.

83. *Völker aus Gottes Athem: Atlantis-Helgoland, das arisch-germanische Rassenhochzucht-und Kolonisations-Mutterland* (Leipzig, 1936); *Helgoland: Heiligland* (Leipzig, 1931); *Nachweise für Atlantis* (Leipzig, 1937); 'Neue Nachweise für Atlantis-Helgoland', *Neue Helgoland-Forschungen*, no. 5 (Feb. 1937); 'Bestätigung des geologisch größeren Helgoland', *Neue Helgoland-Forschungen*, no. 6 (Mar. 1937);'Helgoland und das Land der weißen Felsen', *Neue Helgoland-Forschungen*, Beiheft 29 (1941).

84. On Himmler and Germanic mysticism see Josef Ackermann, *Heinrich Himmler als Ideologe* (Göttingen, 1970) and Peter Longerich, *Heinrich Himmler* (Munich, 2008), esp. 285–9.

85. BA (formerly BDC), RK, Heinrich Pudor, NSDAP Kreisleitung Leipzig, Politische Beurteilung Heinrich Pudor, 25 May 1940; ibid., Akten-Vermerk Heinrich Pudor, 2 Aug. 1941; ibid., Reichsminister für Volksaufklärung to Präsident Reichsschrifttumskammer, 29 Oct. 1938.

86. Michael Kater, *Das 'Ahnenerbe' der SS 1935–1945: Ein Beitrag zur Kulturpolitik des Dritten Reiches* (Munich, 1997); Ackermann, *Himmler als Ideologe*, 62; Longerich, *Himmler*, 285–9.

87. Ingo Wiwjorra, 'Herman Wirth: Ein gescheiterter Ideologe zwischen "Ahnenerbe" und Atlantis', in Barbara Danckwortt (ed.), *Historische Rassismusforschung: Ideologen, Täter, Opfer* (Hamburg, 1995), 91–112.

88. BA, NS 19/486, Himmler to Wüst, 5 Sept. 1938; ibid., Oberbefehlshaber der Kriegsmarine to Reichsführer SS, 17 Nov. 1938.

89. BA, NS 19/486, Himmler to Sievers, 29 Apr. 1939. Copy in BA, NS 21/1709.

90. On Wiepert see Johannes Tuchel, 'Reinhard Heydrich und die "Stiftung Nordhav": Die Aktivitäten der SS-Führung auf Fehmarn', *Zeitschrift der Gesellschaft für Schleswig-Holsteinische Geschichte*, 117 (1992), 199–225.

91. BA, NS 19/486, Himmler to Sievers, 29 Apr. 1939; Sievers to Wiepert, 8 Aug. 1939; Sievers to Wiepert, 12 Sept. 1939.

92. Ibid., Wiepert to Sievers, 1 Nov. 1939; Wiepert to Sievers, 19 Nov. 1939. For the context see J. Laurence Hare, *Excavating Nations: Archaeology, Museums, and the German–Danish Borderlands* (Toronto, 2015), ch. 6 and Bettina Arnold, 'The Past as Propaganda: Totalitarian Archaeology in Nazi Germany', *Antiquity*, 64 (1990), 464–78.

93. BA, NS 19/486, Aktenvermerk Sievers, 12 Sept. 1939.

94. Ibid., Sievers to Wolff, 13 Nov. 1939.

95. Ibid., Sievers to Witzell, 5 Apr. 1940.

96. Hansard, HC, 10 Nov. 1920, 239.

97. *Time Magazine*, 13 May 1935.

98. On German rearmament and the shift towards a war economy see Adam Tooze, *The Wages of Destruction: The Making and Breaking of the Nazi Economy* (London, 2006), ch. 7; Richard Overy, *War and Economy in the Third Reich* (Oxford, 1994), ch. 6.

99. BA-MA, RM45/II/115.

100. Kershaw, *Making Friends with Hitler;* Gerwin Strobl, *The Germanic Isle: Nazi Perceptions of Britain* (Cambridge, 2000); Gerhard L. Weinberg, 'Hitler and England, 1933–1945: Pretense and Reality', in Weinberg, *Germany, Hitler, and World War II* (Cambridge, 1998), 85–94; G. T. Waddington, '*Hassgegner.* German Views of Great Britain in the later 1930s', *History,* 81 (1996), 22–39; Josef Henke, *England in Hitlers außenpolitischem Kalkül 1935–1939* (Boppard, 1973); Josef Henke, 'Hitlers England-Konzeption: Formulierung und Realisierungsversuche', in Manfred Funke (ed.), *Hitler, Deutschland und die Mächte* (Düsseldorf, 1976), 584–603.

101. Joachim von Ribbentrop, *Zwischen London und Moskau: Erinnerungen und letzte Aufzeichnungen* (Leoni, 1961), 64.

102. Jost Dülffer, *Weimar, Hitler und die Marine: Reichspolitik und Flottenbau 1920–1939* (Düsseldorf, 1973); Joseph Maiolo, *The Royal Navy and Nazi Germany, 1933–39: A Study in Appeasement and the Origins of the Second World War* (London, 1998); Weinberg, 'Hitler and England'.

103. Hans Bohrmann (ed.), *NS-Presseanweisungen der Vorkriegszeit,* vol. 4, part ii (Munich, 1993), 650–1.

104. *Daily Telegraph,* 17 Oct. 1936.

105. Kershaw, *Making Friends with Hitler;* Keith Middlemas, *Diplomacy of Illusion: The British Government and Germany, 1937–39* (London, 1972); R. A. C. Parker, *Chamberlain and Appeasement: British Policy and the Coming of the Second World War* (London, 1993); Gaines Post, *Dilemmas of Appeasement: British Deterrence and Defense, 1934–1937* (Ithaca, NY, 1993); Benny Morris, *The Roots of Appeasement: The British Weekly Press and Nazi Germany during the 1930s* (London, 1991).

106. Harold Nicolson, *Diaries and Letters 1930–1939* (London, 1966), 254, entry for 23 Mar. 1936.

107. TNA, FO 371/23059, 156; Hansard, HC, 13 July 1936, 639–40.

108. TNA, FO 371/23059, 150–4; Hansard, HC, 20 Mar 1939, 885; Kershaw, *Making Friends with Hitler,* 45–51.

109. Bohrmann, *NS-Presseanweisungen der Vorkriegszeit,* vol. 4, part ii, 820.

110. BA-MA, RM 7/2303, Niederschrift über den Vortrag beim Ob.d.M. am 4.3.1937 betr. Ausbau der Befestigungen von Helgoland.

111. BA-MA, RM7/2304, Geheime Kommandosache, KG-Endziel Helgoland, 5 May 1939. See also Fröhle and Kuhn, *Hochseefestung,* vol. 2, 19–67.

112. See the collection of cuttings in BA, R 901/58686. On the orchestration of the media coverage see Bohrmann, *NS-Presseanweisungen,* vol. 6, part ii, 2209 and 2278.

113. See the case of Pudor's *Festung Helgoland* documented in BA (formerly BDC), RK, Heinrich Pudor, Geheimes Staatspolizeiamt to Reichsminister für Volksaufklärung und Propaganda, 9 Nov. 1939; ibid., Reichsministerium für Volksaufklärung und Propaganda to Präsident der Reichsschrifttumskammer, 30 Nov. 1939.

114. *Die Tagebücher von Joseph Goebbels*, part 1, vol. 6, 56.

115. Hansard, HC, 3 Oct. 1938, 51.

116. Weinberg, 'Hitler and England'; Waddington, '*Hassgegner*'; Henke, *England in Hitlers außenpolitischem Kalkül*; Henke, 'Hitlers England-Konzeption'.

117. Gerhard L. Weinberg, *The Foreign Policy of Hitler's Germany: Starting World War II, 1937–1939* (Chicago, IL, 1980); Ian Kershaw, *Hitler, 1936–1945: Nemesis* (London, 2000), ch. 5; Mark Mazower, *Dark Continent: Europe's Twentieth Century* (London, 1998), ch. 5; Mark Mazower, *Hitler's Empire: Nazi Rule in Occupied Europe* (London, 2008), ch. 3.

118. In doing so Hitler's admirals would draw a line from Heligoland to the various harbours they envisaged as locations for a landing, detailing the distance from the island to the English coast. See 'Geheime Kommandosache: Vorüberlegungen über die Möglichkeiten einer Truppenlandung an der Küste der britischen Inseln', in Karl Klee (ed.), *Dokumente zum Unternehmen 'Seelöwe': Die geplante deutsche Landung in England 1940* (Göttingen, 1959), 281–95 (doc. 6). The role of Heligoland for a potential invasion of Britain remained undefined—the Luftwaffe's failure to gain air superiority over Britain resulted in *Operation 'Sea Lion'* being postponed indefinitely. See Karl Klee, *Das Unternehmen 'Seelöwe': Die geplante deutsche Landung in England 1940* (Göttingen, 1958) and Ronald Wheatley, *Operation Sea Lion: German Plans for the Invasion of England, 1939–42* (Oxford, 1958).

119. Hansard, HC, 18 June 1940, 60.

120. *Hamburger Fremdenblatt*, 8 Aug. 1940; *Bremer Nachrichten*, 11 Aug. 1940. See also the cuttings in HStA Hanover, ZGS 2/1, Nr 223 and StA Hamburg, A 355, ZAS, Helgoland.

121. *Signaal*, 19 (1941), 15, 'Helgoland op Wacht'. On the magazine (here cited in its Dutch version) see Rainer Rutz: '*Signal': Eine deutsche Auslandsillustrierte als Propagandainstrument im Zweiten Weltkrieg* (Essen, 2007).

122. See the Epilogue for Anselm Kiefer and his work on Heligoland as a site of memory.

123. *Große Deutsche Kunstausstellung 1940 im Haus der Deutschen Kunst zu München: Offizieller Ausstellungskatalog* (Munich, 1940), 51. For the role of the *Haus der Deutschen Kunst*, built specifically for these exhibitions, see Sabine Brantl, *Haus der Kunst, München: Ein Ort und seine Geschichte im Nationalsozialismus* (Munich, 2007).

124. Eric Michaud, *The Cult of Art in Nazi Germany* (Stanford, CA., 2004); Jonathan Petropoulos, *The Faustian Bargain: The Art World in Nazi Germany* (Oxford, 2000); Stephanie Barron (ed.), *'Degenerate Art': The Fate of the Avant-Garde in Nazi Germany* (New York, 1991).

125. AWM, REL29394.

126. Arthur Catherall, *Raid on Heligoland* (London, 1940), 248, 77, 246.

127. See the assessment in TNA, AIR 34/681.

128. Hansard, HC, 7 Mar. 1940, 595.

129. See Richard Overy, *The Bombing War: Europe 1939–1945* (London, 2013), 242 on the initial raids.
130. TNA, AIR 40/406.
131. Dietmar Süß, *Tod aus der Luft: Kriegsgesellschaft und Luftkrieg in England und Deutschland* (Munich, 2011), 105–10; Mark Connelly, 'The British People, the Press, and the Strategic Air Campaign against Germany', *Contemporary British History*, 16 (2002), 39–58.
132. StA Oldenburg, Best. 135, Nr 96, Reichsführer-SS, 4 July 1939.
133. Ibid., Sicherungsbereich Helgoland, 18 Mar. 1940.
134. Ibid., Polizeipräsident Wilhelmshaven, 26 Apr. 1940; ibid., Geheime Staatspolizeistelle Wilhelmshaven, 3 June 1940.
135. See StA Hamburg, 331–1 I, 1522 for the intensification of surveillance.
136. BA-MA, RM 7/227, Geheime Kommandosache, 21 Nov. 1944.
137. *Picture Post*, 19 Feb. 1944. See also BA-FA, 24625, 'Festung Helgoland', a Nazi production of 1944. Popular novels paraded Adolf Neumann, the seaman who survived the Battle of Heligoland Bight in August 1914 (see Chapter 6). as an example of German heroism. See Wolfgang Loeff, *Der letzte Mann der 'Köln': Nach 76 Stunden hilflosen Herumtreibens in der Nordsee gerettet. Erzählung aus dem Gefecht bei Helgoland am 28. August 1914* (Gütersloh, 1939).
138. *Picture Post*, 19 Feb. 1944.
139. Ibid.
140. NAA, B883,VX78850.
141. NAA, B884, N274904. For another example see NAA, B884,V145470.
142. BA-MA, RM 45/II/125 (5 Sept. 1939). On the raid in which he had been involved see TNA, CAB 65/2/23.
143. Kropatscheck, *Nächte und Tage*, 70.
144. Ibid.
145. Ibid., 26, 70, 83.
146. In many cases their bodies were repatriated after the war. Compare NAA, A705, 163/103/193; NAA, A705, 163/120/451; NAA, A705, 163/160/200; NAA, A705, 166/6/760; NAA, A705, 166/9/416; NAA, A705, 166/14/408; NAA, A705, 166/21/83; NAA, A705, 166/38/718.
147. *Sydney Morning Herald*, 11 May 1943; 11 May 1944; 11 May 1945; 11 May 1946. On Scouller see NAA, A705, 163/160/200 and AWM 65, 4596.
148. Overy, *Bombing War*, 327–38. See Süß, *Tod aus der Luft*, 88–90 on public reactions to the destruction of Hamburg.
149. Ian Kershaw, *The End: Hitler's Germany, 1944–45* (London, 2011), 261–2, 316, 324–6, 343–4. See also Jörg Hillmann and John Zimmermann (eds), *Kriegsende 1945 in Deutschland* (Munich, 2002) and Richard Bessel, *Germany 1945: From War to Peace* (London, 2009).
150. StA Hamburg, 331–1 I, 1522.
151. On definitions of resistance see Ian Kershaw, *The Nazi Dictatorship: Problems and Perspectives of Interpretation*, 4th edn (London, 2000), ch. 8. For the

Heligolanders' post-war perspective see Astrid Friedrichs, *Wir wollten Helgoland retten: Auf den Spuren der Widerstandsgruppe von 1945* (Helgoland, 2010).

152. BA-MA, RM 7/227, Fernschreiben, 19 Apr 1945.

153. BA-MA, RM 7/851, Admiral Deutsche Bucht to Oberkommando der Marine, 19 Apr. 1945; Werner Rahn and Gerhard Schreiber (eds), *Kriegstagebuch der Seekriegsleitung 1939–1945*, part A, vol. 68 (Herford, 1997), 305, Lagebesprechung, 20 Apr. 1945.

154. The mission is documented in TNA, AIR 34/672. See also TNA, CAB/66/65/11.

155. IWM, 80/30/1, Operations Diary R. E. Wannop, 68–9.

156. TNA, CAB, 66/65/19, General Eisenhower to Combined Chiefs of Staff, repeated to the British Chiefs of Staff and Field-Marshal Alexander, 14 Apr. 1945.

157. IWM, 80/30/1, 68–9.

158. TNA, AIR 34/672, Heligoland and Dune, Daylight Attack, 18 Apr. 1945.

159. See the film footage in AWM, P04198.002 and the photographs in TNA, AIR 34/672.

160. BA-MA, RM 45/II/124, 169.

161. BA-MA, RM 7/193, Teilnahme des Ob.d.M. an der Führerlage, 18 Apr. 1945.

162. See AWM, F02598 for a film of the attack on 19 April.

163. Klaus Kröhn, 'Kindertage auf Helgoland', in Wallmann, *Zerstörung*, 55. On the evacuation see StA Stade, Rep. 98, Nr 677; Kropatscheck, *Nächte und Tage*, 102–8.

164. BA-BA, RM 45 II/134, Tagesbefehl, 28 Apr. 1945. This echoed the High Command's general order of that day, for which see Werner Rahn and Gerhard Schreiber (eds), *Kriegstagebuch der Seekriegsleitung 1939–1945*, vol. 68 (Herford, 1997), 405-A. For the context: Michael Geyer, 'Endkampf 1918 and 1945: German Nationalism, Annihilation, and Self-Destruction', in Alf Lüdtke and Bernd Weisbrod (eds), *No Man's Land of Violence: Extreme Wars in the 20th Century* (Göttingen, 2006), 35–68.

165. TNA, CAB 66/65/43, Cessation of Hostilities in Europe. See also Percy Ernst Schramm (ed.), *Kriegstagebuch des Oberkommandos der Wehrmacht*, vol. 4 (Frankfurt, 1961), 1670.

166. Gareth Pritchard, *Niemandsland: A History of Unoccupied Germany, 1944–1945* (Cambridge, 2012).

167. Max Domarus (ed.), *Hitler: Reden und Proklamationen 1932–1945*, vol. 1/2 (Wiesbaden, 1977), 933 (Goebbels concluding Hitler's Sportpalast speech, 26 Sept. 1938); ibid., vol. 2/1, 1316 (Hitler's Reichstag speech, 1 Sept. 1939).

168. BA-MA, RM 7/854, Waffenruhe, 5 May 1945.

169. Kropatscheck, *Nächte und Tage*, 118.

170. Ibid.

171. Ibid., 119.

172. TNA, CAB 66/65/61. Muirhead-Gould had sent an advance detachment of marines to secure the island before his arrival; see TNA, ADM 199/2382, 256.

173. The Act of Military Surrender was first signed on 7 May at Rheims. In order to meet Russian demands a second version was signed at Karlshorst, outside Berlin, in the early hours of 9 May. This second version was backdated to 8 May, to comply with the terms of the agreement the Allies had come to at Rheims. See Kershaw, *The End*, 371–2.

174. *The Times*, 15 May 1945; TNA, ADM 1/18270, Report of Proceedings of Occupation of Heligoland and Dune from 11 to 17 May 1945. For the official Admiralty photograph, see IWM, A.28580. See also Chris Madsen, *The Royal Navy and German Naval Disarmament, 1942–1947* (London, 1998), 62.

175. Kropatscheck, *Nächte und Tage*, 121.

176. Grey to House, 3 June 1919, qtd in Macmillan, *Peacemakers*, 187. See Chapter 7.

CHAPTER 9: OUT OF RUINS

1. IWM, 83/24/1, Unreported Events, 1. Copy in TNA, PRO 30/26/197.

2. TNA, ADM 228/48, Walker to Secretary of the Admiralty, 25 Nov. 1946.

3. IWM, 83/24/1, Unreported Events, 1.

4. The details are recorded in TNA, ADM 228/48. See also IWM, 83/24/1, Demolition of the Fortifications of Heligoland (Operation Big Bang), report by F. T. Woosnam, 3 May 1947. A copy is in TNA, PRO 30/26/197.

5. TNA, ADM 228/48, Secretary of the Admiralty to Walker, 13 Dec. 1947.

6. NAS, GD40/17/65, Memorandum on Heligoland, A. J. Balfour, 14 Apr. 1919.

7. Marder (ed.), *Fear God and Dread Nought*, vol. 2, 435, Fisher to Churchill, 5 Mar. 1912. See Chapter 5.

8. TNA, ADM 228/48, Communications Office, HQ, RN, Berlin, 'Press Coverage Heligoland Demolitions'.

9. Dunkirk at the very north-western fringes of France had been the scene of the hasty evacuation of the British Expeditionary Force in late May and early June 1940.

10. TNA, ADM 228/48, Wigglesworth to Walker, 27 Mar. 1947. Compare Madsen, *Royal Navy and German Naval Disarmament*, 205–7, on the publicity arrangements.

11. See the correspondence between Lord Portal and Richard Meinertzhagen contained in IWM, 10526, on this point.

12. TNA, ADM 228/53, Bischof Halfmann to Governor of Schleswig-Holstein, 14 Feb. 1947.

13. Ibid., Landesregierung Schleswig-Holstein to Governor of Schleswig-Holstein, 14 Feb. 1947.

14. TNA, ADM 228/48, Press Release Concerning Heligoland, 7 Feb. 1947.

15. The firing was done from two ships. E. C. Jellis operated the submarine cable control on board HMS *Lasso*, the primary firing mechanism. A secondary one, using radio transmission, was operated by Lieutenant Commander Frank Graves on board HMS *Bleasdale*. See TNA, ADM 228/48, *Demolition of the*

Fortifications of Heligoland (Operation Big Bang), 24 and IWM, 83/24/1, Unreported Events, 3.

16. British Pathé Archive, 1183.06, 'Heligoland Goes Up'.

17. IWM, 83/24/1, Unreported Events, 5.

18. TNA, BJ 1/267, Information given to the Press, 18 Apr. 1947. For similar observations at Cambridge see the correspondence between Edward Bullard and Arthur Beer, contained in TNA, BJ 1/267.

19. See the press digest in TNA, ADM 228/48 and the cuttings in BA, N 1222/396.

20. TNA, ADM 228/48, Demolition of the Fortifications of Heligoland.

21. *Die Welt*, 19 Apr. 1947.

22. *Dokumente deutscher Kriegsschäden*, vol. 4/3 (Bonn, 1971), 'Der Kampf um die Insel', 28. See also the cuttings in BA, Z 35/187 and StA Hanover, Nds. 50 Acc. 96/88, Nr 106/1.

23. *Die Tagebücher von Joseph Goebbels*, part 1, vol. 6, 56.

24. On the politics of victimhood in post-war Germany see Robert G. Moeller, *War Stories: The Search for a Usable Past in the Federal Republic of Germany* (Berkeley, CA, 2001); Robert G. Moeller, 'Germans as Victims? Thoughts on a Post-Cold War History of World War II's Legacies', *History and Memory*, 17 (2005), 147–94; Frank Biess, *Homecomings: Returning POWs and the Legacies of Defeat in Postwar Germany* (Princeton, NJ, 2006); Bill Niven (ed.), *Germans as Victims: Remembering the Past in Contemporary Germany* (Basingstoke, 2006); Josef Foschepoth, 'German Reactions to Defeat and Occupation', in Robert G. Moeller (ed.), *West Germany under Construction: Politics, Society, and Culture in the Adenauer Era* (Ann Arbor, MI, 1997), 73–89.

25. Kershaw, *The End*, ch. 9; Bessel, *Germany 1945*, ch. 2. See also Christian Meier, 'Erinnern—Verdrängen—Vergessen', *Merkur*, 50 (1996), 937–52, who echoes Hermann Lübbe, 'Der Nationalsozialismus im politischen Bewußtsein der Gegenwart', in Martin Broszat (ed.), *Deutschlands Weg in die Diktatur* (Berlin, 1983), 329–49. On the debate about the political function of self-victimization see Norbert Frei, *Vergangenheitspolitik: Die Anfänge der Bundesrepublik und die NS-Vergangenheit* (Munich, 1996) in contrast to Manfred Kittel, *Die Legende von der 'zweiten Schuld': Vergangenheitsbewältigung in der Ära Adenauer* (Frankfurt and Berlin, 1993).

26. It is obvious that this suited all those who found a comparably smooth transition from having served the Nazi regime to serving the West German authorities. See Axel Schildt, 'Der Umgang mit der NS-Vergangenheit in der Öffentlichkeit der Nachkriegszeit', in Wilfried Loth and Bernd A. Rusinek (eds), *Verwandlungspolitik: NS-Eliten in der westdeutschen Nachkriegsgesellschaft* (Frankfurt and New York, 1998), 19–54 and Ulrich Herbert, 'NS-Eliten in der Bundesrepublik', ibid., 93–115.

27. Klaus Naumann, *Der Krieg als Text: Das Jahr 1945 im kulturellen Gedächtnis der Presse* (Hamburg, 1998); Moeller, *War Stories*; Biess, *Homecomings*; Peter Fritzsche, *Life and Death in the Third Reich* (Cambridge, MA, 2008), ch. 4; Süß,

Tod aus der Luft, ch. 9; Eckart Conze, *Die Suche nach Sicherheit: Eine Geschichte der Bundesrepublik Deutschland von 1949 bis in die Gegenwart* (Munich, 2009), 214–25.

28. Parliamentary questions and answers on the future of Heligoland are documented in TNA, FO 371/39135.

29. *Die Frage Helgoland: The Heligoland Issue* (Hamburg, 1948). On the preparation of the pamphlet see StA Hamburg, 131–1 II, 375 and BA, Z 35/187, Z35/523, Z 21/1235.

30. BA, Z 35/187, Kirchliches Aussenamt der Evangelischen Kirche in Deutschland (Martin Niemöller) to Deutsches Büro für Friedensfragen, 2 Aug. 1949. The Bremen government was the only one to voice reservations about the pamphlet. See StA Hamburg, 131–1 II, 375, Meineke to Stödter, 1 July 1848.

31. For his involvement see StA Hamburg, 131–1 II, 375. On his role during the Third Reich see Christian Joerges and Navraj S. Ghaleigh (eds), *Darker Legacies of Law in Europe: The Shadow of National Socialism and Fascism over Europe and its Legal Traditions* (Portland, OR., 2003), 182–4.

32. For the British response to the pamphlet see BA, Z35/523, Statement on British Bombing Policy to Heligoland, 5 Oct. 1949.

33. *Daily Mirror*, 10 Mar. 1948. See also *Die Welt*, 13 Mar. 1948 and BA, Z 35/523.

34. Ray M. Douglas, *Orderly and Humane: The Expulsion of the Germans after the Second World War* (New Haven, CT, and London, 2012); Andrew Demshuk, *The Lost German East: Forced Migration and the Politics of Memory, 1945–1970* (Cambridge, 2012); Pertti Ahonen, *After the Expulsion: West Germany and Eastern Europe 1945–1990* (Oxford, 2003); Rainer Schulze, 'The German Refugees and Expellees from the East and the Creation of a Western German Identity after World War II', in Philipp Ther and Ana Siljak (eds), *Redrawing Nations: Ethnic Cleansing in East-Central Europe 1944–1948* (Lanham, MD, 2001), 307–25.

35. *Helgoland (Mitteilungsblatt für Hallunner Moats)* appeared bi-monthly. Most Heligolanders subscribed to it, as did the British High Commission and the ministries in Kiel and Bonn.

36. The biographies of some of those contributing to the journal mirrored the amnesia about the Nazi past. Hartmuth Merleker, for example, had written anti-Semitic comments about Heligoland's Jewish guests and had welcomed the rise of the Nazis on the island in the 1930s. After the war he concentrated on local news and the documentation of British 'atrocities' against the island. Compare Merleker, *Helgoland*, 8; Merleker, 'So War Es', *Helgoland*, no. 1/2 (1948); Merleker, 'Chronik 1945–1952', in James Packroß and Peter Rickmers (eds), *Helgoland Ruft* (Hamburg, 1952), 159–68.

37. *Das alte Helgoland photographiert von Franz Schenksy* Rösing, *Franz Schenksy*.

38. *Dokumente Deutscher Kriegsschäden: Evakuierte, Kriegssachgeschädigte, Währungsgeschädigte. Die geschichtliche und rechtliche Entwicklung*, 5 vols (Bonn, 1958–71).

The main lobby group involved in the documentation was the *Zentralverband der Flieger- und Währungsgeschädigten* (ZvF). See Süß, *Tod aus der Luft*, 503–4.

39. Theodor Oberländer, 'Zum Geleit', in *Dokumente Deutscher Kriegsschäden*, vol. I, vii.

40. Philipp-Christian Wachs, *Der Fall Theodor Oberländer (1905 bis 1998): Ein Lehrstück deutscher Geschichte* (Frankfurt, 2000); Michael Burleigh, *Germany Turns Eastwards: A Study of Ostforschung in the Third Reich* (Cambridge, 1988), 144–6 and 317–18.

41. *Dokumente deutscher Kriegsschäden*, vol. 4/3.

42. *Sten. Ber.*, 1 Dec. 1949, 551. Merkatz, who had been a lawyer and academic in the Third Reich, was to be minister for expellees, refugees, and war injured from 1960 to 1961.

43. Ibid., 552.

44. Adenauer's staff made sure that the professor felt he had the chancellor's attention. See the account of meetings with and gifts from Adenauer in BA, B 136/4365, Savory to Staatssekretär des Bundeskanzleramtes, 8 Sept. 1958. Compare PRONI, D3015/1/B/4, Savory to Adenauer, 18 July 1958. Savory had been a *Lektor* at the University of Marburg before the First World War; see Douglas Savory, 'Recollections of a German University', *Contemporary Review*, 190 (1956). Other public figures lobbying on behalf of the Heligolanders in the UK included Lord Malcolm Douglas-Hamilton, a former RAF commander. See PRONI, D3015/1/B/4, Douglas-Hamilton to Savory, 11 Aug. 1950.

45. See Douglas Savory, 'Heligoland Past and Present', *Contemporary Review*, 191 (1957). For a recent publication written in this vein see George Drower, *Heligoland: The True Story of German Bight and the Island that Britain Betrayed* (Stroud, 2002).

46. For Savory's petitions see TNA, FO 371/85274 and PRONI, D3015/1/B/4.

47. Hansard, HC, 28 July 1950, 912.

48. Hansard, HC, 29 June 1949, 1262–4.

49. Winston S. Churchill, *The Second World War*, vol. 2 (London, 1948), 39; Winston S. Churchill, *A History of the English-Speaking Peoples*, vol. 3 (London, 1957), 277; Winston S. Churchill, *A History of the English-Speaking Peoples*, vol. 4, *The Great Democracies* (London, 1958), 282. See also Churchill, *World Crisis*, vol. 1, 18; vol. 2, 41.

50. Hansard, HC, 22 Nov. 1950, 321.

51. PA-AA, B 10, vol. 429, Wilhelm Blank (*Kölnische Rundschau*) to Adenauer, 30 Nov. 1949. Compare ibid., Strauß to Adenauer, 12 Dec. 1950.

52. Ibid., Strohm to Dittmann, n.d., but immediately after Bevin's statement in the Commons of 22 November. Gustav Strohm and Herbert Dittmann belonged to the key personnel running Adenauer's *Verbindungsstelle zur Alliierten Hohen Komission*, which became later part of the West German Foreign Office.

53. Georg von Hatzfeld, 'Tagebuch der Helgolandfahrer', in Packroß and Rickmers, *Helgoland Ruft*, 170.

54. On Löwenstein see especially his papers in BA, N 1222 and his MI5 file in TNA, KV 2/3716.

55. Prince Rupert Loewenstein, the London-based financier who was to manage the Rolling Stones for four decades, was Löwenstein's second cousin. See Prince Rupert Loewenstein, *A Prince Among Stones* (London, 2013).

56. TNA, KV 2/3716, Report on the Recent Political Activities and Future Plans of Prince Hubertus Loewenstein, 15 May 1935.

57. Ibid., Internal Memorandum, Robson-Scott to Byrde, 10 Nov. 1942.

58. Hubertus Prinz zu Löwenstein, *The Tragedy of a Nation* (London, 1934).

59. TNA, KV 2/3716, Vernon Kell to James MacBrien, 4 June 1936.

60. Hubertus Prinz zu Löwenstein, *Was ist Deutsche Aktion?* (Amorbach, 1950). See also the files of the *Deutsche Aktion* in BA, N 1222/292.

61. BA, N 1222/298, Löwenstein to Secretary Deutsche Aktion, 29 Dec. 1950, given to the press in *Mitteilungen der Deutschen Aktion*, 2 Jan. 1951. René Leudesdorff, who, in contrast to Hatzfeld, did not know Löwenstein, was clearly taken aback. His version of the events is rather more critical than Hatzfeld's; see René Leudesdorff, *Wir befreiten Helgoland: Ein historischer Krimi* (Stade, 2007).

62. TNA, FO 1050/474, Luce to Kirkpatrick, 22 Jan. 1951.

63. Compare the cuttings in BA, N 1222/393, N 1222/305, N 1222/339, N 1222/340, N 1222/377, N 1222/394, and N 1222/396.

64. *Die Stimme der Vertriebenen*, 7 Jan. 1951. See also Hubertus Prinz von Löwenstein, 'Beispiel Helgoland', *Die Zeit*, 11 Jan. 1951.

65. *Time Magazine*, 15 Jan. 1951. See also *Frankfurter Rundschau*, 4 Jan. 1951.

66. *Dokumente deutscher Kriegsschäden*, vol. 4/3, 55, Press Release, High Commission, 29 Dec. 1950.

67. TNA, FO 1006/238, Land Commissioner to Chancery, High Commission, 11 Jan. 1951.

68. Ibid., Kirkpatrick to Bevin, 12 Jan. 1951.

69. Anne Deighton, *The Impossible Peace: Britain, the Division of Germany, and the Origins of the Cold War* (Oxford, 1990); R. Gerald Hughes, *Britain, Germany and the Cold War: The Search for a European Détente 1949–1967* (London, 2007), ch. 1.

70. Ivone Kirkpatrick, *The Inner Circle* (London, 1959).

71. TNA, FO 1014/589, Kirkpatrick to Bevin, 6 Jan. 1951.

72. *The Times*, 9 Jan. 1951.

73. *The Times*, 15 Jan. 1951. The West German consul general in London replied promptly to Berry that the issue was affecting 'mass sentiment in Germany in a very serious manner. The average German will say: "On the one hand we are to furnish soldiers to help in defending the West and on the other hand we are being treated like this."' See PA-AA, B 10, vol. 430, Schlange-Schöningen to

Berry, n.d., but after 17 and before 23 Jan. 1951. On Berry see Michael Ahrens, *Die Briten in Hamburg: Besatzerleben 1945–1958* (Munich, 2011) and *Hamburgische Biografie*, vol. 6 (Göttingen, 2012), 29–31.

74. TNA, AIR 2/10012, Foreign Office to Wahnerheide, 2 Jan. 1951.

75. Ibid., 15 Jan. 1951.

76. TNA, PREM 8/474, Foreign Office to Chiefs of Staff, 18 Jan. 1947.

77. TNA, CAB 129/44/74, Policy Towards Germany, 9 Mar. 1951.

78. For an example of Britain's contradictory occupation policy more generally see Jessica Reinisch, *The Perils of Peace: The Public Health Crisis in Occupied Germany* (Oxford, 2013), ch. 5.

79. BA, DY 24/2404, Protokoll des Sekretariats, Zentralbüro FDJ, 4 Jan. 1951. See also Patrick Major, *The Death of the KPD: Communism and Anti-Communism in West Germany, 1945–1956* (Oxford, 1998); Ulrich Mählert and Gerd-Rüdiger Stephan, *Blaue Hemden, Rote Fahnen: Die Geschichte der Freien Deutschen Jugend* (Opladen, 1996); Michael Herms, *Hinter den Linien: Westarbeit der FDJ 1945–1956* (Berlin, 2001), esp. 214–18.

80. PA-AA, B 10, vol. 430, Aufzeichnung Strohm, 9 Feb. 1951.

81. BA, SGY 27/2 contains a selection.

82. TNA, PREM 8/1375, Memorandum, Secretary of State for Air, 20 Feb. 1951.

83. Ibid., Foreign Office to Wahnerheide, 21 Feb. 1951.

84. TNA, AIR 2/10012, British Communiqué, Bonn, 26 Feb. 1951.

85. BA, DY 24 FDJ 2407, Protokoll der Sitzung des Sekretariats des Zentralrats der Freien Deutschen Jugend, 28 Feb. 1951.

86. *Neues Deutschland*, 4 Mar. 1951.

87. BA, BY1/2153, Deutsche Bewegung Helgoland, Albrecht Müller, 23 Jan. 1952.

88. PA-AA, B 10, vol. 431, Bundesverfassungsamt to Bundesminister des Innern und Auswärtiges Amt, 7 Dec. 1951. See also StA Hamburg, 614-2/20, 1.

89. For the statements made by those whom the West German police arrested see TNA, FO 1014/590, Statement Hans Raimund Werner; ibid., Statement Kurt Christen; ibid., Statement Willi Entelman. For the material collected by the East German secret police, the future Stasi, who assumed that some of the 'squatters' were being approached by Western intelligence during their prison terms, see BstU, MfS, AU 262/51, Zwischenbericht, 28 Aug. 1951; Vernehmungsprotokoll, 9 Oct. 1951; Anklageschrift, 11 Dec. 1951.

90. BA, DY 24 FDJ 2407, Protokoll der Sitzung des Sekretariats des Zentralrats der Freien Deutschen Jugend, 4 April 1951, Anlage 2, Protesttelegramm.

91. For examples see BA, DY 24 FDJ 2413, Protokoll der Sitzung des Sekretariats des Zentralrats der FDJ, 22 July 1951.

92. Peter Martin Lampel, *Kampf um Helgoland: Schauspiel in einem Vorspiel, 5 Akten und einem Nachspiel* (Berlin, 1952). The Ulbricht government orchestrated and funded the staging of the play at Berlin's main youth theatre. See Archiv

Theater in der Aue (Junges Staatstheater), Berlin, GDR State Commission for Artistic Affairs to Theater der Freundschaft, 6 Aug. 1951.

93. Archiv Theater in der Aue (Junges Staatstheater), Berlin, ADN Kulturdienst, 11 Mar. 1952. *Kampf um Helgoland* was well received in the East German press, though some critics felt that the main villains—the British judge and West German police inspector—were played more convincingly than the Socialist students, who looked 'pale and unimpressive' (*Berliner Zeitung*, 15 Mar. 1952). See also *Der Morgen*, 13 Mar. 1952.

94. On the petition, the 'Referendum Against Re-Militarisation and for a Peace Treaty', see Beatrice Vierneisel, 'Die Volksbefragung 1951', *Deutschlandarchiv*, 40 (2007), 436–44.

95. PA-AA, B 10, vol. 430, Bartram to Adenauer, 21 May 1951.

96. TNA, FO 1014/590, Luce to Kirkpatrick, 3 May 1951.

97. Jeffrey Herf, *The Jewish Enemy: Nazi Propaganda during World War II and the Holocaust* (Cambridge, MA, 2006), 27.

98. Major, *Death of the KPD*, 260–1, 269–70.

99. Mathias Friedel, *Der Volksbund für Frieden und Freiheit (VFF): Eine Teiluntersuchung über westdeutsche antikommunistische Propaganda im Kalten Krieg und deren Wurzeln im Nationalsozialismus* (Sankt Augustin, 2001).

100. William Glenn Gray, *Germany's Cold War: The Global Campaign to Isolate East Germany, 1949–1969* (Chapel Hill, NC, 2003). On Lippmann, who fell out with the SED leadership in 1953 and fled to West Germany, see Michael Herms, *Heinz Lippmann: Porträt eines Stellvertreters* (Berlin, 1996). See also Jeffrey Herf, *Divided Memory: The Nazi Past in the Two Germanys* (Cambridge, MA, 1997) and David Engerman, 'Ideology and the Origins of the Cold War, 1917–1962', in Melvyl Leffler and Odd Arne Westad (eds), *Cambridge History of the Cold War*, vol. 1 (Cambridge, 2010), 20–43.

101. For a selection of the VFF's posters and brochures see WL, 550.

102. See the statements by arrested 'squatters' contained in TNA, FO 1050/474 and FO 1014/590.

103. BA-FA, MAVIS 578330, *Insel der Entscheidung* (1951).

104. BA, B 136/4365 and 4366, Eingaben und Zuschriften aus der Bevölkerung; BA, B 122/2206, Petitionen aus der Bevölkerung. See also the petitions contained in PA-AA, B 10, vol. 430.

105. StA Hamburg, 131-1II, Peter Knuts Michels, 15 Jan. 1951, emphasis in the original.

106. PA-AA, B 10, vol. 431, Adenauer to Kirkpatrick, 14 Nov. 1951.

107. The controversy surrounding the Großer Knechtsand is documented in StA Hanover, Nds. 50 Acc. 96/88, Nr 106/3-9. Compare the summary in BA, B 122/2206, Aufzeichnung betr. Luftwaffenübungsziel 'Großer Knechtsand', 8 Mar. 1952 and the brief, retrospective survey in BA, B 136/4365, Brentano to Steel, 22 May 1957.

108. PA-AA, B 10, vol. 431, Kirkpatrick to Adenauer, 28 Feb. 1952.

109. Ibid., Kurzprotokoll über die Besprechung im Bundesministerium des Innern über den Festakt zur Feier der Freigabe der Insel Helgoland. The preparations are documented in BA, M 136/4365 and BA, B 122/2206.

110. Adenauer's instructions of 15 January 1952 are quoted in PA-AA, B 10, vol. 431, Bundesminister des Innern to Staatssekretär Bundeskanzleramt, 30 Apr. 1952.

111. PA-AA, B 10, vol. 431, Bundesminister für Verkehr to Staatssekretär, Bundeskanzleramt, 21 May 1952.

112. BA, B 145/993, Ansprache des Ministerpräsidenten Friedrich-Wilhelm Lübke, 1 Mar. 1952.

113. BA, B 136/20694, Rundfunkansprache des Bundeskanzlers anläßlich der Übergabe von Helgoland, 29 Feb. 1952.

114. TNA, FO 1006/242, Kirkpatrick to Eden, 10 Mar. 1952.

115. Marc Trachtenberg, *A Constructed Peace: The Making of the European Settlement, 1945–1963* (Princeton, NJ, 1999); Ronald Granieri, *The Ambivalent Alliance: Konrad Adenauer, the CDU/CSU, and the West, 1949–1966* (New York and Oxford, 2003); Tony Judt, *Post-War: A History of Europe Since 1945* (London, 2005), chs 4–5; Adam Tooze, 'Reassessing the Moral Economy of Post-War Reconstruction: The Terms of the West German Settlement in 1952', in Mark Mazower, Jessica Reinisch, and David Feldman (eds), *Post-War Reconstruction in Europe: International Perspectives, 1945–1949* (Oxford, 2011), 47–90; David Clay Large, *Germans to the Front: West German Rearmament in the Adenauer Era* (Chapel Hill, NC, 1996); Hans-Peter Schwarz, *Die Ära Adenauer: Gründerjahre der Republik. 1949–1957* (Stuttgart, 1981).

116. BA, B 145/115, Aufzeichnung, 11 Feb. 1952.

117. Ibid., Helgoland, Günther Schnabel, 11 Feb. 1952.

118. BA, B 136/4365, Konstituierende Sitzung des Helgoland-Kuratoriums, 28 Feb. 1952.

119. BA, B 136/4366, Finanzierungsplan für den Wiederaufbau der Insel Helgoland. Compare ibid., Bundesminister der Finanzen to Staatssekretär des Bundeskanzleramtes, 4 Feb. 1953, with enclosed revisions.

120. PA-AA, B 10, vol. 431, 'Gebt für Helgoland!' See also BA, B 122/5024 on the *Stiftung Helgoland*.

121. Payments are documented in PA-AA, B 10, vol. 430.

122. PA-AA, B 10, vol. 433, Bassler to Dehler, 27 Nov. 1953. On the Adenauer government actively discouraging all compensation claims against Britain see ibid., Vermerk Bassler, 26 Nov. 1952.

123. TNA, FO 1014/590, Helmers to Dunlop, 4 Mar. 1952.

124. Ibid., Dunlop to Helmers, 12 Mar. 1952 (letter in German in the original).

125. TNA, FO 1014/590, Helmers to Dunlop, 15 Mar. 1952.

126. Blackbourn, *Conquest of Nature*; Lekan, *Imagining the Nation*; Thomas Zeller, *Driving Germany: The Landscape of the German Autobahn, 1930–1970* (Oxford and New York, 1997); Frank Uekötter, *The Green and the Brown: A History of Conservation in Nazi Germany* (Cambridge, 2006).

127. BA, B 136/20694, Rundfunkansprache des Bundeskanzlers anläßlich der Übergabe von Helgoland.

128. See Epilogue.

129. *Ideenwettbewerb für den Wiederaufbau der Insel Helgoland* (Pinneberg, 1951), 39.

130. Otto Bartning, 'Ketzerische Gedanken am Rande der Trümmerhaufen', *Frankfurter Hefte*, 1 (1946), 63–72. On Bartning see Jürgen Bredow and Helmut Lerch (eds), *Materialien zum Werk des Architekten Otto Bartning* (Darmstadt, 1983).

131. On the competition see Ulrich Höhns, *Eine Insel im Aufbau: Helgoland, 1952–62* (Otterndorf, 1990), 43–91. The prototypes for the new Heligoland houses are documented in BA, B 134/4864.

132. Höhns, *Insel im Aufbau*, 125–7.

133. Iain Boyd Whyte, *Bruno Taut and the Architecture of Activism* (Cambridge, 2010), 166–8; Maiken Umbach, 'The *Deutscher Werkbund*, Globalization, and the Invention of Modern Vernaculars', in Maiken Umbach and Bernd-Rüdiger Hüppauf (eds), *Vernacular Modernism: Heimat, Globalization, and the Built Environment* (Stanford, CA, 2005), 138–9.

134. *The Times*, 14 May 1964, 'Heligoland Arises from the Ashes'. For the conflation of 'Europe' and 'Germany' see Timothy Garton Ash, *In Europe's Name: Germany and the Divided Continent* (London and New York, 1993); Mazower, *Hitler's Empire*, ch. 7; and Ute Frevert, 'Europeanizing Germany's Twentieth Century', *History & Memory*, 17 (2005), 87–116.

135. SLNSW B2785, *Deutschlandspiegel*, no. 131 (1965).

136. Höhns, *Insel im Aufbau*, 121.

EPILOGUE

1. Anselm Kiefer, *Hoffmann von Fallersleben auf Helgoland* (1978), private collection. See also Anselm Kiefer, *Verbrennen, Verholzen, Versenken, Versanden: XXXIX Biennale* (Venice, 1980) and, for Kiefer's books more generally, Götz Adriani, *The Books of Anselm Kiefer 1969–1990* (London and New York, 1991). *Hoffmann von Fallersleben auf Helgoland* was subsequently published in an edition of 500 (Groningen, 1980).

2. Caspar David Friedrich, *Das Eismeer* (1823–4), Kunsthalle Hamburg. The painting was for a long time knows as *The Wreck of Hope* (*Gescheiterte Hoffnung*). Compare Peter Märker, *Geschichte als Natur: Untersuchungen zur Entwicklungsvorstellung bei Caspar David Friedrich* (Kiel, 1994) and Peter Rautmann, *Caspar David Friedrich: Das Eismeer* (Frankfurt, 2001). Kiefer had invoked Germany's most revered nineteenth-century landscape painter before, provocatively so in one of his performative 'occupations' of historical landmarks, where he stood overlooking the sea in imitation of Friedrich's *Traveller Looking Over a Sea of Fog*, while raising the Hitler salute. See Anselm Kiefer, 'Zwischen Sommer und Herbst habe ich die Schweiz, Frankreich und Italien besetzt', *Interfunktionen*, no. 122 (1969). For a juxtaposition of Friedrich's

painting and Kiefer's 'occupation' see Simon Schama, *Landscape and Memory* (London, 1995), 122–3.

3. *Operation 'Sea Lion'* (1975), one of the earliest of Kiefer's history paintings, features the same zinc tub as *Hoffmann von Fallersleben auf Helgoland*, the photo book. See Royal Academy of Arts, *Anselm Kiefer* (London, 2014), 50.

4. Anselm Kiefer, *Hoffmann von Fallersleben auf Helgoland* (1983–6), Nationalgalerie im Hamburger Bahnhof, Berlin. The painting echoes in material, composition, and theme the second *Operation Seelöwe* (1983/4) which Kiefer worked on in parallel to the Fallersleben/Heligoland canvass. See also *Für Velimir Chlenikov: Die Lehre vom Krieg. Seeschlachten* (2004–10), a series of paintings depicting naval battles in similar colours and materials, and Adriani, *Books*, 170–89, for further Kiefer works on *Operation 'Sea Lion'*.

5. Fallersleben, *Mein Leben*, 210–11. See Chapter 2 for the origins of the *Lied der Deutschen*.

6. Schama, *Landscape and Memory*, 120–35; Aleida Assmann, *Erinnerungsräume: Formen und Wandlungen des kulturellen Gedächtnisses* (Munich, 1999), 360–3; Lisa Saltzman, *Anselm Kiefer and Art after Auschwitz* (Cambridge, 1999); Andréa Lauterwein, *Anselm Kiefer/Paul Celan: Myth, Mourning and Memory* (London, 2007).

7. Alfred Mahlau, *Die Insel Helgoland: Ein Skizzenbuch* (Frankfurt, 1961); Horst Janssen, *Helgoland—Der Walfisch* (1970), Kunsthalle Hamburg.

8. Jeismann, 'Die Nationalhymne', 661–4.

9. Peter Reichel, Harald Schmid, and Peter Steinbach (eds), *Der Nationalsozialismus: Die zweite Geschichte* (Munich, 2009); Dirk Moses, *German Intellectuals and the Nazi Past* (Cambridge, 2007); Stefan Aust and Gerhard Spörl (eds), *Die Gegenwart der Vergangenheit: Der lange Schatten des Dritten Reichs* (Munich, 2004); Nicolas Berg, *Der Holocaust und die westdeutschen Historiker* (Göttingen, 2003); Norbert Frei and Sybille Steinbacher (eds), *Beschweigen und Bekennen: Die deutsche Nachkriegsgesellschaft und der Holocaust* (Göttingen, 2001); Richard J. Evans, *In Hitler's Shadow: West German Historians and the Attempt to Escape from the Nazi Past* (London, 1989).

10. TNA, FO 371/183181, Roberts to Stewart, 18 Aug. 1965.

11. For the details see TNA, PRO 56/227.

12. TNA, FO 371/183181, Roberts to Stewart, 18 Aug. 1965.

13. TNA, FO 371/183181, Speech by Her Majesty's Ambassador at Heligoland Reception, 9 Aug. 1965.

14. See especially the two prominent documentaries which styled the *Helgoland* as a symbol of West German pacifism during the Vietnam War: *Nur leichte Kämpfe im Raum Da Nang* (1970) and *Die Helgoland in Da Nang* (1970). The *Helgoland* had previously served as a tourist steamer on the Hamburg to Heligoland route and was refitted for its role in Vietnam. Over the five years while it was stationed at Saigon and Da Nang its medical teams treated more than 200,000 patients. See BA, B 145/6456; B 145/3008; B 136/3658; and B 136/4241, the latter documenting Willy Brandt's public address to the crew of the *Helgoland*.

15. 'Grusswort des Bundeskanzlers', in *Helgoland 100 Jahre deutsch: Festschrift im Auftrage der Gemeinde Helgoland herausgegeben von H. P. Rickmers und H. Huster* (Otterndorf and Helgoland, 1990).

16. Joschka Fischer, the German foreign secretary, was still complaining in 2004: 'Co-operation between our two countries is excellent on the official level. But people-to-people there is a problem, and I think the media are playing a very important role' (*The Guardian*, 21 Oct. 2004).

17. John Ramsden, *Don't Mention the War: The British and the Germans Since 1890* (London, 2006), ch. 10.

18. State Banquet Speech, Berlin, 24 June 2015. See <https://www.royal.uk/queens-speech-german-state-banquet-24-june-2015>, accessed on 29 Sept. 2016.

19. *Der Helgoländer*, Aug. 2015, '125 Jahre zugehörig zu Deutschland'.

20. TNA, FO 371/183181, Roberts to Stewart, 18 Aug. 1965.

21. Shena Mackay, *Heligoland* (London, 2003), 8.

22. Mackay, *Heligoland*, 7. See also the role the island plays in Michael Frayn, *Copenhagen* (London, 1998) and in Rhidian Brook, *The Aftermath* (London, 2013). See also the album *Heligoland* by Massive Attack (2010); the song of the same title by Overseer, contained in the 2002 album *Wreckage*; the dance by Lindsay Seers (<www.lindsayseers.info/blog/dancing-helgoland>, accessed on 26 Sept. 2016); and the historical novella by Ray Furness, *On Heligoland* (Oxford, 2008).

23. Neil MacGregor, *Germany: Memories of a Nation* (London, 2014), xxv–xxviii; Klaus Neumann, 'Mahnmale', in François and Schulze (eds), *Deutsche Erinnerungsorte*, vol. 1, 622–37; Rudy Koshar, *From Monuments to Traces: Artifacts of German Memory, 1870–1990* (Berkeley, CA, 2000); Bill Niven and Chloe Paver (eds), *Memorialization in Germany since 1945* (Basingstoke, 2010).

Sources

ARCHIVES

Altonaer Museum, Hamburg
Helgoland-Sammlung

Archiv Theater in der Aue (Junges Staatstheater), Berlin
Kampf um Helgoland (Peter Martin Lampel)

Australian War Memorial, Canberra
Photographic and film collections
Heraldry

Behörde des Bundesbeauftragten für die Unterlagen des Staatssicherheitsdienstes der ehemaligen Deutschen Demokratischen Republik, Berlin
MfS, AU 262/51 (Deutsche Bewegung Helgoland)

British Library, London
Cunningham Papers
Charles Pasley Papers
Melville Papers
Willoughby Gordon Papers
Jellicoe Papers
Liverpool Papers
Wellesley Papers

British Pathé Archive, London
Pathé Newsreels
Pathé Animated Gazette

Bundesarchiv, Berlin
BILD 111 (Ausland-Abteilung des Lichtbild-Dienstes)
BY 1/2153 (Wolfgang Plat, Deutsche Bewegung Helgoland)
DB 52/12, 53/36, 59/20 (Seegefecht Helgoland, 1849)
DY 6/196 (Nationalrat der Nationalen Front, Protest Helgoland)
DY 24 (Zentralrat, Freie Deutsche Jugend)
DY 27/782 (Kulturbund, 'Kampf um Helgoland')
DY 31/992 (Demokratischer Frauenbund Deutschlands, Protestaktion gegen die Bombardierung der Insel Helgoland)

DY 60/4105 (Demokratische Bauernpartei Deutschlands, Briefe aus Westdeutschland)
NS 19 (Persönlicher Stab Reichsführer-SS)
NS 21 (Forschungs- und Lehrgemeinschaft 'Das Ahnenerbe')
OPG (Oberstes Parteigericht der NSDAP)
R 2/4482 (Finanzministerium, Gemeinde Helgoland)
R 32/374 (Reichskunstwart, Denkmal des Kolonialpioniers Carl Peters auf der Insel Helgoland)
R 43 (Reichskanzlei)
R 58/1493 (Reichssicherheitshauptamt, Johann Krüss)
R 901 (Auswärtiges Amt)
R 1001 (Reichskolonialamt)
R 1401 (Reichskanzleramt)
R 1401/153 (Großbritannien, Helgoland)
R 1507 (Reichskommissar für Überwachung der öffentlichen Ordnung)
R 2301 (Rechnungshof des Deutsche Reiches)
R 3003 (Akten des Oberreichsanwalts)
R 4901 (Staatliche Biologische Anstalt auf Helgoland)
R 8034II (Reichslandbund, Pressearchiv)
Sgy 27/2 (Deutsches Arbeiterkomitee gegen die Remilitarisierung Deutschlands)

Bundesarchiv, Koblenz
Z 21/1235 (Sekretariat Friedensvertrag, Senatskanzlei der Hansestadt Hamburg)
Z 35 (Deutsches Büro für Friedensfragen)
B 122 (Bundespräsidialamt)
B 134/4864 (Wiederaufbau Helgoland)
B 136 (Bundeskanzleramt)
B 145 (Presse- und Informationsamt der Bundesregierung)
N 1222 (Nachlass Hubertus Friedrich Prinz zu Löwenstein)

Bundesarchiv-Filmarchiv, Berlin
Heligoland newsreels and films

Bundesarchiv-Militärarchiv, Freiburg
RM 2 (Kaiserliches Marinekabinett)
RM 3 (Reichsmarineamt)
RM 5 (Admiralstab)
RM 7 (Oberkommando der Marine)
RM 43 (Kaiserliche Kommandantur Helgoland)
RM 45/II (Kommandant im Abschnitt Helgoland)
RM 47 (Kommando der Hochseestreitkräfte)
N 253 (Nachlass Alfred von Tirpitz)

Cambridge University Library
Sedley Taylor Papers
Henry Seebohm Papers
Alfred Newton Papers

John Ward Correspondence
Royal Commonwealth Society

Churchill Archives Centre, Churchill College, Cambridge
Winston Churchill Papers
Leopold Amery Papers
John Fisher Papers
Reginald McKenna Papers

Deutsches Rundfunkarchiv, Frankfurt
Die Stunde der Nation
Reichs-Rundfunk-Gesellschaft (RRG)
Nordische Rundfunk AG (NORAG)

Durham County Record Office, Durham
Register of the Court of Summary Jurisdictions

Ellerman Family Archive, Canberra
Unpublished biography of Sir Abraham Ellerman by William Alexander Ellerman

Geheimes Staatsarchiv Preußischer Kulturbesitz, Berlin
I. HA Rep. 77, Tit. 50 Nr 89, 1–4 (Vereinigung der Insel Helgoland mit dem preußischen Staat)
I. HA Rep. 77, Tit. 50 Nr 90 (Einführung von Reichsgesetzen und preußischen Landesgesetzen auf der Insel Helgoland)
I. HA Rep. 77, Tit. 311 a Nr 147 (Entfestung Helgolands)
I. HA Rep. 77, Tit. 332 r Nr 95, 1–3 (Unterbringung der aus militärischen Gründen abgeschobenen Zivilbevölkerung der Insel Helgoland)
I. HA Rep. 77, Tit. 872 Nr 12, 10 (Spionageabwehr auf Helgoland)
I. HA Rep. 77, Tit. 1278 Nr 1 (Militärische Einrichtungen auf der Insel Helgoland)
I. HA Rep. 81, Hamburg Nr 916 (Abschluß des deutsch-englischen Abkommens vom 1. Juli 1890)
I. HA Rep. 151, HB Nr 1177 (Notstandsmaßnahmen aus Anlaß der Räumung von Festungen und befestigten Plätzen)
I. HA Rep. 151, IB Nr 2571–4 (Finanz-Ministerium, Insel Helgoland)
I. HA Rep. 197, A I h Nr 50, Beiheft 2 (Rückführung der Bewohner Helgolands)
III. HA Nr 1192 (Angelegenheiten der Insel Helgoland)
III. HA II Nr 207 (Vizekonsulat auf Helgoland)
Charts, maps, and drawings

Hampshire Record Office, Winchester
Augustus Phillimore Papers

Imperial War Museum, London
J. J. Eames
F. H. H. Goodhart
W. A. Jenkins

G. M. Levick
D. Lorimer
H. Miller
W. R. C. Steele
R. R. Stewart
H. K. Thorold
P. E. Vaux
R. E. Wannop
F. T. Woosnam

Landesarchiv Schleswig-Holstein, Schleswig
Abt. 174 (Colonial Government Heligoland)
Abt. 131 (Landgemeinde Helgoland)
Abt. 320.22 (Landrat Helgoland)

National Archives, Kew
ADM 1 (Admiralty Correspondence and Papers)
ADM 30/47 (Heligoland Yard, Musters, 1808–15)
ADM 37/425 (Heligoland, Shore Establishment)
ADM 37/8607 (Heligoland Yard, 1813–15)
ADM 106/2031 (Heligoland Yard, Letters to Navy Board, 1808–15)
AMD 116/1981 (Naval Inter-Allied Commission)
ADM 188/548 (Service Records)
ADM 228/48, 53 (Office of the British Naval Commander in Chief, Germany)
AIR 2/10012 (Air Ministry and Ministry of Defence, Heligoland)
AIR 34/672, 681 (Air Ministry, Heligoland)
AIR 40/406 (Mission Reports, Heligoland)
BJ 1/267 (Kew Observatory, Explosions at Heligoland)
BT 351/1 (James Temple)
CAB 1, 17, 24, 37, 38, 41, 65, 66, and 129 (Cabinet Papers)
CO 118 (Heligoland, Original Correspondence)
CO 119 (Entry Books)
CO 122 (Blue Books)
CO 346 (Register of Correspondence)
CO 347 (Register of Out-letters)
CO 537/17 (Treatment of Persons Opting for British Nationality)
CO 885 (Colonial Office Confidential Print)
FO 36 (General Correspondence before 1906, Heligoland)
FO 64 (Prussia and Germany)
FO 84/2031–7 (Germany, Dispatches)
FO 93/36 (Protocols of Treaties, Germany)
FO 93/41 (Protocols of Treaties, Hanse Towns)
FO 371 (Germany)
FO 608 (Peace Conference)

FO 800 (Private Office papers)
FO 881 (Foreign Office Confidential Print)
FO 893 (Ambassadors to the Peace Conference, Minutes)
FO 918/54 (Ampthill Papers)
FO 933/24 (Thornton Papers)
FO 1006 (Control Commission for Germany, Schleswig-Holstein)
FO 1008 (High Commissioner, Chancery Files)
FO 1014 (Control Commission for Germany, Hamburg)
FO 1035 (Chief of Staff, High Commission)
FO 1049 (Control Commission for Germany, Political Division)
FO 1050 (Control Commission for Germany, Office of the Public Safety Adviser)
FO 1056 (Control Commission for Germany, Public Relations and Information Services Division)
HO 45 (Home Office Correspondence, 1839–1979)
HO 144 (Home Office Correspondence, 1868–1959)
HO 396 (Aliens Department)
KV 2/3716 (Security Service, Prinz Löwenstein)
PREM 8 (Prime Minister's Office Records)
PRO 30/26/197 (Demolition of Fortifications on Heligoland)
PRO 56/227 (Loan of Public Records, Heligoland)
PROB 11/1798/183 (Abraham Ellerman)
TS 25 (Treasury Solicitor)

National Archives, Washington, DC
Newsreels

National Archives of Australia, Canberra
Department of External Affairs
Department of Defence
Service Records

National Archives of Canada, Ottawa
Sir Henry Fitzhardinge Berkeley Maxse, correspondence and personal papers

National Film Archives, British Film Institute, London
British and Colonial Kinematography Company
Pathé newsreels

National Maritime Museum, Greenwich
Admiral of the Fleet David Earl Beatty
Sir William Wordsworth Fisher
Eugene Hollingworth
Michael Henley & Son
Telegraph Construction and Maintainance Company Ltd
Arnold White
James Whitworth

Niedersächsisches Landesarchiv, Hauptstaatsarchiv Hanover

Dep. 110, A, Nr 50, 109, 114, 120 (Nachlass Ernst Friedrich Herbert Graf Münster)

Hann. 51, Nr 1406 (Beschlagnahme eines nach Helgoland bestimmten Schmugglers durch französische Douaniers)

Hann. 80, Nr 650 (Königliche Landvogtei, Zusammenkünfte Hannoverscher Opponenten auf Helgoland)

Hann. 87 Acc. 92/84, Nr 69/1 (Sicherungsbereich Helgoland)

Nds. 50 Acc. 96/88, Nr 106/1–2 (Wiederaufbau der Insel Helgoland)

Nds. 100 Acc. 144/81, Nr 697 (Öffentliche Sammlungen und Spendenaktionen)

Nds. 600 Acc. 37/85, Nr 177–82 (Insel Helgoland und Knechtsand, Bombenziel)

VVP 17, Nr 235–6 (Zeitungsauschnittsammlung)

ZGS 2/1 (Zeitungsauschnittsammlung)

Niedersächsisches Landesarchiv, Staatsarchiv Bückeburg

Adolf von Trotha, papers and letters

Photographic collection

Niedersächsisches Landesarchiv, Staatsarchiv Oldenburg

Best. 82 Nr 362 (Handel mit den Engländern über Helgoland)

Best. 135 Nr 96 (Aufenthaltsverbot für Ausländer auf der Insel Helgoland)

Best. 166-5 Nr 12 (Personalakte, Prof. Dr. Friedrich Heincke)

Best. 231-3 Nr 232 (Erklärung der Insel Helgoland zum Sicherungsbereich)

Best. 231-4 Nr 2284 (Erklärung der Insel Helgoland zum militärischen Sicherungsbereich)

Niedersächsisches Landesarchiv, Staatsarchiv Stade

Rep. 72/172 (Amtsgericht Cuxhaven)

Rep. 80, Nr 01231 (Versammlungen der Oppositionspartei auf Helgoland)

Charts and drawings

Niedersächsisches Landesarchiv, Staatsarchiv Wolfenbüttel

VI Hs 11 Nr 242 (August Vasels Reise nach Helgoland)

24 Neu Nr 31 (Aussage des Jägers Ernst Meyer über seine Flucht aus der Gefangenschaft nach Helgoland)

27 Neu 1 Nr 648 (Untersuchung gegen den Soldaten Carl Wilhelm Schönian)

27 Neu 1 Nr 666 (Untersuchung gegen den nach Blankenburg beurlaubten Jäger Johann Georg Heinrich Wilhelm Knigge)

27 Neu 2 Nr 135 (Untersuchung gegen den Kanonier Theodor Charles Friedrich August Schmidt)

Niels Bohr Archive, Copenhagen

Niels Bohr, correspondence

Nordseemuseum Helgoland

Ephemera

Photographic collection

Österreichische Nationalbibliothek, Vienna
Handschriften Abteilung

Parliamentary Archives, London
Sir George Smyth Baden-Powell Papers
John St Loe Strachey Papers

Politisches Archiv des Auswärtigen Amtes, Berlin
Botschaft London
B 10, 429–33 (Politische Abteilung, Helgoland)
R 2417–20 (Verhandlungen mit England)
R 5835–53 (Frage einer Verständigung Deutschlands mit England)
R 5663–798 (Die politischen Beziehungen Englands zu Deutschland)
R 5612–44 (Die englische Presse)
R 2490–9 (Deutschland)
R 6114–15 (England)
R 19552–3 (Die Verhältnisse der Insel Helgoland)
R 22574 (Delegation Versailles, Helgoland)
R 33213–17 (Entfestigung von Helgoland)
R 77407–9 (Abteilung III, Helgoland)
R 98398 (Schleswig-Holstein, Helgoland)

Public Record Office of Northern Ireland, Belfast
Sir Douglas Savory Papers

Rigsarkivet, Copenhagen
Departementet for de Udenlandske Anliggender, England

Rothschild Archives, London
XI (Correspondence, N. M. Rothschild)
T3 (Correspondence, N. M. Rothschild)

Royal Archives, Windsor
Queen Victoria, journals

Scottish Record Office, Edinburgh
Balfour Papers
Sederunt books

Staatsarchiv Hamburg
111-1, 4001 (Senat Hamburg, Badecommissariat Helgoland)
111-2, B II g 2 (Senat, Kriegsakten)
131-1 II, 375, 4021–2 (Senatskanzlei, Helgoland Frage)
212-1, B 51 (Schleichhandel)
331-1 I, 1522 (Staatspolizeiliche Überwachung der Insel Helgoland)
331-2, 1821, Nr 287 (Untersuchungsakten betr. englische Werbungen auf Helgoland)
331-3, SA 217 (Club Helgoland)

331-3, S 4417 (Helgoländer Anarchisten)
362-2/5, 29 (Emilie Wüstenfeld Gymnasium)
363-6, B 89 (Kunstbehörde und Landeskunstschule)
364-5 I, M 90.16 (Hamburgische Universität)
411-2_II J 4568 (Conrad Wilhelm Block)
614-2/20, 1 (Deutsche Bewegung Helgoland)
621-1/95 (HAPAG, Mobilmachungsverträge, Evakuierung der Helgoländer Bevölkerung)
622-1/138, B1 (John Parish)
731-8_A 355 (Zeitungsausschnittsammlung, Helgoland)

State Library of New South Wales, Sydney
Deutschlandspiegel newsreels
George Milner Stephen, diary and papers

Warburg Institute, London
Aby Warburg Family Correspondence
Aby Warburg General Correspondence

Ward Library, Peterhouse, Cambridge
John Ward Papers

Wiener Library, London
Centralverein deutscher Staatsbürger jüdischen Glaubens
Philipp Manes Collection
Volksbund für Frieden und Freiheit

Wiltshire and Swindon Archives, Chippenham
Walter Long Papers

NEWSPAPERS AND PERIODICALS

Berliner Abendblätter
Berliner Lokal-Anzeiger
Berliner Morgenpost
Berliner Politische Nachrichten
Berliner Tageblatt
Berliner Zeitung
Bremer Nachrichten
Bremer Tageblatt
Central-Vereins-Zeitung
Cuxhavener Zeitung
Daily Express
Daily Mail
Daily Mirror
Daily News

Daily Telegraph
Der Helgoländer
Der Morgen
Der Stahlhelm
Der Stürmer
Deutsche Allgemeine Zeitung
Deutsche Rundschau
Deutsches Tagesblatt
Die Gartenlaube
Die Stimme der Vertriebenen
Die Welt
Die Zeit
Evening Post
Financial News
Frankfurter Rundschau
Frankfurter Zeitung
Fraser's Magazine for Town and Country
Hamburger Correspondent
Hamburger Echo
Hamburger Fremdenblatt
Hamburger Nachrichten
Hamburger Volksblatt
Helgoland (Mitteilungsblatt für Hallunner Moats)
Helgoländer Heimat-Bund
Helgoländer Zeitung
Illustrated London News
Jugend
Kreuzzeitung
London Gazette
The (Manchester) Guardian
Morning Post
Münchner Neueste Nachrichten
Nathurn (Helgoländer Volks- und Heimatbote)
Nationalzeitung
Neues Deutschland
Neueste Mittheilungen
Norddeutsche Allgemeine Zeitung
The Observer
Pall Mall Gazette
Picture Post
Punch
Reichs- und Staats-Anzeiger

Simplicissimus
Sydney Morning Herald
Time Magazine
The Times
Ulk
Völkischer Beobachter
Vorwärts
Vossische Zeitung

WORKS CITED

Aaslestad, Katherine B., 'Lost Neutrality and Economic Warfare: Napoleonic Warfare in Northern Europe, 1795–1815', in Roger Chickering and Stig Förster (eds), *War in an Age of Revolution, 1775–1815* (Cambridge, 2010), 373–94.

Aaslestad, Katherine B. and Johan Joor (eds), *Revisiting Napoleon's Continental System: Local, Regional and European Experiences* (Basingstoke, 2014).

An Account of the Interesting Island of Helgoland, its Inhabitants, &c (London, 1811).

Achilles, Manuela, 'With a Passion for Reason: Celebrating the Constitution in Weimar Germany', *Central European History*, 43 (2010), 666–89.

Ackermann, Josef, *Heinrich Himmler als Ideologe* (Göttingen, 1970).

Adler, H. G., *Theresienstadt 1941–1945: Das Antlitz einer Zwangsgemeinschaft* (Göttingen, 2005).

Adriani, Götz, *The Books of Anselm Kiefer 1969–1990* (London and New York, 1991).

Afflerbach, Holger and David Stevenson (eds), *An Improbable War? The Outbreak of World War I and European Political Culture before 1914* (New York and Oxford, 2007).

Ahonen, Pertti, *After the Expulsion: West Germany and Eastern Europe 1945–1990* (Oxford, 2003).

Ahrens, Michael, *Die Briten in Hamburg: Besatzerleben 1945–1958* (Munich, 2011).

Allen, William Sheridan, *The Nazi Seizure of Power: The Experience of a Single German Town, 1922–1945*, 2nd, rev. edn (New York, 1984).

Applegate, Celia, *A Nation of Provincials: The German Idea of Heimat* (Berkeley, CA, 1990).

Applegate, Celia and Pamela Potter (eds), *Music and German National Identity* (Chicago, IL, 2002).

Archer, E. G., *Gibraltar: Identity and Empire* (New York and London, 2006).

Assmann, Aleida, *Erinnerungsräume: Formen und Wandlungen des kulturellen Gedächtnisses* (Munich, 1999).

Bach, Steven, *Leni—The Life and Work of Leni Riefenstahl* (New York, 2007).

Badedirektion Helgoland (ed.), *Der deutschen Nordsee Kronjuwel: Helgoland. Kleiner Führer* (Cuxhaven, 1910).

Bajohr, Frank, *Unser Hotel ist judenfrei: Bäder-Antisemitismus im 19. und 20. Jahrhundert* (Frankfurt, 2003).

Bajohr, Frank and Michael Wildt (eds), *Volksgemeinschaft: Neue Forschungen zur Gesellschaft des Nationalsozialismus* (Frankfurt, 2009).

Baranowski, Shelley, *Strength through Joy: Consumerism and Mass Tourism in the Third Reich* (Cambridge, 2004).

Baranowski, Shelley, *Nazi Empire: German Colonialism and Imperialism from Bismarck to Hitler* (Cambridge, 2011).

Barkai, Avraham, *'Wehr dich!' Der Centralverein deutscher Staatsbürger jüdischen Glaubens (C. V.) 1893–1938* (Munich, 2002).

Barkly, Fanny A., *From the Tropics to the North Sea* (Westminster, 1897).

Barron, Stephanie (ed.), *'Degenerate Art': The Fate of the Avant-Garde in Nazi Germany* (New York, 1991).

Barth, Boris, *Dolchstoßlegenden und politische Desintegration: Das Trauma der deutschen Niederlage im ersten Weltkrieg 1914–1933* (Düsseldorf, 2003).

Bartning, Otto, 'Ketzerische Gedanken am Rande der Trümmerhaufen', *Frankfurter Hefte*, 1 (1946), 63–72.

Battle of the Bight: Being the Official Narrative of the Naval Engagement between the British and German Fleets in the Heligoland Bight on Friday, August 28th, 1914 (London, 1914).

Bayley, Charles Calvert, *Mercenaries for the Crimea: The German, Swiss, and Italian Legions in British Service, 1854–1856* (Montreal, 1977).

Bayly, C. A., *The Birth of the Modern World 1780–1914* (Oxford, 2004).

The Beatty Papers: Selections from the Private and Official Correspondence of Admiral of the Fleet Earl Beatty, ed. Bryan Ranft, 2 vols (Aldershot, 1989–93).

Beaufort, J. M., 'A Voyage of Discovery in Germany', *Quarterly Review*, 226 (1916).

Beaufort, J. M., *Behind the German Veil: A Record of a Journalistic War Pilgrimage*, 2nd edn (London, 1917).

Behnken, Klaus (ed.), *Deutschland-Berichte der Sozialdemokratischen Partei Deutschlands (Sopade) 1934–1940*, 7 vols (Frankfurt, 1980).

Bell, Christopher M., 'Sir John Fisher's Naval Revolution Reconsidered: Winston Churchill at the Admiralty, 1911–14', *War in History*, 18 (2011), 333–56.

Bell, Christopher M., *Churchill and Sea Power* (Oxford, 2013).

Bell, Duncan, *Building Greater Britain: Empire, Ideology, and the Future of World Order, 1860–1900* (Princeton, NJ, 2007).

Benton, Lauren, *Law and Colonial Cultures: Legal Regimes in World History, 1400–1900* (Cambridge, 2002).

Benton, Lauren, *A Search for Sovereignty: Law and Geography in European Empires, 1400–1900* (Cambridge, 2010).

Berbig, Roland (ed.), *Fontane als Biograph* (Berlin and New York, 2010).

Berg, Nicolas, *Der Holocaust und die westdeutschen Historiker* (Göttingen, 2003).

Berghahn, Volker R., *Der Tirpitz-Plan: Genesis und Verfall einer innenpolitischen Krisenstrategie unter Wilhelm II.* (Düsseldorf, 1971).

Berghahn, Volker R., *Rüstung und Machtpolitik: Zur Anatomie des 'kalten Krieges' vor 1914* (Düsseldorf, 1973).

Berghahn, Volker R. and Wilhelm Deist (eds), *Rüstung im Zeichen der wilhelminischen Weltpolitik: Grundlegende Dokumente 1890–1914* (Düsseldorf, 1988).

Beschwerdeschrift der Helgolander Bürgerschaft wider den Gouverneur Maxse wegen Verletzung der der Insel Helgoland garantirten Rechte und Privilegien (Husum, 1866).

Bessel, Richard, *Germany after the First World War* (Oxford, 1993).

Bessel, Richard, '1918–1919 in der deutschen Geschichte', in Dieter Papenfuß and Wolfgang Schieder (eds), *Deutsche Umbrüche im 20. Jahrhundert* (Cologne, 2000).

Bessel, Richard, *Germany 1945: From War to Peace* (London, 2009).

Bickers, Robert (ed.), *Settlers and Expatriates: Britons over the Seas* (Oxford, 2010).

Biess, Frank, *Homecomings: Returning POWs and the Legacies of Defeat in Postwar Germany* (Princeton, NJ, 2006).

Bird, J. C., *Control of Enemy Alien Civilians in Great Britain 1914–1918* (London and New York, 1986).

[Bismarck, Otto von,] *Die politischen Reden des Fürsten Bismarck*, ed. Horst Kohl, 14 vols (Stuttgart, 1892–1905).

Bismarck, Otto von, *Gedanken und Erinnerungen*, 3 vols (Stuttgart, 1898–1922).

Bjork, James E., *Neither German nor Pole: Catholicism and National Indifference in a Central European Borderland* (Ann Arbor, MI, 2008).

Black, William George, *Heligoland and the Islands of the North Sea* (London, 1888).

Black, William George, 'From Heligoland to Helgoland', *National Review*, 58 (1911).

Blackbourn, David, *Marpingen: Apparitions of the Virgin Mary in Nineteenth-Century Germany* (Oxford, 1993).

Blackbourn, David, '"Taking the Waters": Meeting Places of the Fashionable World', in Martin H. Geyer and Johannes Paulmann (eds), *The Mechanics of Internationalism* (Oxford, 2001), 435–57.

Blackbourn, David, *The Conquest of Nature: Water, Landscape and the Making of Modern Germany* (London, 2006).

Blackbourn, David, '"As Dependent on Each Other as Man and Wife": Cultural Contacts and Transfers', in Dominik Geppert and Robert Gerwarth (eds), *Wilhelmine Germany and Edwardian Britain: Cultural Contacts and Transfers* (Oxford, 2008), 15–37.

Blackbourn, David and Geoff Eley, *The Peculiarities of German History: Bourgeois Society and Politics in Nineteenth-Century Germany* (Oxford, 1984).

Blatchford, Robert, *Germany and England* (London, 1909).

Blickle, Peter, *Heimat: A Critical Theory of the German Idea of Homeland* (Rochester, NY, 2002).

Blyth, Robert, Andrew Lambert, and Jan Rüger (eds), *The Dreadnought and the Edwardian Age* (Farnham, 2011).

Bödewadt, Jakob, 'Helgoland', in Hermann Krumm and Fritz Stoltenberg (eds), *Unsere meerumschlungene Nordmark*, vol. 1 (Kiel, 1914).

Bohrmann, Hans (ed.), *NS-Presseanweisungen der Vorkriegszeit*, 7 vols (Munich, 1984–2000).

Bönker, Dirk, *Militarism in a Global Age: Naval Ambitions in Germany and the United States before World War I* (Ithaca, NY, 2012).

Borutta, Manuel and Sakis Gekas, 'A Colonial Sea: The Mediterranean, 1798–1956', *European Review of History*, 19 (2012), 1–13.

Bracher, Karl Dietrich, Wolfgang Sauer, and Gerhard Schulz, *Die nationalsozialistische Machtergreifung: Studien zur Errichtung des totalitären Herrschaftssystems in Deutschland 1933/34* (Cologne and Opladen, 1960).

Bracher, Karl Dietrich, *Die deutsche Diktatur* (Cologne, 1979).

Brantl, Sabine, *Haus der Kunst, München: Ein Ort und seine Geschichte im Nationalsozialismus* (Munich, 2007).

Brassey, Annie, 'Heligoland', *Macmillan's Magazine*, 37 (1878).

Braudel, Fernand, *The Mediterranean and the Mediterranean World in the Age of Philip II*, vol. 1 (New York, 1972).

Bredow, Jürgen and Helmut Lerch (eds), *Materialien zum Werk des Architekten Otto Bartning* (Darmstadt, 1983).

Bremer, Otto, *Ethnographie der germanischen Stämme* (Strassburg, 1904).

Brewer, John, 'Microhistory and the Histories of Everyday Life', *Cultural and Social History*, 7 (2010) 87–109.

Brézet, François-Emmanuel, *Le Plan Tirpitz, 1897–1914: une flotte de combat allemande contre l'Angleterre* (Paris, 1998).

British Documents on Foreign Affairs: Reports and Papers from the Foreign Office Confidential Print, ed. Kenneth Bourne and D. C. Watt, series F, parts 1–5 (Frederick, MD, 1987–91).

British Documents on the Origins of the War, 1898–1914, ed. G. P. Gooch and Harold W. V. Temperley, 11 vols (London, 1926–38).

British Envoys to Germany, 1816–1866, vol. 1: *1816–1829*, ed. Sabine Freitag and Peter Wende; vol. 2: *1830–1847*, ed. Markus Mösslang, Sabine Freitag, and Peter Wende; vol. 3: *1848– 1850*, ed. Markus Mösslang, Torsten Riotte, and Hagen Schulze; vol. 4: *1851–1866*, ed. Markus Mösslang, Chris Manias, and Torsten Riotte (Cambridge, 2000–10).

British Naval Documents, 1204–1960, ed. John B. Hattendorf, R. J. B. Knight, A. W. H. Pearsall, N. A. M. Rodger, and Geoffrey Till (Aldershot, 1993).

Bröhan, Margrit, *Walter Leistikow* (Berlin, 1988).

Broszat, Martin (ed.), *Deutschlands Weg in die Diktatur* (Berlin, 1983).

Broszat, Martin, *Die Machtergreifung: Der Aufstieg der NSDAP und die Zerstörung der Weimarer Republik* (Munich, 1984).

Broszat, Martin et al. (eds), *Bayern in der NS-Zeit*, 6 vols (Munich, 1977–83).

Brown, Judith and W. Roger Louis (eds), *The Oxford History of the British Empire*, vol. 4 (Oxford, 1999).

Bryant, G., *The Postage Stamps of Heligoland and their History* (Swansea, 1895).

Bruckner, Anton, *Sämtliche Werke*, vol. 22/8, *Helgoland* (Vienna, 1993).

Burbank, Jane and Frederick Cooper, *Empires in World History: Power and the Politics of Difference* (Princeton, NJ, 2010).

Burleigh, Michael, *Germany Turns Eastwards: A Study of Ostforschung in the Third Reich* (Cambridge, 1988).

Burton, Antoinette (ed.), *After the Imperial Turn: Thinking with and through the Nation* (Durham, NC, 2003).

Burton, Antoinette, 'Not Even Remotely Global? Method and Scale in World History', *History Workshop Journal*, 64 (2007), 323–8.

Burton, Antoinette, *Empire in Question: Reading, Writing, and Teaching British Imperialism* (Durham, NC, and London, 2011).

Busch, Fritz Otto, *Das Buch von Helgoland* (Braunschweig, 1935).

Buschhorn, Gerd W. and Helmut Rechenberg, *Werner Heisenberg auf Helgoland: Zur 75jährigen Wiederkehr der Entdeckung der Quantenmechanik durch Werner Heisenberg im Juni 1925* (Munich, 2000).

Butler, E. M., 'Heine and the Saint-Simonians: The Date of the Letters from Heligoland', *Modern Language Review*, 18 (1923), 68–85.

Cain, Peter and Tony Hopkins, *British Imperialism 1688–2000*, 2nd edn (London, 2001).

[Campbell, Thomas,] *The Poetical Works of Thomas Campbell* (London, 1837).

Canis, Konrad, *Der Weg in den Abgrund: Deutsche Außenpolitik 1902–1914* (Paderborn, 2011).

Cannadine, David, *Ornamentalism: How the British Saw their Empire* (London, 2001).

Canning, Kathleen, Kerstin Barndt, and Kirsten McGuire (eds), *Weimar Publics/Weimar Subjects: Rethinking the Political Culture of Germany in the 1920s* (New York and Oxford, 2010).

Caplan, Jane (ed.), *Short Oxford History of Germany: Nazi Germany* (Oxford, 2008).

[Caprivi, Leo von,] *Die Reden des Grafen von Caprivi im deutschen Reichstage, Preußischen Landtage und bei besonderen Anlässen*, ed. Rudolf Arndt (Berlin, 1894).

Caprivi, Leopold von, 'Die Ostafrikanische Frage und der Helgoland-Sansibar-Vertrag' (Ph.D. dissertation, Rheinische Friedrich-Wilhelms-Universität, Bonn, 1934).

Carl, Horst, Hans-Henning Kortüm, Dieter Langewiesche, and Friedrich Lenger (eds), *Kriegsniederlagen: Erfahrungen und Erinnerungen* (Berlin, 2004).

Carter, Paul, *Living in a New Country: History, Travelling and Language* (London, 1992).

Cassidy, David C., *Uncertainty: The Life and Science of Werner Heisenberg* (New York, 1992).

Catherall, Arthur, *Raid on Heligoland* (London, 1940).

Chalmers, W. S., *The Life and Letters of David, Earl Beatty, Admiral of the Fleet* (London, 1951).

Cheney, C. Emma, 'A Crown Jewel: Heligoland', *Scribner's Magazine*, 8 (1890), 377–88.

Chickering, Roger, *We Men Who Feel Most German: A Cultural Study of the Pan-German League, 1886–1914* (London, 1984).

Chickering, Roger and Stig Förster (eds), *War in an Age of Revolution, 1775–1815* (Cambridge, 2010).

Childers, Erskine, *The Riddle of the Sands: A Record of Secret Service* (London, 1903).

Churchill, Winston S., *The World Crisis*, 5 vols (London, 1923–32).

Churchill, Winston S., *The Second World War*, 6 vols (London, 1948–53).

Churchill, Winston S., *A History of the English-Speaking Peoples*, 4 vols (London, 1956–8).

Clark, Christopher, *Iron Kingdom: The Rise and Downfall of Prussia, 1600–1947* (London, 2006).

Clark, Christopher, *Kaiser Wilhelm II: A Life in Power* (London, 2009).

Clark, Christopher, *The Sleepwalkers: How Europe Went to War in 1914* (London, 2012).

Colley, Linda, *Britons: Forging the Nation 1707–1837* (London, 1994).

Colley, Linda, *The Ordeal of Elizabeth Marsh: A Woman in World History* (London, and New York, 2007).

Colley, Linda, 'Empires of Writing: Britain, America and Constitutions, 1776–1848', *LHR*, 32 (2014), 237–66.

Colquhoun, Patrick, *A Treatise on the Wealth, Power, and Resources of the British Empire* (London, 1814).

Confino, Alon, *The Nation as a Local Metaphor: Württemberg, Imperial Germany, and National Memory, 1871–1918* (Chapel Hill, NC, 1997).

Connelly, Mark, 'The British People, the Press, and the Strategic Air Campaign against Germany', *Contemporary British History*, 16 (2002), 39–58.

Conrad, Sebastian, *Globalisierung und Nation im deutschen Kaiserreich* (Munich, 2006).

Constantine, Stephen, *Community and Identity: The Making of Modern Gibraltar Since 1704* (Manchester, 2009).

Conze, Eckart, *Die Suche nach Sicherheit: Eine Geschichte der Bundesrepublik Deutschland von 1949 bis in die Gegenwart* (Munich, 2009).

Corbin, Alain, *The Lure of the Sea: Discovery of the Seaside 1750–1840* (Berkeley, CA, 1994).

Crampton, R. J., *The Hollow Détente: Anglo-German Relations in the Balkans, 1911–1914* (London, 1980).

Cunningham, Andrew, *A Sailor's Odyssey: The Autobiography of Admiral of the Fleet, Viscount Cunningham of Hyndhope* (London, 1951).

Daly, Gavin, 'English Smugglers, the Channel, and the Napoleonic Wars, 1800–1814', *Journal of British Studies*, 46 (2007), 30–46.

Danckwortt, Barbara (ed.), *Historische Rassismusforschung: Ideologen, Täter, Opfer* (Hamburg, 1995).

D'Andrea, Diletta, 'The "Insular" Strategy of Gould Francis Leckie in the Mediterranean during the Napoleonic Wars', *Journal of Mediterranean Studies*, 16 (2006), 79–89.

D'Angelo, Michela, *Mercanti inglesi a Malta 1800–1825* (Milan, 1990).

Darwin, John, 'Imperialism and the Victorians: The Dynamics of Territorial Expansion', *EHR*, 112 (1997), 614–42.

Darwin, John, *The Empire Project: The Rise and Fall of the British World-System, 1830–1970* (Cambridge, 2009).

Darwin, John, 'Orphans of Empire', in Robert Bickers (ed.), *Settlers and Expatriates: Britons over the Seas* (Oxford, 2010), 329–45.

Davis, John R., *Britain and the German Zollverein, 1848–66* (Basingstoke, 1997).

Davis, John R., *The Victorians and Germany* (Frankfurt, 2007).

Davis, John R., Stefan Manz, and Margrit Schulte Beerbühl (eds), *Transnational Networks: German Migrants in the British Empire, 1660–1914* (Leiden, 2012).

Decken, Friedrich von der, *Philosophisch-historisch-geographische Untersuchungen über die Insel Helgoland oder Heiligenland und ihre Bewohner* (Hanover, 1826).

Deighton, Anne, *The Impossible Peace: Britain, the Division of Germany, and the Origins of the Cold War* (Oxford, 1990).

Deist, Wilhelm, *Flottenpolitik und Flottenpropaganda: Das Nachrichtenbureau des Reichsmarineamtes 1897–1914* (Stuttgart, 1976).

Demshuk, Andrew, *The Lost German East: Forced Migration and the Politics of Memory, 1945–1970* (Cambridge, 2012).

Dening, Greg, *Islands and Beaches: Discourse on a Silent Land, Marquesas 1774–1880* (Honolulu, HI, 1980).

Dincklage-Campe, Friedrich von, *Helgoland: Unsere Reichsinsel* (Berlin, 1894).

Doering-Manteuffel, Anselm, *Vom Wiener Kongress zur Pariser Konferenz: England, die deutsche Frage und das Mächtesystem, 1815–1856* (Göttingen, 1991).

Dohrn, Anton, 'Der gegenwärtige Stand der Zoologie und die Gründung zoologischer Stationen', *Preußische Jahrbücher*, 30 (1872), 137–61.

Dokumente deutscher Kriegsschäden: Evakuierte, Kriegssachgeschädigte, Währungsgeschädigte. Die geschichtliche und rechtliche Entwicklung, 5 vols (Bonn, 1958–71).

Domarus, Max (ed.), *Hitler: Reden und Proklamationen 1932–1945*, 2 vols (Wiesbaden, 1977).

Douglas, Ray M., *Orderly and Humane: The Expulsion of the Germans after the Second World War* (New Haven, CT, and London, 2012).

Dülffer, Jost, *Weimar, Hitler und die Marine: Reichspolitik und Flottenbau 1920–1939* (Düsseldorf, 1973).

Dülffer, Jost, Martin Kroger, and Rolf-Harald Wippich, *Vermiedene Kriege: Deeskalation von Konflikten der Großmächte zwischen Krimkrieg und Erstem Weltkrieg 1865–1914* (Munich, 1997).

Dummett, Ann and Andrew Nicol, *Subjects, Citizens, Aliens and Others: Nationality and Immigration Law* (London, 1990).

Duppler, Hansjörg and Gerhard P. Groß (eds), *Kriegsende 1918* (Munich, 1999).

Dwyer, Philip G. (ed.), *Napoleon and Europe* (Harlow, 2001).

Eberle, Henrik (ed.), *Briefe an Hitler: Ein Volk schreibt seinem Führer* (Bergisch Gladbach, 2007).

Eckardstein, Hermann von, *Lebenserinnerungen und politische Denkwürdigkeiten* (Leipzig, 1919).

Eckermann, Johann Peter, *Gespräche mit Goethe in den letzten Jahren seines Lebens* (Zurich, 1948).

Egerton, Hugh Edward, *The Origin and Growth of the English Colonies and of their System of Government* (Oxford, 1903).

Ehrman, John, *The Younger Pitt*, 3 vols (Palo Alto, CA, 1969–96).

Eichner, Barbara, *History in Mighty Sounds: Musical Constructions of German National Identity, 1848–1914* (Woodbridge, 2012).

Eley, Geoff, *Reshaping the German Right: Radical Nationalism and Political Change after Bismarck* (New Haven, CT, and London, 1980).

Eley, Geoff, 'The View from the Throne: The Personal Rule of Kaiser Wilhelm II', *HJ*, 28 (1985), 469–85.

Eley, Geoff, *From Unification to Nazism: Reinterpreting the German Past* (London, 1986).

Eley, Geoff, 'Hitler's Silent Majority? Conformity and Resistance Under the Third Reich', *Michigan Quarterly Review*, 42 (2003), 389–425, 550–83.

Epkenhans, Michael, *Die wilhelminische Flottenrüstung 1908–1914: Weltmachtstreben, industrieller Fortschritt, soziale Integration* (Munich, 1991).

Epkenhans, Michael, 'Was a Peaceful Outcome Thinkable? The Naval Race before 1914', in Holger Afflerbach and David Stevenson (eds), *An Improbable War? The Outbreak of World War I and European Political Culture Before 1914* (New York and Oxford, 2007).

Epkenhans, Michael, 'Dreadnought: A "Golden Opportunity" for Germany's Naval Aspirations?', in Robert Blyth, Andrew Lambert, and Jan Rüger (eds), *The Dreadnought and the Edwardian Age* (Farnham, 2011).

Evans, Richard J., *Death in Hamburg: Society and Politics in the Cholera Years, 1830–1910* (Oxford, 1987).

Evans, Richard J., *Rethinking German History: Nineteenth-Century Germany and the Origins of the Third Reich* (London, 1987).

Evans, Richard J., *In Hitler's Shadow: West German Historians and the Attempt to Escape from the Nazi Past* (London, 1989).

Evans, Richard J., *The Coming of the Third Reich* (London, 2003).

Evans, Richard J., *The Third Reich in Power* (London, 2005).

Evans, Richard J., *The Third Reich at War* (London, 2008).

Evans, Richard J., *The Pursuit of Power: Europe 1815–1914* (London, 2016).

Facts Relating to the Trial which Took Place in the Court of King's Bench, 23 February 1816, in which Mr John Anderson was Plaintiff and Sir William Hamilton was Defendant (London, 1816).

Fahrmeir, Andreas, *Citizens and Aliens: Foreigners and the Law in Britain and the German States, 1789–1870* (New York and Oxford, 2000).

Fairbanks, Charles H. Jr., 'The Origins of the Dreadnought Revolution: A Historiographical Essay', *IHR*, 13 (1991), 246–72.

Fallersleben, August Heinrich Hoffmann von, *Unpolitische Lieder*, 2 vols (Hamburg, 1840–1).

Fallersleben, August Heinrich Hoffmann von, *Mein Leben: Aufzeichnungen und Erinnerungen*, vol. 3 (Hanover, 1868).

Feldbaek, Ole, 'Denmark and the Baltic, 1720–1864', in Göran Rystad, Klaus-Richard Böhme, and Wilhelm M. Carlgren (eds), *In Quest of Trade and Security: The Baltic in Power Politics, 1500–1990*, vol. 1 (Lund, 1994), 257–93.

Feldbaek, Ole, 'Denmark in the Napoleonic Wars', *Scandinavian Journal of History*, 26 (2001), 89–101.

Ferguson, Niall, *The World's Banker: A History of the House of Rothschild* (London, 2000).

Fesser, Gerd, *Reichskanzler von Bülow: Architekt der deutschen Weltpolitik* (Leipzig, 2003).

Finamore, Daniel (ed.), *Maritime History as Global History* (Gainesville, FL, 2004).

Firchow, Peter E., *The Death of the German Cousin: Variations on a Literary Stereotype, 1890–1920* (Lewisburg, PA, 1986).

Fisher, John Arbuthnot, *Records by the Admiral of the Fleet, Lord Fisher* (London, 1919).

Fitzpatrick, Matthew, 'A Fall from Grace? National Unity and the Search for Naval Power and Colonial Possessions 1848–1884,' *German History*, 25 (2007), 135–61.

Fitzpatrick, Matthew, *Liberal Imperialism in Germany: Expansionism and Nationalism, 1848–1884* (New York and Oxford, 2008).

Fitzpatrick, Matthew, *Purging the Empire: Mass Expulsions in Germany, 1871–1914* (Oxford, 2015).

Fligge, Jörg, *Lübecker Schulen im 'Dritten Reich': Eine Studie zum Bildungswesen in der NS-Zeit im Kontext der Entwicklung im Reichsgebiet* (Lübeck, 2014).

Fontane, Theodor, 'Rudolf Lindau: Ein Besuch', in Theodor Fontane, *Werke, Schriften und Briefe*, ed. Walter Keitel and Helmuth Nürnberger, 3. Abteilung, vol. 1 (Munich, 1969).

Fontane, Emilie and Theodor Fontane, *Der Ehebriefwechsel 1873–1898*, ed. Gotthard Erler, 3 vols (Berlin, 1998).

Die Frage Helgoland: The Heligoland Issue (Hamburg, 1948).

François, Étienne and Hagen Schulze (eds), *Deutsche Erinnerungsorte*, 3 vols (Munich, 2001).

Fremantle, Edmund Robert, *The Navy as I Have Known It* (London, 1904).

Frei, Norbert, *Vergangenheitspolitik: Die Anfänge der Bundesrepublik und die NS-Vergangenheit* (Munich, 1996).

Frei, Norbert and Sybille Steinbacher (eds), *Beschweigen und Bekennen: Die deutsche Nachkriegsgesellschaft und der Holocaust* (Göttingen, 2001).

French, David, 'Spy Fever in Britain, 1900–1915', *HJ*, 21 (1978), 355–70.

Frevert, Ute, 'Europeanizing Germany's Twentieth Century', *History & Memory*, 17 (2005), 87–116.

Friedel, Mathias, *Der Volksbund für Frieden und Freiheit (VFF): Eine Teiluntersuchung über westdeutsche antikommunistische Propaganda im Kalten Krieg und deren Wurzeln im Nationalsozialismus* (Sankt Augustin, 2001).

Friedrichsmeyer, Sara, Sara Lennox, and Susanne Zantop (eds), *The Imperialist Imagination: German Colonialism and Its Legacy* (Ann Arbor, MI, 1998).

Fritzsche, Peter, *Germans into Nazis* (Cambridge, MA, 1998).

Fritzsche, Peter, *Life and Death in the Third Reich* (Cambridge, MA, 2008).

Führer des Nordseebades Helgoland (Leipzig, 1928).

Fulbrook, Mary, *A Small Town Near Auschwitz: Ordinary Nazis and the Holocaust* (Oxford, 2012).

Gade, Christel, *Gleichgewichtspolitik oder Bündnispflege? Maximen britischer Außenpolitik, 1909–1914* (Göttingen and Zurich, 1997).

Gall, Lothar, 'Bismarck und England', in Paul Kluke and Peter Alter (eds), *Aspekte der deutsch-britischen Beziehungen im Laufe der Jahrhunderte* (Stuttgart, 1978), 46–59.

Gall, Lothar, *Bismarck: Der weiße Revolutionär* (Frankfurt, 1980).

Garton Ash, Timothy, *In Europe's Name: Germany and the Divided Continent* (London, 1993).

Garvin, James L. and Julian Amery, *The Life of Joseph Chamberlain*, 6 vols (London, 1932–69).

Gätke, Heinrich, *Die Vogelwarte Helgoland* (Braunschweig, 1891).

Geisthövel, Alexa, *Eigentümlichkeit und Macht: Deutscher Nationalismus 1830–1851. Der Fall Schleswig-Holstein* (Stuttgart, 2003).

Gellately, Robert, *The Gestapo and German Society: Enforcing Racial Policy 1933–1945* (Oxford, 1991).

Gellately, Robert, 'Denunciations in Twentieth-Century Germany: Aspects of Self-Policing in the Third Reich and the German Democratic Republic', *JMH*, 68 (1996), 931–67.

[George III,] *The Later Correspondence of George III*, ed. Arthur Aspinall, 5 vols (Cambridge, 1962–70).

Geppert, Dominik, *Pressekriege: Öffentlichkeit und Diplomatie in den deutsch–britischen Beziehungen 1896–1912* (Munich, 2007).

Geppert, Dominik and Robert Gerwarth (eds), *Wilhelmine Germany and Edwardian Britain: Cultural Contacts and Transfers* (Oxford, 2008).

Geppert, Dominik and Andreas Rose, 'Machtpolitik und Flottenbau vor 1914: Zur Neuinterpretation britischer Außenpolitik im Zeitalter des Hochimperialismus', *HZ*, 293 (2011), 401–37.

Gerwarth, Robert, 'The Past in Weimar History', *Contemporary European History*, 15 (2006), 1–22.

Gerwarth, Robert, *Hitler's Hangman: The Life of Heydrich* (New Haven, CT, and London, 2011).

Geyer, Michael, ' "Endkampf" 1918 and 1945: German Nationalism, Annihilation, and Self-Destruction', in Alf Lüdtke and Bernd Weisbrod (eds), *No Man's Land of Violence: Extreme Wars in the 20th Century* (Göttingen, 2006), 35–68.

Gifford, Prosser and W. Roger Louis (eds), *Britain and Germany in Africa: Imperial Rivalry and Colonial Rule* (New Haven, CT, 1967).

Gillard, D. R., 'Salisbury's African Policy and the Heligoland Offer of 1890', *EHR*, 75 (1960), 631–35.

Gillard, D. R., 'Salisbury's Heligoland Offer: The Case Against the "Witu Thesis"', *EHR*, 80 (1965), 538–52.

Gillessen, Günther, *Lord Palmerston und die Einigung Deutschlands: Die englische Politik von der Paulskirche bis zu den Dresdner Konferenzen, 1848–1851* (Lübeck, 1961).

Gillis, John R., *Islands of the Mind: How the Human Imagination Created the Atlantic World* (London and New York, 2004).

Ginzburg, Carlo, *Clues, Myths, and the Historical Method* (Baltimore, MD, 1989).

[Goebbels, Joseph,] *Die Tagebücher von Joseph Goebbels*, ed. Elke Fröhlich, 3 parts (Munich, 1987–2008).

Göllerich, August and Max Auer, *Anton Bruckner: Ein Lebens- und Schaffensbild*, 4 vols (Regensburg, 1922–37).

Görtemaker, Manfred (ed.), *Britain and Germany in the 20th Century* (New York and Oxford, 2006).

Gombrich, Ernst H., *Aby Warburg: An Intellectual Biography* (Chicago, IL, 1986).

[Goschen, Edward,] *The Diary of Edward Goschen 1900–1914*, ed. Christopher Howard (London, 1980).

Granieri, Ronald, *The Ambivalent Alliance: Konrad Adenauer, the CDU/CSU, and the West, 1949–1966* (New York and Oxford, 2003).

Gray, William Glenn, *Germany's Cold War: The Global Campaign to Isolate East Germany, 1949–1969* (Chapel Hill, NC, 2003).

Gregory, Desmond, *Sicily, the Insecure Base: A History of the British Occupation of Sicily, 1806–1815* (London and Toronto, 1988).

Gregory, Desmond, *Malta, Britain and the European Powers, 1793–1815* (London, 1996).

Griebens Reiseführer, *Die Insel Helgoland* (Berlin, 1925).

Groeben, Christiane (ed.), *Charles Darwin–Anton Dohrn Correspondence* (Naples, 1982).

Große Deutsche Kunstausstellung 1940 im Haus der Deutschen Kunst zu München: Offizieller Ausstellungskatalog (Munich, 1940).

Die Große Politik der Europäischen Kabinette 1871–1914: Sammlung der Diplomatischen Akten des Auswärtigen Amtes, ed. Johannes Lepsius, Albrecht Mendelssohn Bartholdy, and Friedrich Thimme (Berlin, 1922–7).

Hagen, Maximilian von, *Geschichte und Bedeutung des Helgolandvertrages* (Munich, 1916).

Hall, Catherine, *Civilising Subjects: Metropole and Colony in the English Imagination 1830–67* (Cambridge, 2002).

Hall, Catherine and Sonya O. Rose (eds.), *At Home with the Empire: Metropolitan Culture and the Imperial World* (Cambridge, 2006).

Hall, Catherine and Keith McClellan (eds.), *Race, Nation and Empire: Making Histories, 1750 to the Present* (Manchester, 2010).

Hallier, Ernst, *Helgoland unter deutscher Flagge* (Hamburg, 1892).

Hamilton, Frederic, *The Days before Yesterday* (London, 1920).

Hansard Parliamentary Debates, House of Commons, House of Lords (London, 1807–1952).

Häntzschel, Günter, 'Das literarische Helgoland: Eine Insel zwischen Utopie und Apologie', in Jürgen Barkhoff, Gilbert Carr, and Roger Paulin (eds), *Das schwierige neunzehnte Jahrhundert: Festschrift für Eda Sagarra* (Tübingen, 2000), 27–40.

Harding, Nick, *Hanover and the British Empire 1700–1837* (Woodbridge, 2007).

Hare, J. Laurence, *Excavating Nations: Archaeology, Museums, and the German–Danish Borderlands* (Toronto, 2015).

Harring, Harro, *Die Passions-Möwe: Psalmen eines Verbannten* (London, 1838).

Harrison, Austin, *England and Germany* (London, 1907).

Harvey, Elizabeth, 'Pilgrimages to the "Bleeding Border": Gender and Rituals of Nationalist Protest in Germany, 1919–39', *Women's History Review*, 9 (2000), 201–29.

Heiber, Helmut (ed.), *Goebbels-Reden*, 2 vols (Düsseldorf, 1971–2).

Heine, Heinrich, *Historisch-kritische Gesamtausgabe der Werke*, vol. 11, *Ludwig Börne: Eine Denkschrift* (Hamburg, 1978).

Heinemann, Ulrich, *Die verdrängte Niederlage: Politische Öffentlichkeit und Kriegsschuldfrage in der Weimarer Republik* (Göttingen, 1983).

Heintel, Brigitte and Helmut Heintel, 'Franz Kafka: 1901 allein auf Norderney und Helgoland?', *Freibeuter*, 17 (1983), 20–5.

Heinzen, Jasper, 'Transnational Affinities and Invented Traditions: The Napoleonic Wars in British and Hanoverian Memory, 1815–1915', *EHR*, 127 (2012), 1404–34.

Heinzen, Jasper, 'Die Königlich Deutsche Legion: Waffenbrüderschaft als Medium des transnationalen Gesellschaftsdialogs, 1803–1850', in Ronald G. Asch (ed.), *Hannover,*

Großbritannien und Europa: Erfahrungsraum Personalunion 1714–1837 (Göttingen, 2014), 310–34.

Heinzen, Jasper and Mark Wishon, 'A Patriotic Mercenary? Sir Julius von Hartmann as a Hanoverian Officer in British Service (1803–16)', *Comparativ*, 23 (2013), 13–26.

Heisenberg, Werner, 'Über quantentheoretische Umdeutung kinematischer und mechanischer Beziehungen', *Zeitschrift für Physik*, 33 (1925), 879–93.

Heisenberg, Werner, *Physics and Beyond: Encounters and Conversations* (London, 1971).

Helfritz, Hans, *Rechtsgutachten über den Fortbestand der der Gemeinde Helgoland gewähr-leisteten Gesetze und Gewohnheiten* (Berlin, 1929).

Helgoland 100 Jahre deutsch: Festschrift im Auftrage der Gemeinde Helgoland herausgegeben von H. P. Rickmers und H. Huster (Otterndorf and Helgoland, 1990).

Helgoland: Deutschlands Fels im Meer (Hamburg, 1935).

Helgoland: Gedicht von Dr August Silberstein für Männerchor und großes Orchester von Dr Anton Bruckner (Leipzig, 1893).

Henke, Josef, *England in Hitlers außenpolitischem Kalkül 1935–1939* (Boppard, 1973).

Henke, Josef, 'Hitlers England-Konzeption: Formulierung und Realisierungsversuche', in Manfred Funke (ed.), *Hitler, Deutschland und die Mächte* (Düsseldorf, 1976), 584–603.

Herf, Jeffrey, *Divided Memory: The Nazi Past in the Two Germanys* (Cambridge, MA, 1997).

Herf, Jeffrey, *The Jewish Enemy: Nazi Propaganda during World War II and the Holocaust* (Cambridge, MA, 2006).

Hermand, Jost, 'On the History of the *Deutschlandlied*', in Celia Applegate and Pamela Potter (eds), *Music and German National Identity* (Chicago, IL, 2002), 251–68.

Hermand, Jost and James Steakley (eds), *Heimat, Nation, Fatherland: The German Sense of Belonging* (New York, 1997).

Herms, Michael, *Heinz Lippmann: Porträt eines Stellvertreters* (Berlin, 1996).

Herms, Michael, *Hinter den Linien: Westarbeit der FDJ 1945–1956* (Berlin, 2001).

Herms, Michael, *Flaggenwechsel auf Helgoland: Der Kampf um einen militärischen Vorposten in der Nordsee* (Berlin, 2002).

Heron-Fermor, Robert, *Speech in Condemnation of the Cession of Heligoland* (Brighton, 1890).

Herwig, Holger, *The German Naval Officer Corps: A Social and Political History, 1890–1918* (Oxford, 1973).

Herwig, Holger, 'The Failure of German Sea Power, 1914–1915: Mahan, Tirpitz, and Raeder Reconsidered', *IHR*, 10 (1988), 68–105.

Herwig, Holger, 'The German Reaction to the Dreadnought Revolution', *IHR*, 13 (1991), 273–83.

Herzog, Dagmar (ed.), *Sexuality and German Fascism* (Oxford and New York, 2004).

Hibberd, John, 'Heinrich Von Kleist's Report on Heligoland', *German Life and Letters*, 51 (1998), 431–42.

Hildebrand, Klaus, '"British Interests" und "Pax Britannica": Grundfragen engli-scher Außenpolitik im 19. und 20. Jahrhundert', *HZ*, 221 (1975), 623–39.

Hildebrand, Klaus, 'Zwischen Allianz und Antagonismus: Das Problem bilateraler Normalität in den britisch–deutschen Beziehungen des 19. Jahrhunderts (1870–1914)', in *Weltpolitik. Europagedanke. Regionalismus: Festschrift für Heinz Gollwitzer* (Münster, 1982), 305–31.

Hildebrand, Klaus, *Das vergangene Reich: Deutsche Außenpolitik von Bismarck bis Hitler 1871–1945* (Stuttgart, 1995).

Hildebrand, Klaus, *No Intervention: Die Pax Britannica und Preußen, 1865/66–1869/70* (Munich, 1997).

Hillmann, Jörg and John Zimmermann (eds), *Kriegsende 1945 in Deutschland* (Munich, 2002).

Hislam, Percival A., *The North Sea Problem* (London, 1914).

Hjelholt, Holger, *British Mediation in the Danish–German Conflict*, 2 vols (Copenhagen, 1965–6).

Hjelholt, Holger, *Great Britain, the Danish–German Conflict and the Danish Succession, 1850–1852* (Copenhagen, 1971).

Hobsbawm, Eric, *The Age of Revolution: Europe, 1789–1848* (London, 1962).

Hobsbawm, Eric, *The Age of Capital, 1848–1875* (London, 1975).

Hobsbawm, Eric, *The Age of Empire, 1875–1914* (London, 1987).

Hobson, Rolf, *Imperialism at Sea: Naval Strategic Thought, the Ideology of Sea Power and the Tirpitz Plan, 1875–1914* (Boston, MA, 2002).

Höcker, Oskar, *Der Seekadett von Helgoland* (Leipzig, 1916).

Höhns, Ulrich, *Eine Insel im Aufbau: Helgoland, 1952–62* (Otterndorf, 1990).

Hollenberg, Günter, *Englisches Interesse am Kaiserreich: Die Attraktivität Preußen-Deutschlands für konservative und liberale Kreise in Großbritannien 1860–1914* (Wiesbaden, 1974).

[Holstein, Friedrich von,] *Die geheimen Papiere Friedrich von Holsteins*, ed. Werner Frauendienst, 4 vols (Göttingen, 1956–63).

Hopman, Albert, *Das Logbuch eines deutschen Seeoffiziers* (Berlin, 1924).

Hopman, Albert, *Das ereignisreiche Leben eines 'Wilhelminers': Tagebücher, Briefe, Aufzeichnungen 1901 bis 1920*, ed. Michael Epkenhans (Munich, 2004).

Horden, Peregrine and Nicholas Purcell, *The Corrupting Sea: A Study of Mediterranean History* (Oxford, 2000).

Horden, Peregrine and Nicholas Purcell, 'The Mediterranean and "the New Thalassology"', *AHR*, 111 (2006), 722–40.

Horne, John, 'Defeat and Memory in Modern History', in Jenny Macleod (ed.), *Defeat and Memory: Cultural Histories of Defeat in the Modern Era* (London, 2008), 11–29.

Horne, John and Alan Kramer, *German Atrocities, 1914: A History of Denial* (London and New Haven, CT, 2001).

Hough, Richard, *First Sea Lord: An Authorized Biography of Admiral Lord Fisher* (London, 1969).

Howie, Crawford, *Anton Bruckner: A Documentary Biography*, vol. 2 (Lewiston, NY, 2002).

Howoldt, Jenns E. and Andreas Baur (eds), *Die Gemälde des 19. Jahrhunderts in der Hamburger Kunsthalle* (Hamburg 1993).

Hubatsch, Walter, *Die Ära Tirpitz: Studien zur deutschen Marinepolitik 1890–1918* (Göttingen, 1955).

Hubbell, Paul E., 'The Helgoland–Zanzibar Treaty of 1890' (Ph.D. dissertation, University of Michigan, 1937).

Hughes, R. Gerald, *Britain, Germany and the Cold War: The Search for a European Détente 1949–1967* (London, 2007).

Hull, Isabel V., *A Scrap of Paper: Breaking and Making International Law during the Great War* (Ithaca, NY, 2014).

Hurd, Archibald and H. C. Bywater, *From Heligoland to Keeling Island: One Hundred Days of Naval War* (London, 1914).

Hussain, Nasser, *Jurisprudence of Emergency: Colonialism and the Rule of Law* (Ann Arbor, MI, 2003).

Ideenwettbewerb für den Wiederaufbau der Insel Helgoland (Pinneberg, 1951).

Isabella, Maurizio, 'Italian Revolutionaries and the Making of a Colonial Sea, 1800–1830', in Maurizio Isabella and Konstantina Zanou (eds), *Mediterranean Diasporas: Politics and Ideas in the Long 19th Century* (London, 2015).

Jäckh, Ernst (ed.), *Kiderlen-Wächter der Staatsmann und Mensch: Briefwechsel und Nachlaß*, 2 vols (Stuttgart, 1924).

James, William, *A Great Seaman: The Life of Admiral of the Fleet Sir Henry F. Oliver* (London, 1956).

Jane, L. Cecil, *The Action off Heligoland, August 1914* (London, 1915).

Jarausch, Konrad H., *The Enigmatic Chancellor: Bethmann Hollweg and the Hubris of Imperial Germany* (New Haven, CT, 1973).

Jarausch, Konrad H., *Out of Ashes: A New History of Europe in the Twentieth Century* (Princeton, NJ, 2015).

Jellicoe, Admiral Viscount, *The Grand Fleet 1914–1916: Its Creation, Development and Work* (London, 1919).

Jellonnek, Burkhard, *Homosexuelle unter dem Hakenkreuz: Die Verfolgung von Homosexuellen im Dritten Reich* (Paderborn, 1990).

Jellonnek, Burkhard and Rüdiger Lautmann (eds), *Nationalsozialistischer Terror gegen Homosexuelle* (Paderborn, 2002).

Johnson, Gaynor, *The Berlin Embassy of Lord D'Abernon, 1920–1926* (Basingstoke, 2002).

Jubiläumsjahr des Nordseebades Helgoland: 1826–1926 (Helgoland, 1926).

Judt, Tony, *Post-War: A History of Europe Since 1945* (London, 2005).

Karatani, Rieko, *Defining British Citizenship: Empire, Commonwealth and Modern Britain* (London, 2003).

Kater, Michael, *Das 'Ahnenerbe' der SS 1935–1945: Ein Beitrag zur Kulturpolitik des Dritten Reiches* (Munich, 1997).

Kehr, Eckart, *Schlachtflottenbau und Parteipolitik 1894–1901: Versuch eines Querschnitts durch die innenpolitischen, sozialen und ideologischen Voraussetzungen des deutschen Imperialismus* (Berlin, 1930).

Kehr, Eckart, *Der Primat der Innenpolitik: Gesammelte Aufsätze zur preußisch-deutschen Sozialgeschichte im 19. und 20. Jahrhundert*, ed. Hans-Ulrich Wehler, second edition (Berlin, 1970).

Kelly, Patrick J., *Tirpitz and the Imperial German Navy* (Bloomington, IN, 2011).

Kemp, Wolfgang, *'Foreign Affairs': Die Abenteuer einiger Engländer in Deutschland 1900–1945* (Munich, 2010).

Kennedy, Paul M., 'German World Policy and the Alliance Negotiations with England, 1897–1900', *JMH*, 45 (1973), 605–25.

Kennedy, Paul M., 'Idealists and Realists: British Views of Germany, 1864–1939', *Transactions of the Royal Historical Society*, 5th Series, 24 (1975), 137–56.

Kennedy, Paul M., 'The Tradition of Appeasement in British Foreign Policy 1865–1939', *British Journal of International Studies*, 2 (1976), 195–215.

Kennedy, Paul M., *The Rise of the Anglo-German Antagonism 1860–1914* (London, 1980).

Kennedy, Paul M., *The Rise and Fall of British Naval Mastery*, 3rd edn (London, 1991).

Kershaw, Ian, *Hitler, 1889–1936: Hubris* (London, 1998).

Kershaw, Ian, *Hitler, 1936–1945: Nemesis* (London, 2000).

Kershaw, Ian, *The Nazi Dictatorship: Problems and Perspectives of Interpretation*, 4th edn (London, 2000).

Kershaw, Ian, *Making Friends with Hitler: Lord Londonderry and Britain's Road to War* (London, 2004).

Kershaw, Ian, *The End: Hitler's Germany, 1944–45* (London, 2011).

Kershaw, Ian, *To Hell and Back: Europe 1914–1949* (London, 2015).

Keyes, Roger, *The Naval Memoirs of Admiral of the Fleet Sir Roger Keyes: The Narrow Seas to the Dardanelles, 1910–1918* (London, 1936).

The Keyes Papers: Selections from the Private and Official Correspondence of Admiral of the Fleet Baron Keyes of Zeebrugge, ed. Paul G. Halpern, 3 vols (London, 1972–81).

Kießling, Friedrich, *Gegen den 'großen Krieg'? Entspannung in den internationalen Beziehungen 1911–1914* (Munich, 2002).

Kirchberger, Ulrike, *Aspekte deutsch–britischer Expansion: Die Überseeinteressen der deutschen Migranten in Großbritannien in der Mitte des 19. Jahrhunderts* (Stuttgart, 1999).

Kirkpatrick, Ivone, *The Inner Circle: Memoirs* (London, 1959).

Kittel, Manfred, *Die Legende von der 'zweiten Schuld': Vergangenheitsbewältigung in der Ära Adenauer* (Frankfurt and Berlin, 1993).

Klee, Karl, *Das Unternehmen 'Seelöwe': Die geplante deutsche Landung in England 1940* (Göttingen, 1958).

Klee, Karl (ed.), *Dokumente zum Unternehmen 'Seelöwe': Die geplante deutsche Landung in England 1940* (Göttingen, 1959).

Klein, Bernhard and Gesa Mackenthun (eds), *Sea Changes: Historicizing the Ocean* (New York, 2004).

Kleist, Heinrich von, 'Geographische Nachricht von der Insel Helgoland', *Berliner Abendblätter*, 4 Dec. 1810.

Klönne, Arno (ed.), *Jugendkriminalität und Jugendopposition im NS-Staat: Ein sozial-geschichtliches Dokument* (Münster, 1981).

Knight, Roger, *Britain against Napoleon: The Organisation of Victory, 1793–1815* (London, 2013).

Knupp, Christine, 'Walter Leistikow (1865–1908): Helgoland, 1890', *Jahrbuch Altonaer Museum*, 12/13 (1974–75).

Kobbe, Theodor von, *Briefe über Helgoland* (Bremen, 1840).

Koditschek, Theodore, *Liberalism, Imperialism, and the Historical Imagination: Nineteenth-Century Visions of a Greater Britain* (Cambridge, 2011).

Kolsky, Elizabeth, *Colonial Justice in British India: White Violence and the Rule of Law* (Cambridge, 2010).

Koopmann, Helmut, 'Die Helgoländer Briefe', in Heinrich Heine, *Historisch-kritische Gesamtausgabe*, vol. 11 (Hamburg, 1978), 251–67.

Koshar, Rudy, *From Monuments to Traces: Artifacts of German Memory, 1870–1990* (Berkeley, CA, 2000).

Koshar, Rudy, *German Travel Cultures* (Oxford, 2000).

Koss, Stephen E., *Lord Haldane: Scapegoat for Liberalism* (New York, 1969).

Kracauer, Siegfried, *From Caligari to Hitler: A Psychological History of the German Film* (Princeton, NJ 1947).

Kraft, Zdenko von, *Die Stimme von Helgoland* (Leipzig, 1916).

Krause, Andreas, *Scapa Flow: Die Selbstversenkung der wilhelminischen Flotte* (Berlin, 1999).

Krogmann, Willy, *Die heilige Insel: Ein Beitrag zur altfriesischen Religionsgeschichte* (Assen, 1942).

Kropatscheck, Walter, *Nächte und Tage auf Helgoland: Aufzeichnungen des Inselarztes* (Pfullingen, 1972).

Kuckuck, Paul, *Der Nordseelotse: Lehrreiches und lustiges Vademekum für Helgoländer Badegäste und Besucher der Nordsee* (Hamburg, 1908).

Laband, John, 'From Mercenaries to Military Settlers: The British German Legion, 1854–1861', in Stephen M. Miller (ed.), *Soldiers and Settlers in Africa, 1850–1918* (Leiden, 2009), 85–122.

Ladurie, Emmanuel Le Roy, *Montaillou,* (London, 1978).

Lambert, Andrew, 'The Royal Navy 1856–1914: Deterrence and the Strategy of World Power', in Keith Neilson and Elizabeth Jane Errington (eds), *Navies and Global Defense: Theories and Strategy* (Westport, CT, 1995).

Lambert, David and Alan Lester (eds), *Colonial Lives across the British Empire: Imperial Careering in the Long Nineteenth Century* (Cambridge, 2000).

Lambert, Nicholas A., *Sir John Fisher's Naval Revolution* (Columbia, SC, 1999).

Lambi, Ivo, *The Navy and German Power Politics, 1862–1914* (Boston, MA, 1984).

Lampel, Peter Martin, *Kampf um Helgoland: Schauspiel in einem Vorspiel, 5 Akten und einem Nachspiel* (Berlin, 1952).

Lansing, Robert, *The Peace Negotiations: A Personal Narrative* (Boston, MA, and New York, 1921).

Lappenberg, Johann Martin, *Über den ehemaligen Umfang und die alte Geschichte Helgolands: Ein Vortrag bei der Versammlung der deutsche Naturforscher im September 1830* (Hamburg, 1831).

Large, David Clay, *Germans to the Front: West German Rearmament in the Adenauer Era* (Chapel Hill, NC, 1996).

Lattek, Christine, *Revolutionary Refugees: German Socialism in Britain, 1840–1860* (London, 2006).

Lauterwein, Andréa, *Anselm Kiefer/Paul Celan: Myth, Mourning and Memory* (London, 2007).

Leckie, Gould Francis, *An Historical Survey of the Foreign Affairs of Great Britain* (London, 1808).

Leed, Eric, *The Mind of the Traveller: From Gilgamesh to Global Tourism* (New York, 1991).

Leffler, Melvyl L. and Odd Arne Westad (eds), *Cambridge History of the Cold War*, 3 vols (Cambridge, 2010).

Lehnert, Detlef and Klaus Megerle (eds), *Politische Identität und nationale Gedenktage: Zur politischen Kultur der Weimarer Republik* (Opladen, 1989).

Lekan, Thomas M., *Imagining the Nation in Nature: Landscape Preservation and German Identity, 1885–1945* (Cambridge, MA, 2004).

L'Estrange, M., *Heligoland: or, Reminiscences of Childhood: A Genuine Narrative of Facts by an Officer's Daughter* (London, 1851).

Leudesdorff, René, *Wir befreiten Helgoland: Ein historischer Krimi* (Stade, 2007).

Levi, Giovanni, 'On Microhistory', in Peter Burke (ed.), *New Perspectives in Historical Writing* (Cambridge, 1991), 97–119.

Lewin, Evans, 'The Heligoland Mistake', *Contemporary Review*, 110 (1916), 68–77.

[Lindau, Rudolf,] *Die politische und literarische Korrespondenz Rudolf Lindaus*, ed. Rainer Hillenbrand, 2 vols (Frankfurt, 2007).

Lindemann, Emil, *Das deutsche Helgoland* (Berlin, 1913).

Lindemann, Emil, *Helgoländer Badeplauderei* (Stuttgart, 1920).

Lindemann, Emil, *Helgoland-Führer* (Cuxhaven, 1925).

Lindner, Ulrike, *Koloniale Begegnungen: Deutschland und Großbritannien als Imperialmächte in Afrika 1880–1914* (Frankfurt, 2011).

Lipsius, Adolf, *Helgoland: Beschreibung der Insel und des Badelebens*, 2nd edn (Leipzig, 1895).

Lockley, R. M., *I Know an Island* (London, 1938).

Loeff, Wolfgang, *Der letzte Mann der 'Köln': Nach 76 Stunden hilflosen Herumtreibens in der Nordsee gerettet. Erzählung aus dem Gefecht bei Helgoland am 28. August 1914* (Gütersloh, 1939).

Longerich, Peter, *Heinrich Himmler* (Munich, 2008).

Loth, Wilfried and Bernd A. Rusinek (eds), *Verwandlungspolitik: NS-Eliten in der westdeutschen Nachkriegsgesellschaft* (Frankfurt and New York, 1998).

Löwenstein, Hubertus Prinz zu, *The Tragedy of a Nation* (London, 1934).

Löwenstein, Hubertus Prinz zu, *Was ist Deutsche Aktion?* (Amorbach, 1950).

Lucas, Charles Prestwood, *A Historical Geography of the British Colonies* (Oxford, 1888).

Lynder, Frank, *Spione in Hamburg und auf Helgoland* (Hamburg, 1964).

Lynn-Jones, Sean M., 'Détente and Deterrence: Anglo–German Relations, 1911–1914', *International Security*, 11 (1986), 121–50.

McDonough, Frank, *The Conservative Party and Anglo-German Relations, 1905–1914* (Basingstoke, 2007).

Macfarlane, Robert, *Mountains of the Mind: A History of a Fascination* (London, 2008).

Mackay, Shena, *Heligoland* (London, 2003).

Macmillan, Margaret, *Peacemakers: The Paris Conference of 1919 and its Attempt to End War* (London, 2001).

Madsen, Chris, *The Royal Navy and German Naval Disarmament, 1942–1947* (London, 1998).

Mahlau, Alfred, *Die Insel Helgoland: Ein Skizzenbuch* (Frankfurt, 1961).

Mählert, Ulrich and Gerd-Rüdiger Stephan, *Blaue Hemden, Rote Fahnen: Die Geschichte der Freien Deutschen Jugend* (Opladen, 1996).

Maiolo, Joseph, *The Royal Navy and Nazi Germany, 1933–39: A Study in Appeasement and the Origins of the Second World War* (London, 1998).

Major, Patrick, *The Death of the KPD: Communism and Anti-Communism in West Germany, 1945–1956* (Oxford, 1998).

Manes, Philipp, *Als ob's ein Leben wär: Tatsachenbericht Theresienstadt 1942 bis 1944*, ed. Ben Barkow and Klaus Leist (Berlin, 2005).

Mantoux, Paul, *The Deliberations of the Council of Four*, ed. and trans. A. S. Link, vol. 1 (Princeton, NJ, 1992).

Marder, Arthur J. (ed.), *Fear God and Dread Nought: The Correspondence of Admiral of the Fleet Lord Fisher of Kilverstone*, 3 vols (London, 1952–9).

Marder, Arthur J., *From the Dreadnought to Scapa Flow: The Royal Navy in the Fisher Era, 1904–1919*, 5 vols (London, 1961–78).

Marder, Arthur J., *The Anatomy of British Sea Power: A History of British Naval Policy in the Pre-Dreadnought Era, 1880–1905*, 2nd edn (London, 1964).

Märker, Peter, *Geschichte als Natur: Untersuchungen zur Entwicklungsvorstellung bei Caspar David Friedrich* (Kiel, 1994).

Martin, Robert Montgomery, *History of the Colonies of the British Empire in the West Indies, South America, North America, Asia, Austral-Asia, Africa, and Europe* (London, 1843).

Marx, Karl and Friedrich Engels, *Werke*, vol. 3 (Berlin, 1969).

Marxen, Klaus, *Das Volk und sein Gerichtshof: Eine Studie zum nationalsozialistischen Volksgerichtshof* (Frankfurt, 1994).

Mason, Tim, 'The Legacy of 1918 for National Socialism', in Anthony Nicholls and Erich Matthias (eds), *German Democracy and the Triumph of Hitler* (London, 1971), 215–39.

Massie, Robert K., *Dreadnought: Britain, Germany and the Coming of the Great War* (London, 1991).

Massie, Robert K., *Castles of Steel: Britain, Germany and the Winning of the War at Sea* (London, 2003).

Mastnak, Jens, 'Werbung und Ersatzwesen der Königlich Deutschen Legion 1803 bis 1813', *MGZ*, 60 (2001), 119–42.

Mauch, Christof (ed.), *Nature in German History* (New York, 2004).

Mazower, Mark, *Dark Continent: Europe's Twentieth Century* (London, 1998).

Mazower, Mark, *Hitler's Empire: Nazi Rule in Occupied Europe* (London, 2008).

Mazower, Mark, Jessica Reinisch, and David Feldman (eds), *Post-War Reconstruction in Europe: International Perspectives, 1945–1949* (Oxford, 2011).

Mehra, Jagdish and Helmut Rechenberg, *The Historical Development of Quantum Theory*, vol. 1, *The Discovery of Quantum Mechanics, 1925* (New York and Heidelberg, 1982).

Meier, Christian, 'Erinnern—Verdrängen—Vergessen', *Merkur*, 50 (1996), 937–52.

Meinecke, Friedrich, *Geschichte des deutsch–englischen Bündnisproblems 1890–1901* (Munich, 1927).

Merleker, Hartmuth, *Helgoland* (Hamburg, 1938).

Michaud, Eric, *The Cult of Art in Nazi Germany* (Stanford, CA, 2004).

Middlemas, Keith, *Diplomacy of Illusion: The British Government and Germany, 1937–39* (London, 1972).

Militärgeschichtliches Forschungsamt (ed.), *Das Deutsche Reich und der Zweite Weltkrieg*, 12 vols (Stuttgart, 1979–2008).

Millar, Delia, *The Victorian Watercolours in the Collection of H.M. The Queen* (London, 1995).

Miller, Michael B., *Europe and the Maritime World: A Twentieth-Century History* (Cambridge, 2012).

Minor, Ryan, *Choral Fantasies: Music, Festivity, and Nationhood in Nineteenth-Century Germany* (Cambridge, 2013).

Moeller, Ernst von, *Rechtsgeschichte der Insel Helgoland* (Weimar, 1904).

Moeller, Robert G. (ed.), *West Germany under Construction: Politics, Society, and Culture in the Adenauer Era* (Ann Arbor, MI, 1997).

Moeller, Robert G., *War Stories: The Search for a Usable Past in the Federal Republic of Germany* (Berkeley, CA, 2001).

Moeller, Robert G., 'Germans as Victims? Thoughts on a Post-Cold War History of World War II's Legacies', *History and Memory*, 17 (2005), 147–94.

Moens, Jean-Baptiste, *Heligoland, et ses timbres: Étude suivie du catalogue général de toutes les émissions postales* (Brussels, 1897).

Mohrhenn, Wernher, *Helgoland zur Zeit der Kontinentalsperre* (Berlin, 1926).

Möller, Horst, Andreas Wirsching, and Walter Ziegler (eds), *Nationalsozialismus in der Region: Beiträge zur regionalen und lokalen Forschung und zum internationalen Vergleich* (Munich, 1996).

Mombauer, Annika and Wilhelm Deist (eds), *The Kaiser: New Research on Wilhelm II's Role in Imperial Germany* (Cambridge, 2003).

Mommsen, Wolfgang J., 'Zur Entwicklung des Englandbildes der Deutschen seit dem Ende des 18. Jahrhunderts', in *Studien zur Geschichte Englands und der deutsch–britischen Beziehungen: Festschrift für Paul Kluke* (Munich, 1981).

Mommsen, Wolfgang J., *Two Centuries of Anglo-German Relations: A Reappraisal* (London, 1984).

Mommsen, Wolfgang J. (ed.), *Die ungleichen Partner: Deutsch–Britische Beziehungen im 19. und 20. Jahrhundert* (Stuttgart, 1999).

Morieux, Renaud, 'Diplomacy from Below and Belonging: Fishermen and Cross-Channel Relations in the Eighteenth Century', *P&P*, 202 (2009), 83–125.

Mordal, Jacques, *Héligoland: Gibraltar allemand de la mer du Nord* (Paris, 1967).

Morris, Benny, *The Roots of Appeasement: The British Weekly Press and Nazi Germany during the 1930s* (London, 1991).

Moses, Dirk, *German Intellectuals and the Nazi Past* (Cambridge, 2007).

Mosse, George L., *The Crisis of German Ideology: Intellectual Origins of the Third Reich* (London, 1966).

Mosse, W. E., *The European Powers and the German Question, 1848–1871* (Cambridge, 1958).

Muhs, Rudolf, Johannes Paulmann, and Wilibald Steinmetz (eds), *Aneignung und Abwehr: Interkultureller Transfer zwischen Deutschland und Großbritannien im 19. Jahrhundert* (Bodenheim, 1998).

Müller, Frank Lorenz, *Britain and the German Question: Perceptions of Nationalism and Political Reform, 1830–63* (Basingstoke, 2002).

Müller, Sven Oliver, *Die Nation als Waffe und Vorstellung: Nationalismus in Deutschland und Grossbritannien im Ersten Weltkrieg* (Göttingen, 2002).

Mulligan, William, 'We Can't be More Russian than the Russians: British Policy in the Liman von Sanders Crisis, 1913–14', *Diplomacy & Statecraft*, 17 (2006), 261–82.

Mulligan, William, 'From Case to Narrative: The Marquess of Lansdowne, Sir Edward Grey, and the Threat from Germany, 1900–1906', *IHR*, 30 (2008), 273–302.

Munch-Petersen, Thomas, 'Colin Alexander Mackenzie: A British Agent at Tilsit', *Northern Studies*, 37 (2003), 9–16.

Murray, Scott W., *Liberal Diplomacy and German Unification: The Early Career of Robert Morier* (Westport, CT, 2000).

Mustafa, Sam, *The Long Ride of Major von Schill* (Boulder, CO, 2008).

Naujoks, Eberhard, 'Rudolf Lindau und die Neuorientierung der auswärtigen Pressepolitik Bismarcks (1871/78)', *HZ*, 215 (1972), 299–344.

Naumann, Klaus, *Der Krieg als Text: Das Jahr 1945 im kulturellen Gedächtnis der Presse* (Hamburg, 1998).

Naval Staff Monographs, vol. 3, *The Battle of Heligoland Bight 28 Aug 1914* (London, 1921).

Neilson, Keith, *Britain and the Last Tsar: British Policy and Russia, 1894–1917* (Oxford, 1995).

Neilson, Keith, 'The Russo-Japanese War and British Strategic Foreign Policy', in Rotem Kowner (ed.), *Rethinking the Russo-Japanese War, 1904–5*, vol. 1 (Folkestone, 2007), 307–17.

Nicolson, Harold, *Peacemaking, 1919* (London, 1933).

Nicolson, Harold, *Diaries and Letters 1930–1939* (London, 1966).

Nipperdey, Thomas, *Deutsche Geschichte 1866–1918*, 2 vols (Munich, 1994–5).

Niven, Bill (ed.), *Germans as Victims: Remembering the Past in Contemporary Germany* (Basingstoke, 2006).

Niven, Bill and Chloe Paver (eds), *Memorialization in Germany since 1945* (Basingstoke, 2010).

Noakes, Jeremy, *The Nazi Party in Lower Saxony, 1921–1933* (Oxford, 1971).

Norbert, Willy, *Die deutsche Nordsee* (Bielefeld and Leipzig, 1925).

Oetker, Friedrich, *Helgoland: Schilderungen und Erörterungen* (Berlin, 1855).

Olivier, David H., *German Naval Strategy 1856–1888: Forerunners of Tirpitz* (London, 2004).

Olshausen, Otto, *Zur Vorgeschichte Helgolands* (Berlin, 1893).

Ompteda, Christian, *In the King's German Legion* (London, 1894).

Osborne, Eric W., *The Battle of Heligoland Bight* (Bloomington, IN, 2006).

Osterhammel, Jürgen, *Die Verwandlung der Welt: Eine Geschichte des 19. Jahrhunderts* (Munich, 2009).

Otte, T. G., 'Eyre Crowe and British Foreign Policy: A Cognitive Map', in T. G. Otte and Constantine A. Pagedas (eds), *Personalities, War and Diplomacy: Essays in International History* (London, 1997), 14–37.

Otte, T. G., 'The Fragmenting of the Old World Order: Britain, the Great Powers and the War', in Rotem Kowner (ed.), *The Impact of the Russo-Japanese War* (London, 2007), 91–108.

Otte, T. G., 'A "German Paperchase": The "Scrap of Paper" Controversy and the Problem of Myth and Memory in International History', *Diplomacy & Statecraft*, 18 (2007), 53–87.

Otte, T. G., *The China Question: Great Power Rivalry and British Isolation, 1894–1905* (Oxford, 2007).

Otte, T. G., *The Foreign Office Mind: The Making of British Foreign Policy, 1865–1914* (Cambridge, 2013).

Otte, T. G., *July Crisis: The World's Descent into War, Summer 1914* (Cambridge, 2014).

Overy, Richard, *War and Economy in the Third Reich* (Oxford, 1994).

Overy, Richard, *The Bombing War: Europe 1939–1945* (London, 2013).

Packroß, James and Peter Rickmers (eds), *Helgoland Ruft* (Hamburg, 1952).

Panayi, Panikos, *German Immigrants in Britain during the Nineteenth Century, 1815–1914* (Oxford and New York, 1995).

Panayi, Panikos (ed.), *Germans in Britain since 1500* (London, 1996).

Panayi, Panikos, *Prisoners of Britain: German Civilian and Combatant Internees during the First World War* (Manchester, 2012).

Papers Relating to the Foreign Relations of the United States, 1919: The Paris Peace Conference, vol. 4 (Washington, DC, 1943).

Parker, R. A. C., *Chamberlain and Appeasement: British Policy and the Coming of the Second World War* (London, 1993).

Parry, Jonathan, *The Politics of Patriotism: English Liberalism, National Identity and Europe, 1830–1886* (Cambridge, 2006).

Pasley, Charles, *Essay on the Military Policy and Institutions of the British Empire* (London, 1810).

Paulmann, Johannes, 'Verwandtschaft, Vorbild und Rivalität: Britisch–deutsche Beziehungen von der Wiener Ordnung bis zum Imperialismus', *Westfälische Forschungen*, 44 (1994), 343–66.

Paul von Hintze: Marineoffizier, Diplomat, Staatssekretär. Dokumente einer Karriere zwischen Militär und Politik, 1903–1918, ed. Johannes Hürter (Munich, 1998).

Pedersen, Susan, *The Guardians: The League of Nations and the Crisis of Empire* (Oxford, 2015).

Perras, Arne, *Carl Peters and German Imperialism 1856–1918* (Oxford, 2004).

Peters, Carl, *Die Gründung von Deutsch-Ostafrika: Kolonialpolitische Erinnerungen und Betrachtungen* (Berlin, 1906).

Petersen, Lorenz, 'Zur Geschichte der Verfassung und Verwaltung auf Helgoland', *Zeitschrift der Gesellschaft für Schleswig-Holsteinische Geschichte*, 67 (1939), 29–190.

Petropoulos, Jonathan, *The Faustian Bargain: The Art World in Nazi Germany* (Oxford, 2000).

Petzold, Joachim, *Die Dolchstoßlegende* (Berlin, 1963).

Peukert, Detlev, *Inside Nazi Germany: Conformity, Opposition, and Racism in Everyday Life* (New Haven, CT, and London, 1989).

Pfannkuche, Adolf, *Die königlich deutsche Legion 1803–1816* (Hanover, 1926).

[Phipps, Sir Eric,] *Our Man in Berlin: The Diary of Sir Eric Phipps, 1933–1937*, ed. Gaynor Johnson (Basingstoke, 2008).

Pietsch, Ernst Robert, *Reise nach Helgoland über Berlin und Bremen im Jahre 1912*, ed. Stefan Wolter (Göttingen, 2001).

Pietsch, Tamson, *Empire of Scholars: Universities, Networks and the British Academic World, 1850–1939* (Manchester, 2013).

Pitts, Jennifer, *A Turn to Empire: The Rise of Imperial Liberalism in Britain and France* (Princeton, NJ 2005).

Plagemann, Volker (ed.), *Übersee: Seefahrt und Seemacht im deutschen Kaiserreich* (Munich, 1988).

Pommerin, Reiner and Michael Fröhlich (eds.), *Quellen zu den deutsch-britischen Beziehungen 1815–1914*, vol. 3 of *Quellen zu den Beziehungen Deutschlands zu seinen Nachbarn im 19. und 20. Jahrhundert* (Darmstadt, 1997).

Porter, Andrew (ed.), *The Oxford History of the British Empire*, vol. 3 (Oxford, 1999).

Post, Gaines, *Dilemmas of Appeasement: British Deterrence and Defense, 1934–1937* (Ithaca, NY, 1993).

Prior, Robin, *Churchill's 'World Crisis' as History* (London, 1983).

Pritchard, Gareth, *Niemandsland: A History of Unoccupied Germany, 1944–1945* (Cambridge, 2012).

Pudor, Heinrich, *Helgoland: Heiligland* (Leipzig, 1931).

Pudor, Heinrich, *Völker aus Gottes Athem: Atlantis-Helgoland, das arisch-germanische Rassenhochzucht- und Kolonisations-Mutterland* (Leipzig, 1936).

Pudor, Heinrich, *Nachweise für Atlantis* (Leipzig, 1937).

Puschner, Uwe, Walter Schmitz, and Justus H. Ulbricht (eds), *Handbuch zur 'Völkischen Bewegung' 1871–1918* (Munich, 1996).

Radkau, Joachim, *Das Zeitalter der Nervosität: Deutschland zwischen Bismarck und Hitler* (Munich, 1998).

Radkau, Joachim, *Natur und Macht: Eine Weltgeschichte der Umwelt* (Munich, 2000).

Raeder, Erich, *Mein Leben* (Tübingen, 1956).

Rahn, Werner and Gerhard Schreiber (eds), *Kriegstagebuch der Seekriegsleitung 1939–1945*, 68 vols (Herford, 1988–97).

Ramsden, John, *Don't Mention the War: The British and the Germans since 1890* (London, 2006).

Rebentisch, Jost, *Die vielen Gesichter des Kaisers: Wilhelm II. in der deutschen und britischen Karikatur, 1888–1918* (Berlin, 2000).

Rehding, Alexander, *Music and Monumentality: Commemoration and Wonderment in Nineteenth-Century Germany* (Oxford, 2009).

Reichel, Peter, Harald Schmid, and Peter Steinbach (eds), *Der Nationalsozialismus: Die zweite Geschichte* (Munich, 2009).

Reinermann, Lothar, *Der Kaiser in England: Wilhelm II. und sein Bild in der britischen Öffentlichkeit* (Paderborn, 2001).

Reinhardt, Karl, *Von Hamburg nach Helgoland* (Leipzig, 1856).

Reinisch, Jessica, *The Perils of Peace: The Public Health Crisis in Occupied Germany* (Oxford, 2013).

Reuter, Ludwig von, *Scapa Flow: Das Grab der deutschen Flotte* (Leipzig, 1921).

Riall, Lucy, *Under the Volcano: Revolution in a Sicilian Town* (Oxford, 2013).

Ribbentrop, Joachim von, *Zwischen London und Moskau: Erinnerungen und letzte Aufzeichnungen* (Leoni, 1961).

Riefenstahl, Leni, *Memoiren* (Munich, 1987).

Ring, Jim, *Erskine Childers: A Biography* (London, 1996).

Ringer, Alexander L., '*Germanenzug* bis *Helgoland*: Zu Bruckners Deutschtum', in Albrecht Riethmüller (ed.), *Bruckner-Probleme: Beiheft zum Archiv für Musikwissenschaft*, 45 (Stuttgart, 1999), 25–34.

Riotte, Torsten, *Hannover in der britischen Politik 1792–1815: Dynastische Verbindung als Element außenpolitischer Entscheidungsprozesse* (Münster, 2005).

Rittschlag, Georg, *Das Asyl auf dem Felseneiland* (Weimar, 1840).

Robertson, James, *Narrative of a Secret Mission to the Danish Islands in 1808* (London, 1863).

Rodger, N. A. M., *The Command of the Ocean: A Naval History of Britain, 1649–1815* (London, 2004).

Rodowicz-Oświęcimsky, Theodor von, *Unter Englands Fahnen zur Zeit des Krimkrieges: Humoristisch-satyrische Reminiscenzen*, 2 vols (Hanover, 1875).

Röhl, John C. G., *The Kaiser and his Court: Wilhelm II and the Government of Germany* (Cambridge, 1994).

Röhl, John C. G., *Young Wilhelm: The Kaiser's Early Life, 1859–1888* (Cambridge, 1998).

Röhl, John C. G., *Wilhelm II: The Kaiser's Personal Monarchy, 1888–1900* (Cambridge, 2004).

Röhl, John C. G., *Wilhelm II: Into the Abyss of War and Exile, 1900–1941* (Cambridge, 2014).

Röhl, John C. G. and Nicolaus Sombart (eds), *Kaiser Wilhelm II: New Interpretations* (Cambridge, 1982).

Rose, Andreas, *Zwischen Empire und Kontinent: Zur Transformation britischer Außen- und Sicherheitspolitik im Vorfeld des Ersten Weltkrieg* (Munich, 2011).

Rose, John Holland, 'A British Agent at Tilsit', *EHR*, 16 (1901), 712–16.

Rose, John Holland, 'British West Indian Commerce as a Factor in the Napoleonic War', *HJ*, 3 (1929), 34–46.

Rösing, Wilhelm, *Franz Schensky: Der Fotograf und das Meer* (Kiel and Hamburg, 2015).

Rothschild, Emma, *The Inner Life of Empires* (Princeton, NJ, 2011).

Rüger, Jan, *The Great Naval Game: Britain and Germany in the Age of Empire* (Cambridge, 2007).

Rüger, Jan, 'OXO: Or, The Challenges of Transnational History', *EHQ*, 40 (2010), 656–68.

Rüger, Jan, 'Revisiting the Anglo-German Antagonism', *JMH*, 83 (2011), 579–617.

Rüger, Jan, 'Sovereignty and Empire in the North Sea, 1807–1918', *AHR*, 119 (2014), 313–38.

Ruggiero, Guido (ed.), *Microhistory and the Lost Peoples of Europe* (Baltimore, MD, 1991).

Russell, Mark, *Aby Warburg and the Public Purposes of Art in Hamburg* (Oxford and New York, 2007).

Rutz, Rainer, *'Signal': Eine deutsche Auslandsillustrierte als Propagandainstrument im Zweiten Weltkrieg* (Essen, 2007).

Ryan, A. N., 'The Causes of the British Attack on Copenhagen in 1807', *EHR*, 68 (1953), 37–55.

Sahlins, Marshall, *Islands of History* (Chicago, IL, 1985).

Sahlins, Peter, *Boundaries: The Making of France and Spain in the Pyrenees* (Berkeley, CA, 1989).

Salewski, Michael, *Tirpitz: Aufstieg, Macht, Scheitern* (Göttingen, 1979).

Salewski, Michael, *Die Deutschen und die See* (Stuttgart, 1998).

Salewski, Michael, 'Das historische Lehrstück: Helgoland', *Zeitschrift der Gesellschaft für Schleswig-Holsteinische Geschichte*, 116 (1991), 173–92.

Salomon, Gotthold, *Erinnerungen an das Seebad auf Helgoland im Jahr 1834* (Hamburg, 1835).

Saltzman, Lisa, *Anselm Kiefer and Art after Auschwitz* (Cambridge, 1999).

Salvator, Ludwig, *Helgoland: Eine Reise-Skizze* (Leipzig, 1901).

Samuel, Raphael, *Island Stories: Unravelling Britain* (London, 1998).

Sanderson, G. N., 'The Anglo-German Agreement of 1890 and the Upper Nile', *EHR*, 78 (1963), 49–72.

Sandiford, Keith, *Great Britain and the Schleswig-Holstein Question, 1848–64: A Study in Diplomacy, Politics, and Public Opinion* (Toronto, 1975).

Sartori, Andrew, 'The British Empire and its Liberal Mission', *JMH*, 78 (2006), 623–42.

Savile, Leopold, 'The Demolition of the Harbour and Defence Works of Heligoland', *Minutes of the Proceedings of the Institution of Civil Engineers*, 220 (1924–5), 55–96.

Savory, Douglas, 'Heligoland Past and Present', *Contemporary Review*, 191 (1957).

Schama, Simon, *Landscape and Memory* (New York, 1995).

Scheer, Reinhard, *Deutschlands Hochseeflotte im Weltkrieg: Persönliche Erinnerungen* (Berlin, 1920).

Scheidemann, Philipp, *Politische Reden 1914–1945*, ed. Peter Wende (Frankfurt, 1994).

Schensky, Franz, *Das alte Helgoland photographiert von Franz Schensky*, ed. Evelin Schultheiß, 2nd edn (Helgoland, 2001).

Scherer, Georg and Franz Lipperheide (eds), *Die Wacht am Rhein* (Berlin, 1871).

Schivelbusch, Wolfgang, *Die Kultur der Niederlage: Der amerikanische Süden 1865, Frankreich 1871, Deutschland 1918* (Berlin, 2001).

Schlink, Roland, *Hoffmann von Fallerslebens vaterländische und gesellschaftskritische Lyrik* (Stuttgart, 1981).

Schneider, Fred D., 'Deadlock on the Rock: Constitutionalism and Counteraction in Heligoland 1864–1868', *Canadian Journal of History*, 8 (1973), 23–35.

Schöllgen, Gregor, *Imperialismus und Gleichgewicht: Deutschland, England und die orientalische Frage 1871–1914*, 2nd edn (Munich, 1992).

Schramm, Martin, *Das Deutschlandbild in der britischen Presse 1912–1919* (Berlin, 2007).

Schramm, Percy Ernst (ed.), *Kriegstagebuch des Oberkommandos der Wehrmacht*, 6 vols (Frankfurt, 1961–79).

Schreiber-Loetzenburg, Arno, *Das Finanzrecht der Gemeinde Helgoland* (Steglitz, 1931).

Schröder, Joachim, *Die U-Boote des Kaisers: Die Geschichte des deutschen U-Boot-Krieges gegen Großbritannien im Ersten Weltkrieg* (Bonn, 2003).

Schroeder, Paul W., *The Transformation of European Politics 1763–1848* (Oxford, 1994).

Schroeder, Paul W., 'International Politics, Peace, and War, 1815–1914', in Tim Blanning (ed.), *Short Oxford History of Europe*, vol. 9: *The Nineteenth Century* (Oxford, 2000).

Schulte Beerbühl, Margrit, 'Crossing the Channel: Nathan Mayer Rothschild and his Trade with the Continent during the Early Years of the Blockades (1803–1808)', *The Rothschild Archive Annual Review* (London, 2008), 41–8.

Schulte Beerbühl, Margrit, 'Trading Networks across the Blockades', in Katherine B. Aaslestad and Johan Joor (eds), *Revisiting Napoleon's Continental System: Local, Regional and European Experiences* (Basingstoke, 2014).

Schulze, Rainer, 'The German Refugees and Expellees from the East and the Creation of a Western German Identity after World War II', in Philipp Ther and Ana Siljak (eds), *Redrawing Nations: Ethnic Cleansing in East-Central Europe 1944–1948* (Lanham, MD, 2001), 307–25.

Schulze-Berghof, Paul, *Das letzte Nerthusfest auf Helgoland* (Leipzig, 1935).

Schütte, Gisela, 'Helgolandfahrten und Seebäderdienst', in Volker Plagemann (ed.), *Übersee: Seefahrt und Seemacht im deutschen Kaiserreich* (Munich, 1988), 186–8.

Schwarz, Bill (ed.), *The Expansion of England: Race, Ethnicity and Cultural History* (London and New York, 1996).

Schwarz, Hans-Peter, *Die Ära Adenauer: Gründerjahre der Republik, 1949–1957* (Stuttgart, 1981).

Schweizer, Claudia, *Johann Wolfgang Goethe und Kaspar Maria von Sternberg: Naturforscher und Gleichgesinnte* (Vienna, 2004).

Schwerk, Ekkehard, *Die Meisterdiebe von Berlin: Die goldenen Zwanziger der Gebrüder Sass* (Berlin, 1984).

Schwertfeger, Bernhard, *Geschichte der königlich deutschen Legion*, 2 vols (Hanover and Leipzig, 1907).

Scott, James C., *The Art of Not Being Governed: An Anarchist History of Southeast Asia* (New Haven, CT, 2009).

Scully, Richard, *British Images of Germany: Admiration, Antagonism and Ambivalence, 1860–1914* (Basingstoke, 2012).

Segrè, Gino, *Faust in Copenhagen: A Struggle for the Soul of Physics* (London, 2007).

Seligmann, Matthew S. (ed.), *Naval Intelligence from Germany: The Reports of the British Naval Attachés in Berlin, 1906–1914* (Aldershot, 2007).

Seligmann, Matthew S., *The Royal Navy and the German Threat 1901–1914* (Oxford, 2012).

Seligmann, Matthew S., Frank Nägler, and Michael Epkenhans (eds), *The Naval Route to the Abyss: The Anglo-German Naval Race 1895–1914* (Aldershot, 2015).

Sell, Manfred, *Die deutsche öffentliche Meinung und das Helgolandabkommen im Jahre 1890* (Berlin, 1926).

Semmens, Kristin, *Seeing Hitler's Germany: Tourism in the Third Reich* (Basingstoke, 2005).

Sherwig, John M., *Guineas and Gunpowder: British and Foreign Aid in the War with France, 1793–1815* (Cambridge, MA, 1969).

Siebs, Benno, *Helgoland und die Helgoländer* (Kiel, 1953).

Siebs, Theodor, *Helgoland und seine Sprache: Beiträge zur Volks- und Sprachkunde* (Cuxhaven, 1909).

Simms, Brendan, 'Britain and Napoleon', in Philip G. Dwyer (ed.), *Napoleon and Europe* (Harlow, 2001), 195–200.

Simms, Brendan, *The Longest Afternoon: The 400 Men Who Decided the Battle of Waterloo* (London, 2014).

Simms, Brendan and Torsten Riotte (eds), *The Hanoverian Dimension in British History, 1714–1837* (Cambridge, 2007).

Simpson, Michael, *A Life of Admiral of the Fleet Andrew Cunningham* (London, 2004).

Sivasundaram, Sujit, *Islanded: Britain, Sri Lanka, and the Bounds of an Indian Ocean Colony* (Chicago, IL, 2013).

Soames, Mary (ed.), *Speaking for Themselves: The Personal Letters of Sir Winston and Lady Churchill* (London, 1999).

Sondhaus, Lawrence, *Preparing for Weltpolitik: German Sea Power before the Tirpitz Era* (Annapolis, MD, 1997).

Sontag, Raymond J., *Germany and England: Background of Conflict, 1848–1894*, 2nd edn (New York, 1969).

Spiero, Heinrich, *Rudolf Lindau* (Berlin, 1909).

Stargardt, Nicholas, *The German War: A Nation under Arms, 1939–1945* (London, 2015).

Steber, Martina and Bernhard Gotto (eds), *Visions of Community in Nazi Germany: Social Engineering and Private Lives* (Oxford, 2014).

Stein, Ludwig (ed.), *England and Germany* (London, 1912).

[Steinbart, Gustav,] *The Letters and Journal of Gustav Steinbart, German Military Colonist to British Kaffraria, Cape Province, South Africa*, 2 vols (Port Elizabeth, 1975–8).

Steinberg, Jonathan, *Yesterday's Deterrent: Tirpitz and the Birth of the German Battle Fleet* (London, 1965).

Steinberg, Jonathan, 'The Copenhagen Complex', *JCH*, 1 (1966), 23–46.

Steinberg, Jonathan, 'Diplomatie als Wille und Vorstellung: Die Berliner Mission Lord Haldanes im February 1912', in Herbert Schottelius and Wilhelm Deist (eds), *Marine und Marinepolitik im kaiserlichen Deutschland, 1871–1914* (Düsseldorf, 1972), 263–82.

Steinberg, Jonathan, *Bismarck: A Life* (Oxford, 2011).

Steiner, Zara, *The Foreign Office and Foreign Policy, 1898–1914* (Cambridge, 1969).

Steiner, Zara, *The Lights that Failed: European International History 1919–1933* (Oxford, 2007).

Steiner, Zara, *The Triumph of the Dark: European International History, 1933–1939* (Oxford, 2011).

Steiner, Zara and Keith Neilson, *Britain and the Origins of the First World War* (Basingstoke, 2003).

Steinhauer, Gustav, *Der Meisterspion des Kaisers: Was der Detektiv Wilhelms II. in seiner Praxis erlebte* (Berlin, 1930).

Stenographische Berichte über die Verhandlungen des Reichstages (Berlin, 1871–1942).

Stenzel, Alfred, *Helgoland und die deutsche Flotte* (Berlin, 1891).

Stevenson, David, *The First World War and International Politics* (Oxford, 1988).

Stevenson, David, *Armaments and the Coming of War: Europe, 1904–1914* (Oxford, 1996).

Stevenson, David, *1914–1918: The History of the First World War* (London, 2004).

Stibbe, Matthew, *German Anglophobia and the Great War, 1914–1918* (Cambridge, 2001).

Stibbe, Matthew, *British Civilian Internees in Germany: The Ruhleben Camp, 1914–1918* (Manchester, 2008).

Stocks, Heinrich, *Helgoland im Versailler Friedensvertrag* (Leipzig, 1927).

Stoler, Ann Laura and Fredrick Cooper (eds.), *Tensions of Empire: Colonial Cultures in a Bourgeois World* (Berkeley, CA, 1997).

Storer, Colin, *Britain and the Weimar Republic: The History of a Cultural Relationship* (London, 2010).

Strauss, Monica J., *Cruel Banquet: The Life and Loves of Frida Strindberg* (New York, 2000).

Strindberg, Frida, *Marriage with Genius* (London, 1937).

Strobl, Gerwin, *The Germanic Isle: Nazi Perceptions of Britain* (Cambridge, 2000).

Stuchtey, Benedikt and Peter Wende (eds), *British and German Historiography, 1750–1950: Traditions, Perceptions, and Transfers* (Oxford, 2000).

Sumida, Jon Tetsuro, *In Defence of Naval Supremacy: Finance, Technology and British Naval Policy, 1889–1914* (Boston, MA, 1989).

Sundermann, Sabine, *Deutscher Nationalismus im englischen Exil: Zum sozialen und politischen Innenleben der deutschen Kolonie in London 1848–1871* (Paderborn, 1997).

Süß, Dietmar, *Tod aus der Luft: Kriegsgesellschaft und Luftkrieg in England und Deutschland* (Munich, 2011).

Thaler, Peter, *Of Mind and Matter: The Duality of National Identity in the German–Danish Borderlands* (Lafayette, IN, 2009).

Thimme, Friedrich, 'Die hannoverschen Aufstandspläne im Jahre 1809 und England', *Zeitschrift des historischen Vereins für Niedersachsen*, 62 (1897), 278–381.

Tirpitz, Alfred von, *Erinnerungen* (Leipzig, 1919).

Tirpitz, Alfred von, *Politische Dokumente: Der Aufbau der deutschen Weltmacht* (Stuttgart, 1924).

Toepser-Ziegert, Gabriele (ed.), *NS-Presseanweisungen der Vorkriegszeit*, 7 vols (Munich, 1984–2001).

Tooze, Adam, *The Wages of Destruction: The Making and Breaking of the Nazi Economy* (London, 2006).

Trachtenberg, Marc, *A Constructed Peace: The Making of the European Settlement, 1945–1963* (Princeton, NJ, 1999).

Trimborn, Jürgen, *Riefenstahl: Eine deutsche Karriere* (Berlin, 2002).

Tuchel, Johannes, 'Reinhard Heydrich und die "Stiftung Nordhav": Die Aktivitäten der SS-Führung auf Fehmarn', *Zeitschrift der Gesellschaft für Schleswig-Holsteinische Geschichte*, 117 (1992), 199–225.

Tyler, W. B., 'The British German Legion, 1854–1862', *Journal of the Society of Army Historical Research*, 54 (1976), 14–29.

Uekötter, Frank, *The Green and the Brown: A History of Conservation in Nazi Germany* (Cambridge, 2006).

Umbach, Maiken and Bernd-Rüdiger Hüppauf (eds), *Vernacular Modernism: Heimat, Globalization, and the Built Environment* (Stanford, CA, 2005).

Unterberger, Siegfried, Felix Billeter, and Ute Strimmer (eds), *Die Scholle: Eine Künstlergruppe zwischen Sezession und Blauer Reiter* (Munich, 2007).

Urbach, Karina, *Bismarck's Favourite Englishman: Lord Odo Russell's Mission to Berlin* (London, 1999).

Urban, Frank, *Ned's Navy: The Private Letters of Edward Charlton from Cadet to Admiral* (Shrewsbury, 1995).

[Valentiner, Christian August,] *Erinnerungen aus Kriegs- und Friedenszeiten, geschrieben auf einer Reise von Hamburg nach Helgoland im August 1851. Von einem abgesetzten Schleswigschen Geistlichen* (Altona, 1852).

[Victoria,] *The Letters of Queen Victoria*, ed. George Earl Buckle, third series, vol. 1 (London, 1930).

Vierneisel, Beatrice, 'Die Volksbefragung 1951', *Deutschlandarchiv*, 40 (2007), 436–44.

Virchow, Rudolf, *Beiträge zur physischen Anthropologie der Deutschen mit besonderer Berücksichtigung der Friesen* (Berlin, 1876).

Vlossak, Elizabeth, *Marianne or Germania? Nationalizing Women in Alsace, 1870–1946* (Oxford, 2010).

Wachs, Philipp-Christian, *Der Fall Theodor Oberländer (1905 bis 1998): Ein Lehrstück deutscher Geschichte* (Frankfurt, 2000).

Wachsmann, Nikolaus, *Hitler's Prisons: Legal Terror in Nazi Germany* (New Haven, CT, and London, 2004).

Wachsmann, Nikolaus, *KL: A History of the Nazi Concentration Camps* (London and New York, 2015).

Waddington, G. T., 'Hassgegner. German Views of Great Britain in the Later 1930s', *History*, 81 (1996), 22–39.

Wagenbach, Klaus, *Franzk Kafka: Eine Biographie seiner Jugend, 1883–1912* (Berlin, 2006).

Wagner, Patrick, *Volksgemeinschaft ohne Verbrecher: Konzeptionen und Praxis der Kriminalpolizei in der Zeit der Weimarer Republik und des Nationalsozialismus* (Hamburg, 1996).

Wahl, Alfred, *L'option et l'émigration des Alsaciens-Lorrains, 1871–1872* (Paris, 1972).

Waller, Horace, *Heligoland for Zanzibar, or One Island Full of Free Men to Two Full of Slaves* (London, 1893).

Wallmann, Eckhard, *Eine Kolonie wird deutsch: Helgoland zwischen den Weltkriegen* (Bredstedt, 2012).

Wallmann, Elisabeth (ed.), *Die Zerstörung Helgolands* (Helgoland, 1996).

Warburg, Aby, *Images from the Region of the Pueblo Indians of North America*, trans. Michael P. Steinberg (Ithaca, NY, and London, 1995).

[Ward, Sir Adolphus William,] *The Collected Papers of Sir Adolphus William Ward*, 5 vols (Cambridge, 1921).

Wawro, Geoffrey, *The Franco-Prussian War: The German Conquest of France in 1870–1871* (Cambridge, 2003).

Weber, Thomas, *Our Friend 'The Enemy': Elite Education in Britain and Germany before World War I* (Stanford, CA, 2008).

Wehl, Feodor, *Der kleine illustrirte Fremdenführer nach und auf Helgoland* (Hamburg, 1848).

Wehler, Hans-Ulrich, *Bismarck und der Imperialismus* (Cologne, 1969).

Wehler, Hans-Ulrich, *Deutsche Gesellschaftsgeschichte*, 5 vols (Munich, 1987–2008).

Weinberg, Gerhard L., *The Foreign Policy of Hitler's Germany: Diplomatic Revolution in Europe, 1933–36* (Chicago, IL, 1970).

Weinberg, Gerhard L., *The Foreign Policy of Hitler's Germany: Starting World War II, 1937–1939* (Chicago, IL, 1980).

Weinberg, Gerhard L., *Germany, Hitler, and World War II* (Cambridge, 1998).

Weinberg, Gerhard L., *A World at Arms: A Global History of World War II*, rev. edn (Cambridge, 2005).

Weir, Gary, *Building the Kaiser's Navy: The Imperial Naval Office and the German Industry in the von Tirpitz Era, 1890–1919* (Annapolis, MD, 1992).

[Weizsäcker, Ernst von,] *Die Weizsäcker-Papiere 1900–1932*, ed. Leonidas E. Hill (Berlin, 1974).

Wells, H. G., *The War in the Air* (London, 1908).

[Wemyss, Lord Wester,] *The Life and Letters of Lord Wester Wemyss* (London, 1935).

Wendt, Bernd-Jürgen (ed.), *Das britische Deutschlandbild im Wandel des 19. und 20. Jahrhunderts* (Bochum, 1984).

Wermuth, Adolf, *Ein Beamtenleben: Erinnerungen* (Berlin, 1922).

Werner, Petra, 'Die Gründung der Königlichen Biologischen Anstalt auf Helgoland und ihre Geschichte bis 1945', *Helgoländer Meeresuntersuchungen*, supplement, 47 (1993).

Westad, Odd Arne (ed.), *Reviewing the Cold War: Approaches, Interpretations, Theory* (London, 2000).

Westerman, Percy Francis, *The Sea-Girt Fortress: A Story of Heligoland* (London, 1914).

Westphal, William, *Ten Years in South Africa: Only Complete and Authentic History of the British German Legion in South Africa and the East Indies* (Chicago, IL, 1892).

Wheatley, Ronald, *Operation Sea Lion: German Plans for the Invasion of England, 1939–42* (Oxford, 1958).

Widenmann, Wilhelm, *Marine-Attaché an der kaiserlich-deutschen Botschaft in London 1907–1912* (Göttingen, 1952).

Wienbarg, Ludolf, *Tagebuch von Helgoland* (Hamburg, 1838).

Wigen, Kären, 'Oceans of History', *AHR*, 111 (2006), 717–21.

Wildt, Michael, '"Der muß hinaus! Der muß hinaus!" Antisemitismus in deutschen Nord- und Ostseebädern 1920–1935', *Mittelweg*, 36 (2001), 3–25.

Wile, Frederic William, *Who's Who in Hunland* (London, 1916).

Wile, Frederic William, *News Is Where You Find It: Forty Years Reporting at Home and Abroad* (Indianapolis, IN, 1939).

[Wilhelm II.,] *Die Reden Kaiser Wilhelms II.*, ed. Johannes Penzler, 4 vols (Leipzig, 1897–1913).

Wilhelm II., *Ereignisse und Gestalten aus den Jahren 1878–1918* (Leipzig and Berlin, 1922).

Winter, Jay, *Sites of Memory, Sites of Mourning: The Great War in European Cultural History* (Cambridge, 1995).

Winzen, Peter, *Bülows Weltmachtkonzept: Untersuchungen zur Frühphase seiner Außenpolitik, 1897–1901* (Boppard, 1977).

Wippermann, Wolfgang, *Politische Propaganda und staatsbürgerliche Erziehung: Die Reichszentrale für Heimatdienst in der Weimarer Republik* (Bonn, 1976).

Wolz, Nicolas, *Das lange Warten: Kriegserfahrungen deutscher und britischer Seeoffiziere 1914–1918* (Paderborn, 2008).

Zadoff, Mirjam, *Next Year in Marienbad: The Lost Worlds of Jewish Spa Culture* (Philadelphia, PA, 2012).

Zantop, Susanne, *Colonial Fantasies: Conquest, Family, and Nation in Precolonial Germany, 1770–1870* (Durham, NC, 1997).

Zeiß-Horbach, Auguste, *Der Verein zur Abwehr des Antisemitismus: Zum Verhältnis von Protestantismus und Judentum im Kaiserreich und in der Weimarer Republik* (Leipzig, 2008).

Ziemann, Benjamin, *Contested Commemorations: Republican War Veterans and Weimar Political Culture* (Cambridge, 2013).

Acknowledgements

I would like to thank those first who have shaped my thinking about this book most: Nik Wachsmann, Richard Evans, Mark Mazower, Linda Colley, Francis Markham, and the late Greg Dening. I am extremely grateful to them for their comments and advice.

I began this project when I was Sackler-Caird fellow at the National Maritime Museum in Greenwich, a treasure trove for historians. My thanks to Robert Blyth, Margarette Lincoln, and Nigel Rigby for making my time there so rewarding. The first portion of the book was written while I held a visiting fellowship at the Humanities Research Center at the Australian National University, followed by a stint at the School of History at the same institution. I thank Angela Woollacott, Debjani Ganguly, Gemma Betros, Christian Goeschel, Frank Bongiorno, and Alexander Cook for the enjoyable months in Canberra. The second phase of writing was greatly facilitated by a research fellowship which the Arts and Humanities Research Council awarded me. I am very grateful to Richard Evans, Jay Winter, Geoff Eley, Catherine Hall, and Linda Colley for supporting my applications over the years.

Birkbeck has nurtured this project with crucial early funding and the generous provision of research leave. I thank the friends and colleagues who make the College the exceptional place that it is: Fred Anscombe, John Arnold, Jen Baird, Joanna Bourke, Sean Brady, Matthew Champion, Matt Cook, Serafina Cuomo, Rebecca Darley, Filippo de Vivo, Catharine Edwards, David Feldman, Caroline Goodson, Sarah Howard, Matthew Innes, Julia Laite, Julia Lovell, Lesley McFayden, Carmen Mangion, Caspar Meyer, Jessica Reinisch, Hilary Sapire, Julian Swann, Frank Trentmann, Nik Wachsmann, Brodie Waddell, Jerry White, and Miriam Zukas. Special thanks are due to those at Birkbeck who read versions of the manuscript and made important suggestions for its improvement: John Arnold, Joanna Bourke, Jesscia Reinisch, and Nik Wachsmann. I am also grateful for the many fruitful discussions I had with students at Birkbeck, especially Charles Dick, Colin Hand, Johnny Johnson, Alina Khatib, Rebecka Klette, David Sutherland, and Jack Watling.

For comments and suggestions along the way I thank Tobias Becker, Carolyn Birdsall, David Blaazer, Charles Carter, John Connor, Sebastian Conrad, Norman Domeir, Martin Dusinberre, Matthew Fitzpatrick, Stefan Goebel, Christian Goeschel, Victoria Harris, Jasper Heinzen, Maurizio Isabella, Pieter Judson, Andrew Lambert, Tim Livsey, Chris Manias, Peter Monteath, Dirk Moses, Markus Mößlang,

William Mulligan, Paul Nolte, Dan Outram, Alexandra Phillips, Tamson Pietsch, Alexander Rehding, Lucy Riall, Torsten Riotte, Margrit Schulte Beerbühl, Richard Scully, Matthew Seligmann, Naoko Shimazu, Zoë Slotover, Kate Slotover, Glenda Sluga, Anne Thidemann, Andrekos Varnava, Brian Vick, Dagmar Walach, Eckhard Wallmann, Natasha Wheatley, Kim Wünschmann, and Marshall Yokell.

Eugen Blume (Nationalgalerie im Hamburger Bahnhof, Berlin), Helen Hyland (National Gallery of Australia, Canberra), Ursula Trieloff (Hamburger Kunsthalle), Charlotte Topsfield (Scottish National Gallery, Edinburgh), and Frank Zöllner (Universität Leipzig) gave me some crucial advice on the paintings that feature in the book. I am very grateful to them.

I am glad to be able to thank the many archivists and librarians without whose help my research would have been impossible, in particular Frank Anton (Bundesarchiv-Militärarchiv, Freiburg), Gabriela Baumer (Altonaer Museum für Kunst und Kulturgeschichte), Malte Bischoff (Landesarchiv Schleswig-Holstein), Mary Bond (Library and Archives Canada, Ottawa), Liz Bregazzi (Durham County Office), Natalie Broad and Justin Cavernelis-Frost (Rothschild Archive, London), Andres Christensen (Statens Arkiver, Copenhagen), Julie Crocker (Royal Archives, Windsor), Howard Falksohn (Wiener Library, London), Gudrun Fiedler (Niedersächsisches Landesarchiv, Stade), Katherine Ford (Dana Research Centre and Library, Science Museum, London), Sara Greer (Public Record Office of Northern Ireland, Belfast), Kirsten Hoffmann (Niedersächsisches Landesarchiv, Hanover), Katrin Jilek (Österreichische Nationalbibliothek, Vienna), Ute Klawitter (Bundesarchiv-Filmarchiv, Berlin), Alexandra Kosubek (Bundesarchiv, Koblenz), Constanze Krause (Geheimes Staatsarchiv Preußischer Kulturbesitz, Berlin), Klaus-Joachim Lorenzen-Schmidt (Staatsarchiv Hamburg), Jo Maddocks (Rare Books, British Library), Hans-Peter Maus (Theater an der Parkaue, Berlin), Constanze von Moltke (Staats- und Universitätsbibliothek, Hamburg), Petra Moritz (Behörde des Bundesbeauftragten für die Stasi-Unterlagen, Berlin), Solveig Nestler (Bundesarchiv, Berlin), Felicity Pors (Niels Bohr Archive, Copenhagen), Chris Read (State Library of South Australia, Adelaide), Sigrun Reinhardt (Geheimes Staatsarchiv Preußischer Kulturbesitz, Berlin), Jana Remy (German Historical Institute London), Andrew Sergeant (National Library of Australia, Canberra), Paul Skinner (Philatelic Collections, British Library), Samantha Smart (National Archives Scotland, Edinburgh), Brian Thynne (National Maritime Museum, Greenwich), Anne Vogt (Staatsarchiv Oldenburg), Jodie Walker (Ward Library, Peterhouse, Cambridge), Claudia Wedepohl (Warburg Institute, London), Jörg Wyrschowy (Deutsches Rundfunkarchiv, Frankfurt), and Liz Young (Shropshire Archives, Shrewsbury).

For permission to consult and quote archival material I thank Her Majesty Queen Elizabeth II, His Royal Highness The Duke of Oldenburg, John M. Parish, John Ellerman, and Peter Maaß at Hapag-Lloyd.

I am immensely grateful to Georgina Capel for finding the ideal publisher for the book and to Luciana O'Flaherty for taking *Heligoland* on. I have been most fortunate in the people with whom I have worked at OUP. Matthew Cotton edited the manuscript with admirable attention and care, Virginia Catmur went through the proofs with exemplary thoroughness, Erica Martin researched the illustrations and Franziska Bröckl oversaw the production process with much appreciated Anglo-German expertise. All of them were invariably patient and professional.

The biggest debt I owe to my family who have been a constant source of support. No words can convey my gratitude to Jayne whose kindness has made everything possible. The book is dedicated to our children with love.

Picture Credits

Index